CONTESTING RURAL SPACE

Mary Anne Gyves and grandson Robert (Bob) Akerman.
"Mixed-race" families were common on Saltspring Island in the
nineteenth century. Saltspring Island Archives (SSIA)

Contesting Rural Space

Land Policy and the Practices of Resettlement on Saltspring Island 1859–1891

R.W. SANDWELL

McGill–Queen's University Press
Montreal & Kingston · London · Ithaca

© McGill-Queen's University Press 2005
ISBN 0-7735-2859-8 (cloth)
ISBN 0-7735-2952-7 (paper)

Legal deposit second quarter 2005
Bibliothèque nationale du Québec

Printed in Canada on acid-free paper that is 100% ancient forest free
(100% post-consumer recycled), processed chlorine free.

This book has been published with the help of a grant from the Canadian
Federation for the Humanities and Social Sciences, through the Aid to
Scholarly Publications Programme, using funds provided by the Social
Sciences and Humanities Research Council of Canada.

McGill-Queen's University Press acknowledges the support of the Canada
Council for the Arts for our publishing program. We also acknowledge
the financial support of the Government of Canada through the Book
Publishing Industry Development Program (BPIDP) for our publishing
activities.

Library and Archives Canada Cataloguing in Publication

Sandwell, R. W. (Ruth Wells), 1955–
    Contesting rural space: land policy and practices of resettlement on
    Saltspring Island, 1859-1891/R.W. Sandwell.

Includes bibliographical references and index.
ISBN 0-7735-2859-8 (bound)
ISBN 0-7735-2952-7 (pbk)

1. Land settlement – British Columbia – Saltspring Island – History – 19th century.
2. Land use – British Columbia – Saltspring Island – Planning – History –
19th century. 3. Saltspring Island (B.C.) – History – 19th century. I. Title.

HN110.B8S25 2005   971.1′28   C2004–906920-9

This book was typeset by Interscript Inc. in 10/12 Sabon.

To Keith Ralston
historian and friend

Contents

Tables

Figures and Maps

FIGURES

MAPS

Illustrations

Acknowledgments

This book owes its development over the years to a great many colleagues and friends. Mary Davidson, whose energy, knowledge, and enthusiasm led to the founding of the Saltspring Island archives, first roused my interest in the island. Her assistance and encouragement made this book possible. Marvin Cohodas not only encouraged me to take on this project, but introduced me, through long discussions, to a broad literature about power and society that helped me to situate "my" island in a wider intellectual context. Jack Little, professor of history at Simon Fraser University, supervised the research and writing of the doctoral dissertation on which this book is based. Throughout that process, his detailed knowledge of rural Canadian history, and his sensitivity to the difficulties and richness of microhistorical investigations, were invaluable. I would also like to thank John Herd Thompson for his appreciation of my work.

The work of British Columbia historians provided an important context for this book, and I was fortunate to have been able to discuss this work with so many in person. Jean Barman, of the Educational Studies Department at the University of British Columbia, provided me with important information about Saltspring Island families, and has generously shared her own insights into British Columbia and Saltspring Island history. Bob McDonald has been generous with his time and his knowledge of British Columbia history, guiding my research by challenging my interpretations. I would like to thank Cole Harris for sharing his understanding of rural British Columbia with me. Peter Baskerville at the University of Victoria has been important in helping me to clarify my own thoughts about rural populations. I would like to thank Ian McPherson, whose knowledge and enthusiasm for rural history first got me thinking about the need to challenge the urban focus of so much Canadian history. Conversations with Ken Favreholdt,

Bruce Stadfeld, Carol Williams, David Peterson del Mar, Dan Marshall, Adele Perry, Duane Thomson, and Duncan Stacey helped me to understand the larger contours of British Columbia history. Ben Bradley, a former student, inspired me with his unflagging enthusiasm for my topic and my approach as he developed his own historical expertise and knowledge. George Brandak, archivist at Special Collections at the University of British Columbia, and Richard Mackie, the most knowledgeable scholar in the field of British Columbia history, shared their knowledge and insights with me, for which I am most grateful. I would particularly like to thank John Belshaw, whose work on the demographic, gender, and social history of other local communities in British Columbia has been both helpful and inspirational to me. John Lutz's extensive knowledge of Aboriginal peoples in British Columbia has helped me formulate my own ideas about rural society and culture on this coast. His knowledge and insights were invaluable to me in a general way throughout the course of my research. Chapter 7 in particular owes much to the long conversations that we had about racism and violence in nineteenth-century British Columbia, as we worked together on the educational website "Who Killed William Robinson?" which is based on the research for this chapter.

I am also indebted to numerous discussions with historians outside the field of British Columbia history, whose work has challenged and directed my own. Philip Greven's study, *Four Generations*, first introduced me to microhistorical research, and his interest and encouragement have been extremely helpful and important to me. Chad Gaffield first introduced me to the history of the family in Canada, and his commitment to the importance of the family and rural populations has provided an important model for my own work. Over the course of many discussions, Desmond Morton generously shared his knowledge of Canadian history with me, and encouraged me in my work. Discussions and correspondence with rural historians Colin Coates, Royden Loewen, and Danny Samson provided me with a deeper understanding of the varieties of experience contained in rural populations and how to understand them. Cecilia Danysk, rural and labour historian, not only spent many hours discussing nineteenth-century rural Canada with me but, heroically, also spent an entire four-hour ferry ride from the mainland to Saltspring Island entrapped in a detailed discussion of this manuscript. I would also like to thank Lyle Dick, whose work as a historian has provided me with a fine example of how to combine theory and practice, and whose conversations have inspired and challenged me. Megan Davies, an expert in the fields of British Columbia, gender, and rural history, not only helped with the writing of this manuscript, but provided a splendid example of how to be both a scholar and a splendid human being.

I would like to thank the people at McGill-Queen's University Press, especially Roger Martin for his continuing support of this manuscript. I would like to acknowledge the financial assistance of Simon Fraser University, the SSHRC, and the Canada Council, who supported various phases of the research and writing of this book.

My children, Rachel and Katie, grew up with this book, and their love and support throughout this long process sustained me. I would like to thank Colin Duncan, not only for his immediate enthusiasm for this study but also for his sympathy with the larger goals of my work. He also helped in the final preparation of this manuscript in a myriad ways, for which I am extremely grateful.

Finally, I would like to thank those people who lived on Saltspring Island between 1859 and 1891, and who shared their lives with me, albeit posthumously. Keith Ralston, now retired from UBC, often overwhelmed me with his knowledge of British Columbia history. His probing questions about my research, particularly concerning racism and power, encouraged me to question earlier interpretations of island history. It is because of his unflagging confidence in me as a scholar and as a person that I dedicate this book to him.

Preface

In the case of the liberal order, the new framework had to be constructed
against or alongside radically different ways of conceptualizing human beings
and societies.

Ian McKay[1]

I discovered Saltspring Island, as thousands of others have in recent
years, by visiting it as a tourist destination. In the twenty-first century,
the island is famed as much for the counter-cultural "back to the
landers" who settled there in the 1960s and for its artistic communities
as it is for its natural beauty and Mediterranean climate. Wanting a
break from urban life, I was fortunate to be able to spend almost an entire summer on the island with my husband and two small children.
Curious to learn more about the community within which we were to
spend the summer, I became involved with an oral history project at the
island archives. Under the able direction of island archivist Mary
Davidson, I spent a good part of that summer driving around the island
with my tape recorder, interviewing old timers and listening as they
told me, a stranger from "off island," about a world that I thought had
disappeared with the nineteenth century.

   I learned a lot in the first few days of interviewing – how to get men
to talk to a city woman about logging in spite of cultural prohibitions
against "shop talk," and how to get women to tell me about their
"work" when they thought that I wanted them to tell me about secre-
tarial waged labour, alien to most of them. I was soon able to grasp
some of the more salient features of living without indoor plumbing or
electricity, as almost all of them did growing up in the 1920s and 30s. I
became used to stories documenting the antipathy that most of these
elderly residents felt, as their parents had before them, to any form of
official interference in their lives (no matter how reasonable it seemed
to me), particularly if it came from off-island in the form of a game
warden, tax man, or police officer. Particularly poignant was the story
of the pregnant mother, killed along with her unborn twins at the end
of the nineteenth century by a drunken and violent husband. "What

happened to him?" I asked, aghast. "Did he go to jail?" "No," my interviewee responded, "No one ever did go to the police about it. It was our business. We all knew by the time of the funeral how sorry he was about what he had done."

The most difficult problem I had, however, was simply *hearing* what my interview subjects were telling me about the flexible and infinitely varied contours of their lives. My epiphany finally occurred as I was interviewing the great granddaughter of one of the first settler families on the island; one that had, according to my research, clearly succeeded in creating the kind of successful farm operation whose absence in the rest of the island had been puzzling me since I began the interviews. My interview questions for this family involved a number of straightforward and, I believed, clear questions about the farm operation. Listening to the tape after the interview, I could hear the impatience creep into my voice as the interview subject repeatedly failed to provide adequate answers to my eminently sensible questions (garnered from some detailed research into Canadian farming practices) about varieties of wheat and oats, breeds of livestock, profit margins, and production yields. Finally, the granddaughter interrupted my line of questioning, saying, "I don't think you understand. The farming never did pay. We always had to do something else to keep the farm going."[2] She then went on to explain in considerable detail the wide variety of waged and non-waged, self-provisioning, and market-oriented economic activities, carried out on an irregular, seasonal, or ever-changing basis, that made up a good portion of social life within their household and the community as she was growing up.

After this encounter, I was forced to acknowledge that I had brought with me, albeit unconsciously, a model of rural life that informed the questions I was asking of this rural society, but did little to uncover its dynamics. I was forced to seriously consider the challenge to liberal economic theories of individualism and the maximization of self-interest implied by that granddaughter's words. Well into the twentieth century, only a few short miles from the growing cities of Victoria and Vancouver, the people of Saltspring Island continued to catch, hunt, grow, gather, raise, and preserve much of what they ate. While waged labour had been an important part of island life since the 1860s, as I later learned, formal employment punctuated but did not define the complex and varied activities by which most island families made a living, made a life. Living close to nature did not, however, create the kind of community that most city dwellers like to associate with rural life. On the contrary, the society on the island, in the 1930s as in the 1860s, was both fragmented and contentious; under a veneer of civility, deep divisions and old wounds festered, breaking out in violent altercations at irregular intervals.

I spent the following months back home in Vancouver transcribing and indexing the archives' extensive collection of taped interviews, over a hundred in all, some of which dated back to the 1960s. Little in my knowledge of Canada, including my studies as a Master's student in Canadian history, had prepared me for what I listened to over those remarkable months. This whole book is, in an important sense, my response to questions raised by those interviews. The period examined in this book is that of the first generation of non-Native settlement on the island, a time that was no longer alive, in any real sense, in the public memory of the islanders I spoke with that summer. And much of the evidence used in this book seems a long way from those interviews; a quantitative database, allowing for a detailed examination of aggregate data pertaining to landholdings and geographical persistence, made up the foundation of my research here. Nevertheless, the interviews played an invaluable role in reminding this city researcher that formal narratives and official representations of rural life need to be tempered by evidence that might shed light on the ways that rural people understood their own experience and created their own lives.

Later, when I decided to return to university and write a doctoral dissertation about the island, I discovered that I was not alone in finding a disjuncture between the evidence provided by microhistorical research into rural societies on the one hand and the familiar narratives of national history on the other. Historians in Britain, France, Germany, and the United States, I have since learned, have noticed similar disjunctures between the narratives of progress and development associated with modernity, and the changes that occurred in the countryside. Like me, they are struggling to find ways of understanding societies in which we find ghostly contours of today's more regularized existences, mixed in with features that are so different from our own that they are difficult to see, let alone measure.

Ian McKay has recently addressed this particular problem of difference in the Canadian context, drawing attention to the naturalness that historians have attributed to the "progress" of our society over the past hundred and fifty years, and commenting on their reluctance to discuss the societies, and the world views, that modernity has replaced. He recommends a "reconnaissance of liberalism" that would problematize the changes that characterized the transition to the liberal order in Canada. He suggests that "at the close of the twentieth century, liberal assumptions have been so successfully and massively diffused through the population that it is difficult to see, let alone treat accurately and with scholarly empathy, the a-liberal positions they have replaced."[3] At the heart of the liberal order is the deep and enduring belief that Canada can be understood, and meaning found in its history, through the study of the individual's progress towards freedom, equality, justice, property, and rational citizenship. These beliefs are so deeply embedded in our own contemporary consciousness that they function as "something more akin to a secular religion or a totalizing philosophy than to an easily manipulated set of political ideas."[4] It is the very pervasiveness of the liberal project, its "taken-for-granted-ness" that helps to explain why the massive transition in social values, structures of power, and daily practices that eventually led to the liberal order has been strangely invisible to Canadian historians. "It was not merely a weekend's work" he argues, "to wrench 'values' from the fabric of the cosmos, where, inter alia, Aristotle and the church fathers had found them, and to assert the 'individual's' right and duty to justify his own norms."[5]

This book provides a long look at one community where "antithetical traditions and forms that had functioned for centuries and even millennia" continued, co-existing with, sometimes conflicting with, and at times accommodating "the new conceptions of the human being and society"[6] that were integral to the new liberal order. Neither a "traditional" society nor a modern one, Saltspring Island in the nineteenth century provides a window on a world that fits few of our preconceptions. I thank the islanders for sharing this world, and for showing me how varied, complex, and profound the differences between past and present can be.

CONTESTING RURAL SPACE

Introduction: Reading the Rural
with a Microhistorical Eye

This book describes how a remarkably varied collection of people first created and then sustained a distinctive economy, society, and culture in one particular part of nineteenth-century Canada. The place is Saltspring Island during the homesteading years. This study begins in 1859 with the first non-Native settlers. I end it in 1891 with the second decennial census, when the homesteading phase had all but ended. Saltspring Island was the first area in the colonies of Vancouver Island and British Columbia, and indeed the first place west of present day Ontario, where cheap country lands were made widely available to prospective farmers under a pre-emption, or homesteading, system. Of greater significance than this little-known "first" is the unusually rich documentation available about the people who lived on Saltspring Island, documentation that provides a rare view of the process of "resettlement" in nineteenth-century British Columbia.[1]

Saltspring Island forms part of the archipelago of islands located at the southerly end of the Gulf of Georgia, between the mainland of British Columbia and Vancouver Island and just within the rain shadow of the Olympic Mountains of Washington State to the south and west (see map on page 16). The earliest Spanish and British explorers in the area are still remembered in the place names of the islands, which stretch from the American San Juan Islands in the south to the Canadian Gulf Islands that include Saturna, Main, Pender, Galiano, Valdez, Gabriola, Hornby, and Denman. Saltspring is the largest of these Gulf Islands, occupying about one hundred and eighty square kilometres; since the mid-nineteenth century it has been the most populous of the Canadian island chain.

In July 1859, almost seventy-five years after the first explorers charted these waters on European maps, the first non-Native settlers arrived on the island. Within months, Saltspring Island contained a number of small settlements and a larger number of isolated homesteads, inhabited by mostly English, but also European, African-American, Irish, Scottish, Aboriginal, and (later) Hawaiian individuals and families. Archaeological evidence, some of it still visible in the form of clam shell middens on the island's shores, reveals that it had been used by generations of Aboriginal peoples before the mid-nineteenth century. But by all accounts, by the time non-Natives arrived, regular (seasonal) occupation of village sites had ceased. Epidemics, warfare, and changing patterns of trade had de-populated many areas of south-western British Columbia long before non-Native settlers began to arrive in the 1850s.[2] Aboriginal peoples did, however, return to Saltspring Island during the resettlement period; a number of women, usually from neighbouring Cowichan and Sto:lo bands, set up households with incoming settlers, forming the ethnically mixed families that added a distinct character to the economy and society of Saltspring Island.

The first generation of settlers varied not only in origin but also in the range of life experience they brought to the island: goldminers, teachers, slaves, landed gentry, farmers, labourers. People were drawn to the area by many factors, including the fur trade, the gold rush, family ties, the desire to avoid family ties, and the search for adventure. The decision to take up land and "settle," however, shows a coherent response to government policies that promised cheap and easy access to agricultural lands. The vast majority of those taking up land on Saltspring Island in the nineteenth century took advantage of the homesteading laws, the "pre-emption system" of land acquisition that allowed them to occupy and develop their lands before paying for them.

The emphasis here on the practice of settlement is, in part, a response to the paucity of land-related studies about British Columbia. The particular system of land registration has made it especially difficult to study the history of land settlement,[3] but pragmatic difficulties have been exacerbated by several thematic imbalances in the way the province's history has been imagined. The rural in British Columbia has been narrowly conceived. Historians' blinkered pre-occupation with resource extraction and large-scale capitalist enterprise has resulted in the neglect of agrarian themes. The fact of European settlement has not, of course, been ignored. It normally functions as the starting point, and defines the content, of British Columbia history. Over the last decade, some of the injustices to Aboriginal peoples in British Columbia, born of nineteenth-century land distributions, have been successfully redressed in the courts. In this connection, important research has been conducted on the history of land in British Columbia, but studies have tended to focus either on the general ideological framework of colonial land legislation or specifically on its devastating consequences for the Aboriginal populations concerned.

What has been missing from the picture are the details of how the rural resettlement areas were actually used.[4] So far, the predominant focus on the Euro-Aboriginal clash has resulted, paradoxically, in an excessively racialized approach to British Columbia history, which tends to construct the population as only two segregated and polarized groups.[5] As John Lutz has argued, this reification is inappropriate for many parts of British Columbia, in both the nineteenth and the twentieth centuries.[6] It is especially so for the period and the topics under consideration here. I will indicate that, notwithstanding the general fact of racism in nineteenth-century British Columbia, the experience of resettlement *on the ground* involved complex, varied, and changeable relations amongst *all* the populations involved (First Nations, African-Americans, English, etc.).[7] The model that polarizes Native and non-Native cultures and economies cannot capture the complexity of the rural in a place like Saltspring Island. So this study is more than a rural reclamation project.

Using the methods and approaches of microhistory to explore the minutiae of daily life in one particular rural society, this study does more than document the interactions amongst different peoples in one place. It also challenges historians' assumptions about non-Native colonists in nineteenth-century British Columbia. Most of the settlers living on Saltspring Island by 1891 came from a European background; but after living on the island for a time, most did not embrace the liberal and colonial ideals of maximizing their own self-interest through either proletarian or market activities. They did not transform their rural lands to conform to the images of rural felicity so much beloved by journalists and colonial writers of the time. Instead, after a brief period of frantic agricultural development in the early 1860s, most islanders relaxed into a way of life that, according to important indicators, resembled the lifeways of their Aboriginal neighbours, or the peasantry of Europe, more closely than it did that of their urban countrymen. Research presented here thus challenges the very notion of a coherent white-settler society that could be understood as the colonizing "other" of nineteenth-century British Columbia.

This book describes a kind of conversation between two groups of people – loosely defined as urban policy makers and rural settlers – about the appropriate uses of country lands, and the type of society to best build on them. Even when difference and conflict turned this long conversation into an argument, the dialogue did not usually take place in a public forum, nor was it articulated through the kinds of verbal or written exchanges most accessible to historians. By means of painstaking research, I have traced the terms of the debate in the dissonance between the behaviour of Saltspring Island residents – their rural practice

– and the various prescriptive narratives through which urban bureaucrats and policy makers sought to define the rural populations of what is now British Columbia. There were important differences between the respectable, reasonable, and profitable rural life being prescribed for settlers and the rural life they experienced. And it is in this intricate dialogue between prescription and practice, between the ideologies of land and the behaviours of a land-based society that we can see a rural culture emerging, one that differed in important ways both from urban society and from the kind of rural society represented in most nineteenth-century writing.

Only by making distinctions between discourse and settler practice can the peculiarities of the island's history be brought to light. Of the hundreds of aspiring rural residents taking up land on Saltspring Island in the later nineteenth century, most stayed less than a year. Those who remained walked a careful line between adherence to the mandatory provisions of land policies that guaranteed their continued residence on the land and the manipulation of these policies for their own purposes. On the one hand deterred by the poor quality of farmland, but on the other encouraged by the variety of part-time, off-farm remunerative occupations, as well as by the temperate climate and the natural abundance of the Gulf Island environment, the settlers on Saltspring Island made their own choices about the appropriate uses of rural lands. These choices were circumscribed, but not determined, by policies and prescriptions that sought to define rural in a very particular way. The behaviour of most island residents regarding their land suggests that they favoured security over risk, ease over hard work, and a modest sufficiency over the accumulation of wealth. These goals were often incompatible with the vision of rural society that lay at the heart of the policies that sought to both discipline and define rural settlement in North America as commercially successful family farms run by sober and respectable men. The residents of Saltspring Island did not conform in any regular way to the hegemonic discourse of colonialism that gave nineteenth-century British Columbia its dominant rural ideology.

Finding, defining, and understanding the alternative non-urban cultures that, as I argue, co-existed with nineteenth-century capitalism, colonialism, urbanization, and modernization is frustratingly difficult. Most of the Saltspring Island population was able to write, but few left behind their own narrative impressions of rural life.[8] In trying to discover the terms on which islanders understood land and rural community, the most accessible narratives from which we can infer their motivations, or even "see" their behaviours, are the modernizing, colonizing discourses through which nineteenth-century urban observers described rural society. Rejecting the notion that any historical documents can be read simply as literal descriptions of empirical reality, I will argue that the wide range of evidence available about this rural society can do much more than reveal that single, colonial, urban gaze upon rural British Columbia. In contrast to the tendency among contemporary post-colonial theorists to read a text "back" to a single narrative of conquest and oppression, I will suggest that it is also possible to read it against the grain, or "out, to the ways in which its meanings became constructed."[9] Microhistorical theory and method offer some important tools to historians who, impatient with hierarchies of knowledge imposed by a focused gaze on the centre, want to explore what lies outside the dominant discursive structures of historical representation.

When microhistory – the detailed observation and analysis of the minutiae of daily life in one small community or region – emerged as an identifiable form of European historical writing in the 1970s and 1980s, it did so within a historiographic context that was increasingly critical of the positivist, monolithic, and one-dimensional analyses of social change identified with Enlightenment thought and its successors. Fundamental to this post-modern critique has been the realization that, as Dirks, Eley, and Ortner have argued, "'society' as a unitary object can no longer be maintained," because "the commitment to grasping society as a whole, to conceptualizing its underlying principles of unity – which is now conventionally described as the specifically 'modern' or Enlightenment project – has passed into crisis ... The grand ideals that allowed us to read history in a particular direction, as a story of progress and emancipation, from the Industrial Revolution and the triumph of science over nature to the emancipation of the working class, the victory of socialism and the equality of women, no longer persuade. All bets are off."[10]

While few historians accept the complete breakdown of coherent systems of representation, many have become much more sensitive than previous generations were to the complexity and variability contained in human history. As Chad Gaffield has argued, historians now find themselves mediating generalizations with the questions "to what extent?" and "according to whom?"[11] Microhistorical research is particularly adept at seeking out this kind of complexity. Giovanni Levi has argued that the rich and multi-layered minutiae of historical experience revealed in microhistorical studies have not only contributed to our understanding of the complexities of societies in the past but have also helped to disrupt ideological perspectives that chart social change as a "regular progression through a uniform and predictable series of stages" in which individuals respond to social and economic structures in a way that seemed to be "given, natural and inevitable."[12] The microhistorian does not seek changes originating in large structures imposed in a general way and evaluated in terms appropriate to an implied centre, but rather in the "minute and endless strategies and choices operating within the interstices of contradictory normative systems."[13] It is in their day-to-day practices that people make "innumerable and infinitesimal transformations of and within the dominant cultural economy in order to adapt it to their own interests and their own rules."[14] It is only at the level of microhistorical research that these practices, and the strategies they contain, become visible.

Microhistorians' emphasis on processes and relationships, on the local and the specific, and on the variety of human experience has made important contributions to the work of rural historians. At first glance (and at a particular time in the research agenda), the microhistorian's attempt to cut a broad swath across a wide variety of sources about a narrowly defined place in the past seems to support what many see as the fatal weaknesses of post-modern historical analysis: the creation of endless contradiction rather than unanimity, passivity rather than agency, individuality rather than community, fragmentation rather than coherence, and plurality rather than uniformity, all of which culminate in chaos and irrelevance in lieu of a comprehensible view of the past. If, as some theorists argue, the only coherent account of history can be found in an analysis of the "discourse" articulated in a particular type of source, this will provide cold comfort to those historians wanting to understand the experiences, the "real" contexts, of social relations in the past.[15]

At the heart of this post-modern angst is the troubling question "Is the past knowable in any intelligible way?" In this study I assume that it is. While our understanding of the past is limited, partial, and mediated by particular cultural, social, and political forces now and in the past, I argue that the historian can indeed construct meaningful cross-sections of historical experience from available sources. Of course, in an important sense, creating a total history is impossible. Experience, past and present, even for one individual, is so complex and varied that it is ultimately unknowable. In this sense the past is irretrievable. Fortunately, however, people through the ages have disguised and/or tamed this chaos. In their attempts to survive and prosper in the midst of a largely unknowable world, they have often superimposed order and meaning onto their relations with each other and with their environment, trying to live *as if* the world did make sense. To some extent, they have succeeded. And, fortunately for the historian, some people have preserved documentary evidence charting their attempts to explain these ever-changing structures of meanings to each other. So while it is impossible to know the chaos that may be, on one level, the single reality of the past, it *is* possible to look at primary sources to find the locally and historically specific generalizations on which order and structure were created, explained, and imposed by people attempting to make their world comprehensible and controllable. Primary sources let us know both how people situated themselves in relation to others and how they explained themselves to each other. Therefore, while considerable suspicion still surrounds the supposition that "all the world is a text," the detailed examination of social interaction via primary sources and microhistorical investigation nevertheless illustrates some of the benefits of reading the historical record *as if it were* a text.[16] Levi uses the term "bounded rationalities" to describe the specific behaviours by which peoples of the past attempted to both create and subvert order and meaning in their lives.[17] In the broadest sense, this study is an attempt to uncover the "bounded rationalities" by which people in nineteenth-century British Columbia understood rural society in general and Saltspring Island in particular.

As one of the oldest surviving immigrant communities in the province, Saltspring Island is an obvious target for microhistorical investigation. Levi begins his argument for the significance of microhistory – the detailed description and analysis of the minutiae of life in a specific geographic area – by arguing that "phenomena previously considered to be sufficiently described and understood assume completely new meanings by altering the scale of observation."[18] Levi's argument became increasingly relevant to me, as, over the course of my research, I became more and more aware that the view from the government sources and community "boosters" on Saltspring Island was at considerable variance with the glimpses that I was able to obtain of views from the countryside.[19] Neither successful farmers nor full-time waged workers, self-provisioners, or profit-maximizers, squatters or *bona-fide* landowners, capitalists or proletarians, traditional or modern, and not predominantly male, these people lived lives that are as far from the economic, political, and geographical centres of British Columbia historiography as they were from nineteenth-century ideals of rural life. Where the dominant historiographical discourse of Canadian progress, like the nineteenth-century colonial discourse, suggests that change on the island should and would be measured by progress from frontier subsistence to agricultural capitalism, the day-to-day practices of island residents indicated an economy consistently based on the labour of all household members, characterized by a wildly fluctuating combination

John Maxwell, one of the first settlers to arrive in the Burgoyne
Valley in the late 1860s, with one of his sons (on the wagon);
the rugged island landscape forms the background. (SSIA)

of subsistence activities, waged labour (often off-farm work), and commercial agricultural production. The people of Saltspring Island – resistant to the growth of the modern state, religiously diverse, and influenced by Aboriginal practices – demonstrated, furthermore, few of the characteristics of that hegemonic, racialized, and colonizing society that has recently come to define the resettlement of British Columbia by Europeans.[20]

The normal categories of British Columbia historical analysis – occupation, wage labour, capital accumulation, profit maximization –

seemed strangely ill-suited to the household-based, land-centred, economically diverse population I was studying. So beyond looking at the narratives by which urban British Columbians understood the people of Saltspring Island, this study analyses available aggregate data to examine the ways in which Saltspring Islanders structured their own experience to create their own rural culture.[21] The following chapters examine land acquisition, land usage, geographic persistence, economic activities, demographic behaviour, and community formation as the "cultural co-ordinates" of Saltspring Island society.[22] These provide an excellent framework for understanding the structures of meaning, the "bounded rationalities," through which the population of Saltspring Island created and sustained their understanding of the world.

The machine-readable database that I created for this study contains the names of every person who is mentioned in the documents available for the island between 1859 and 1916, particularly in a variety of land records. This presented some difficulties, as nineteenth-century names were not standardized as they are today. To trace people over time and space, I had to standardize the spellings of all the names in my database first, always being as careful as possible to establish the correct identity of the individuals concerned. The documents also include parish records; business directories; assessment rolls (available only after 1891); censuses of 1881, 1891, and 1901; listings in voters' lists and in reports from the Departments of Education, Agriculture, and Public Accounts found in the British Columbia Sessional Papers; probate files; court records (particularly inquests); and newspapers. These data have been used to link individuals over time and to link them to other kinds of information to glimpse patterns in their behaviour. Such evidence provides the foundation of rural practice in this study, while newspapers, government reports, land policies, and the written reflections of a few visitors and residents document the dominant rural discourse.

The first three chapters of this study examine the ways in which the coherent, official discourse represented country lands in general, and Saltspring Island in particular. Chapter 1 begins the discussion of "rural" in British Columbia with a look at the first country lands legislation in the province, and its peculiar relationship to the settlement of Saltspring Island. Writers and policy makers of the time had their own vision of rural culture and society, and were charting its relation to the province's destiny. For many of these public figures, rural was a problematic concept within the discourse of laissez-faire liberalism. Tensions in the official discourse of rural – impatience with stability and apprehensions about progress – can be found neatly contained in the pre-emption system that dominated land acquisition on Saltspring

Island in the time under study. Small-scale and family-centred capitalism was to be a foil against too vibrant, socially disruptive capitalist activity and liberal individualism in other parts of the province.

Relying heavily on government-generated land records, chapters 2 and 3 examine the ways in which the official discourse of rural, implemented through land policies, directed and shaped land settlement and land use on Saltspring Island. Chapter 2 explores in some detail the discourse of the sturdy yeoman that dominated the official view of the island in the nineteenth century. Here we find considerable evidence that the society of Saltspring Island was seen as tending towards petty commodity production on family farms. Chapter 3 evaluates the practice of pre-emption from the vantage point of policy makers and finds that land settlement policies did succeed in limiting land speculation and ensuring landowners' residence on their land. The surprisingly high rates of geographical persistence for landholders on the island argue that the pre-emption system provided an effective bridge between government expectations and settler aspirations for those remaining for more than a year on the island. Thus chapters 2 and 3 suggest that the official discourse of rural did find considerable resonance in the island population.

In chapter 4, focusing largely on census data, land records, and Department of Agriculture statistics, I argue that, notwithstanding the tendency of observers to describe the island in terms of its commercial agricultural success, both land clearance and the production of agricultural commodities for markets were, by 1891, extremely limited – few Saltspring Island farmers were making a living from farming in the usual sense of the word. How do we reconcile the absence of commercially viable farms with the identity of the island as an area of commercially successful agricultural enterprises? The remaining chapters explore in closer detail the rural experience for those living on country lands. Chapter 5 begins this exploration by viewing land as a contact zone between settler culture and government prescription – as the physical site on which different views of what the rural experience should be were negotiated. The focus on the details of landholders' practice over time, rather than on policy-makers' prescriptions, confirms that some pre-emptors clearly used the system as a foundation for a family farm. Most settlers, although acquiescing to pre-emption regulations, were simultaneously manipulating its provisions in ways not at all intended by policy makers. Chapter 6 explores the varied economic and familial advantages that ready and secure access to land, in an area rich in natural resources, brought to those who chose to stay on Saltspring Island. Chapters 4, 5, and 6, therefore, explore the society on Saltspring Island through the lens of land- and household-based economic activity.

Willis Stark, who arrived on the island in 1860 at the age of two, standing beside the house built by his parents. Note the lush growth, one of the advantages of the island's mild Mediterranean climate. (SSIA)

The final two chapters examine the varieties of rural experience that co-existed with the official discourse of rural outlined in the first three. Chapter 7 provides a microhistory within this microhistory, focusing narrowly on a series of murders in the island's African-American community to explore violence, ethnicity, and power on the island. Chapter 8 examines the ways in which religion, gender, age, and class organized social and political relations on the island. It concludes with an examination of the fractious social formations that were appearing by the later nineteenth century. The majority of people – backed by the economic security inherent in their land tenure – demonstrated a considerable disinclination to recognize formal social, political, and bureaucratic power. The land-based and household-oriented society on Saltspring Island showed a decided reluctance to incorporate the new liberal ideals of civic behaviour contained in the official discourse of rural: the community was a very long way from being the idyllic, stable, and coherent rural community envisaged by urban observers.

In nineteenth-century British Columbia, conceptions of rural were neither fixed nor uniform. Rural society was defined from the outside by nineteenth-century urban bureaucrats and by a popular bucolic vision of rural harmony. It was defined from the inside by the behaviours,

expectations, and beliefs of those living on the island. Rural history in
British Columbia, by contrast, has been constructed by the ideological
proclivities of bureaucrats and historians alike. On the one hand, the
emphasis of British Columbia historians on waged labour and large-
scale, successful, capitalist enterprises has directed attention away from
rural communities like Saltspring Island, whose economy was rooted in
intermittent wage labour, small-scale investments in land, and an em-
barrassingly atavistic reliance on subsistence activities. Sources from
the nineteenth century, on the other hand, have a good deal to say
about rural society, but their view reflects a positivistic predisposition
to limit farming to agricultural occupations, agricultural occupations
to cash flow, and both to men only. Neither approach allows much
room for the description and analysis of the types of experiences – occupational plurality; a reliance on the informal economic activity of
men, women, and children; and the marginality of cash incomes – that
characterized the practice of Saltspring Island residents in the nineteenth century. This study clarifies the official discourse that mediated
between urban populations and the rural societies they observed, and
then looks beyond it to the more varied terms on which this rural community understood its own experiences.

Because land was central to the process of resettlement and because
extensive records document both land policy and practice, this study
"reads" land-related sources as a discursive space on which different
groups of people have recorded their interpretations of rural life. The
settlement of families on agricultural lands was clearly a matter of importance to many of those living in, and thinking about, nineteenth-
century British Columbia. It was a cause of great concern to those
formulating policy about land settlement, immigration, and economic
development. It was a subject that, judging by the impassioned discussions it generated on a wide range of issues, touched the heart of the
great questions about the new society slowly emerging in the Pacific
Northwest: What kind of society would it be? What were the personal
values and social goals that would regulate and direct its course? How
would these social and moral questions be reconciled with the economic development of the region and the liberty of individuals?

Land Policies and the Agricultural Vision in British Columbia

The historical record provides few details about the motives and experiences of the individual settlers taking up their first lands on Saltspring Island in 1859. Only two narrative accounts detailing early land resettlement on the island exist. One is a memoir written in old age by the freed slave Sylvia Stark. We know from her unpublished memoir that the Stark family – Howard Estes with his daughter Sylvia Stark, her husband Louis, and their infant son – were fleeing racial persecution in the American south, and had been invited by Vancouver Island governor James Douglas to take up farmland in the new colony as part of a larger African-American group of settlers.[1] Like the other African-Americans arriving on Saltspring Island at that time, including young men like Fielding Spott, William K. Brown, and Armstead Buckner, Lewis Stark was pursuing an opportunity to own agricultural land that was not available to African-Americans in the American West. A similar desire to own country lands motivated Jonathan Begg, a young Englishman who took up land a few miles from the Stark family. In a series of letters written between 1858 and 1862, Begg wrote of the goals and aspirations that brought him from England to Saltspring Island in 1859, via Toronto and a "fruit ranch" in California. Once on the island, Begg worked enthusiastically to transform his land into a successful agricultural enterprise, and the island into a thriving rural community of sturdy yeomen farmers.[2] Scattered and fragmentary records hint at the importance of landownership in drawing other settlers to the island in the early years of settlement.

In spite of differences between their respective origins, goals, and eventual accomplishments – Jonathan Begg was more interested in, and successful at, the commercial aspects of farming than were Sylvia Stark and her family, for example, and the Stark family was more successful at making a living on rural lands than Begg, who was a single man – their testimonies reveal some common beliefs about the social meaning

1.1 Saltspring Island

of country land and some common ideas about its legitimate uses. The vast majority of first-generation Saltspring Island settlers did not write about their experiences, however, and so their motives in coming to the island, like their expectations of rural life, have to be inferred from other sources. Later chapters turn to the abundant but fragmentary evidence documenting their land-related practices, finding in such evidence a window through which to see and understand some of the meanings that land held for these islanders. This chapter has a more specific aim. It sets out to examine the expectations that brought the first settlers to the island and the practices that kept them there, through the lens of colonialism. For, in an important sense, the presence of non-Natives on Saltspring Island in 1859 owes as much to a particular colonial vision, itself intimately intertwined with a particular rural ideology, as it does to the choices made by individual settlers.

The colonial project – the attempt to replace Native with non-Native peoples, landscapes, and economies in nineteenth-century British Columbia – rested on a set of coherent cultural beliefs about the meaning and purposes of country lands, and on a set of political decisions designed to mobilize those beliefs into economic and social practices. Whatever their personal motives and individual experiences, therefore, and whether or not they shared with Begg and Stark a set of colonial beliefs about land, early settlers were directed to the island by ideologically informed land policies that identified the foundations of colonial society with commercially successful agricultural activity on the family farm. The intersection of the local and the international, of the personal and the political that constituted colonialism can be seen with particular clarity in the early resettlement of Saltspring Island. For the first "homesteading" policy west of Ontario not only was designed within the larger context of British (and later Canadian) colonialism but also was created as a specific and localized response to the settlers who wanted to take up country lands on Saltspring Island and neighbouring Chemainus in 1859. An examination of land policies and the rich and varied literature written by government officials, journalists, and policy makers about land and rural society in mid-nineteenth-century British Columbia provides a view of the cultural, political, and economic contexts within which the first Euro-Canadians made their individual decisions to take up land on Saltspring Island.

THE COLONIAL CONTEXT OF EARLY SETTLEMENT ON SALTSPRING ISLAND, 1859

Land mattered to people living in British Colulmbia in the mid-nineteenth century. Natives and non-Natives, although they had very different ideas about its legitimate uses, depended on the land to provide much of the material, as well as the ideological foundations, of their respective societies. Socially complex, economically varied, and intermittent, land use was a key component of the larger social and cultural meanings of land to Aboriginal populations long before the arrival of Europeans.[3] Colonization involved the transformation of these "wild" and "empty" Aboriginal lands into the civilized, civilizing spaces of Euro-Canadian society.[4] For the colonial administrators contemplating the future of the colony before the advent of mass long-distance transportation systems, a local agriculture was essential for a food supply. Agriculture was also central to the meaning of land, and to the material and ideological processes of re-making British Columbia as settler space. For, "publicly and privately, agriculture introduced a vision of the future that was anchored to long pasts in distant places; as vision, it embodied some of an immigrant society's most essential values. It also introduced assumptions about nature and the ordering of space and time that most immigrants took for granted, but that were relatively new in British Columbia. As a result, farm landscapes were expressions of introduced cultural and ecological arrangements, and were drastic departures from indigenous pasts."[5]

As Cole Harris has argued, the process of colonization involved the re-imagining of Native space, but this was predicated both on Natives' legal alienation and on their physical removal from what was increasingly defined as "settler lands."[6] British eighteenth-century law had recognized Native ownership of colonial lands in British North America, and had insisted on a legal process by which Aboriginal title was to be extinguished before settlers could take up Native lands. Devastating epidemics, European military technologies, and the creation of reserves facilitated the physical removal of Native peoples from their lands in the 1850s and 60s, but the problem of legal title continued to be much more difficult to settle. Aside from fourteen treaties negotiated by James Douglas in the early 1850s, which involved only a tiny portion of the lands to which Aboriginal peoples held legal title, no other Native lands were legally transferred to the British crown as the law required.[7] In lieu of the legal transfer of title, the process of replacing Native peoples with Euro-Canadians, as Cole Harris explains in *Making Native Space*, was carried out within a "shifting set of assumptions and practices that turned variously on the issue of title without resolving it one way or the other."[8] The legacy of this disordered and mostly sub-legal process of alienating Native people from their lands has haunted Aboriginal societies for more than a century. As the growing number and success of Native land claims in the British Columbia courts in the early twenty-first century suggest, the issue is returning to haunt non-Natives as well.[9]

Cutting Hay on Glenshiels Farm. Alexander McLennan arrived from Victoria in the 1880s and settled in the Beaver Point area of the island's south end. He is shown here mowing grain with his son Douglas and daughter Anne. (SSIA)

The settlers making their way to Saltspring Island in July 1859 were some of the first aspiring Euro-Canadian agricultural settlers in what would become British Columbia. Little agricultural settlement had occurred in either Vancouver Island or British Columbia before this date. Fur-trading posts in Fort St James, Fort Langley, and Fort Victoria, established under the authority of the Hudson's Bay Company in 1811, 1824, and 1843 respectively, provided the sites of the first European agricultural activity in present-day British Columbia, but they did little to create agriculturally based communities. Whether the Hudson's Bay Company was unwilling to promote settlement in British Columbia, as historians have generally assumed, or whether it was simply unable to do so, as Richard Mackie has suggested, non-Native settlement in the area was extremely limited before 1858.[10] Few disagree, however, that the Fraser River gold rush of 1858 provided the first impetus for permanent European settlement in the area. This influx stimulated the government to re-evaluate the suitability of the Wakefield system, an unofficial system of land disbursement designed to sustain traditional class relations by limiting the access of the lower orders to land by keeping the price of land high.[11] While the first land laws of the new colonies were formulated with particular reference to the needs of miners flooding into the Fraser River area, they went far beyond the requirements of a mining population. Their focus was to address the need, felt by administrators, capitalists, and workers alike, to settle immigrants from Europe, the Canadas, and the United States on country lands throughout the province.[12]

The British government believed that the availability of arable rural lands was essential to the successful settlement of the young colonies, but, even after Wakefield's conservative vision was abandoned by colonial legislators, their determination that the Pacific colonies should be self-supporting considerably affected the formation of policies that would encourage land settlement.[13] Although in principle the twin goals of establishing settlers on the land and raising revenue by so doing seemed reasonable to the Colonial Office in Britain, James Douglas, the first governor of the mainland and Vancouver Island colonies, had great difficulty establishing land policies that could do both simultaneously. Town sites had been laid out at Fort Langley, Fort Hope, and Fort Yale shortly after the colonial government was installed in 1858, and a number of lots had been sold that year at £1 per acre, the price fixed by the crown. In spite of a system of deferred payment and public auction, revenues from land sales fell far short of expectations.[14] By early 1859 it was becoming clear to Governor Douglas that Sir Edward Bulwer-Lytton, colonial secretary in Britain, had seriously underestimated the difficulty in attracting permanent settlers to an isolated area of high-priced, heavily treed land on the edge of the Empire.[15]

Problems with high land prices in the British colonies were exacerbated by the availability of cheap lands to the south, in the Oregon Territory. Because the British presence on the Pacific coast was so fragile, Douglas believed that these cheap lands could have serious consequences for the continued security and existence of the mainland and Vancouver Island colonies. Although Douglas was deeply concerned with raising revenue, and land sales were one of the few means the government could use to do so, he disagreed with Bulwer-Lytton that high-priced land was the answer to the revenue problem. Although cheap land might result in expensive labour as Wakefield predicted, cheap land, he maintained, was essential to encourage "the sturdy yeomen expected this year from Canada, Australia, and other British Colonies" to take up land in British territory rather than on American lands to the south.[16] Furthermore, Douglas maintained that a low price for country lands would inhibit rather than promote the land speculation that both administrators identified as so detrimental to the agricultural foundation and the community base essential to the new colonies.[17]

Even though Native land title had still not been settled, in February 1859 Douglas made some concessions to the growing pressure for cheaper land by publishing the first proclamation concerning public country lands. Lands outside towns would, it declared, now be available under auction as the town lots were, but at the lower price of ten shillings per acre. The practice of deferred payment established in 1858 could be applied to half the purchase price. In an attempt to stave off rampant land speculation, no land was to be offered for sale until it had been mapped and surveyed under the government's authority.[18] While the government was concerned with raising desperately needed revenue and maintaining the British presence on the coast, the poor and unemployed men pouring into Victoria were increasingly concerned with finding economic support and security through the acquisition of land in the new colonies. The reduced price for country lands announced in February did little to meet the needs of many of the potential settlers, who simply did not possess sufficient capital to make land purchases under these terms. As the Victoria *British Colonist* argued in June 1859:

Foremost among the objects we wish to secure by a good land system, is the locating of actual settlers upon the soil. To induce them to do this, now that they have been driven away [by the high price of land], the public lands ought to be open to pre-emption, in quantities of 100 or 160 acres, on condition of actual residence and the cultivation of a certain number of acres with improvements; and a reasonable period allowed to pay for the land ... To compel the poor and industrious emigrant to compete with a set of land-sharks, bespeaks little, either for the intelligence, humanity or justice of the government. We view the public domain as the patrimony of the people.[19]

In the words of Jonathan Begg, who would become one of the first settlers on Saltspring Island and one of the first to be granted pre-emptive land in the colony, the land system in the Vancouver Island colony in June, 1859 was "in such a deplorable condition that no one out of the employment of the HB Coy could procure an acre of the public domain. I saw that justice and reform was necessary. So I commenced a movement which has since changed the whole land system in the colony. I got up a public meeting in one of the principal hotels where strong resolutions accompanied by an urgent petition to the governor and local legislature was carried."[20] Following his sister to North America, Begg had left England for Toronto, and then California, where he took up fruit ranching in 1858. Disillusioned with the republican frontier society of California, he moved north to Victoria in June

1859.[21] Discovering that he could "get no work of any kind as there were hundreds more out of employment," he tried to support himself by raising produce on a vacant lot until he obtained gardening work from the local banker some weeks later.[22]

While the seminal role that he gives himself in his correspondence for changing land laws is not entirely consistent with other evidence, Begg certainly was present at the Colonial Hotel in Victoria on June 22 when a group of would-be settlers first organized to pressure the government to address their need, as settlers, for land.[23] The petition, drawn up at this meeting by Amor de Cosmos (editor of the *British Colonist* and later provincial premier) and seconded by Begg, put forward resolutions on a number of land issues. "The history of nations and the experience of ages," petitioners unanimously resolved, "dictate a liberal encouragement of the art of agriculture as the only sure guarantee of the enduring prosperity and wealth of a country."[24] In their petition, submitted to Governor Douglas in early July 1859, this group of would-be-settlers further resolved that "the true policy as well as duty of government is to encourage agricultural pursuits above all others; to induce immigration to the country; to invite the hardy pioneer to occupy its territory; to furnish the actual settler cheap access to the soil – whereon to permanently invest his labor, and rear his home."[25] The petition went on to outline a system of land pre-emption whereby "a preference should be given to actual settlers in the choice of the public lands."[26] The competition provided by cheaper land available south of the border, they argued, was drawing off desirable settlers, and with them the potential success of the British colony. They were, in effect, requesting an imitation of the American system in which settlers could take up land before paying for it, on condition that they improve it and reside on it. The legitimacy of their petition rested on the conviction that arable land was essential to the subsistence and growth of the colony.

The petition received a "courteous reception" from Douglas, who maintained that while he was "personally opposed to the present system," he was unable to alter it because he had no authority to change the terms of the colonies' land policies.[27] To illustrate his support in principle for their goals of land settlement, however, Douglas went on to request that "if there are a hundred farmers ready to settle in the Cowitchen [sic] valley, let them present themselves and facilities will be afforded them, the Indian title extinguished as soon as practicable, ... no immediate payment will be required for the land, and the price [will] be determined by the legislature."[28]

On July 11 a number of people, "mostly Canadians," met at the offices of John Copland, an Edinburgh lawyer who had arrived in Victoria via Australia and had presented himself as a land agent to those wishing to obtain cheap country lands for settlement.[29] He drew up a list of twenty-six people wishing to settle on land around Cowichan and Saltspring. At this meeting, the aspiring landowners declared "their desire to settle in Cowitchan [sic], that they were farmers; that they engage to settle on condition of actual occupancy and improvement, and if they fail to do so, their lands [are] to be forfeited."[30] On July 13 a deputation of thirty or forty people waited upon Douglas, presenting a petition signed by over a hundred people, requesting the right to take up land in the Cowichan valley on these terms. Again, Douglas responded that the price had been set by the crown, and he could not alter it.[31]

The next day, however, Douglas found a potential loophole and took his first practical step to support his previously stated belief that "the practice of making the public lands a source of revenue is unwise and impolitic."[32] He decided that he could get around the stipulations limiting his ability to grant land by looking to the large tracts of unsurveyed lands outside Victoria, which did not have either the £1 or ten shillings per acre upset price attached. In these unsurveyed districts, "actual settlers would be allowed to go on the land upon payment of one shilling per acre at the time of settlement, and no other payement [sic] would be required of them until the land was surveyed, which would not probably be for at least one year."[33] The fertile Cowichan lands being already surveyed, he decided to open up lands in "the Chemainus country, which is unsurveyed and commences ten miles north of the southern end of Cowichan, towards Nanaimo."[34] This area included Saltspring Island.

After the July 14 revision of the terms of land settlement, prospective settlers lost little time in pursuing this opportunity, and a group of about thirty "farmers" left aboard the *Nanaimo Packet* to look at the Chemainus lands. On July 18 the first handful of settlers arrived on Saltspring. As they reported back to the Victoria *British Colonist*, they were "highly pleased with the country, and consider it to be a beautiful agricultural country."[35] Begg was "one of the eighteen adventurers who went out to view the land," and he was favourably impressed with what he saw on Saltspring Island:

This is one of the most romantic regions I was ever in. Scotland is nowhere in that respect in comparison ... The band of adventurers ... finding the island beautifully situated in the midst of an archipelago more beautiful than the 1000 Islands of the St. Lawrence ... This being the most convenient to Victoria, ... we determined to form a settlement here. We drew for choices of selection. My lot fronts a quarter of a mile in a nice little bay ... Behind my lot, on its rear it borders a beautiful fresh water lake of some 2 miles in length, teeming with fish. I have about 80 acres of prairies on the farm. It is not exactly a prairie as it more resembles an English park or pleasure ground, and here and there is a clump of beautiful balsam growing.[36]

They returned on July 24, two days before the Colonial Surveyor, Joseph Pemberton, gave his reply to John Copland's petition.

As Begg summarized in a letter written the next year, "so the movement went until the HB Governor and councel [sic] had to submit to the popular demand."[37] On July 26 the colonial surveyor replied to Copland's petition for the settlement of twenty-nine settlers on Saltspring. Acknowledging their "want of funds to settle on surveyed lands elsewhere in which cases an immediate installment is required," Pemberton agreed "to delay the survey of that portion of Tuan [Saltspring] Island on which these persons shall settle for [left blank] years or until requested at an earlier period to survey and issue titles by the majority of the holders."[38] He went on to state that "after the survey of the lands in question shall have been made, preemptive rights in those of the number stated who shall have effected most improvements in the way of Buildings, fencing, or cultivation on any government section shall be recognised."[39]

Pemberton's reply constitutes the first official statement granting pre-emptive rights to land in the Canadian West, pre-dating by some three years the American Homestead System, by four months the first official pre-emption proclamation on the mainland colony of British Columbia, and by a full eighteen months the official pre-emption proclamation in the Vancouver Island colony.[40] Although historians have correctly identified the mainland colony as having the first pre-emption legislation, the Vancouver Island colony played a pivotal role. Not only did community action against high land prices first crystallize in Victoria, but the first pre-emptions were granted and taken up in the Vancouver Island colony, albeit it in un-legislated form.[41] In the letter outlining the first homesteading system, Pemberton also endorsed three out of the four main principles that informed rural land settlement over the next half century: cheap land, deferred payment, and the purchase of such land on condition that it had been cleared, fenced, and built on. The "essential requirement of the preemptive system,"[42] the personal residence of the pre-emptor, was not included explicitly until the 4 January 1860 Land Ordinance.

At the end of July, prospective settlers on the mainland colony presented to Douglas a petition similar to the Vancouver Island petition, stating that the "want of a proper and liberal land system, is the first and most important grievance of which the People of this Colony have to complain."[43] Like those in Victoria, these petitioners asked for a policy that would allow settlers with little or no capital to take up rural lands. There is no evidence that this petition spawned any of the unofficial pre-emptions of the type being granted in the Vancouver Island colony, as the earliest pre-emptions are dated after the 1860 Land Ordinance.[44]

By contrast, unofficial pre-emptions continued to be offered in the Vancouver Island colony, including Saltspring Island, throughout the summer and fall of 1859 and through 1860. On July 30 Pemberton had extended the terms applicable to Saltspring Island to 212 settlers wanting to take up lands in the Chemainus area.[45] At the end of August Copland wrote to Pemberton and noted that the first twenty-nine settlers "have now nearly all settled their lands," adding that "there is ample land left for the present applicants," an additional thirty-two settlers.[46] In November Copland sent the Land Office a list of another thirty potential settlers, and before the end of the year another seventy-two had applied.[47] In December, having granted pre-emptive rights to over three hundred people in the Saltspring and Chemainus area under the terms outlined in his July 26 letter, Pemberton wrote to Douglas, "earnestly and respectfully" urging him to formalize the pre-emption system. He argued that while a great deal of land near Victoria "has been put up to public auction," it was not being purchased, "even at that low price because the land, although containing many fertile spots is, generally speaking, covered with forest and rock or swamp. I would therefore ... suggest that these sections ... be thrown open to pre-emption, believing that many persons who now wish to occupy lands at a distance, at Salt Spring Island for instance, or Chemainus, would thereby be induced to seek out and occupy the fertile spots alluded [sic] and that an Impetus would be given to settle up lands which, although so near Victoria are too wild to sell at present."[48] The result was the Land Ordinance of January 1860, outlining a pre-emption system for the mainland on almost exactly the same terms as outlined in Pemberton's July 26 letter.

Under this proclamation, a single man could take up 160 acres of unsurveyed land, on condition that he occupy and improve it and that he pay up to ten shillings an acre when the land was surveyed and the legal title obtained. Douglas's support for this system of settlement in both colonies cannot be doubted. As he declared in the Colonial Legislature on 1 March 1860, "I am prepared also to concur in any measures which may tend more directly to encourage settlers to occupy and cultivate the country; and I believe that the cheap and easy acquisition of public lands, and the construction of roads, to facilitate and reduce the cost of transit to and from the settlements will tend materially to the advancement of these objects."[49] It is not clear why this piece of legislation was not expanded beyond the mainland colony to include

Victorians from south of the border, such as
Howard Estes and his wife Hannah and her
children (including Sylvia Stark as a child),
were drawn to Saltspring Island by the
colonial homesteading policy and driven
by racist land policies in the United States.
(SSIA)

lands on Vancouver Island, except that, as Robert Cail suggests, Douglas was "so preoccupied in guiding the development of the mainland colony that he had found little time to consider the state of affairs closer to home."[50]

Douglas was still vexed, however, by the problem of Native title to the lands. As Tennant and Harris have argued, he advocated a revolutionary (in colonial circles) plan to include Aboriginal peoples within the pre-emption system on similar terms to whites.[51] He believed that this would provide a way of solving the legal problem of land title, the cultural problem of "uncivilized" hunters and gatherers in the colony, and the social, economic, and military problems that might be presented by dispossessed Native peoples. Under what Tennant terms the "Douglas System," Natives were to have, in Douglas's words, "precisely the same rights of acquiring and possessing land in their individual capacity, either by purchase or by occupation under the Pre-emption law, as other classes of Her Majesty's subjects, provided they in all respects comply with the legal conditions of tenure by which land is held in the colony."[52] Douglas also advocated relocating dispossessed Natives onto reserves, but this was to provide a temporary solution, a bridge to help "civilize" Natives who were unwilling or unable to take up land under the system of pre-emption. In March 1860 he requested that the House of Assembly "provide the means for extinguishing, by purchase, the native Title to the lands" in Chemainus, Cowichan, and Saltspring Island, lest the Natives "regard the settlers as trespassers and become troublesome." The assemblymen agreed that the land should be paid for, but they believed that the British, and not the colonial government, should pick up the tab, and so took no action.[53]

No Aboriginal men appear in the pre-emption records relating to Saltspring Island. Of the hundreds of pre-emptions taken out on Saltspring Island before 1866, when legislation explicitly forbade Aboriginal peoples to pre-empt land, none seems to be in an Native person's name. A small reserve was established on Saltspring Island in 1876, long after the Douglas System had been abandoned in favour of a more punitive and restrictive system of reserves, but fewer than thirteen people lived on it at any point during these years. A Native presence on "settler" lands continued throughout the colonies and on Saltspring well into the third decade of non-Native settlement, marked at one extreme by murderous violence between Natives and non-Natives, and at the other by high rates of inter-marriage among the two groups.[54]

If the issue of land title created devastating problems for Native peoples on the coast, alienating them from their economic support and cultural foundations, the sub-legal status of pre-emptions on Saltspring Island created some thorny difficulties for settlers in these early years. It must have been a source of concern to the settlers on the island when, for example, on 5 October 1859 Pemberton declared that the settlers on Saltspring and Chemainus had no legal title to the land they had been granted in July, and were nothing more than squatters.[55] Mr Copland quickly responded on behalf of the settlers, presenting Pemberton with a copy of his July 26 letter, and Pemberton's statement was retracted publicly in the October 5 edition of the *British Colonist*.[56] The confusion of names and claims in the early pre-emption records can, in part, be attributed to the sub-legal status of these early claims, as it was not until 1861 that a formal registration process for pre-emptions was instituted for the Vancouver Island colony. The confusion did not, however, end with formal registration – overlapping claims and registration duplication continued to characterize the pre-emption system throughout the nineteenth century.

In spite of these problems, settlement was definitely taking place on Saltspring Island in 1859. On September 20 Jonathan Begg wrote to the *New Westminster Times,* informing its readers that "the settlement of the land is progressing favorably, and considering all circumstances, rapidly. Cabins are being built, ground being cleared and other difficulties disappearing before the energetic labourers who have undertaken the task of pioneers."[57] Begg had taken up his land in one of the first settlements on the island, which soon became known as Begg's Settlement. A number of British settlers, many of whom had worked for the Hudson's Bay Company, lived in the vicinity of this north-eastern settlement.[58] By early spring 1860 settlers had begun clearing their land. In September of that year, the visiting Bishop George Hills noted that he "visited most of the log houses that are built on each lot. The land is ... quite park-like and the soil is sometimes rich black loam."[59]

Begg's Settlement was not the only area settled in 1859. Another group of settlers took up land in the vicinity of Vesuvius Bay, lying a few short miles to the southwest, in 1859 and early 1860. Unlike those in Begg's Settlement, many of these settlers were African-Americans from the United States, with an added mixture of Canadian (from what is now Ontario), British, and European settlers. Within a few months, settlers were also living near the Fulford Valley, at the south end of the island.[60] Settlers were obliged to build roads, in addition to working towards the improvement of their own lands as required under the pre-emption system.[61] By the middle of December 1859, when Pemberton wrote to Douglas arguing for the adoption of a pre-emption system, the island already possessed a store, a nursery, and a post office, and had a population of forty or fifty settlers.[62] The first colonial elections on Saltspring Island were held in January 1860. By April 1861 the *Daily Press* could report that ninety-four "bonafide agricultural settlers" resided on Saltspring Island.[63]

THE PRE-EMPTION LEGISLATION

Notwithstanding the difficulties of implementing the pre-emption system of land settlement, by 1868 Joseph Trutch, surveyor-general of the united colonies of Vancouver Island and British Columbia, was convinced that the system was exactly suited to the needs of the colonies. In a long letter he outlined why. He noted that in the mainland colony, almost 1,700 pre-emption claims had been taken out by 1867, and about 30 per cent of these, comprising about 90,000 acres of land, had been "actually settled upon and improved." In the Vancouver Island colony, just over a thousand claims had been recorded by 1867, and about 70 per cent had been settled and improved. Noting that "almost the entire farming settlements of Vancouver Island as well as the Mainland of British Columbia have been made on lands acquired under the pre-emption system," Trutch argued that this system worked far better than the original one of sale by auction. In contrast to the system of outright sale, "in which large tracts of land purchased at auction for purely speculative purposes remain still in the same primitive condition as when they were sold – not a tree felled – not an acre ploughed up – totally unproductive to the owners – and retarding the general progress of the Country," he maintained that pre-emption was "most important when regarded as the first steps towards development of the capabilities of the Colony."[64]

As Robert Cail has outlined in some detail, the Land Ordinances of 1860 and 1861 had provided the backbone of the land legislation in effect in 1867 when Trutch provided this evaluation of the land system. Similar legislation remained in force throughout the nineteenth century. The 1861 Land Ordinance outlined in detail the pre-emption regulations roughly drawn up in 1860. It stated that all British male subjects over eighteen years of age could pre-empt land, provided the claim was not on an Indian reserve or settlement.[65] Each man could take up 150 acres if single, and 200 acres if married. Applications for pre-emption had to be accompanied by a description of the land. When the land was surveyed, the settler was required to pay the price of four shillings and two pence per acre, and three years were allowed for full payment. If, after two years, the settler could demonstrate that he had been in continuous occupation of his land, and that he had made improvements amounting to two shillings per acre, he could obtain a certificate of improvement. After receiving this certificate, the pre-emptor was allowed to mortgage, transfer, or purchase his land at the special price of ten shillings per acre. An absence of no more than two months from the claim was allowed, or it would be forfeit.[66]

The Land Ordinance of 1870, in effect when the colonies entered Confederation, closely resembled this legislation. There were a few changes. Pre-emptions of unsurveyed lands were, for example, restricted to 320 acres east and 160 acres west of the Cascades. Also, pre-emptors were not allowed to take out more than one claim at a time, and improvements had to be made to the amount of $2.50 per acre. Bona-fide personal residence of the owner on the claim was insisted on, replacing the earlier edict that anyone could be appointed to occupy the claim. The purchase price, after improvement, was set at $1 per acre, and a crown grant was obtainable after a survey and payment of all fees.[67] Revisions in the 1875 Land Act provided for pre-emptions of smaller plots of land, and of surveyed, as well as unsurveyed, land, but upheld the single pre-emption rule, and the same acreages as the 1870 Ordinance. Free land grants, also established in 1875, did not stimulate land settlement, and were no longer offered after revisions to the Land Act in 1879.[68] By 1879 the provincial government had also decided to tighten up its regulations concerning payment for improved land, allowing for payment by installment, but requiring it within four years.[69]

The Land Act of 1884 raised the price of surveyed and unsurveyed agricultural lands from $1 to $2.50 per acre, but the price of pre-empted land remained at $1 per acre. A ceiling of 640 acres was placed on the extent of unsurveyed land that could be purchased. Another land act in 1888 broke new ground by classifying different kinds of land as agricultural or timber lands, and facilitating grazing leases for the growing cattle industry. Again, reflecting the increasing realization of the relative scarcity of agricultural lands, and the desire to protect such lands from speculators, restrictions on the amount of surveyed and unsurveyed land that could be taken up came into effect with the Land Act of 1891. Classifications of types of agricultural lands were also refined.[70] Although there were many variations in land legislation throughout the century, the principles of cheap rural land, deferred payment, the purchase of such land on condition that it had been cleared, fenced, and built on, and the residence of the bona-fide settler on the land remained intact from 1860 to the end of the century.

THE MEANING OF RURAL LANDS: AGRICULTURE AND THE FAMILY FARM

The factors discussed above provided the immediate context of early land settlement in the colonies of Vancouver Island and British Columbia. To understand the wider significance of both the pre-emption system and the vision of country lands on which it was based, we must step back a little to look at the broader context of rural land settlement in the colony and province throughout the later nineteenth century. Policy makers, editorialists, and a growing stream of settlers repeatedly stressed that "the mining as well as the other interests in the colony are dependent on its agricultural development for their prosperity."[71] Rural was clearly identified with agricultural land, settled by small producers and their families. To rural society fell the task of providing the foundation of wealth, establishing the white population, and ensuring social stability in the growing colony and province.[72]

The concern with land settlement was not limited to administrators and policy makers – it is one of the striking features of a broad range of evidence available from the nineteenth-century. Despite the propensity of twentieth-century historians to look to capital enterprise in logging, mining, and fishing as the foundation of wealth and settlement in British Columbia, newspapers, colonial correspondence, personal memoirs, and land legislation (which discouraged land speculation and encouraged agricultural settlement) suggest that this other, more agrarian vision preoccupied many in the nineteenth century. When the Victoria *Weekly British Colonist* declared in May 1860 that "there is no interest here so important as that of agriculture,"[73] it was not indulging in rural nostalgia, nor was it simply expressing the view of a group of disillusioned miners. It was reflecting a commonly held view that land was the basis of security and wealth in society. "Get settlers into British Columbia," argued the *Colonist*, "and they will raise provisions, make roads, and generally develope [sic] the resources of the country."[74]

Although it would eventually become clear to governors and governed that British Columbia was going to have an economy rooted in something other than agriculture, this was not yet apparent to many of those living in the province throughout the later nineteenth century. The conviction that individual landownership would provide the foundation of the provincial economy was clearly expressed in the debates leading up to British Columbia's union with Canada. Amor De Cosmos, member for the Victoria District, declared in 1870, "If the terms between British Columbia and Canada do not protect the farming interest, the largest and only permanent interest in this Colony, Confederation will do no good. If it does not protect the farming interest, I vote against Confederation, first, last and all the time."[75] Daniel Marshall's detailed study of voting patterns in the provincial legislature of the early 1870s reveals a clear pattern in pre-party politics: the tariff question, centring on the protection of markets for the benefit of farmers in the province, was the single most important political issue that divided members of the Legislative Assembly as the province entered its first years in confederation with Canada.[76]

The agricultural potential of the province provided a standard theme in the literature enticing immigrants to colony and province; pamphlets and guidebooks promised that "circumstances here greatly favour the prosecution of small farming."[77] The *Handbook of British Columbia and Emigrant's Guide to the Gold Fields* (1862) began with the assertion that "British Columbia is apparently a second England, with the added advantages of gold fields the richest in the world. It is computed to contain about 200,000 square miles of land, fitted to the labor of the agriculturist."[78] Maintaining that "its agricultural capabilities are almost illimitable," the author argues that "men of steady and industrious habits, possessed of small capital, ... would, there is little doubt, do well in following agricultural pursuits in British Columbia."[79] An 1883 pamphlet urged the settler to appreciate the "immense advantage to a settler to be in mineral country, because the mines give, or will give, work to those able to undertake it, and will create local markets which otherwise might not exist for generations." Everything that brought people to the province, pamphlets argued, "specially benefits the farming settler."[80] Immigration literature reassured potential settlers about the viability of farming by reference to the imports of food from the United States and elsewhere.[81]

Immigrants were being drawn by the benefits of capital accumulation through farming, but the ideal of independence inherent in landownership was also of great importance. For large numbers of nineteenth-century Canadians, a farm was not simply, or even mainly, a money-making business enterprise; it was the best security for a family in a world where neither the market economy nor the state could be relied on to provide the foundations of economic support.[82] As one pamphlet urged, "Why should a farmer in the old country continue to pay rent ... when, with one year's rental, he can purchase a partially prepared farm with buildings on it in the thoroughly British province of British Columbia?"[83] In 1895 the Reverend Wilson, Anglican minister of Saltspring Island, explained the advantages of farming to prospective settlers in this way: "A farm on the Pacific coast may not, perhaps, yield its owner a fortune, but it will at any rate enable him to make a living and to bring up a family with comparative ease and comfort."[84] Agriculture in British Columbia was to provide a safe and secure living for those "who would be glad, untrammeled by conventions, to make a home for themselves by work, bring up their children to a healthy, independent life, and gratify those tastes for shooting and fishing which their means will not permit in the Old Country."[85]

In trying to establish what social commentators and reformers found so compelling about this particular rural vision, it is important to remember that the economic advantages of agriculture were inseparable from a particular set of cultural values: land was not simply to provide for the subsistence needs of the province; it was to do so in a way that was compatible with particular ideas about the family, liberal democracy, and the progress of civilization; ideas that were inseparable from colonial settlement. As a result of the encounter with "America," Europeans as early as the seventeenth century came to a new appreciation of the relative importance of their agriculture and commerce.[86] This privileging of agriculture persisted. By the late nineteenth century, Europeans had "constructed a pyramidal evolutionary model with their own culture occupying the apex and all others ranked on an ascending scale from hunting to farming to industrial society."[87] As Adele Perry argues, reformers were actively working throughout the later nineteenth century to "create an orderly, white settler colony anchored in respectable gender and racial behaviours and identities."[88] Land settlement played a key role in this process.

Land policies in the process of being realized. This small unidentified wooden cabin among the stumps was typical of island houses in the later nineteenth century when houses made of sawn lumber were beginning to replace the older log cabins. (SSIA)

The construction of British Columbia as an empty wilderness awaiting civilized use, no less than the literature surrounding agricultural development, provides evidence of this evolutionist, ethnocentric paradigm. The large Aboriginal populations on the coast, designated primitives, were transformed by the colonial discourse into part of this empty, natural landscape, waiting to be turned to productive use, civilized just as the land they lived on was cultivated. As Edward Mallandaine (architect, teacher, and early landowner on Saltspring Island) stated in his *First Victoria Directory* of 1860: "Land, wild, tenanted only by the bear, the wolf and deer is valueless; but land obtained gratuitously by industrious men, and by them made to produce the 'fruits of the earth' is valuable, because turned to its natural and intended use, and enhances the value (gives it, then, in fact) of the remainder."[89] As historians of Aboriginal British Columbia have demonstrated, the discourse of land settlement and the agrarian ideology it contained are inseparable from the political, economic, and ideological context of colonial expansion.[90]

Settler culture in British Columbia has been identified with the "raw self-interest" manifested by settlers caught up in "overwhelming European technological supremacy."[91] But the discourse that associated rural land use with the commercially viable family farm differs in some significant ways from parallel discourses of progress rooted in industrial and other forms of capitalist development. How do we reconcile this family-based bucolic vision with the aggressive liberal individualism that has been used to categorize social and economic relations in nineteenth-century British Columbia? Notwithstanding the importance of the gold rush, the discovery of coal, and, later, of the commercial value of timber, the discourse of laissez-faire capitalism was, as land legislation suggests, mediated by the discordant voice of small-scale production on the family farm.[92]

In his study of liberalism, nation building, and family property law in British Columbia in the 1860s, Christopher Clarkson argues that the family was particularly important in the liberal discourse that identified rural with small-scale landownership of agrarian lands. He suggests that this particular construction of rural shared some important points with some strands of liberal capitalist ideology in Britain and America: "while economic development and liberalism's theoretical economic equality of opportunity appealed to most Pacific north western reformers, the social effects of capitalistic acquisitive individualism did not. They, like republicans, clear grits and British radical Liberals, idealized property-based democracy and economic equality for yeomen smallholders, artisans, tradesmen, merchants and entrepreneurial businessmen. The prospect of industrial monopolies, widespread wage labour and a large landless proletariat was abhorrent to them."[93]

Clarkson argues that British Columbia reformers such as Amor de Cosmos and John Robson, recoiling against fears concerning the consequences of laissez-faire capitalism, nevertheless kept their faith in this system by looking to the families who would constitute the household-based and small-scale capitalism of rural society. The family, and the values it represented as an extra- or sub-capitalist formation, would provide a foil against the worst aspects of capitalism and shore up nation-building in a number of important ways.[94] Demographically, land-based families would establish a permanent Anglo-Saxon base for nation-building; for, as Adele Perry has argued, white women would "raise the moral tone of the white, male-dominated society, quell the rapid development of a mixed-blood community, and ensure that British law, mores and economic development flourished."[95] Furthermore, because the discourse of liberal economics positioned families outside the relentless search for rational self-interest, it was the family that could best allay fears that competition would escalate "to the point where self-gratifying desire and instinctual self-preservation over-ruled altruism, morality and social cooperation."[96] Finally, small-scale agricultural production, as a household-based industry, would prevent capitalism from destroying the family at the same time that it limited proletarianization, thereby curtailing the social and cultural alienation that capitalism too often entailed. The family, in its rural setting, was the "stable social institution" in the reformers' nation-building agenda, reflecting, in Clarkson's words, "desires for progress, order and individual equality, all of which were threatened by lasissez-faire capitalism."[97]

At the same time that agriculture would provide the economic foundation of the province's resource industries, therefore, petty commodity production on the family farm would provide the ideological underpinnings, through economic independence, necessary for a fully functioning liberal state.[98] This helps to explain why, in spite of the hyperbole about free enterprise, land policies continued throughout this period to identify beneficial use with the settlement of small-scale agricultural producers on the land.[99] It also explains the ideological appeal of the pre-emption system, which expressly limited the rights of individual landowners to treat their land as a commodity, so as to preserve it for family farms. The pre-emption system resolved tensions in the official discourse of rural – impatience with stability on the one hand and apprehensions about progress on the other – by allocating to the rural family the responsibility for preventing the self-destruction of the capitalist state.

By the 1890s discussions surrounding land settlement were taking place within the increasingly detailed context of agricultural land use. Like so many other Victorian-era bureaucracies in the Western world, the British Columbia government demonstrated its interest in the subject by creating reports and compiling detailed statistics.[100] In 1891 the Department of Agriculture published its first report, which aimed to provide detailed statistical support of the government's belief that "this Province is thoroughly suited in every way, by soil and climate, for good farming."[101] In addition to educating farmers in modern agricultural practices, the Department of Agriculture reports served the explicit goal of providing information to prospective immigrants who would be drawn by the agricultural potential of the province.[102] As James Anderson, statistician, proclaimed in the First Report on Agriculture in the Province in 1891: "enough information has been obtained to prove that the Province is not the 'Sea of Mountains' it has been represented [sic], and although it cannot be compared in extent as a grain growing country to the Great North West, nor can it aspire to produce 70,000 or 80,000 turkeys in a season like the County of Lanark, Ontario, ... it will, with improved means of communication, and transport, yet show that it is not to be ignored in the matter of agricultural production, while its climatic excellence is too well known to need descanting upon."[103]

In the process of industriously creating reports detailing the growth of agriculture in the province, bureaucrats and statisticians have provided

By the late 1880s the Akerman family had a thriving farm in the Burgoyne Valley.
(SSIA)

historians with a view of the "process by which visions of reality, models
of social structure, were elaborated and revised."[104] When we turn to the
statistical record, the vision of social order we see is portrayed in the cash
value of farms and the market value of produce. It is a vision of rural life
understood within the context of an efficient and scientifically informed
industry, and defined by the presence of the commercial farmer.

Statistics provided the material standard against which agricultural
success or failure was measured, but the moral imperative that was always present in the literature took on an increasingly dominant tone
over time. In British Columbia, as in the rest of Canada, governments
looked to rural areas for the stability and security that seemed to be
quickly disappearing from urban and industrial life. Farm schools, soldiers' settlements, and agricultural education programmes are examples of the ways that the government looked to the countryside to
compensate for the demoralizing modernization of urban areas.[105] As
this federal Agricultural Bulletin from 1919 suggests, by the inter-war
period discussions on rural life had taken on a typically Edwardian
moral fervour:

Agriculture is the basic science upon which rests the superstructure of our economic wealth; a most important industry, which makes for the highest development and the moral and physical well-being of the people ... no other vocation

Figure 1.1
Number of Pre-emptions by Year and Region, British Columbia, 1873–1901

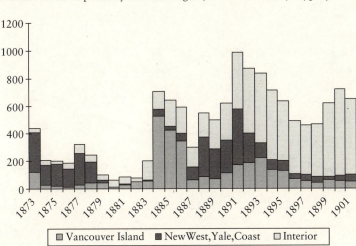

Source: Cail, *Land, Man and the Law,* Appendix B, Table 1.

has so many claims to preeminence as this, the oldest pursuit in the world ... the farmer alone adds to the common wealth; his calling is a co-operative triumph of nature and science, which exemplifies the faithfulness of mother earth in rewarding the mental and physical energy of man, when intelligently applied to unlocking the secrets of nature's treasure vaults ... The success of agriculture is absolutely necessary to the existence of a stable and prosperous nature.[106]

How successful were the attempts of the government to turn British Columbia into a province of farmers? As Robert Cail argues in *Land, Man and the Law,* government administrators devoted considerable time, effort, and money to developing and overseeing land policies that identified "beneficial use" of country lands with the installation of "bona-fide settlers" on such lands. Records suggest that many people must have found the prospect of landownership appealing: before 1871, when the non-Native population stood at about 9,000, over 4,000 pre-emptions had been granted in the British Columbia and Vancouver Island colonies.[107]

Between 1873 and 1900 the number of pre-emptions grew to 18,000 and, by 1913, over 37,000 pre-emptions had been taken out by prospective settlers (Figure 1.1).[108] For these people, the real opportunities offered by the province seemed to lie in small-scale landownership. Government records suggest that many of the stated objectives with

Figure 1.2
Total Value of Production in British Columbia Primary Industries, in millions of
dollars, 1915–30

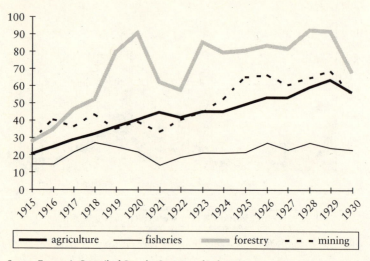

Source: Economic Council of Canada, *Statistics of Industry in B.C. 1871–1934* (1935);
1915–1920 agricultural figures are extrapolated from Census of Canada, 1931, Vol. 8,
Table 1.

regard to land settlement were achieved by the early decades of the
twentieth century. While one historian has claimed that statistics show
that "farming for many people was on the limits of marginaliza-
tion,"[109] his view is not borne out by the numbers of people taking out
pre-emptions, or reportedly involved in farming in the province.[110]
Farmers' Institutes, and their women's auxiliary, the Women's Institutes, flourished as the rural population flaunted its agricultural character. An editorial in the *Vancouver Province* in 1927 declared British
Columbia a "farming province," and suggested that while agriculture
still trailed behind forestry as the most lucrative industry, "it promises,
very shortly, to assume the leading position."[111] As Figure 1.2 demonstrates, farming continued to be an important industry well into the
twentieth century.

CONCLUSION

Although we know little about the motives and intentions of the first
settlers to arrive on Saltspring Island in 1859, we know a great deal
more about the legal and cultural contexts of their settlement. Even
though British law required that Native title be extinguished on lands

being opened up for settlement in the late 1850s, this did not, for the most part, occur. Instead, a special series of colonial land policies provided the ideological and legal foundation on which settlers carved immigrant societies out of Native space. Whatever personal feelings about country lands settlers had, or whatever their particular personal contexts, when the first non-Native settlers arrived on Saltspring Island in 1859, they did so because a particular and ideologically informed system of colonial land acquisition and land use framed their right to do so. This system also directed the way that they took up and used their land. Policy makers developed land policies and regulations that reflected their own cultural beliefs about the countryside, about families, about the Empire, and about the nature of a good society.

The dominant public discourse about country lands, visible in land legislation, land regulations, government reports, and some settlers' reflections and journalists' musings, identified beneficial land use with the establishment of would-be farmers on agricultural lands. This public discourse was visible in the pre-emption system, which encouraged settlers with little capital to settle on country lands, where government agents actively encouraged the pursuit of small-scale agricultural production on the family farm. These policies had their ideological roots in the belief that the independent yeomen and their families would naturally create thriving agricultural economies that would provide a moral and economic foundation for the new colony. These beliefs about land and settlement reflected not only their experience in Britain but also the deeply held liberal beliefs in the colony and province about civilization, progress, individualism, and the growth of capitalism. The next two chapters explore in more detail some of the specific ways in which this discourse shaped the rural society growing up on Saltspring Island in the second half of the nineteenth century.

2

Settling Up the Wild Lands

In a letter to his sister and brother-in-law early in 1860, just a few short months after taking up land at the north end of Saltspring Island, Jonathan Begg explained the advantages that the island held for a settler like himself, and the benefits that a settler like himself brought to the new colony. "I need not tell you that commencing in the wilderness without capital and a stranger to boot has been a hard task," he wrote, "but I have perseverance and industry. I have so far surmounted all my difficulties in a very satisfactory way, and am now in possession of 200 acres on the Pacific coast. I have got about three acres inclosed [sic] and under cultivation, which I am at present at work on. We will be able to put in 1 acre of vegetables, 1 acre turnips and cabbage, 1 acre potatoes. I have planted 75 apple trees this spring, and put in a number of gooseberries and current [sic] bushes in addition to the crop already referred to." Ever cognizant of the commercial potential of his agricultural land and works, Begg went on to write that "you may imagine how vegetables pay here, when green peas sell at 10 to 20 cts per bu., cabbages from 2 1/2 to 10 cts, turnips 2 1/2 cts, etc. etc."[1] Two years later, he argued that in Canada or the Northern States, "you see no growth of fruit trees like what we have here." Begg confidently asserted that "my commencing that trade here has been a decided hit. A large local demand has sprung up, owing to the number of settlers just now settling up the wild lands."[2]

The story of "settling up the wild lands" that Begg narrates in his colourful letters of the late 1850s and early 1860s is familiar to historians, history buffs, and anyone who watches television dramas like "Little House on the Prairie," which portray nineteenth-century families in the North American West. Hard-working, optimistic, respectable but needing ready money, always with an eye to the main agricultural chance, Begg seemed to be exactly the kind of settler (as he claimed)

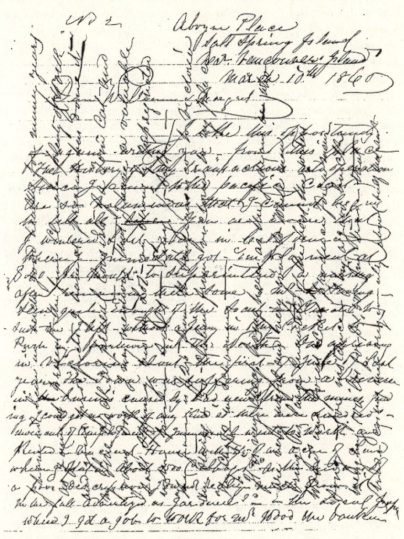

Like many people sending letters in the nineteenth century, Jonathan Begg kept the cost of mailing lower by writing "cross hatch" style to conserve paper.

that could tame the wilderness and transform it into productive farm-land. He was, in other words, just the kind of man to realize the partic-ular vision of rural success that was so clear in his mind's eye. Less transparent to Begg were the specific and yet fragile assumptions he was taking for granted about rural life on the island, most particularly about the inevitability of its progress towards a rural, commercial agri-cultural future.[3]

A very particular discourse about rural life, which equated rural set-tlement with the progress of commercial agriculture, framed the way that Begg and other newcomers saw the rural lands around Victoria. It encouraged them to see Saltspring Island and other country lands as a harbinger of British Columbia's agricultural future. The newspaper re-ports, government documents, travel accounts, and personal memoirs relating to Saltspring Island in these early years evince this discourse as they document changes in the colony. They seem to tell the coherent story of aspiring farm families treading the well-worn path from pio-neer subsistence to commercial agriculture as lands were slowly cleared and brought into production.[4] By 1891 even the bureaucrats in the provincial Department of Agriculture had embraced a hyperbolic rhet-oric of boosterism to describe and quantify the rich agricultural bounty that they perceived in the southern Vancouver Island region in general and Saltspring Island in particular.

This discourse was more prescriptive than descriptive. It was at best selective, and, in its most extreme manifestations, a serious misrepresen-tation of the kind of rural society, economy, and culture experienced by most Saltspring Islanders. The discourse that appears in so many writ-ten sources purporting to describe Saltspring Island in the 1859–1891 period (and presented in this chapter in a deliberately uncritical manner) does not provide an "accurate" representation of lived experience. It does, however, accord us a fine view of how rural society, economy, and culture were framed and understood by those writing about colonial British Columbia. And this discourse had teeth: it shaped the behav-iours of settlers like Begg directly by narrowing and limiting the way they imagined community and the uses of rural land; and it shaped their behaviours indirectly, most significantly through land regulations de-signed to create the kind of rural society imagined within the discourse.

Those writing about Saltspring Island before the 1880s, seeing it through this discursive lens, commonly identified it as a community in the pioneer stages of development. The railway boom of the 1880s marked the maturing of the agricultural economy, at least in the eyes of island observers, for after this time, it was generally assumed that its commercial agricultural promise had been realized. Implicit in the terms of the pre-emption system, and most explicit in newspaper and government reports, the discourse constituted the outer shell, as it were, of Saltspring Island's identity, an outer shell that perhaps appeared smoothest and firmest to those who were farthest away in space and time.

PIONEER SETTLEMENT, 1859–81

Even though it is clear that those writing about the island measured its progress and evaluated its success against a very particular vision of rural life, unfortunately almost no statistical data are available concerning production or land clearances for the 1859–1881 period. The first dominion census was not conducted until 1881, and the Department of Agriculture did not start publishing an annual report until 1891. Little household-level data are available to attest to the state of British Columbia agriculture, as the household agricultural schedules after 1871 have been destroyed. Even though a specific model of family-based commercial agriculture defined the general discourse of settlement, we know – as I will make clear – that people on Saltspring often actually lived by substantially non-agricultural means through this entire period. For example, the Aboriginal settlers who married or partnered with non-Native men on the island helped to augment the hunting, fishing, and gathering skills of immigrants, providing them with local knowledge that made it possible to live off the rich bounty that had supported thousands of years of human settlement in coastal British Columbia. But such people and activities were seldom represented within the colonial discourse and, when they were, they figured as exceptions in an otherwise coherent pattern of European settlement. Certainly, they were not identified as the early stages of a new, or hybrid, culture on the coast.

When Begg wrote to his sister and brother-in-law in 1862 that he was living in a "a country we can grow stuff in," he was clearly thinking of the benefits that would accrue to the agricultural capitalist, as the rest of his letter (and indeed most of his correspondence) attests: "There are many good openings in the way of farming in this country; in fact no country in the globe shows the like. I know farms that have netted 30,000 dollars. I know some farmers that have made $10,000 in cutting and stacking wild hay in the course of 6 weeks. Barley and oats for fodder brings 20 to 25 cents per lb. and it costs me $4 1/2 a night at some points to keep a horse in hay. When will your Iowa prices compare with that? There is no country that presents the openings for a working man that this does."[5]

Begg was not alone in his aspirations to develop systems of agricultural commodity production and commercial distribution. Newspapers frequently reported on the market opportunities offered by the island's agricultural potential. In a series of articles about the island and the promise it held for the future of commercial agriculture in British Columbia, the Victoria *Daily Press* noted in 1861 that the island, like neighbouring Vancouver Island, is "intersected with rocky hills, running S.E. and S.W. Between these there are many valleys of extremely rich land. There are many open plats." The article goes on to note the island's suitability for livestock raising: "cattle thrive all year round upon the herbage and some parts are well suited for sheep walks ... Springs abound and the water is good;" and its suitability for growing a variety of crops suitable for home consumption and commercial production: "There are all kinds of grain and a great variety of vegetables ... The Indian corn grown here is very fair ... The wild fruits are very plentiful ... and orchards and strawberry beds are likely to prove profitable."[6]

Saltspring Island was perceived from its earliest days as a community that could, and would, realize its potential as a commercially successful farming settlement. Begg, dubbed "one of the first and most respectable of the [Saltspring Island] settlers," by the *New Westminster Times*,[7] and its most vocal booster, was able to report to that newspaper in September 1859 that "the settlement of the land is progressing favorably."[8] By December 1859, "having obtained the agency for the sale of Fruit Trees from some of the best Nurseries in Oregon and California,"[9] Begg had established Balmoral nursery and general store on his property. From here he sold nursery stock and his expertise in planting and maintaining orchards, and he also bought and sold island produce. Just five months after the first settlers arrived, the island had a population forty or fifty settlers, a small store, and a post office.[10]

Begg had taken up his land in what soon became known as Begg's Settlement. In the vicinity of this north-eastern settlement were a number of British settlers, many of whom had worked for the Hudson's Bay Company.[11] By early spring, 1860, settlers had begun clearing their land, and by September of that year some 8,000 acres had been taken up, and "A log barn has been built upon each." Three to five acres had been cultivated on each lot and "garden produce of all sorts is to be seen. Cabbages, potatoes, beetroots, onions, tomatoes, peas, cucumbers, watermelons, carrots and wheat and oats, pigs, poultry and calves."[12] Political activity was also developing on the island, launched with the first colonial elections in January 1860. By April 1861 the *Daily Press* could report that ninety-four "bona fide agricultural settlers" resided on Saltspring Island.[13] In May 1860 Begg had expanded his agricultural frontier beyond the limits of his own property and, with five other island residents, had formed the Saltspring Island Agricultural

Association. As Begg promoted in the notice he issued to the *British Colonist*, "the probabilities are that if like societies are formed throughout the island, and farming engaged in energetically and systematically, we shall be enabled in a short time to export, instead of importing nearly every article of daily consumption."[14]

The indefatigable Begg had cleared and fenced a lot of land, built two houses, and planted 7,000 fruit and other trees by the time he applied for his certificate of improvement in 1862. In that same year he applied for a Leave of Absence from his claim to broaden his entrepreneurial scope by heading for the Cariboo goldfields. He travelled "some 1500 miles with my blankets and grub on my back," hoping to make a quick profit out of selling produce to the miners. The journey was not a commercial success, however, because of the exigencies of production and trade on "the frontier"; as he noted in a letter to his sister, "I packed cabbage plants right into the mines and planted them out also. I should have realized $2.50 per head if I had not got starved out before they matured."[15]

Those occupying neighbouring properties on Saltspring Island did not reach the dizzy entrepreneurial heights aspired to by Begg, but neighbours such as Englishman Henry Sampson and Irishmen James McFadden and George Mills seemed to have worked hard to establish viable agricultural properties in these early years. All three had been employed by the Hudson's Bay Company at a variety of locations, including Fort Langley and Fort Victoria, before coming to Saltspring in 1859.[16] By 1862 Sampson and his partner, Mr Baker, had built a house, fenced some land, and were in possession of twelve cows and a horse.[17] Mills, like Begg, stayed only a few years on his land – both were gone by 1865 – but each had made some substantial improvements to their land before transferring it, as they both did, to Thomas Griffiths. In 1864 the Victoria *Colonist* noted that fellow Welshmen, Mssrs Brinn and Griffiths, who had purchased Begg's nursery earlier that year, were in possession of a "nursery for fruit trees ... [that] may safely be set down as the largest in the whole colony of Vancouver Island."[18] More than ten years later, the *Guide to The Province of British Columbia* noted that Griffiths was still making his living by selling – in Nanaimo and Victoria – raspberries, apples, grain-fed fowl, and eggs from the farms of Saltspring Island.[19]

Begg's Settlement was but one of three major settlements on the island in which people took up land in these early years. Geography exerted a considerable influence on patterns of settlement. Prospective farmers like Begg and Sampson were attracted to the island's arable lands, but these fertile areas were restricted to valley bottoms separated by rocky hills and mountains that provided serious obstacles not only

Integrated schooling at North Vesuvius School, Fernwood (Begg's Settlement).
Schools reflected the African-American, Irish, English, Scots, Hawaiian, Aboriginal,
and European population of the island. (SSIA)

to farming but also to the transportation of farm goods. In a country
where roads were difficult to build, the ocean still provided the easiest
trade route between the island communities, as well as the only route
between the island and the coastal communities growing up around it.
A mountain range separated Begg's Settlement from its nearest neighbouring settlement, one that stretched between Ganges Harbour and
Vesuvius Bay. A petition from settlers at Begg's Settlement in 1865,
protesting the new route of the steamship that bypassed their community, announced: "it seems that the steamer calls regularly at Vesuvius
Bay, on the west side of the Island, and communication with which
point lies over a mountainous range, rendering it difficult and at this
season of the year out of the question to send any of their produce
there for shipment to a market."[20]

The trade preferences thereby granted to the Vesuvius settlement over
Begg's Settlement contributed to political friction between the two communities, and may have exacerbated racial tensions between the predominantly British Begg's Settlement, and the African-American settlement
of Vesuvius Bay. For unlike Begg's Settlement, which was first settled
by Canadians (from present-day Ontario), Europeans, some British settlers, and the Aboriginal wives who took up with them, the Ganges-
Vesuvius settlement was settled primarily by African-Americans.[21] In

1858 Governor James Douglas had invited the original African-American settlers, including Louis Stark and his family, whom we met briefly in chapter 1, to take up land, and the citizenship rights that accompanied landownership, in the new colony.[22] A number of these made their way up the Saanich Peninsula, and about twenty families took up land on Saltspring Island in the 1859–1869 period.

Like other families throughout Saltspring Island, African-American settlers took up country lands under a homesteading system that required them to clear, fence, and build on their lands in order to purchase them at a low and deferred purchase price. The *Daily Press* reported in 1861 that it had received "samples of wheat, oats, and barley grown on the farm of Mr. Abraham Copeland, which are certainly not to be surpassed on the coast. This gentleman has about fifteen acres under cultivation."[23] Stark, moving with his family from Missouri, took up land in Vesuvius Bay in 1859 and began work clearing and fencing it. Like many of the early settlers, Stark also worked hard to fulfill his responsibility to build roads on the island. The Reverend Ebenezer Robson, visiting the island as a Methodist preacher in 1861, was particularly impressed by the accomplishments of the Stark family:

We came up to Mr Stark's. He met us at the landing. We found a pleasant and pious person in Mr Stark's wife. They once were slaves in the Southern United States, that land of liberty. Mr Stark bought himself for $1500. Mrs S.'s father [Howard Estes] bought her. They were married in California. They came up to the Island 2 years ago and now they with their children 3 in number are living on their own farm. It is good land and they only pay $1 per acre for it. Mr Stark has about 39 head of cattle. He sowed one quart of wheat near his house last winter and reaped 180 quarts in the summer. One grain of wheat produced 2360 grains on 59 branches. His turnips of which he has a large quantity are beautiful and large – also cabbage etc etc. His wife who was converted about 2 months ago filled my sacks with good things – 4 lbs fresh butter, 2 qts new milk.[24]

The Starks abandoned this piece of land in the early 1870s after a series of murders in the community, widely rumoured to be the result of Aboriginal attacks, prompted them to take up land away from the coast. The issue of Aboriginal land title took on a very personal meaning for many of the settlers on Saltspring, as in other areas of the two colonies in these years.[25]

African-American John Craven Jones took up 100 acres in the Vesuvius area in 1861, and by 1874 he had built a house, a barn, and some outbuildings, in addition to clearing land and erecting a "large quantity of fencing."[26] Jones taught at the two earliest schools on the island from their inception until the time he left the island in the mid-1870s.[27]

Another range, aptly called the Divide, runs between the north half of the island and the south. The south end was geographically closer to markets in Victoria, but better harbours, greater availability of arable land, and easy proximity to the new commercial and coal mining town of Nanaimo, encouraged the first non-Natives to take up land in the northern area. Ethnic clustering and chain migrations of both British and African-American settlers may also have been responsible for the decision of a number of people to settle in northern areas in the first two decades of non-Native settlement. In 1866 the Reverend Cave visited the island and estimated the population on the north end at "17 couples, 22 single men, and 42 children."[28]

Land in the south end of island was taken up more slowly. By 1866 228 pre-emptions had been taken out in the north end of the island, the vast majority of which were quickly abandoned. By that date only nineteen pre-emptions had been taken out in the south end,[29] and of these only eight families remained in that year. Cave was "unable to reach" the south end community at Burgoyne Bay during his survey of the island in 1866, but he was told that about fifteen people lived there.[30] By 1874, when Ashdown Green conducted an informal census of the island, the population of the south end was still small, enumerated at twenty-one men, thirteen women, and twenty children (see Table 2.1).[31] With no Jonathan Begg to spur them along, and no steamboat service at Beaver Point, only forty-two settlers had taken out pre-emptions in the south end of the island by 1881, as compared with ninety-six in the north end.

Although the south end attracted fewer people to take up lands, those who did were more inclined than their counterparts on the northern part of the island to stay: only a quarter of those pre-empting northern Saltspring lands up to 1881 stayed more than ten years, whereas more than half of the south-end settlers remained on the island for over a decade.[32] Steamer and post-office service was established at the south end in the 1880s, and more people began moving into the area in the late 1870s. The increased settlement at this time, in combination with the higher persistence rates and larger families, resulted in a higher population in south Saltspring Island than in the north in 1881: 148 people in thirty-nine families, as opposed to 110 people in thirty-two families.[33]

Settlers in the south end of the island included George Mitchell, another former Hudson's Bay Company employee. He had cleared and cultivated about six acres by 1874, and had 160 acres fenced, presumably for grazing. Michael Gyves, an Irishman and a wheelwright by trade, had arrived from Ireland via New York, where he had joined the United States army. His name appears on a plaque commemorating

Table 2.1
Ashdown Green's Survey of South Saltspring Island, November 1874

Name	Men	Women	Children	Horses	Cattle	Sheep	Pigs
Mitchell	1	1	3	2			
McDonald	1	1					
Cairnes	1	1	2		9		
Purser	1	x	3		7		20
Foord	1	1					
Williams	1	1					
Sparrow	1	x	3	1	30		
Gyves	1	x					
Welch	1						
Meinerstorf	1			1	12		8
Trage and Spikerman	2	x	1		13		28
Ruckle	1				17		20
Howmere (Kanaka)	1	x			2		12
Nuan (Kanaka)	1	x					
Shepherd	1	x	4				
Pimburys	3				2	350	
Akerman	1	1	4				
Weston	1						
Total	21	13	20	4	92	350	88

Source: 20 November 1874; Ashdown Green, Diary of a Survey of Saltspring Island, 8 June –
22 November 1874, Add Mss 437, BCA.
Note: x connotes a Native woman.

those who fought on the San Juan Islands during the Pig War, when
Britain and the United States were dividing up lands in the Pacific
Northwest. He left the army for the Fraser and Cariboo goldrush, according to his granddaughter. In Victoria he met John Maxwell, who
encouraged him to come to Saltspring. Gyves settled in Burgoyne Bay
in 1866, when he was thirty-three years old.[34] He met his wife Mary
Ann on the island. She was a cousin of Theodore Trage's wife, and was
of the Penelkut people, daughter of Chief Tzouhalem. By the time
Gyves obtained an improvement certificate for his land, he had built a
house, cleared fifteen acres, and fenced an additional twenty.[35]

Maxwell had arrived on Saltspring Island with his lifelong friend and
fellow Irishman, James Lunney, who also had been in the goldfields of

Theodore Trage

Susannah Trage, nee Swanac

Theodore Trage and three of his children. Trage arrived on Saltspring Island from Germany in the early 1860s with his partner, Heinrich Spikerman. Spikerman never married, but Trage soon married Susannah Swanac, of the Cowichan Band; she was a sister of John Maxwell's wife. Theodore and Susannah raised four children on the island. (SSIA)

the Cariboo in 1861, where they may have first met Gyves. Arriving with what was rumoured to be a large sum of money, they pre-empted about 360 acres of land in the rich Burgoyne Valley. They established a large cattle-raising operation, with Maxwell quickly importing about one hundred Texas Longhorns from Oregon to Victoria and then to Saltspring Island via Cowichan.[36] The pair expanded their property through a five-year grazing lease from the provincial government in 1870, where they "scattered grass seed so there is some good feed for stock."[37] Maxwell soon married a Native woman, but Lunney stayed single all his life, taking up residence near the Maxwell's. Another Burgoyne Valley neighbour at this date was Norwegian John C. Sparrow. He arrived on the island in 1862, having once been quartermaster on board an American government surveying vessel on this coast. He took up two hundred acres, which he had improved by 1866, and purchased in 1881, on which he raised hogs.[38] Like Maxwell, Sparrow married a Native wife, and raised his family on the island. The Pimbury brothers, a wealthy family of English stock, who took up land in the mountainous area of Musgrave's Landing, had 650 acres and 350 sheep by 1875.

By the late 1870s, Henry Ruckle, who had arrived from Ontario early in that decade to take up land in the Beaver Point area, was well on his way to establishing what would become the most extensive commercial farming operation on Saltspring Island. In 1874 Ruckle was living alone in a log cabin, and had cleared about thirty acres of land.[39] He married a Norwegian woman, and the family began selling their produce by means of the steamers that stopped at first at Vesuvius and, by the later 1880s, at Beaver Point and Burgoyne Bay.[40] Local lore claims that Henry Ruckle's eloquence about the benefits of Saltspring Island life was responsible for drawing a number of worthy settlers to the south end of the island in the late 1870s and early 80s.[41]

Hawaiians, most of them former Hudson's Bay Company employees, were prohibited from taking up lands in the neighbouring American San Juan Islands in the early 1870s, when the islands were formally given to the United States as part of an international boundary settlement. As a result, a number moved north to nearby Saltspring Island, married Native women, and pre-empted land around Isabella Point in the south end. These settlers show up as "Kanakas" in Ashdown Green's survey and in land records.[42] According to Green's census, the Hawaiian Howmere had an Indian wife, two cows, and twelve pigs. On 26 September 1874 when Green surveyed the land, he noted that Bill Howmere "has about 4 acres under cultivation principally with Indian corn or potatoes and estimates that he can get about 7 acres more on his claim."[43] Another Hawaiian settler, Naukana, born in Hawaii in 1813, may have arrived as early as 1835 in the Pacific Northwest, and worked through the 1840s and 1850s at Hudson's Bay forts in Fort Vancouver, Washington, New Caledonia, Fort Langley, Thompson River, Kamloops, and Fort Victoria, probably ending up in the San Juan Islands. Naukana and his friend John Palua took up land on Portland Island in 1872, becoming naturalized British subjects in 1889.[44]

Although Saltspring Island presented Begg with a vision of nascent commercial agricultural success, most observers were aware that any pioneer community had many obstacles to overcome before that vision could be realized. The occupational plurality that characterized work on the island was usually identified as a necessary, if transitional, part of the maturing process of the agricultural community. Observers were not surprised that commercial activity in these early years was not limited to growing and selling agricultural produce. Settlers throughout the island turned as well to other sources of income to buy provisions, and for money to invest in their farms. Joseph Akerman, for example, who arrived from England in 1863, took up rich land in the Burgoyne Valley and raised cows and sheep. But, like Begg in the north end of the island, he started a market garden on his property to provide produce and seed plants to incoming settlers and a cash income to help start up his growing farm. As a side business, he opened the first hotel on the island, the Traveller's Rest, in the 1870s.[45]

Many islanders were involved in secondary industries, most notably in the field of transportation, a characteristic of settler communities across North America.[46] For example, Captain Walker, another former Hudson's Bay Company employee who took up land in Begg's Settlement in 1859, was one of the early owners of the *Nanaimo Packet*, the ship that brought the first settlers to look at Saltspring in July 1859 and continued to freight goods and people along the coast well after Walker's retirement from the Company.[47]

Walker's boat also carried stone from a quarry established early in the 1860s at the north end of the island. A group of four Yorkshiremen, Henry Elliott, Robert Leach, John Lee, and William Senior, preempted land in the north end for this purpose.[48] Stone was taken from this quarry on Saltspring Island throughout the 1860s to Seattle, San Francisco, and Victoria, where it was used for building.[49] William Isaacs, another north Saltspring Island settler who was involved in maritime trade in the 1860s, was the master of the *Industry*, which carried both wood and stone from the island. In spite of this off-farm employment, Isaacs was one of the earliest to improve his land near Ganges Harbour.[50]

The mineral potential of the island provided the basis for much speculation, both figuratively and practically, but little mineral wealth was ever realized. Ashdown Green noted the ruins of a copper mine when he surveyed the island in 1874. Gold, copper, and coal were reportedly discovered on the island at different times, but nothing materialized from these discoveries. Hopes for discovering coal oil were also raised.[51] It was not until after the railway boom of the 1880s, however, that a large company became interested in mineral exploration: by1892, the Vancouver Coal Company had taken out a 600-acre claim at the south end of the island, but no coal or copper was ever commercially mined.[52] From the earliest days of resettlement, however, a variety of settlers expressed interested in exploiting a very different kind of mineral wealth: the salt springs at the island's north end that gave the island its name. A number of settlers thought that they might provide a source of money, either as salt mines or as health spas. Like the other plans to exploit mineral wealth on the island, this was not realized in the nineteenth century. It was not until the late twentieth century that a small, self-styled "health spa" resort was built to exploit the salt springs on Begg's original claim.

Logging fared much better than mineral exploitation as a commercial venture. Michael Gyves supported himself and his Native wife in part through selling cedar shakes from the huge trees on his property and transporting them from Fulford Harbour to Victoria via Indian canoe. He also worked throughout his life as a carpenter, building barns on and around Saltspring.[53] Theodore Trage, a settler from Germany living in the Beaver Point area of south Saltspring Island with his Native wife, was remembered by other early settlers as rowing his strawberries to market in Victoria.[54] Trage, his lifelong friend Heinrich Spikerman, and other Germans lived near Fulford Harbour. Bishop Hills, who visited the Fulford Harbour area in 1860, commented on this tiny German community on the island:

These industrious men are occupied in cutting shingles for roofing and staves for salmon casks from the cedar. They are friends who came out from Germany together, who lived at the mines in California together and who have come here and decided to remain. They are Roman Catholics, one a Protestant. They appear quiet and respectable ... The chief speaker was a fine young man who unhappily several times took the name of God in vain. They have no land yet under cultivation. They take their work to Victoria and bring back food. They clear 3 1/2 dollars on the 1000 shingles. They have a constant supply of venison ... The spot is pleasant. Some Englishmen lived a short distance off but have left for a while.[55]

Strange as it seems for British Columbians today it was not until the very end of the nineteenth century that the economic potential of British Columbia's trees was realized, and it was not until the twentieth century that logging became an important industry on the island.[56]

Of all the non-agricultural sources of wealth that were imagined by settlers trying to support themselves in the 1860s and 1870s on their still unproductive farms, tourism eventually proved to be the most sustainable; the booming retirement and tourism economy of Saltspring Island in the twenty-first century vindicates this 1861 prediction: "The time may not be very distant when neat cottages, and elegant villas will ornament the hill-sides, as summer residences for those who have to retire from the bustle of town life."[57] In 1861 that vision was still almost a hundred years in the future.

Many settlers recognized occupational plurality as a strategy to allow families to stay on lands that were not, as yet, commercially viable. Settlers were aware of many other problems of pioneer life that intervened between their vision of rural life and its realization on Saltspring Island. Land clearing and the construction of dwellings for people and livestock were foremost among those difficulties. The huge trees of the Pacific coast provided ample materials for constructing the small log cabins that were typical of the earliest homes on the island. Cutting down these giants posed formidable problems, however, for the axes commonly used in eastern areas of North America and Europe were not well-suited to the task.[58] Early settlers reported boring holes into the trees with an auger, and filling the holes with hot coals, to slowly burn the tree down. "Stumping powder" (gunpowder) was used until World War II as a means of getting rid of stumps.[59] Throughout the entire period under study here, "felling trees, burning them, digging among the stumps to plant potatoes with vegetables and different grains, getting some fowls and, later on, cattle by degrees" remained a lengthy and difficult processes.[60]

Without either cash or ready access to markets in the first decade of non-Native settlement, settlers were heavily reliant on self-provisioning. Reports about Saltspring consistently stress the variety and quantity of foodstuffs readily available to the pioneers. Bishop Hills, who visited Saltspring Island in September 1860, noted that "grouse are to be had. Deer in abundance and good. Fish plentiful."[61] Another visitor to the island in the 1860s noted, "there is also Deer, grouse and pheasants, ducks and geese swarme in the numerous inlets that indent the island."[62] Even Begg was diverted from his habitual raptures about the commercial potential of agricultural production to note that "this is the most bountiful country for wild berries."[63]

Problems with transportation created the most sustained chorus of complaint from island farmers. Frontier conditions on the island forced settlers to import a number of foods, particularly sugar, flour, and tea,[64] via Victoria or Nanaimo. Settlers frequently complained of the difficulty of sending and receiving mail.[65] Most of the complaints about transportation seem to have been rooted in the difficulties of shipping produce off the island. The early commercial aspirations of island farmers can be seen in these frustrations with transportation systems that, although better than those in other colonial areas, were a long way from meeting the standards of enthusiastic entrepreneurs like Begg.[66] In 1877 petitioners for a south-end post office were still complaining that they were "entirely shut out from the Nanaimo market, which all the rest of the coast enjoy," because "the steamer only calls on her down trip so that our letters cannot be answered until the next week, although she runs past the Bay within three quarters of a mile of our wharf and calls at other places with less populations."[67] The grave consequences that would accrue to the island's commercial agriculture without improved steamer service were emphasized in a letter from the Minister of Agriculture that accompanied another Saltspring Island petition in the same year.[68] The days of dependence on Indian canoes and rowboats for the transportation of goods on and off the island were fast disappearing by the early 1880s, however, when transportation and communication links to the island by steamer gradually began to improve.

Transportation difficulties made land acquisition unattractive to many land speculators and agriculturalists, but the relative isolation of the island should not be overstated, especially in the first two decades of settlement. At a time of few roads, and in a region where roads were sometimes impossible to construct across rocky terrain, Saltspring Island's strategic situation with regard to water-borne transportation, like its location at the centre of the growing British Columbian population, was often seen as a positive factor by contemporaries. As Begg noted, "My farm contains 200 acres of the best land in the colony and is admirably situated midway between New Westminster and Victoria, the respective capitals of British Columbia and Vancouver Island."[69] The advantages of Saltspring Island, relative to other agricultural areas, clearly declined with the growth of roads throughout the province.

In spite of poverty and the difficulties involved in clearing the land, by the fall of 1860, just over a year after the first non-Native settlers had arrived, a new community was emerging. In November 1861 the Victoria *Daily Press* concluded that the pre-emption system on Saltspring had been most effective in furthering the economic health of the region and, by so doing, had provided an important moral lesson to less enterprising members of the colony:

The encouraging policy adopted towards Saltspring Island enabled men of limited means to clear, fence and cultivate a much larger portion of their land than their neighbors in Vancouver Island could do, in fact many, but for this judicious system, would have been excluded, who now enjoy a good homestead which they can make more valuable every year. To the inexperienced, it would be a matter of surprise when observing what has been accomplished in so short a space of time by individual exertion without hired labor; but when they contrast the industry and perseverance of the many with the indolence and neglect of the few, the matter is explained.[70]

The Reverend Cave declared in 1866 that "Saltspring Island is one of the most promising settlements I have ever visited." Many of those taking up land in the 1860s would have shared Bishop Hills' conviction that on Saltspring Island "there is not better land in British Columbia that I have seen, or on Vancouver Island."[71] According to promotional literature and newspapers, then, the promise of Saltspring Island's agricultural future seemed well on its way to fruition by the beginning of the railway boom decade of the 1880s. In spite of the problems that delayed the development of the island as a commercially successful agricultural community, commentators seemed convinced that the mixed economic activity and poverty that characterized the early years of settlement represented but a stage in the inevitable progress of the community towards a more stable and successful commercial agricultural community.

CONSOLIDATING COMMERCIAL AGRICULTURAL SUCCESS: 1882–91

When the Canadian government finally agreed to fulfill its promise to the new province of British Columbia to build a transcontinental railroad linking it to the rest of Canada, communities grew up almost overnight in areas rumoured to be on, or even near, the main routes. Vancouver, which in 1886 became the western terminus, grew rapidly in the 1880s to accommodate the influx of commerce following in the wake of the railway. By 1891 British Columbia had finally come of age, politicians and community boosters argued, catapulted into the modern era by the power of steam and steel.[72]

Although Saltspring Island was a long way from both the western terminus of Vancouver and the proposed E&N railroad line between Nanaimo and Victoria, it too was influenced by the railway boom of the early 1880s. Contrary to A.F. Flucke's contention that "neither the fur trade, nor the gold rush, nor the railroad boom so much as touched the shores of Saltspring Island,"[73] land records clearly document a boom in land sales in the 1880s. Between 1881 and 1891, 183 pre-emptions – just about half the total of the entire period between 1860 and 1891 – were taken out on the island, totalling almost 24,000 acres of land.[74] Furthermore, nearly 10,000 acres of pre-empted land were purchased from the crown during this decade, compared to just over 2,000 acres in the twenty-two years before 1882.[75] For the first time in the island's history, however, outright purchases – land obtained without a prior pre-emption certificate – dominated land alienated from the crown. Over 15,000 acres of land was purchased in this way between 1882 and 1891, compared to under a thousand acres before 1882.[76] The number of acres occupied on the island increased from 8,845 in 1881 to almost 40,000 in 1891.[77] The number of landowners more than doubled, from fifty-three to 125, and the population of the island grew from 257 to 436.

Throughout the 1880s, journalists, government agents, and the settlers themselves wrote as if the island economy was finally fulfilling its agricultural destiny. For example, in 1894 petitioners for a Beaver Point Post Office noted that "those on Saltspring Island in the vicinity of Beaver Point are engaged almost wholly in agriculture, and the quality of the land being favorable and easily obtained, it is anticipated that the settlement will rapidly increase."[78] Newspapers in Victoria had their interest in the agricultural progress of Saltspring diverted by the series of political scandals that rocked the island in the 1870s, but by the time the Department of Agriculture published its first report in 1891, government reports, immigration literature, memoirs, and business directories seemed assured that Saltspring Island, like many other areas in the southern Vancouver Island area, was well on its way to fulfilling its destiny as an agricultural community.[79] Begg's optimistic 1860 prediction that "farming will be a paying business here for a long time to come"[80] seemed, by 1891, to have been realized.

Saltspring Island was caught up in the hyperbole of agricultural opportunity that characterized the official discourse of rural by the end of the century. The 1891 Report of the Department of Agriculture expressed an enthusiasm about the commercial potential of the island that is reminiscent of Begg's raptures on the same theme:

Surrounded as it is by the salt water, the valleys protected alike from the cold northerly winds of winter and the southerly sea breezes of summer, offer the very best facilities for peach, apricot, nectarine and melon growing, while the hot rocky slopes of the hills seem to be intended by nature for grape culture ... Grain comes to prefection [sic] and can, on account of the small rainfall, be well saved in ordinary seasons ... Root crops did well and gave excellent returns. A considerable number of cattle are kept and a quantity of butter was manufactured and disposed of in the Nanaimo and Victoria markets. The absence of wild animals, and the excellent runs the hills afford, make sheep raising more profitable here than in most places.[81]

Detailed statistics on the island's agricultural production were compiled in a number of returns published by the Department of Agriculture throughout the 1890s,[82] further boosting the glowing reports of Saltspring Island's agricultural potential in the earliest newspaper accounts. As the 1892 Report on Agriculture noted, although the island "has a rugged appearance, having several high, rocky hills on it," this did not preclude the potential for agricultural success: "the fact that nearly one hundred farmers live on the island goes to prove that there is a great deal of good land in the valleys. These valleys are for the most part wooded, in some parts lightly, and are of great fertility, the soil being a red sandy loam and a somewhat heavy black loam, according to locality."[83] The virtues of Saltspring Island as an area of great agricultural promise lay particularly in its fruit-growing potential: "as a fruit growing district and also for sheep raising it stands unrivaled."[84] The Report on Agriculture for 1894 reflected this interest, noting that 14,000 apple trees and a further 3,600 pear, plum, and cherry trees were being grown on Saltspring in that year.[85]

While sheep and fruit trees were identified as providing the most lucrative cash commodities for export, island informants for the Department of Agriculture continued to emphasize the importance of mixed farming to the community. Trage noted in 1891 that "nearly everybody has hens and all agree that they are very profitable," and many farm women sold eggs.[86] Potatoes were "extensively grown," he noted in 1895, while "other vegetables are grown for home consumption."[87] Sheep, horses, hogs, and poultry were extensively kept. The two stores on the island provided a venue for the sales of some produce, but many islanders chose to ship their produce off-island to take direct advantage of the higher prices available in Nanaimo, Ladysmith, and Victoria.[88] In 1891 the Dominion Census considered Saltspring Island important enough to be included as a separate district in the aggregate agricultural statistics. These statistics indicated that almost three thousand bushels of wheat, six thousand bushels of oats, three thousand bushels of peas, and almost twenty thousand bushels of potatoes were being grown on Saltspring Island in 1891.[89]

By the mid-1880s lines of communication and transportation had improved dramatically from the pre-railway boom years. Steamers were stopping at Vesuvius Bay, Burgoyne Bay, and Beaver Point, providing mails twice a week to these localities from Nanaimo and Victoria.[90] Post offices, which not only facilitated trade but also provided for the transfer of money through an essential money-order service, were established at Vesuvius in 1873, Burgoyne Bay in 1880, Beaver Point in 1884, and Fulford Harbour in 1893.[91] By 1887 mail service to the north end had increased to four times a week.[92] Scottish-born shepherd Alexander Aitken, who in 1891 dutifully recorded each vessel that he

This work crew is clearing land and building fences on Henry Bullock's property. Bullock was one of the few landowners who could afford to hire labourers regularly. (SSIA)

saw from his vantage point at the south end of the island as he tended sheep for the Musgrave family, perceived a busy commercial thoroughfare: "while waiting for the [steamer] Isabel we saw the Sady, the Isabel, a large sloop, one boat and two canoes all out there at once; quite a busy place this [is] getting to be."[93] Aitken's detailed diary of activities in 1891 notes trips off-island to buy and sell produce as often as twice a week when the weather allowed.[94]

But it was farming that dominated definitions of the island's economic base. The success of farming, detailed in promotional literature, newspapers, and Department of Agriculture statistics, is echoed in residents' self-definition. Memoirs of Saltspring Islanders habitually define the community as a farming area.[95] More significant evidence for occupational self-definition is provided by the censuses, directories, and voters' lists, in which household heads were asked to provide their occupation. Between 1871 and 1891, 84 per cent of the 434 people on Saltspring who listed their occupation in provincial business directories gave their occupation as farmer, while 92 per cent of those 653 Saltspring men identified as voters and listing occupations between 1862 and 1891 did so. As Table 2.2 indicates, the 1881 and 1891 censuses provide further evidence of the overwhelming proportion of men on the island who considered themselves farmers: 83 per cent of household heads in 1881 were listed as farmers.[96] In 1891 three-quarters of household heads listed themselves as farmers.[97] Those household heads declaring themselves farmers were older, more likely to own land, and had been longer on the island than other segments of the population, suggesting that farming, as

Table 2.2
Occupational Data from the Nominal Censuses, Saltspring Island, 1881 and 1891

Census data on household heads	1881 farmer	1881 non-farmer	1891 farmer	1891 non-farmer
Number	60	11	71	24
% household heads	85	15	75	25
Average age	48	42	46	41
% landowners	78	63	89	56
% living on island >5 yrs	60	23	70	50

Source: Census of Canada, 1881, District no. 191, Vancouver, Cowichan and Saltspring Island, Schedule no. 1 – Nominal; Census of Canada, 1891, District no. 3, Vancouver, M2 – S.D. 14, Saltspring Island, Schedule no. 1 – Nominal.

in so many rural communities across Canada, was a "destination occupation." The nominal census, like the Department of Agriculture reports, suggests that Saltspring Island had achieved the status of a successful agricultural community by the 1890s.

CONCLUSION

By 1891 Saltspring Island was being identified by newspapers, governments, and some settlers themselves as an area of significant commercial agricultural production – the culmination of a promise the island had represented since its earliest pioneer days. There can be little doubt that Begg's vision of rural felicity had been partly realized. Farm families were established on the land, and some were marketing crops. But the identification of Saltspring Island as the kind of agricultural community imagined by Begg was maintained only by ignoring many of the peculiarities that continued to characterize life on the island: the occupational plurality, the gathering and hunting, the off-farm work, the difficulties with transportation and communication. These were all understood only as the vicissitudes of pioneer life, markers of a mere stage in a larger story of commercial progress. To what extent did the life of islanders correspond with that discourse? How can we evaluate the relationship between it and the lives of Saltspring Island residents? Chapter 3 takes a closer look at these questions by examining the extent to which land policies, those specific articulations of the discourse, worked in practice to facilitate "settling up the wild lands."

The Main Support of the Colony: How Pre-emptors Met Policy-Makers' Goals

John Norton, born on the Azores Islands in 1824, came to Saltspring Island in 1861. Almost nothing is known of the first thirty-seven years of his life. If he was like most of the early settlers, he arrived with little money and a desire to own rural land. Norton pre-empted 200 acres in the north end of the island. His immediate neighbours were a family comprising an African-American husband, Henry Robinson (born in Bermuda), his Irish Catholic wife Margaret, and their two children. By 1867, when he was in his mid-forties, Norton had married one of those children, Annie. Unlike most of the settler families, John and Annie had had the first of their fourteen children when Annie was just twelve years old.[1] Two years later, Norton applied for a certificate of improvement for the land, declaring that he had built a house and barns valued at $800, and that he had cleared and fenced his land, bringing its value to $1,300. In 1882 he purchased his pre-emption at the bargain-basement price of $1 per acre. Having paid for his first pre-emption, he was now eligible to stake another claim, which he did almost immediately, right next to land pre-empted in the same year by family member Emanuel Norton. John later abandoned his 1884 pre-emption without listing any improvements on it. No records exist to tell us whether he made any use of this land or its resources before it was taken up by another settler in 1891. Norton went on to purchase two other pieces of land outright in the 1880s, one of them the 160 acres of land that Emanuel Norton had pre-empted in 1884, which had been cancelled "due to non occupation."[2]

By 1891, at sixty-seven years of age, Norton had used the pre-emption system strategically and to his advantage. He had his original 200 acres, of which about forty were cleared, and his land was now valued at $2,000. He had sold off his later land acquisitions, which had probably contributed to the wealth he declared on his 1891 tax assessment. The assessment roll for that year taxed him on $450 of personal property, and listed an impressive collection of livestock: he owned eight cattle, twenty sheep, four horses, and three hogs.[3] Seven of his ten children were living at home, with the elder sons William and John Jr listing their occupation as "farmer." He was well respected within his community, serving as public school trustee in 1883 and 1884.[4] When he died at eighty-eight in 1911, Norton left an estate valued at over $7,000, including land, personal property, and mortgages lent out to other island landholders.[5] As far as John Norton was concerned, the pre-emption system had allowed him to settle on the land and support a large family. It had also provided an economic foundation that allowed him to accumulate capital.

In chapters 1 and 2, I have argued that a particular ideology intended to shape the way that newcomers to British Columbia saw and understood rural lands. In this chapter I want to turn the reader's attention away from rural ideology, the discursive structures of policy formation, and the descriptive narratives that this dominant rural ideology helped to create. I want to focus instead on the ways that settlers like Norton responded to these ideologies in their land-related activities. What did settlers *do* with their land? How closely did they follow the often onerous and always cumbersome requirements of the pre-emption system? To what extent, and in what ways, were the goals of policy makers, articulated so clearly through the ideologically informed pre-emption system, actualized in the behaviours of Norton and his neighbours? What, in other words, was the relationship between the dominant rural discourse and the ways that settlers took up land on Saltspring Island?

In this chapter I will argue that when the success of the pre-emption system is measured by its ability to further policy-makers' specific goals for country lands, the system did indeed provide an effective bridge between government expectations and settler aspirations. Most of the landowners who, like Norton, stayed more than a year on the island seem to have accepted to a considerable extent those conditions of the pre-emption system specifically designed to create the kind of rural society imagined by policy makers. Critical to the colonial project was the installation of "real" farm families on country lands. Evidence suggests that the pre-emption system worked to promote this goal by successfully curtailing land speculation and encouraging permanent residency. By cross-linking land records and census data, I will show that a third goal of the pre-emption system – the installation of families on country lands – was also accomplished. In the remaining chapters I will argue that, while the system achieved considerable success at meeting the specific goals of those who had formulated its provisions,

John Norton arrived on Saltspring Island in the early 1860s. He
and his wife, the young daughter of African-American settler
Mr Robinson and his Irish Catholic wife, had fifteen children.
(SSIA)

it was just flexible enough to accommodate a variety of other land-
related agendas, some of which were frankly antithetical to the spirit of
the original legislation.

THE SYSTEM OF LAND SETTLEMENT I:
THE SOURCES

It is easy to find a colonial ideology of rural lands – and the particular
discourse that framed it – in pre-emption legislation, colonial correspondence, letters, and newspapers in nineteenth-century British Columbia.
Trying to find, let alone analyse, the records of land-related practices
that might shed light on settler experience is much more difficult. Pre-
emption records for Saltspring Island are confusing and disorganized
collections dispersed across several repositories on Vancouver Island.[6]
Research into landownership is agonizingly slow. The following excerpt
(typographical errors all original) comes from my file for claim 749:

Land register [for Saltspring Island North] notes that the east half of section
14, range 1 north property, along with 38 acres in the east half of section 14,

Range 1 south, was pre empted first by Brinn in 1864, and "forfeited"; it was then taken up by in 1883 Francis Lakin, and abandoned. It was taken up again by Lakin in 1891, not as a pre emtion as before, but as a purchase; The east half of section 14, range 1 north was only 43 acres; where is the rest of the pre emtpion? According to pre emption records:100 acres; letter Sept 19, 1864 "We the undersigned settlers on the north side of SSI or Begg's Settlement do certify that the east half of No 14 have been unoccupied for two months and upward" signed Henry Sampson, William Hutson

Although these records are difficult to find, and even more difficult to arrange into a coherent research database, this system of land acquisition offers particular advantages to historians wanting to explore land settlement in British Columbia.[7] The pre-emption system's most important idiosyncrasy within provincial land records is the paper trail it created. Historians of central and eastern Canada can use land registers organized by property address to view a variety of its owners over time, but this is not possible for historians of British Columbia. Under the Torrens system of land registration adopted in British Columbia, once land has been alienated from the crown – once the crown grant has been issued – the ownership of each piece of property is no longer recorded geographically, by address, or in relation to the land. Instead, it is organized by the name of the purchaser and by a number that refers only to the immediately previous land transaction. Tracing one piece of land through a variety of owners is a costly and time consuming practice that usually only clerks in the Land Titles' Office are allowed to do, and for which they charge a considerable fee. Tracing land transactions throughout a whole community over time is, therefore, practically impossible. Before land is alienated from the crown, however, two kinds of sources make it possible to trace the provisional types of ownership offered by the pre-emption system: land registers, organized geographically by district and land address; and pre-emption records, organized by pre-emptor and by region. These provide accessible documentation about who held each piece of land under pre-emptive rights until it was purchased.[8]

Although settlers were able to purchase land outright on Saltspring Island after 1861, land acquisitions on the island were dominated by pre-emptions until 1881. The pre-emption system involved three-stages, the first two of which offered only a provisional form of landholding. Staking a claim and obtaining a certificate of improvement did not result in the legal transfer of title. Only after the conditions attendant on these first two stages had been met could a provisional owner finally apply for legal title to the land, which was confirmed when the land was paid for. Each stage in the pre-emption process generated a document and (in theory and often in practice) a notation in the island land register. By registering a pre-emption claim, settlers obtained full rights to use the land as if they owned it, with the important exception that they could not the sell, trade, or mortgage it. To turn their land into a tradable – or ownable – commodity, pre-emptors had first to register improvements by submitting a sworn statement that they had fenced, cleared, and built permanent dwellings on their land, and that they had permanently resided on their claim. The certificate of improvement, issued if the government was satisfied that the pre-emption requirements had been met, still did not provide clear title to the land; it did, however, allow settlers to apply to purchase the land from the crown at the special price of $1 an acre, contingent on the completion of a survey and the payment of the purchase price. With a certificate of improvement in hand, pre-emptors could trade, mortgage, but still not sell their lands. Only the final stage of the pre-emption process – the payment of the purchase price – provided clear title. With the payment of the purchase price, and the issuing of the crown grant, the land not only passed into private hands but also passed out of the view of historians wanting to trace serial ownership of a piece of land.

As Table 3.1 indicates, only 6 per cent of all pre-emptions in the colonial period, and 40 per cent in the provincial period under study ended in purchase: most claims were pre-empted and abandoned by a number of different people. Pre-emption records, therefore, provide the historian of British Columbia the rarely available documentation to trace the history of landholding by a variety of people over time.[9] Because land transactions on Saltspring Island were dominated by pre-emptions, records about Saltspring Island provide a view of land acquisitions in settler society that is practically impossible to find in later-settled, less-settled, and more rapidly purchased areas of the province.[10]

The value of pre-emption records to the historian is greatly increased when the individuals who appear in the land records are traced over time through other sources. The database created for this study contains information about individuals gathered from a variety of routinely generated sources, including voters' lists, assessment rolls, business directories, inquests, parish records, probate files, family papers, and, particularly, the decennial censuses. Information about landowners is not difficult to find: of a total of 4,652 records gathered about Saltspring Island residents between 1859 and 1891, 3,805 (82 per cent) relate to landowners.[11] Linking individual landowners across a variety of sources allows an examination of landownership in relation to gender, family composition, age, geographical persistence, and occupation. This chapter concentrates on tracing individuals through land records and over time to uncover the patterns of settlement

Table 3.1
History of Pre-emption Claims on Saltspring Island, 1859–91

Number of pre-emption claims	Year taken out	Abandoned with no improvements	Improved but not purchased	Improved and purchased by the pre-emptor
10	1859*	8	2	0
3	1860	1	1	1
39	1861	25	9	5
15	1862	13	1	1
15	1863	13	1	1
10	1864	6	2	2
0	1865	0	0	0
6	1866	3	1	2
8	1867	6	1	1
6	1868	2	3	1
3	1869	2	1	0
7	1870	3	3	1
7	1871	4	2	1
14	1872	7	2	5
15	1873	7	1	7
7	1874	3	2	2
1	1875	0	1	0
1	1876	0	0	1
4	1877	0	0	4
12	1878	4	1	7
14	1879	8	2	4
5	1880	1	2	2
4	1881	2	1	1
12	1882	8	0	4
11	1883	6	0	5
40	1884	26	1	13
35	1885	17	2	16
25	1886	15	0	10
14	1887	10	0	4
8	1888	3	0	5
4	1889	4	0	0
16	1890	7	0	9
15	1891	8	0	7
386		222 (58%)	42 (10%)	122 (32%)

Source: British Columbia Department of Land and Works, Pre-Emption Records, Vancouver and Gulf Islands, GR 766 BCA; British Columbia Department of Land and Works, Certificates of Improvement, Vancouver Island and the Gulf Islands, GR 765, BCA; Land Register for Saltspring Island, Surveyor General's Office, Victoria; Saltspring Island Database.

Note: * Figures for 1859 are highly unreliable. I have included here only the pre-emptions for which certificates of some sort could be located, not those appearing on the multiple lists asking to pre-empt land in 1859.

and geographical persistence that demonstrate the success of the pre-emption system in meeting policy-makers' goals. The terms landholder and landowner are used interchangeably throughout this study, and include the majority with provisional but bona fide landholding status within the pre-emption system, as well as the minority who had clear title to their land.

THE SYSTEM OF LAND SETTLEMENT II: THE PRE-EMPTION PROCESS

Before the mid-1880s almost all of the people acquiring land on Saltspring Island had obtained it through pre-emption rather than outright purchase. Few, apparently, were willing or able to invest cash for lands where uncertain agricultural conditions, distance from markets, and the weakness of economic infrastructures made speculative or agricultural returns uncertain. As Table 3.2 indicates, pre-emptions were central to the process of land acquisition on Saltspring Island in the entire period under study.

All the land acquisitions before 1871 were pre-emptions, and between 1871 and 1881 pre-emptions still accounted for 96 per cent of all lands taken up. Before the railway boom years of the 1880s, the pre-emption system provided virtually the only means of land acquisition. After this time, the number of acres purchased by people without prior pre-emption comes close to rivalling the acres pre-empted. Even during the 1880s, however, outright purchases made up less than half of the land taken up on Saltspring Island, and most of this land was acquired by only three individuals.[12]

What did the process of pre-emption involve? Settlers wishing to pre-empt land needed to pay a small fee to register their claim and to swear that the land they were taking up had been vacant for at least three months. Registration of claims was usually done in Victoria, although a few claims were registered in Cowichan.[13] Regulations changed over time, but throughout this period individuals could pre-empt at least 160 acres, and were able to purchase other lands outright.

As Figure 3.1 indicates, most people took out claims of between 100 and 200 acres. The average size of pre-emptions fell slightly between 1860 and 1891, from 141 acres in the first decade of settlement to 133 acres between 1881 and 1891. This trend can be explained by a shortage of pre-emptable land as time went on and more settlers arrived. The decline can also be explained by the increasing tendency of landowners on Saltspring Island to take out second, third, and even fourth pre-emptions over time: by the 1880s almost a third of all claims were taken out by individuals who had already staked a claim. These subsequent claims

Table 3.2
Acres in Land Transactions on Saltspring Island, 1859–91

Year	Acres Pre-empted	Acres Given Improvement Certificates	Pre-empted Acres Purchased	Acres Purchased Outright, without Pre-emption
1859	2506	0	0	0
1860	479	0	0	0
1861	4182	200	0	0
1862	858	1207	0	0
1863	1807	595	0	0
1864	1210	200	0	0
1865	0	0	0	0
1866	628	200	0	0
1867	906	0	0	0
1868	525	254	0	0
1869	450	400	0	0
1870	709	723	0	0
1871	901	150	0	0
1872	2114	358	0	0
1873	2480	300	0	0
1874	1032	175	0	0
1875	101	943	0	0
1876	170	361	150	160
1877	436	493	0	11
1878	1317	655	89	134
1879	1872	1383	175	100
1880	599	627	964	203
1881	384	62	748	170
1882	1626	902	398	178
1883	977	303	1232	606
1884	6090	973	1089	1263
1885	4739	1289	1318	5288
1886	3249	1332	366	4783
1887	1830	1376	1203	1327
1888	1059	1142	413	754
1889	420	212	874	94
1890	1908	899	1295	965
1891	1628	812	848	207
Total	49,192	18,526	11,162	16,243

Source: British Columbia Department of Land and Works, Pre-Emption Records, Vancouver and Gulf Islands, GR 766 BCA; British Columbia Department of Land and Works, Certificates of Improvement, Vancouver Island and the Gulf Islands, GR 765, BCA; Land Register for Saltspring Island, Surveyor General's Office, Victoria; Saltspring Island Database.

Figure 3.1
Number of Pre-emptors by Pre-emption Acreage, 1860–91

Number of Acres in
Pre-emption

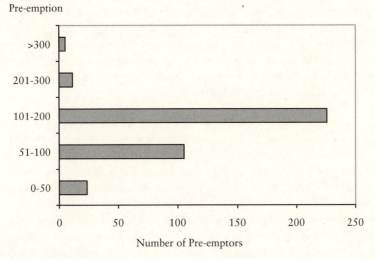

Number of Pre-emptors

Source: Saltspring Island Database.

tended to be smaller than first pre-emptions for a variety of reasons, including the declining availability of land, the tendency of landholders to
take up neighbouring chunks of irregularly sized lands as they became
available, and the regulations limiting the acreage of subsequent parcels
of pre-empted lands.[14] Being on the spot, pre-emptors were well situated
to take up new land, particularly desirable claims abandoned by neighbours. Cross-linkages with the census of 1881 and with both the assessment roll and the census of 1891 confirm that those who stayed longer
on the island owned more land.[15]

Throughout most of the years under study, Saltspring Island seemed a
very long way from the centres of bureaucratic administration in Victoria, because of poor communication and transportation. So it is not surprising that the registration of pre-emption claims proved to be
inefficient and often inaccurate. During the first years of settlement, pre-
emptions could be granted only on lands that had not been surveyed,
which further complicated the situation.[16] Inadequate registration procedures may have been responsible for a number of pre-emptors, such as
Edwin Johnson, Robert Layzell, Henry Sampson, Manuel (probably
Estalon) Bittancourt, William Hutson, and William Meiss, taking up overlapping claims. The loose system of land registration of unsurveyed lands
was probably responsible, for example, for the problems of Bittancourt

and Daniel Fredison. Both were settlers who found themselves in the unfortunate position of having built houses and made improvements on
land that was, in fact, on someone else's claim.[17] Many of these overlapping claims, however, may have existed on paper only, as clerical errors
or delayed claim cancellations. Most were not contested.[18]

Problems with inadequate or non-existent surveys, difficulties with
the registration process, and the tendency of pre-emptors to leave their
claims without notice created a legacy of land-related problems. The
Chief Commissioner of Lands and Work summarized the situation on
Saltspring Island in 1874 as follows:

The position of settlers' claims upon this Island is most confusing, and in no
part of the Province are surveys more urgently required. From the archives of
this Department I gather that, in the early part of 1860, a number of persons
settled on the Island, consequently, prior to any Land Pre-emption Proclamation in the Province. Some of these settlers were permitted to take possession
of, and occupy, 200 acres, others 150 acres; and subsequently, others recorded
100 acres of land. Until the past summer, no regular system of surveys had been
made on the Island. Several disputes, and more than one law suit, have arisen
out of these complications. I am so informed by Mr. Green, the gentleman who
surveyed a portion of the Island this summer, that the Pre-emption Record Map
in the Land Office, shows an extensive acreage of land that has no existence,
and as it is recorded by settlers, who claim that they are entitled to their acreage in that locality, it is impossible to say where these difficulties will end.[19]

Problems did not, unfortunately, end with the official surveys of the island. Although most of the land was officially surveyed in 1874 and
1875 by Ashdown Green, the Surveyor General's office was receiving
complaints as late as 1943 concerning the inaccuracy of acreages surveyed by Green and others in the late nineteenth century.[20]

For those who took up uncontested claims, however, the pre-
emption process seems to have worked well. John Maxwell's history
provides a good example of the practice of pre-emption very much as it
was envisaged by those creating land policy. Maxwell, who we met first
in chapter 1, was an Irishman of about twenty-seven years of age when
he took up excellent agricultural land in the Burgoyne Bay area.[21] On
18 June 1861 he sent a letter to Victoria to register his claim: "Please
record this clame comensing at a stake ate the mouth ofe the creke ate
the south side ofe the Bay and runing due este fore a quarter of a mile
in a similar Poste then runing due north towards whauken mountens
then runing backe to the poste."[22]

To obtain his certificate of improvement, Maxwell needed to prove
that he was a bona fide settler who had cleared, fenced, and constructed

The Furness family farmed in the south end of the island from the 1880s.
Mr Furness died, leaving his wife with young children. Daughter Katie helped to
support the family by working as a teacher on the island. (SSIA)

permanent buildings on portions of his land to the value of ten shillings,
or $2.50 per acre. When Maxwell sent off his application for a certifi-
cate of improvement in March 1875 for his Burgoyne Bay property, he
described his improvements as follows: "dwelling house 34 by 20 =
$500; 2 barns, 32 by 22 and 40 by 20 = $200; 18 acres cleared cultivated and fenced, $1,500; 20 acres cleared fenced and in grass $1,000 =
$3,200; 180 acres improved @2.50/ acre."[23] As was common on
Saltspring Island, Maxwell's neighbours witnessed the improvements
and certified that he had indeed been a resident on the land while making the improvements he claimed.[24]

The fourteen years that John Maxwell took to obtain his certificate of
improvement was a little longer than the average ten years elapsing between pre-emption and improvement for those who pre-empted their land
in 1860s and eventually purchased it. It was also considerably longer than
the two years that the officials who penned the pre-emption acts thought
improvement should take. In the second decade of settlement, the average
had decreased to just under seven years and, by the 1880s, improvement
certificates were being issued after an average of just over five years from
pre-emption.[25] The leisurely pace of land acquisition is reflected in the average length of time from pre-emption to purchase. It decreased from
twenty years for those pre-empting land in the 1860s to nine years, on
average, between 1870 and 1880, and eight years from 1882 to 1891.[26]

Although Maxwell provided detailed descriptions of the improvements he made to his claim, few improvement certificates contain such rich information. Most certificates resembled that of John Christian Sparrow, a Norwegian who, as we have seen, took up land close to Maxwell in 1861.[27] When he applied for an improvement certificate five years after staking his claim, Sparrow simply listed his name and pre-emption number, and noted that he had resided permanently on his claim, making "full improvements of 10 shillings per acre, the amount being 150 acres."[28] Maxwell finally obtained the crown grant and clear title to his land in 1880, almost twenty years from the time he first staked his claim. Like many others, having purchased one claim, he went on to pre-empt more land, taking up 160 acres in 1884, paying the last of four installments on that land in 1892. In 1890 he pre-empted another fifty acres in the same area, paying for it at the same time as his other pre-emption.[29]

While three-quarters of those obtaining a certificate of improvement went on to purchase their claims, this was not the only alternative open to pre-emptors at this point.[30] Once a certificate was granted, land-holders could use the land to raise a mortgage or could transfer their claim to someone else. There are frustratingly few indications of how these transactions worked in practice; but while such records are rare, they are not completely absent. On 9 June 1862, for example, George Mitchell transferred his claim in Begg's Settlement to former fellow-Hudson's Bay employee, William Isbister, in order to take up land in Burgoyne Bay. He wrote to the Land Office in Victoria to register the exchange: "I have this day sold and transferred all my rights and im-provements situated on Saltspring Island, consisting of one dwelling house, cow houses, pig houses etc. to William Isbister in exchange for one cow and calf, signed George Mitchell, witnessed by A. McFarlane, John Isbister."[31] We know from the land register that John Booth transferred much of his land to Arthur Walter after improving it. As with most of these trades, evidence is provided only by the entry of a new name under the "improved" land listing in question, and no indication is given of the amount of money or goods, if any, changing hands in the transaction.[32]

The residency of the landowner on his land was deemed essential to the pre-emption process for two important reasons. First, compulsory residence would prohibit land speculation by absentee landowners. As policy makers were well aware, such speculation was notorious for driving up land prices at the same time that it inhibited the growth of the infrastructure so necessary to the agricultural economy.[33] Second, by compelling residency, policy makers believed that they were setting in motion a natural process by which the hard-working settler would, with his growing family, turn his land into an agriculturally productive living, a living that, it was assumed, would support the family farm deemed so essential for economic, moral, and political stability of the colony and province. Did the pre-emption system succeed on Saltspring Island in accomplishing these goals?

EVALUATING THE SUCCESS OF THE PRE-EMPTION SYSTEM I: ENSURING RESIDENCY

Joseph Trutch explained the importance of residency to the success of the pre-emption system in a letter to the Colonial Secretary in 1868:

Personal residence of the Claimant on the land claimed by him by pre-emption right is in fact the essential requirement of the pre-emption system as it is practically carried out in the neighbouring United States Territories from whence it was adopted into this Colony. His presence on the land (affording the best possible guarantee that his labor and means will be devoted to the utmost to the cultivation of the soil, and thus advance the general interests of the Colony) is the equivalent required for the privilege granted to the pre-emptor of settling on the land in advance of survey without payment and with the secured right of eventual purchase at the upset price.[34]

Trutch credits the pre-emption system with ensuring the growth and development of the colony. It was by ensuring residency through the pre-emption system, he argues, that "we have secured a class of colonists who have not only already contributed in taxes to the Colonial Exchequer many times the sum which the land they hold free of charge would have brought at auction, but by their labor on the land are fast tending to render the Colony self-sustaining, and during the season of depression we are now emerging from, have been the main support of the Colony."[35]

Although residency was central to the pre-emption system, the term "resident," like the term "landowner," was not a simple one in this context and requires a few words of explanation. Residents of Saltspring Island shared with other settlers across Canada serious difficulties in supporting themselves on lands that were not yet productive, and in communities that were not yet established.[36] Although pre-emptors were required to obtain signatures confirming that the land they wanted to pre-empt had been vacant for three months, in a location where it was difficult to support a claim without off-island work, the difference between "claim jumping" and the legal occupation of an abandoned claim was not always easy to ascertain. W.K. Brown, for example, was compelled to return to California to care for his sick wife, having arrived on the island in 1859: "After arriving on the said land, I immediately with the others went to work making a main road several miles long on the Island. After the completion of the road and making the survey, we went to work erecting residences and clearing the land. I erected a house on my land and cleared about 10 acres of land, working all that year and until about the latter part of March 1860 when I was compelled to go to California, my wife being sick."[37] When he returned to his land the following year, he found that John C. Jones had pre-empted and received an improvement certificate for the land. Although Brown had made payments on his original claim, and pursued the case with land officials well into the 1890s, his claim was turned down because he had failed to carry out his "settlement duties" by remaining on the land.[38]

Similarly, James Shaw took up land in August 1859, and wrote on 15 May 1861 to the Surveyor General explaining some of the problems he had encountered when he decided to leave his claim for a short period of time:

I took possession of som land [on Saltspring Island] right opposite Maple Bay on Dec 26, 1859, and improved it by building a [house?] 16 by 21 feet, and cleared som land and planted potatoes and other improvements to the balance of $200. My neighbours all left for the mines in 1860. I remained on the claim four weeks after they left, but found it inconvenient and unprotected from Indians, so I left ... som of my neighbors returned from the mines. I was on the clame on the 26 August 1860 and found the tools and house the same as I left them ... I got an accident I injured one of my hands and was not able to visit my clame until March 18, 1861. I found a man in charge for Lewis Buchard I told the man in charge not to make any improvements I was the first settler on the clame. I have visited the clame since, but I did not see Louis Buckar. Sir I hope you will give me possession of my clame.[39]

Shaw lost the claim to his pre-empted land because he had, in the parlance of the pre-emption system, "abandoned" it by being absent without leave for more than three months.[40]

Jacob Francis was also driven off the island by strictly enforced pre-emption regulations. Even though he had officially registered a leave of absence in Victoria in 1863, and had "left Manuel Anderson on his claim," when Anderson left the claim without notifying Francis, Francis lost his land: his neighbour waited the requisite three months, signed a declaration that the land had been abandoned, and began to occupy it. Despite Francis's insistence that "the spirit of the proclamation has been complied with," and despite protestations that he had spent considerable sums improving his claim, the Land Office refused to overlook his absence, and he lost his right to the claim. Francis shows up in the land records, therefore, as one of the many who had "abandoned" his land.[41]

Others, more punctilious about keeping to the terms of the pre-emption regulations, had more success in establishing claims they had temporarily left.[42] Legislation enacted in 1862 allowed pre-emptors to register a planned interlude off the island,[43] but canny land-watchers continued to take up vacated lands, and were supported by a court system that continued to show little leniency towards those who had transgressed residency regulations.[44] These disputes over pre-emption claims suggest that regulations concerning land residency were rigorously enforced, not so much because of expert policing on the part of land officials, but because of the policy-driven response of pre-emptors themselves: within a system where ownership could not be purchased outright, proof of residency became of central importance, replacing money as the arbiter of the right to land in contested claims.[45]

In spite of difficulties in discovering continuous residency, however, it is possible to estimate the success of residency regulations by using the available data to find those who *never* lived on their pre-emption claims. Evidence suggests that although the year 1859 saw a wave of people taking up land and not residing on it, these non-resident pre-emption claimants became a rapidly decreasing part of the island's history. Because landownership was the most common qualification for suffrage, and pre-emption was the most common means of obtaining land, voters' lists provide a good source of information about pre-emptions. Because these lists include both the location of the land owned, and the place of residence of the voter, they provide the means to establish the extent of landowners' non-residence.

Poll books from the 1862 colonial election indicate that non-residents made up about two-thirds of the voting population (twenty out of thirty), a figure that had declined to less than half (fifteen out of thirty-five) by 1866.[46] Voters' lists from the later provincial period (they appear in 1875–79, 1881–82, 1885, and 1889), indicate a rapidly declining number of non-residents. Only one or two Saltspring Island voters appear as non-residents in each of these years.[47]

A slightly different picture of non-residency is provided by other sources. When the voters' list from 1881 is cross-linked with the census of the same year, eight out of sixty-seven registered voters (12 per cent) show up as owning land but not living on the island.[48] Cross-linkages suggest that three of these were not absentee landowners after all, but did, in fact, reside on the island, though absent from the census listings. Three others had obtained crown grants by 1881, making them absentee landowners but not pre-emptors absent from their claims.[49] Of the remaining two potential absentee pre-emptors appearing on the voters' list, Mr Weston had abandoned his pre-empted lands by 1876, and Mr Jackson abandoned his in 1882.[50] This cross-linkage, therefore, seems to corroborate evidence in the voters' lists alone: non-residency among pre-emptors was not a significant problem.

The assessment rolls contain the most reliable information about residency of landowners, but information is available only for the last year of this study, 1891.[51] This assessment roll records a significantly higher rate of non-residency than is suggested above: twenty-nine out of 124 landowners, or just under a quarter, were *not* resident on the island. A cross-linking of the assessment roll with the land records indicates that most of these individuals had purchased the land they were being taxed for, suggesting that these were tenanted, and not held by delinquent pre-emptors. This leaves seven who were not honouring the residency clauses of their pre-emptions.[52] Six of these seven, however, abandoned their claims shortly after 1891.

The fact that most of the non-resident pre-emptors appearing in the 1891 assessment roll abandoned their land, often within two or three years of 1891, may simply attest to the lag between changes in land status and its transcription in Victoria. However, other sources also indicate a definite trend whereby non-resident pre-emptors did not hang onto their land for long. Most did not realize any profits from their pre-empted lands. The great majority of non-residents seem to have abandoned their claims within a year of taking them up. In many cases, there is little evidence to suggest that they were ever on the island.[53]

Of the 170 non-resident pre-emptors during the period under study, only four ever purchased and only nine improved their claims. That they were able to at all provides a testament to the laxity in enforcing certain aspects of the pre-emption regulations, the inadequacy of sources to document people's residency in these early years, or a combination of both.[54] With an important caveat that will be discussed below, the force of evidence suggests that the pre-emption system usually did succeed in ensuring the residence of pre-emptors on their land.

When residence is measured by geographic persistence, the success of the pre-emption system is remarkable, particularly in the light of studies suggesting high geographic mobility amongst early settlers in British Columbia. Geographic persistence was measured in this study by cross-linking each household head in the censuses of 1881 and 1891 across the entire database for the island. The first and last date for which information on each individual on the island was recorded was noted. Persistence in years was therefore conservatively estimated by subtracting the first date from the last.

Figure 3.2
Average Persistence in Years to Census Date, Landowning and Non-landowning
Household Heads, 1881, 1891

Average
Number of years

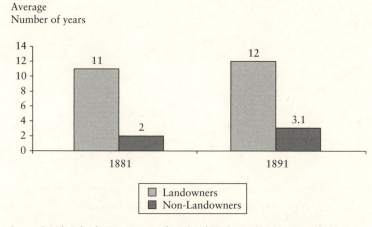

Source: British Columbia Department of Land and Works, Pre-Emption Records, Vancouver and Gulf Islands, GR 766 BCA; British Columbia Department of Land and Works, Certificates of Improvement, Vancouver Island and the Gulf Islands, GR 765, BCA; Land
Register for Saltspring Island, Surveyor General's Office, Victoria. British Columbia Department of Finance, Surveyor of Taxes, 1892 Assessment Roll, Roll B 443, Gulf Islands
Assessment District; Saltspring Island Database.

Figure 3.2 illustrates the average length of time that landowning and
non-landowning household heads had been on the island at the time
the census was taken. Because so many of the documents available for
individuals residing on Saltspring Island were contingent on their status
as landholders, it is much easier to trace landowners than those without land. Notwithstanding this bias in the sources, the correlation of
landownership and geographic persistence over time is persuasive. The
eighteen household heads not owning land in 1881 had been on the island an average of two years, whereas the twenty-nine landowners had
been on the island for just under eleven years, on average. Similar aver-
ages pertain for those appearing on the 1891 census: the seventy-five
landowners had been on the island an average of twelve years by the
census date; the nineteen non-landowners for three years.

These average figures understate the brevity of tenure that characterized the experience of most non-landowners: of the thirteen household
heads who appear in the 1881 census and who *never* owned land on the
island, eleven stayed a year or less. In 1891 ten of the sixteen household
heads who never owned land also stayed a year or less. The centrality of

Figure 3.3
Percentage of All Pre-emptors on Saltspring Island who Remained for 1, 5, 10 and
20 years, by Arrival Period

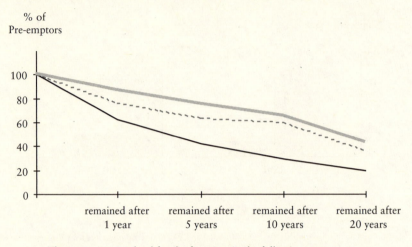

% of
Pre-emptors

Those pre-empting land for the first time in the following years:

———	1860–1870
- - - - -	1871–1881
▬▬▬	1882–1891

Source: British Columbia Department of Land and Works, Pre-Emption Records, Vancouver and Gulf
Islands, GR 766 BCA; British Columbia Department of Land and Works, Certificates of Improvement,
Vancouver Island and the Gulf Islands, GR 765, BCA; Land Register for Saltspring Island, Surveyor
General's Office, Victoria. British Columbia Department of Finance, Surveyor of Taxes, 1892 Assess-
ment Roll, Roll B 443, Gulf Islands Assessment District; Saltspring Island Database.

the landowning experience to adult males in the community can be
stated another way. Of household heads in 1881, fifty-three of the fifty-
nine (90 per cent) who stayed longer than one year were landowners. In
1891 sixty-seven of the seventy-three household heads (92 per cent)
who stayed longer than a year were landowners. The snapshots provided by the censuses suggest that *average* rates of persistence for household heads are conflated with very high rates of mobility in the first year
(particularly among those who did not own land) and stability thereafter for the great majority of landholders.

   Cross-linked land records for all those pre-empting land between
1860 and 1891 confirm the trend seen in the census household heads.
The average length of stay for all of those pre-empting land was just
over fifteen years, while those who pre-empted land and stuck it out for

more than a year stayed, on average, just over twenty-two years.[55] For those taking out their first pre-emption in the first decade of settlement, the average length of stay was just under ten years; those taking out their first pre-emption in the 1870s stayed an average of sixteen years; and those who did so from 1882 and 1891 stayed just under twenty years on average.[56]

But again, average figures hide the distinctive patterns of stability and mobility on the island. As Figure 3.3 illustrates, 30 per cent of those pre-empting lands in the 1860s were still on the island ten years later, a figure that doubled to 60 per cent for those taking out land in the 1870s, and increased to 65 per cent in the 1880s. A fifth of those taking up land in the 1860s were still on the island after twenty years, a figure that rose to 43 per cent for those taking up land in the 1880s and early 1890s. What we are seeing here is a view of the very high mobility of those in their first year on the island, combined with surprisingly stability of tenure thereafter. Like neighbouring Nanaimo, Saltspring Island demonstrated a more permanent core population than average figures suggest, and than historians have tended to assume.[57] Pre-emption regulations were, we can conclude, successful at ensuring residency.

EVALUATING THE SUCCESS OF THE PRE-EMPTION SYSTEM II: PREVENTING LAND SPECULATION

Both the courts and Saltspring Island residents kept a close eye on residency requirements on the island, and settlers were seldom able to purchase pre-empted lands without residing on and improving them. Figure 3.4 presents the information in Table 3.1 in graphic form and demonstrates that throughout the entire period under study, most of the pre-emption claims that were registered on the island resulted in abandonment. Chapter 5 will examine in greater detail the wider significance of these abandoned pre-emptions, but here it will suffice to evaluate briefly the relationship between these high abandonment rates and land speculation.

Some evidence indicates that land abandonment was one of the unforeseen, ironic consequences of the rigorous application of pre-emption regulations, which were intended to stimulate settlement. Attempts to foil land speculation drove off a number of settlers who, having made investments of both time and money in their lands, were anxious to settle on it. As we have seen, in spite of trying very hard to use the pre-emption system to take up land, W.K. Brown and James Shaw had been deprived of their land by the rigorous rules of the system. The potential of the pre-emption system to drive away enterprising settlers,

Figure 3.4
History of Pre-emption Claims, 1859–91

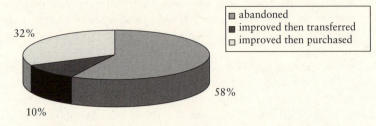

Source: British Columbia Department of Land and Works, Pre-Emption Records, Vancouver and Gulf Islands, GR 766 BCA; British Columbia Department of Land and Works, Certificates of Improvement, Vancouver Island and the Gulf Islands, GR 765, BCA; Land Register for Saltspring Island, Surveyor General's Office, Victoria; British Columbia Department of Finance, Surveyor of Taxes, 1892 Assessment Roll, Roll B 443, Gulf Islands Assessment District; Saltspring Island Database.

whose interests may have expanded to land speculation, can be seen with particular force in the case of John D. Cusheon. Cusheon, a Victoria businessman, was one of the first men to pre-empt land on Saltspring, and was perhaps the most enterprising man to take up land on the island before the boom years of the 1880s. In 1859 he took up about 1,000 acres in the area of the lake now bearing his name. In 1861, "having expended for the improvement of the said land over three thousand dollars in clearing the land, fencing, the erection of a house, and hen house," Cusheon, still a resident of Victoria, applied to purchase the land for a dollar an acre, apparently in the hope of speculating on rising land values.[58]

Although Cusheon had installed someone on the land to fulfill what he understood as the residency clause of the pre-emption regulations, his application for purchase was turned down. This was because he tried to purchase more than the 160 acres that he was, under the pre-emption system, allowed to take up as a single man. Furthermore, regulations allowing the outright purchase of unsurveyed lands at the dollar-an-acre price had not yet been established. Unable to purchase his claim at any price, Cusheon gave it up in disgust, leaving land that he had fenced and partially cleared, but that he had no right to sell, trade, or mortgage.[59]

Other pre-emptors may well have tried to speculate on the first available cheap lands; possibly many of the non-resident pre-emptors who registered a claim and never showed up on the island were aspiring speculators. Most of these abandoned their lands without realizing any

Agricultural success: Haying on the Bullock farm. Henry Bullock, who arrived with considerable capital from Britain, ran one of the most successful agricultural businesses on the island. Hay was an important crop since horses provided much of the labour in farms and forests. (SSIA)

financial gain or turning their land into a commodity through the registration of claim improvements.

Other evidence of land speculation can be found in the number of properties that changed hands in rapid succession without being either improved or purchased, particularly near wharf areas in Ganges, Vesuvius, and Begg's Settlement. If these were attempts at land speculation, they were strikingly unsuccessful, as pre-emption after pre-emption on these lands reverted to the crown instead of being improved or purchased.[60] As Figure 3.1 suggests the promise of increased demand and higher prices for land during the railway boom of the mid-1880s encouraged pre-emptors to take up, improve, and purchase their claims, creating the Saltspring Island land boom of the 1880s. There is little evidence that landowners were transgressing the terms of the pre-emption system to speculate on rising land prices.

The pre-emptors selling their lands in the 1880s and 1890s would have certainly realized considerable profits from their investment of labour, time, and money in their land, but most pre-emptors in the years under study had their ability to turn land into money successfully limited by the terms of the pre-emption system, which ensured that they could not do so without first enduring many years of rural residence and hard work improving their lands.

EVALUATING THE SUCCESS OF THE PRE-EMPTION SYSTEM III: CREATING FAMILIES

The pre-emption system emerged as a legislative development within an official discourse that identified rural settlement with family-based commodity production on agricultural lands: the family was given a crucial role in the development of social stability and economic progress through production on the family farm. How effective was the pre-emption system in placing families on the land?

As Figures 3.5 and 3.6 suggest, by 1881 families were well established on the island. Children (under the age of fifteen) were an important part of island society, making up 40 per cent of the population in both census years.[61] Although the ratio of adult women to men fell from 2:3 in 1881 to 1:3 in 1891, two-thirds of household heads were (or had been) married in both census years, and over half had children.[62] The significance of landownership was not limited to household heads. Married men with children were more likely to own land than were single men: only half of the single people, but three-quarters of the married men with children owned land, a proportion that rose to almost four-fifths in 1891.[63] In both census years, four out of every five people on the island lived with a household head who was a landowner.[64] Although the society on Saltspring Island, with its large number of families and its stable population, did not conform to the norms of British Columbia society in terms of gender and age composition, it did conform to the discourse that equated rural society with families living on the land.

CONCLUSION

Data examined here confirm the importance of the pre-emption system to the settlement of Saltspring Island. The system of land acquisition succeeded in large measure in furthering the specific goals of policy makers regarding country lands. Most of the adult white men living on the island during the first thirty years of European settlement were

Figure 3.5
Ages of Saltspring Island Residents, 1881, by Gender

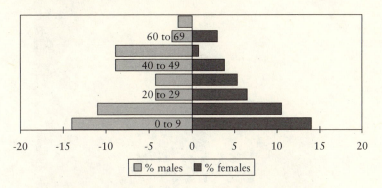

Figure 3.6
Ages of Saltspring Island Residents, 1891, by Gender

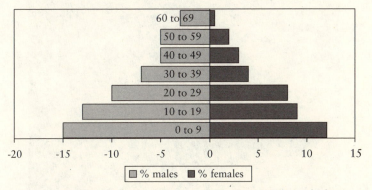

Sources: Census of Canada, 1881, District no. 191, Vancouver, Cowichan and Saltspring Island, Schedule no. 1 – Nominal; Census of Canada, 1891, District no. 3, Vancouver, M2 – s.D. 14, Saltspring Island, Schedule no. 1 – Nominal.

Please see Tables 6.6 and 6.7 for tabular representation of these figures.

resident landowners. Land settlement was encouraged at the expense of land speculation, and landowning household heads were, by 1891, engaged in raising families and staying many years on the island to do so. In spite of high mobility and low persistence among the majority of preemptors who stayed less than a year on the island, a solid core of preemptors had persistence rates that rivalled those of the well-established farmers of southern Ontario during the nineteenth century.

Three generations of the Sampson/McFadden family, who lived on Saltspring Island from the late 1850s on. (SSIA)

4

Commercial Farmers?

Charles Horel, born in England, arrived on Saltspring Island in about 1878 with his wife and five children under twelve. He was in his late forties. His wife Sarah was from the United States, where the first three of their children had been born. The couple had nine children by the time Horel died in 1893. He had pre-empted about 160 acres in the centre of the island in 1878, and received a certificate of improvement for his work on this land in 1884. In the same year, he purchased his original pre-emption, and then pre-empted more land, this time 152 acres nearby. He purchased this land in 1886, at which time he took out a third pre-emption, an additional eighty acres. Horel later abandoned this last pre-emption without making any improvements on it.[1]

The pre-emption system provided the Horels a land base on which to build a farm and a family. Charles was a school trustee in 1883 and 1884. He was active in local politics and was engaged in one of the unfortunate political scandals that characterized public life on the island in the 1880s: he was accused with others of taking funds for his own use.[2] He must have needed them. Poverty plagued the family through the 1880s. Son James started working on the roads in 1888, when he was 18, and he pre-empted land of his own near his parents three years later, while he was still living in the family home. In 1893 he married Lucy Bateman. His sister Georgina married Joseph Jonathan Akerman, son of one of the earliest pioneers. Descendants of the Horel family were still living on the island in the late twentieth century.

While Horel fulfilled the expectations of the policy makers in Victoria by taking up agricultural lands and raising a family on them, the family had less success in turning their land into a commercially viable farm, or themselves into farmers. In 1891 Charles Horel's 464 acres were valued at only $1,200 in the Assessment Roll.[3] Since cleared land on the island was going for between $50 and $150 per acre in the

1890s,[4] we can assume that little of the land had been cleared by 1891, even though the family (with grown sons) had lived on the island for more than fifteen years. Like four out of every five families on the island, the Horel family declared no personal property of any value on the 1891 tax assessments for the island.[5] Horel and his sons regularly took up occasional labour for the provincial government, working on the roads, or doing odd jobs in the schoolhouses on the island, suggesting that agricultural production was not providing a steady income;[6] very likely it was providing no income at all. When Horel died in 1893 he left an estate worth only $500, with five cows, three hogs, seven small pigs, twelve hens, and a plough amounting to an additional $450. His wife, forty-seven years old when he died, with three children under the age of fifteen, remained on the family homestead to eke out a living as best she could.

The discourse of agricultural success outlined in the previous three chapters has provided a view of rural society and agricultural progress that is familiar to students of Canadian and colonial history. Within this context, Horel and his family appear as anomalies, discordant notes in a familiar tune. Their failure to turn their farm into a thriving agricultural business, or to rise out of poverty, might be attributed to unfortunate circumstances, or to the kind of personal failure, poverty, and stagnation that one might expect to see from time to time in any community, particularly in its early stages of development. Microhistorical evidence from the island suggests, however, that Horel's situation was not anomalous or out of step with that of other Saltspring Islanders. In spite of reliable documentation attesting to the existence of cash markets, in spite of the identification of the island's economy as agriculturally based, and in spite of the predominant self-definition of "farmer" among island men, a closer look at land acquisition and land use calls into question any easy assumptions we might make about the relationship between "farmers" and their land. More generally, it calls into question what "rural" signified for those owning country lands. Aggregate data suggests that the experience of the Horel family – poor, subsistence-oriented, economically varied, and family based – was much more typical of life on the island, where few realized the commercially successful farming imagined by colonial policy makers and early settlers such as Jonathan Begg.

In this chapter, I will examine evidence that challenges the identification of rural with successful family-based agricultural development. I will begin by reviewing the extent of poverty on the island, and go on to examine in some detail two vital measures of commercial health in agricultural areas: land clearance and agricultural production. Such evidence provides little support for the contention that commercial agriculture was the basis of the rural economy on Saltspring Island by 1891. An examination of rural behaviours and practices suggests instead that few settlers on Saltspring Island shared the rural ideology articulated so clearly in the public discourse of rural British Columbia.

THE ECONOMIC DOWNSIDE

The public discourse of rural lands in British Columbia consistently identified rural spaces with commercially successful family farms, but writers were well aware that rural life often failed to live up to this ideal. Throughout the later nineteenth century many people, including the more articulate and literate farmers themselves, complained that agricultural ambitions were repeatedly thwarted by the exigencies of island life. A number of island farmers continued to complain, for example, about the high cost and the scarcity of hired help.[7] As Peter Russell has noted in the context of nineteenth-century Ontario, one of the most important factors influencing the rates of land clearance in pioneer communities was the ability to hire the labour to help clear the land.[8] While Begg, like settler J.P. Booth, obviously had some capital (both were able to hire labourers to help with clearing their land), settlers complained about the scarcity and high price of the labour essential for cutting and clearing the huge trees.[9] Saltspring Island correspondents with the Department of Agriculture in the early 1890s were vocal about the problems they experienced with predators, particularly cougars, that ate their livestock, and the deer, jays, and raccoons that ate their produce.[10] As in the pre-1880 period, the difficulties of shipping produce onto and, particularly, off the island remained the most common cause of complaint throughout this entire period. Residents noted problems with transportation and communications, including difficulties with the (part-time) telegraph system at the turn of the century. As late as 1912 the most commonly heard complaint before the Royal Commission into Agriculture in British Columbia made by Saltspring Island residents continued to be transportation problems and the high cost of farm labour.[11] Land clearing remained a costly and difficult practice throughout the nineteenth century. Notwithstanding the increasing value of timber, the steadily growing lumber industry, and better logging tools, even by the turn of the century settlers often considered it too expensive to have the land logged, and found it easier to burn trees down and dynamite the stumps rather than harvest them.[12] Making a living from farming on Saltspring Island was, many agreed, a very difficult task.

Settler activity created dramatic environmental changes on the island, and complaints about these changes surfaced from the 1890s onward. In

1894 Mr Trage, correspondent for the Department of Agriculture on Saltspring noted "very little cedar left; all used for rails and shingles." White and red fir, maple, and alder remained.[13] Anecdotal reports from island residents who were children in the 1920 to 1940 period suggest a drastic reduction in the number of ducks, geese, and sea mammals in and around the island by the 1970s.[14] Although most evidence available in government reports, memoirs, and newspapers, which is summarized in chapters 1 to 3, suggests that the island was well established as an agricultural enclave by 1891, the difficulties of agricultural production were also represented in the literature about this island society.

What of the poverty that characterized life for many of the early pioneers in Canada? Such a concern was a long way from the bureaucratic gaze of the Department of Agriculture, with its emphasis on bountiful agricultural yields and the price of crops; poverty was not mentioned in the published reports. Newspapers also were largely silent on the question of social conditions. When The Reverend E.F. Wilson, recently arrived from Ontario, decided to write a pamphlet boosting the cultural and economic advantages of his new community, his promotional pamphlet noted that "extensive wheat fields, large areas planted with oats, or barley, or peas or roots are not to be found on the Island of Saltspring."[15] Nevertheless, he maintained, farming on the island was a success because, on the small-scale mixed farms that characterized Saltspring's agricultural economy: "ten or fifteen acres with an orchard and a poultry yard and a cow or two ... has probably a greater sustaining power than a hundred acres of land in the prairie regions of the Northwest."[16] Wilson provided a detailed description of the successful commercial agricultural operations of some twenty island farmers, and the general beneficence of the island: "Although the homesteads are so much smaller, and a considerable portion of each farm seems to be the side or base of a timber covered stone spattered mountain, yet for all that there appears to be an air of comfort and content about the place, which is too often wanting on the great prairie farms."[17] Poverty, like most social or political problems, seems to have been banished by the commercial success of island farmers.

A closer look reveals evidence of considerable poverty throughout the entire period under study. Its extent is not easy to measure in a community where most adult men had some considerable, but provisional, landholdings. The concept of landownership was confused by the different types of ownership people had of their lands – preempted, improved, or purchased. Only purchased land could be sold for money, and land without a certificate of improvement had no value as a commodity at all. Land size, therefore, provides only a very rough measure of wealth.[18]

This is the original bridge that linked the Roman Catholic Church, the Fulford Ganges Road, and the Isabella Point Road, with its mixed race Hawaiian population. Fulford Creek, shown in the foreground, is still an important salmon spawning creek. (SSIA)

If its value as a commodity was constrained by the complexities of the system of land acquisition, the production value of land is also obscure: census data and assessment rolls provide little indication of the extent of land improvements, including land clearance. Inequalities of wealth are difficult to assess. Personal property, taxed by the provincial government and therefore included in the assessment rolls for Saltspring Island in 1892, provides one of the few routinely generated sources documenting poverty on the island.

In chapters 5, 6, and 7 I will suggest that ethnicity, age, and length of residence were factors influencing the extent of poverty on the island. As Table 4.1 demonstrates, arrival date also had a significant impact on land size and personal property owned by landholders appearing on the 1892 assessment roll (based on 1891 data). It indicates a strong trend whereby those men who had been on the island longer had more land and more declared personal property. Most landowners, even by these generous standards, which do not consider the production value of land or its value as a tradable commodity, were not wealthy. Most (about two-thirds) held under two hundred acres, and fewer than a quarter of landowners on the assessment rolls declared any personal wealth.[19] Those who declared the most were recent British immigrants who brought substantial wealth with them.[20]

In spite of the landholdings of most household heads on the island, therefore, poverty was common. The poverty of early settlers can be

Table 4.1
Wealth, Landholding, and Geographical Persistence for Household Heads in the 1891 Census

Duration of stay on the island to 1891	No.	No. and percentage, land-holders	No. and percentage, landholders with fewer than 200 acres	No. and percentage with more than 200 acres	Average value of property assessed	No. and percentage declaring personal property
1 year and less	21	8 (38%)	5 (62%)	3 (38%)	$714.00*	0 (0%)
2 to 5 years	13	10 (77%)	8 (80%)	2 (20%)	$920.00	2 (15%)
6 to 10 years	26	25 (96%)	15 (60%)	10 (40%)	$884.00	6 (23%)
11 to 20 years	20	19 (95%)	10 (53%)	9 (47%)	$1131.00	7 (35%)
More than 20 years	15	13 (87%)	6 (46%)	7 (54%)	$1312.00	7 (47%)
Total	95	75 (79%)	44 (60%)	22 (40%)	$1009.70*	

*This average figure does not include the huge piece of land purchased by Chas. Russell (2,441 acres valued at $7,000), even though he is included as one of those owning more than 200 acres. When that is included, the average value of properties rises to $1,500 per person, personal property valued at an average of $650. This difference would also be manifested in the final average of assessed properties, which would be $1090.70 if Russell's land were included.
Source: Land Register for Saltspring Island, Surveyor General's Office, Victoria; British Columbia Department of Finance, Surveyor of Taxes, 1892 Assessment Roll, Roll B 443, Gulf Islands Assessment District; Census of Canada, 1891, District no. 3, Vancouver, M2 – S.D. 14, Saltspring Island, Schedule no. 1 – Nominal; Saltspring Island Database.

glimpsed in many of the documentary sources available for 1860–1881. For example, Saltspring Island was unable to forward any candidates for election to the Legislative Assembly in January 1860. As electoral officer Jonathan Begg reported, "the member had to be worth £1500 so we had to appoint a man from Victoria as no settler could qualify."[21] The poor quality of agricultural implements was also noted by Begg who, in the grand tradition of Old Country visitors assessing North American pioneer agricultural practices,[22] disparaged agricultural tools and methods on the island: "Farming is not conducted here on grand principles. Any little that is done or has been done heretofore has been by old servants of the H.B. Coy. who are more awkward than the animals they drive. One can see here the old carts, farm implements and mode of cultivation in vogue fifty years ago in Britain."[23]

Descriptions and photographs of the earliest cabins provide further evidence of the poverty that characterized life in mid-century. As one early settler described, "cabins were built of fir logs, roofed with shingles of cedar, and chinked with moss or clay. Most had a fireplace, and [were] lighted by candles made by themselves."[24] Most cabins were small, sparsely furnished, and dark.

Many Saltspring Island settlers arrived with families, or soon started them, and difficult living conditions were exacerbated as the size of families grew. Although the Inspector of Schools was willing to blame rates of absenteeism that averaged 25 per cent on the "apathetic carelessness" of Saltspring Island parents,[25] one local teacher believed instead that poverty was to blame. Parents found it difficult to clothe their children adequately, he explained to the school superintendent in 1879: "I expect to get two other young children from Horel," reported school trustee Henry Robinson in 1879, "but he is not very well provided with shoes and clothing for the little ones in this cold damp weather, and that is also the case with Purser."[26]

The difficulties that could beset island families can be seen with particular poignancy in the history of the Purser family. George Purser had taken up land on Saltspring in the early 1870s. Ashdown Green had commented on the poverty of the land: "Purser has a hard old place of it." He noted that "Purser's house stands in a hollow of about 5 acres and I don't think he can get in above 2 or 3 acres more [of cleared land] in his section."[27] Purser, who had a wife and seven children, was struck with paralysis in 1882. To provide support for the family, "the mother, an Indian woman married to Purser, is at Victoria with the baby, she is washing," reported George Stainburn, the Burgoyne Bay teacher, in 1882.[28] Correspondence between Stainburn and the Department of Education documents his attempts to find some support for the family in the face of their deteriorating situation. After the mother left, she failed to send the needed provisions, the eldest daughter ran away from home, and the willingness of the storekeeper, Joseph Akerman to extend further credit to the family was finally exhausted.[29] "The Pursers have been assisted several times by residents here, but most of the settlers are themselves poor ... Altogether Purser and his family are in a very deplorable state,"[30] reported Stainburn. In spite of some aid for the family from the Department of Education, Purser shot and killed himself in 1886. The trial brought to light the human cost of illness and poverty. After swearing that he knew of "no cause why my father should kill himself," his son George Jr declared at the inquest, "he was very weak and ill, paralyzed on one side of his body; has been so for 4 or 5 years. He could walk and get around a little. His wife, my mother, had left him about a year [ago], and the night before he died (I go home every night), he asked me if I knew for sure that my mother had got another man. I told him yes, and he said 'That's all I wanted to know.' We had no gun in the house, the one he shot himself was a borrowed one from George Sheppard."[31] Conditions like these prompted Stainburn to conclude that, "this place is both pecuniarily and otherwise one of the worst places in the province."[32]

Poverty is indicated in other sources. When William Robinson, who occupied one of the most valuable pieces of land on the island, was murdered in his windowless cabin in 1868, the inquest noted that the only contents of his one room were a table, a rifle, a plate and cup, an auger, a hammer, a coat, and a wooden carton that served as a chair.[33] His probate file noted that his total household effects, outside of agricultural produce, some money, and clothing, were worth $8.75.[34] When Armstead Buckner died in 1889, $140 of the $162 worth of his assets was tied up in livestock. Tools, a musket, and a rifle were assessed at $20. Household effects were compiled into two miscellaneous lots valued at $2.50. All of it was sold to pay debts.[35] Settlers on Saltspring Island conform to the pattern identified by Gordon Darroch and Lee Soltow in Ontario, where, "undoubtedly real estate was the principal form of wealth throughout the last century.[36] Scattered and anecdotal evidence suggests that as late as 1914 "for a majority of the farmers, operations were still geared to basic survival."[37]

LAND CLEARANCES

In his study of Emily Township in Ontario, Peter Russell notes that rates of land clearance contain some important information for historians, and not just about the development of settler communities. Land clearance also speaks to the motivations behind settlement, for "those new arrivals from Europe who dreamed of creating farms had to fell that forest. Their rate of clearing is one important measure of how close their dream was to reality."[38] Although limited by factors beyond landowners' control, the rate and extent of land clearance by those who remained for any length of time on Saltspring Island nevertheless speak directly to the expectations they had of life on the island in general, and of farming in particular.

Any study of land clearance must begin with a look at the type of land – soils, topography, geological formation – that characterizes the location in question. For those knowing Saltspring Island only through the glowing terms cited in earlier chapters, it may come as a surprise to find that land and soil surveys of the late twentieth century do not emphasize the fertile valleys that attracted so much attention from nineteenth-century observers; instead, it is the rugged and rocky terrain

Rocks and poor soil characterized much of Saltspring Island. In the early years of resettlement, a stone quarry in the north end provided labour for prospective farmers, and stone for buildings in Victoria and as far away as San Francisco. (SSIA)

covering much of the island that attracts comment. While some arable land certainly exists in the valleys, land-use surveys of Saltspring Island note that steep inclines, rocky soil, and outcroppings of bedrock impose significant limitations on the cultivation of crops.[39] The low rainfall, particularly in August and September, characteristic of Saltspring Island's Mediterranean climate, also limited the type and extent of agricultural production. Although Saltspring, with three large lakes, has more fresh water than the other Gulf Islands, water sources were a problem in many areas of the island, limiting the potential for irrigating on any large scale.[40]

Standing out from the chorus of praise surrounding the island's agricultural potential in the nineteenth century is one discordant voice, that of Ashdown Green, the first official surveyor of the island in 1874. His diaries record his very negative opinion of Saltspring Island's agricultural promise. Much of the land in the south end was rocky but generally believed to be well suited to grazing; Green dismissed it as "worthless except for sheep, but it would require so many acres to keep one sheep that it would not pay to buy it."[41] While he found some good loam in the Burgoyne Valley, particularly on the lands occupied by Gyves, Mitchell, Sparrow, Maxwell, Akerman, and Walsh, Green had little praise for the overall composition of the island. "August 20, 1874: Today we passed over rough worthless country. Gravelly, stony soil with small fir and brush; salal very strong. In whichever direction we looked we could see a rocky bluff, in fact the Island seems to be very little else but ravines and perpendicular rock."[42] A few days later, commenting on the view from Mount Maxwell, the highest point of land on the island, he notes, "from the top of the mountain I had a good view of the country, and a more rocky and worthless place it would be hard to find. In fact it is nothing but steep bluffs and ravines."[43]

It is difficult to reconcile the picture of Saltspring Island found in such land-use reports with the glowing prose of settlers and Department of Agriculture Reports. It is even more difficult to reconcile the statistical returns from the Department of Agriculture with its enthusiastic conclusions about Saltspring's agricultural accomplishments. Any attempt to assess the nature and extent of agricultural production in nineteenth-century British Columbia is hampered by a stark absence of evidence concerning the standard measures of agricultural success: land clearance and crop production. The limited evidence available, however, suggests a large gulf between the aspirations of nineteenth-century agricultural observers and the activities of Saltspring Island farmers.

In the colonial period, the absence of good records about rural land usage can, like so many other areas of the bureaucracy, be traced to the chronic shortage of money and administrative staff available to obtain such information. As Robert Cail argues, however, "even when money became available after 1871, only desultory attempts were made to enforce the regulations [concerning land use]. For thirty years the prevalent attitude was to be that land was plentiful but most of it useless and should anyone have enough initiative to pay a nominal price, no hindrance ought to be placed in his way."[44] Chapter 5 describes in more detail the problems surrounding the collection of even these "nominal prices" for pre-empted land. Routinely generated data concerning clearance rates remain elusive, well into the provincial period. Provisions in the legislation governing land purchase and land use did little to require particular land clearances before 1873 and, when they did appear, they were not rigorously enforced in the province.[45] Even assessment rolls on Saltspring Island fail to distinguish between cleared and uncleared land; instead, they distinguish only between land that was potentially arable and those areas of "marsh, swamp and rock" defined as wild lands and taxed at a lower rate.[46] Similarly, the Department of Agriculture did little to obtain or publish information about agriculture until the early 1890s, when its first reports appeared. Although these reports contain a great deal of important information about agriculture, no data on land clearance were included in the nineteenth century. As a result, evidence of land clearance is problematic for those wanting to provide specific evidence of the extent to which Saltspring Island farmers participated in agricultural pursuits.

Pre-emption improvement certificates are among the few records to mention cleared and cultivated lands. At one Saltspring Island settler's estimate of $180 to clear each acre of land, the required improvements must not have been easy to achieve.[47] Of the 388 pre-emptions granted between 1860 and 1891, only 136 (comprising almost 19,000 acres or 40 per cent of pre-empted lands) had been improved by 1891.[48]

Unfortunately for the historian, the information contained in the individual certificates of improvement provides little insight into the extent of land clearance. Certificates rarely contain detailed figures on the number of acres cleared, fenced, or cultivated. Records are richest in the colonial period and poorest in the era after 1881, but only twenty-two improvement certificates contain any detailed information on the fencing or clearing of land on the island during this whole period. Only fifteen (12 per cent) improved claims contain information about acreages cleared. Results from these sources, although fragmentary, are contained in Table 4.2. A further thirteen records contain information about the value of improvements, but do not specify acreages.

Because the cost per acre of cleared land fluctuates so wildly in the ten records that provide such information, varying from $13 to $50 per acre, it is impossible to estimate acreage values confidently from the value of improvements alone.[49] This small sample, involving claims taken out in the first and second decades of settlement, suggests clearance rates of about two acres per year, on average. This figure is similar to the rates of land clearance suggested by Peter Russell's evidence concerning southern Ontario.[50] Unlike Peter Russell's figures, however, these do not come from tax assessors or census takers, but from a small sample of statements made by the farmer, witnessed by his neighbours and friends, and sent to a bureaucrat in Victoria to substantiate a claim to buy land at a very cheap price.

Fragmentary evidence suggests that these estimates may have been exaggerated by settlers eager to meet the minimum requirements of the pre-emption regulations. John Maxwell, for example, took out a certificate of improvement in March 1875 for land that he had pre-empted in 1861. The certificate, duly signed by Maxwell's neighbours, notes that he has cleared, cultivated, and fenced eighteen acres of land, and cleared and fenced a further twenty acres for pasture.[51] When Ashdown Green surveyed the south end of the island four months later, however, he noted

Table 4.2
Pre-emptors of Land on Saltspring Island Who Included Detailed Information on Land Clearances

Pre-emp. Date (#)	Imp. Cert. Date	Name	Acres cleared	Acres ploughed	Acres fenced	Buildings
n/a	1863/22*	[illegible]	1.5 [?]	3	4	$100
1863 (#619)	1864	Armstead Buckner	15		4000 rails [about 11 acres]	House 20x16, barn 26x24x10
1862 (#423)	Before 1865	Jonathan Begg		7,000 trees planted	20 acres	2 houses built
1874 (#1492)	1874	Louis Stark	100		100	3 houses and 2 barns built
1861 (#84)	1875	John Maxwell	18	18	38	House, 34x20, 2 barns 34x20
1873 (#1448)	1875	George Mitchell	6		160	House 30x30, 16x12 barn 60x25
1871 (#1242)	1875	Joseph Norton	10		25	House, 24x18
1868 (#1082)	[No date]	Ke-awe-hou	6		78	
1864 (#700)	1876	W. Harrison	25		35	House 20x26, barn
1863 (#516)	1877	James McFadden	20		20	House 20x16, barn, cow house
1874 (#1490)	1877	Henry Spikerman	10			
1868 (#1066)	1877	Theodore Trage	100			
1872 (#1326)	1880	Henry Ruckle	60	20	700 rails	
1874 (#1485)	1883	Estalon Bittancourt	7		7	House 23x32, barn 18x24
1866 (#908)	1884	Michael Gyves	15		22	House, $300

Source: British Columbia Deptartment of Land and Works, Pre-Emption Records, Vancouver and Gulf Islands, GR 766 BCA; British Columbia Department of Land and Works, Certificates of Improvement, Vancouver Island and the Gulf Islands, GR 765, BCA; Land Register for Saltspring Island, Surveyor General's Office, Victoria; Saltspring Island Database.
Note: * This is the Certificate of Improvement Number, as name and pre-emption number are not available.

that Maxwell had "a field of grass of about four acres, but not of much account." Even though three days later he noted the "very fair ground occupied garden orchard and buildings,"[52] this assessment does not seem to reflect the thirty-eight cleared acres claimed. Similarly, Armstead Buckner claimed to have cleared fifteen acres and fenced about eleven by 1864. When his property was sold at auction (still without a crown grant) after his death in 1889, probate records suggest that that no improvements had been made to the land, as the property was valued at just over $2 per acre, and finally sold for $6 an acre, a moderate price for unimproved land in the Cowichan area.[53] As the foregoing analysis suggests, historians must be extremely wary about using such data from certificates of improvement to infer the extent of land clearance.

The Dominion Census, the only source to document aggregate figures concerning land clearance, also has serious flaws. While by 1931 the Dominion Census could confidently assert that the term improved lands "is employed in the census to mean all land which has been brought under cultivation and is now fit for the plough, including orchards, gardens and land occupied by buildings,"[54] the meaning of "improved" was not so clearly established in 1881 or 1891. The 1881 census definition of improved land was dramatically different from that of either 1891 or 1901. The tendency of enumerators to regard all lands that received a certificate of improvement as "improved" may have been responsible for some spectacular anomalies in the statistical record in the 1881 census. In that year 184,885 acres of land are listed as improved in the province of British Columbia, a figure that plummeted more than *70 per cent* to 57,881 acres in 1891, notwithstanding the doubling of the population during the decade from 49,459 to 98,173, and the three-fold increase in the number of both occupied farms (from 2,743 to 7,451) and those employed in agriculture (from 2,617 to 8,303).[55] Following a similar pattern, 9,462 acres in Cowichan and Saltspring Island (whose totals are listed together in 1881) are listed as "improved" in 1881, a figure that plummets to 1,592 acres in 1891.[56] My data indicate that 9,286 acres of land had received certificates of improvement by 1881. Because Cowichan lands were not open for pre-emption until early in the 1880s (having been designated as railway lands in the early provincial period in the expectation that the trans-Canada railway would pass through the area[57]), it is likely that most of the agricultural improvements had occurred on Saltspring Island by 1881. If so, this figure supports the contention that all lands that had received a certificate of improvement were considered improved for the purposes of the 1881 census. In most cases, however, only a small proportion of a pre-emption claim needed to be cleared and planted for the entire quarter section to be designated "improved."

Like most island households, the Beddis family cleared only four or five acres of land around their home in the nineteenth century. (SSIA)

In 1891, by contrast, lands were considered improved only if they were explicitly cultivated for crops, fruit trees, or a garden. A number of crops, including hay and hops, were not included in calculations for improved lands, as they fell under the category of pasture lands. This had changed by 1901 to include tracts of timber lands.[58] The 1891 census has the advantage for this study of providing the first reliable aggregate documentation pertaining to land clearance on Saltspring Island. In 1891 the census noted that Saltspring Island had 804 improved acres, i.e., land in gardens, orchards, and crops. A further 455 acres in hay, included in the pasture figures for the 1891 statistics, brings the probable total of land cleared by farmers by 1891 to 1,279 acres, or 4 per cent of the island's 35,105 occupied acres as listed in the census.[59] Department of Agriculture returns for the same year conclude that about 6 per cent of land owned was under cultivation.[60]

These figures suggest that each of the one hundred resident landowners on Saltspring Island in 1891 had cleared an average of about thirteen acres.[61] By this date, three-quarters of landowners had been on the island for more than five years, and over a third had been there more than ten years.[62] Their average stay was just over twelve years, providing an overall average clearance rate of one acre per year by 1891, a rate of land clearing towards the low end of the average of other Canadian agricultural areas in their first decades of settlement.[63] If, as Peter Russell has

Table 4.3
Changes in Agricultural Production, Saltspring Island, 1862–91

Date	Acres Wheat	Acres Barley	Acres Oats	No. Cows	No. Pigs	Acres occupied	Acres cult.	No. HH	Cult. Acres HH
1863	9	37	43	278	200	4,200	163	25	7
1891	104	12	169	354	704	35,105	804	100	8
Increase	x12	x-3	x4	x1.3	x3.5	x8.4	x5	x4	x1

Source: "Miscellaneous notes on Vancouver Island, scrapbooks, 1863–64," Robert Brown, Add Mss 794, vol. I, BCARS; and Table XVI and Table II, Field Produce, *Census of Canada*, 1891.
Note: HH stands for household heads.

suggested, we can infer settlers' goals and aspirations from the rate of land clearance, the slow rate of island clearances suggests that settlers' ideology differed in some important respects from that articulated in the dominant discourse. On a more practical note, the amount of land they cleared is small compared to the twenty acres estimated necessary to support a family in Ontario at this time.[64]

THE PROBLEM OF CROP PRODUCTION

The contrast between the rhetoric of agricultural success constituting the official discourse of rural and the lives of Saltspring Island farmers becomes even more striking when we look beyond both the low yearly rate and total amount of land cleared by 1891 to the detailed evidence of agricultural production. Although statistical information on this subject is not available in routinely generated sources before 1891, some aggregate information is available. Robert Brown stopped to visit the island as his natural history expedition passed by in 1862, and his statistical reporting provides some useful information about settlement and land use at that time. These figures, which provide a point of comparison to those compiled nearly thirty years later in the 1891 census, are provided in Table 4.3.

Brown's data suggest that the average number of acres cultivated per household in 1863 had increased only marginally, from six and a half to eight acres, in 1891. In spite of a six-fold increase in the population (from about seventy-eight to 436), the number of acres under cultivation increased only five-fold from the figures cited by Brown. The differences between the earliest years of pioneer settlement and the time when Saltspring was widely acclaimed as having achieved commercial agricultural success are not, therefore, indicative of sustained agricultural development between 1862 and through the railway boom of the 1880s.

Table 4.4
A Comparison of Agricultural Produce and Producers, Saltspring Island, 1891, 1894

Source	No. of Farmers	Wheat (60 lb./bushel)	Oats (35 lb./bu.)	Peas, Beans, and Corn	Roots	Barley	Hay	Fruit Trees and Gardens	Acres Cultivated	Acres Occupied
1891 census	111	2,836 bu. [85 tons] 104 a.	6,305 bu. [110 tons] 169 a.	3,319 bu. 230 a.*	19,977 bu. 112 a.	450 bu. 12 a.	751 tons 445 a.**	177 a.	804 a.	38,105 a.
1894 Dept of Agriculture	79	2,233 bu. [67 tons] 109 a.	[6,571 bu.] 115 tons 163 a.	81 tons 111 a.	559 tons 125 a.	3 a.	[900 tons] 532 tons	17,343 trees 532 a.	1027	28,514 a.
The Rev. Wilson's Salt Spring Is.	100	950 bu. [28.5 tons]	300 bu.		178 tons		185 tons	4,600 trees	687 a.	14,974 a.
		2 people described	2 people described		4 people described		5 people described	7 people described	11 people described	
Total		3% of the 79 grew 43% of the wheat	3% of the 79 grew 5% of the oats		5% of the 79 grew 32% of the roots		6% of the 79 grew 21% of the hay	9% of the 79 grew 27% of the fruit trees	9% of the 79 owned 67% of the cultivated land	

Source: The Reverend E. Wilson, *Salt Spring Island 1895*; British Columbia Department of Finance, Surveyor of Taxes Assessment Roll for 1894, Gulf Islands Assessment District, Saltspring Division, Roll B 444, BCA; Census of Canada, 1891, District no. 3, Vancouver, M2 – S.D. 14, Saltspring Island, Schedule no. 1 – Nominal; British Columbia, Department of Agriculture Report 1894; British Columbia Sessional Papers, 1895.

Notes: * No acreage is listed for peas, beans, and corn, but the total acreage of wheat, barley, oats, and potatoes and other roots is 397 acres; add to this the 177 acres listed as the total acreage of gardens and orchards, and the total is 574 acres. We know that the total cultivated land for 1891 is listed as 804 acres, so peas, beans, and corn must be 840 minus 574, or 230 acres.

** This acreage was not included in total figures of cultivated lands.

Household-level data from the agricultural schedule of the census are not available for the island in 1891, but three other, slightly later, sources provide the basis for a more detailed analysis of agricultural production at the household level in the early 1890s. While fragmentary, the following evidence gives us the only available means of reaching beyond the average figures discussed above.

The Reverend Wilson's understanding of rural society was framed within the same discursive structure we have seen in newspaper accounts and Department of Agriculture reports, and his promotional pamphlet reflects this construction of Saltspring Island as a successful agricultural community in 1894. Although Wilson's prose is marked by the pastoral hyperbole characteristic of the genre, it also reflects the pre-occupation with yields, crop production, and prices that characterize the bureaucratic discourse on rural British Columbia at that time. The detailed information that Wilson provides about a number of island farmers can be linked to the island assessment roll of 1894, and to Department of Agriculture returns for the same year, to give us a closer look at households on the island.[65] There is good reason to believe the accuracy of the figures he cites: his listings of acreages owned by the nineteen settlers he mentions, for example, are within 2 per cent of the acreages contained in the assessment rolls for 1894.[66] By linking his data on particular individuals with aggregate information in both the Department of Agriculture Reports and the assessment rolls, it is possible to come to some conclusions about average land clearance rates and the types of agricultural activities typical of island residents.

What is most notable about The Reverend Wilson's statistics is the large proportion of all island agricultural activity carried on by the nineteen farmers that he singles out for mention from the 128 farmers that the assessment roll lists as being on the island.[67] As Table 4.4 indicates, even when the farmers he mentions are seen as a proportion of the more modest figure of seventy-nine farmers enumerated by the Department of Agriculture in 1894, the disproportions are striking. For example, the wheat production of the two farmers listed by Wilson who are among the seventy-nine enumerated by the Department of Agriculture in 1894 amounts to 43 per cent of that tabulated by the Department of Agriculture.

Similarly, 5 per cent of the landowners (four people) grew 32 per cent of the root crops, and five farmers (6 per cent of the total) grew 21 per cent of the hay. Eight per cent of the farmers grew a quarter of the fruit. The eleven people for whom Wilson lists cultivated acreages – 14 per cent of the farmers and 9 per cent of the 128 landowners in 1894 – owned 67 per cent of all cultivated lands listed in the Department of Agriculture's report for 1894. A comparison of Wilson's figures with those in the assessment roll indicates that less than a fifth of the farmers

Clark Whims was born on Saltspring, his parents arriving in 1860. Three
generations of the Whims family farmed on the north end of the island. While
African-Americans were relatively poor, even by island standards, like most
islanders they were able to take full advantage of a rich and benign environment to
create a life of modest sufficiency, if not material wealth. (SSIA)

on the island owned more than a third of the land. Their land was, on
average, about four times the size and valued at roughly four times the
price of those farmers' lands not included in Wilson's list. Furthermore,
they had an average amount of personal (i.e., not real) property valued
at almost three times the amount of that belonging to those who are not
mentioned by Wilson.[68]

As these figures suggest, while cultivated land and agricultural production were clearly important aspects of life for some Saltspring Island residents, these seem to have been a distinct minority. Deducting crop
production and land clearances in Wilson's figures from Department of
Agriculture statistics in 1894, we find that the average acreage cleared by
those 109 landowners not mentioned by Wilson is not the thirteen acres
provided to each landowner by general averaging figures: average acreages for the majority were just over three acres per landowner. This was
perhaps enough to support a house, a chicken run, a vegetable garden,
and a few fruit trees. Their crop production, except perhaps of hay, potatoes, and some fruit, must have been extremely small. Therefore, although
the great majority of island householders defined themselves as farmers,
this occupational definition becomes further removed from that of agriculturalist the more closely we look at the details of agricultural production.

CONCLUSION

Any examination of agricultural development on Saltspring Island is frustrated by the absence of detailed information on the most telling of agricultural indicators, land clearance and crop production. A general trend is clear, however: the steady progress of land clearing and cultivation that characterized the earliest years of settlement was not carried out by all people, or in a uniform way, as the century progressed. On the contrary, evidence suggests that land clearance rates declined throughout the 1870s and 1880s, and stood in marked contrast to those in the first year or two of settlement.

How do we reconcile this portrait of Saltspring – a failure in terms of the colonial vision that identified farming with commercial agricultural production on the family farm – with the portrait of the island presented in earlier chapters? Although the official discourse surrounding rural lands in British Columbia suggests that farmers were failing to achieve their desired agricultural aims, a closer look at land acquisition, provided in chapter 5, suggests that Saltspring Island farmers may have had a vision of rural life that differed in some important respects from that usually identified with white settlers in British Columbia.

Appropriating the Land System: Pre-emption Behaviour as Rural Culture

Joseph Akerman was born in England in 1837 and arrived in Canada as a child. In the early 1860s he moved to Victoria, where he met his wife Martha Clay, who had come to British Columbia from Manchester on one of the famous "bride ships," the *Robert Lowe*. Joseph and Martha took up land on Saltspring Island in 1863, and were among the first settlers in the fertile Burgoyne Valley. Akerman abandoned their first pre-emption after four years because, according to the great-grandson Bob Akerman, he disliked the long shadows on that side of the valley. A second pre-emption, taken out in 1865, was abandoned and probably cancelled without ever being lived on by the family. They moved instead to a third pre-emption in 1867 – 150 acres of land on the sunny side of the valley, recently abandoned by another settler. Here they planted some crops, established a nursery to supply island farmers, and, after a few years, built the island's first public guest accommodation, The Travellers' Rest. By 1871 Akerman had improved his 150 acre pre-emption, and five years later he purchased it from the crown, gaining clear title to the land. In 1878 he took out another 100 acres, improving and then purchasing half in 1885 and holding on to the other half without improving it until 1910, when he transferred the pre-emption to his son, Joseph J. Akerman. The unimproved and agriculturally inferior lands were probably used to graze his sheep. In 1885, able to pre-empt more land after his purchase of forty acres in that year, Joseph Sr pre-empted another 75 acres in the Burgoyne Valley. He was granted a certificate of improvement for it in 1894, and then took another thirteen years to purchase it, paying the seventy-five dollars in four installments (plus $11.25 in surveying costs) and finally gaining the crown grant in 1907. Joseph J. followed a similar strategy: he took out a pre-emption in 1885, just after he turned eighteen – 150 acres neighbouring his father's claim. Like his father, he abandoned this claim without improvement in 1907, at which point his son Thomas pre-empted it. In 1886 Joseph Sr purchased another 30 acre parcel nearby, buying it outright without pre-empting it first. Some time in the late 1880s he transferred or sold part of his 1867 pre-emption to his new son-in-law, Joseph Nightingale, who co-owned it with Joseph's sons J.J. and George. By 1903 Nightingale, widowed two years previously when his wife died giving birth to their child, owned it himself. By 1892 Joseph Akerman Sr owned one of the larger farms on the island: 350 acres, most of it paid for. The land was assessed at only $3 an acre overall, however, indicating that it was probably not merely poor agricultural land but largely rocky land suitable only for sheep grazing. Akerman's business ventures – he was calling himself a "storekeeper" rather than a farmer by 1892 – seem to have done well, however, as he had $800 in personal property by that date, a taxable privilege shared by only a fifth of landowners that year.

This complex account of the Akerman family's land-related behaviours over a half-century provides a good sampling of the strategic uses that settlers made of the pre-emption system. Joseph Akerman was one of the most successful "farmers" on Saltspring Island, one who most clearly achieved the kind of success promoted by the land policies of late nineteenth-century British Columbia. Although the material success that the Akerman family achieved on Saltspring Island in these early years was unusual, their complicated and land-based household economy was typical of settlers who stayed for more than a decade. But the complicated and varied transactions that mediated the Akerman family's relation to the land, and the rich and varied uses the family made of it, suggest a much broader understanding of what land had to offer rural families than was contained in the policy-makers' vision.

An approach to Saltspring Island that measures the success of settlers' lives within the parameters set by policy makers – the ability of families to create commercially viable farms – begins by taking for granted what this study seeks to explore: why *did* settlers take up land on Saltspring Island? In this chapter, I try to "see" beyond policy-makers' expectations and beyond a colonial discourse that identified rural with commercial agriculture. A careful examination of land-related behaviours reveals that the settlers of Saltspring Island were frequently acting out very different narratives of rural felicity and very different ideologies of rural from those imagined by policy makers or promoted by carefully formulated land policies. I argue that ironically, in the very terms of the pre-emption system we can find causes of the island's "failure" as an agricultural community, as well as indications of what made it a success for so many island people.

Joe Nightingale and Jim Horel, working on springboards, fell a
tree on Mr Collins' property. Trees were a source of fuel and
provided employment for waged labour. They were also a source
of considerable work for islanders wanting to clear their lands.
(SSIA)

PRE-EMPTION ABANDONMENT

While government policy discouraged land speculation through its residency requirements, its success at ensuring land settlement continued to
be frustrated by high rates of claim abandonment throughout the entire
period under study. By 1881, after more than two decades of non-Native
settlement on the island, only fifteen (4 per cent) of the 358 pre-emptions
taken out on the island had been purchased. By 1891 only a quarter of
pre-emptions taken out since 1859 had been purchased, while two-thirds
were abandoned before any improvements had been registered.[1] Even

Table 5.1
Summary of Lands Pre-Empted on Saltspring Island, 1860–91

Pre-Emption Claims	Number	Percentage
Abandoned	222	58
Improved then transferred	42	10
Improved and purchased	122	32
Total	386	100

Source: Saltspring Island Database.

when the pre-emptions taken out in 1859 – of which an unusually high 96 per cent were abandoned, if all of those who appeared on lists asking to pre-empt land are considered – are left out of the calculation, we still find that more than half of all pre-emptions on the island ended in abandonment, with fewer than a third ending in purchase.

The high rates of abandonment are illustrated in Table 5.1, where the history of each piece of land pre-empted each year is summarized. Although rates of land abandonment fell from 54 per cent for land pre-empted in the 1860–70 period to 50 per cent in 1871–81, they rose to a high of 62 per cent after 1881. How successful was a system of land acquisition from which over half the participants simply walked away?

High rates of claim abandonment, particularly in the first years of non-Native settlement on Saltspring Island, confirm the existence of a highly mobile population in this frontier society. This will come as no surprise to historians of British Columbia, where the transience of a young male work force is a staple of provincial historiography.[2] High rates of mobility were not unique to British Columbia; they have been confirmed in other settler societies across Canada. David Gagan's study of Peel County indicates that about half of the population in mid-century censuses could not be found a decade later, and similar persistence rates have been identified in other Ontario and Quebec locations.[3] This study also suffers from the historiographic exigencies of areas of high mobility typical of the North American frontier: if the majority of pre-emptors who came to the island stayed only a short time, left few records and moved on, it is difficult to describe or explain who they were or what they were doing in any particular place.[4]

Information gleaned about particular settlers does, however, reflect the varieties of settler discontent with the pre-emption system in general, and Saltspring Island in particular. Cross-linked land records and aggregate behaviours tell us a great deal about the problems and promises that pre-emptors found in the land. Some of the pre-emptors who abandoned their claims were the non-resident pre-emptors discussed in chapter 3. Between 1860 and 1881, one quarter of the pre-emption claimants never resided on Saltspring Island, a figure that falls dramatically to 8 per cent in the 1880s.[5] All but two of these elusive pre-emptors abandoned their claims without leaving any evidence that they had ever taken them up.

It is beyond the parameters of this study to follow these itinerant pre-emptors after they abandoned their claims, but histories of British Columbia suggest that they became part of that large group of migrants moving through the colony and province casting about for a way to make a living and a life. For this group, the staking of a pre-emption claim was a speculation in a system of cheap land acquisition that probably involved only the small registration fee and some quixotic thoughts about rural life. The declining number of those who casually registered but did not take up a claim reflects not only the growing number of wage-earning opportunities as colony and province matured but also the increasing seriousness with which land acquisitions were regarded; obtaining cheap lands elsewhere in the southern Vancouver Island area was becoming more difficult, especially in the railway boom years.[6]

The number of these absentee claimants had fallen by 1891, but more than half of pre-emptions were still being abandoned in the 1880s and early 1890s. Although most of these pre-emptors left within a year, a group remained who would eventually abandon their claims, but not until they had made an effort to install themselves on the land. For these people, claim abandonment often reflected their discontent with the exigencies of pioneer life. As we have seen, difficulties with the weather,[7] transportation, and communications created frustrations for settlers.[8]

A number of settlers reported harassment from Aboriginal people, who were probably dissatisfied with the transfer of their lands.[9] James Shaw left his claim in 1860 because of reports of Indian harassment. In 1869 Louis Stark wanted to move to a new pre-emption on the island to protect his family from the violence in the Vesuvius settlement. He wrote to Joseph Trutch, Commissioner of Land and Works, to request a new pre-emption: "I beg leave to inform you that I have ben obliged to move my famerly from my claim as the Indiens is daingeris I cannot get any man to live on the place since Cirtice was killed for this caiss I [would like to pre-empt] a peace of land on the n.e. side of ganges harber and joind on the south east end of david overtons' claim thir is forty or fifty acres of this land near to other settlers which I would be very thankful if you will record this to me and take one hundred acres from my other claim and record to me one hundred onely until I can get a man on it."[10] Trutch replied that Stark must either improve and purchase his claim, or abandon it, if he wanted to pre-empt more land.[11] Stark was in no position to make such a purchase, and so was forced to abandon his first claim.[12] Social conflict and economic difficulties certainly contributed to settler discontent and to claim abandonment; and as we have seen, the strict regulations of the pre-emption system selectively drove a number of serious pre-emptors off the island.

It is clear that numbers of settlers left their pre-emptions before being able to gain any financial return on their investment of time and labour on the land. A close examination of the land records suggests, however, that the significance of an abandoned claim may have been more complex. High claim abandonment rates overstate the extent of mobility on and off the island: although the majority of those staking claims between 1860 and 1891 abandoned their claims, many were doing so without abandoning the island. The 222 claims rescinded after 1860 were abandoned by 156 people; of these, 113 were abandoning their only claim, but forty-three were long-term residents who went on to pre-empt subsequent claims on the island.[13]

Not only were many claim abandoners going on to take up other claims but those who took out only one claim often abandoned it after a very long time. The average length of stay on Saltspring Island for all those who abandoned one or more pieces of land was more than nine years. As Figure 5.1 indicates, of all those who abandoned their claims, more than half were still on the island a year after staking their claim and 40 per cent were still on the island after five years. Almost a third remained after ten years, and, after twenty, almost one out of every five preemptors who had abandoned their first claim was still on the island.[14] For those abandoners who stayed a year or more on the island, however, the average stay was fifteen years, with almost half staying longer than ten years.[15] These figures confirm the pattern seen in earlier chapters: high rates of mobility within the first year of staking a pre-emption claim coexisted with surprisingly high persistence rates thereafter.

The length of time abandoners resided on the island suggests that claim abandonment should not be simply understood as an indicator of pre-emption breakdown; on the contrary, pre-emption abandonment seems to have been used selectively by those remaining for more than a year for a variety of purposes, including graduated and low-risk land acquisition, landholding for the future, and, commonly, a strategy for low-cost continued residence. These will be examined in turn.

For a number of settlers, a first pre-emption seems to have worked as a "starter claim" – land that provided the pre-emptor with the opportunity to get established on the island while looking around for a better location. Joseph Akerman, as we saw at the beginning of this chapter, abandoned his first claim when a more desirable neighbouring location

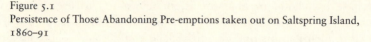

Figure 5.1
Persistence of Those Abandoning Pre-emptions taken out on Saltspring Island,
1860–91

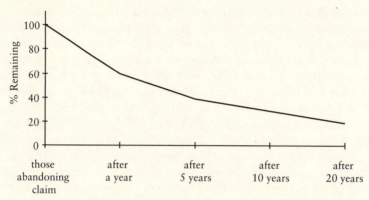

Source: British Columbia Department of Land and Works, Pre-Emption Records, Vancou-
ver and Gulf Islands, GR 766 BCA; British Columbia Department of Land and Works,
Certificates of Improvement, Vancouver Island and the Gulf Islands, GR 765, BCA; Land
Register for Saltspring Island, Surveyor General's Office, Victoria; British Columbia De-
partment of Finance, Surveyor of Taxes, 1892 Assessment Roll, Roll B 443, Gulf Islands
Assessment District; Census of Canada, 1881, District no. 191, Vancouver, Cowichan and
Saltspring Island, Schedule no. 1 – Nominal; Census of Canada, 1891, District no. 3,
Vancouver, M2 – S.D. 14, Saltspring Island, Schedule no. 1 – Nominal; Saltspring Island
Database.

became vacant four years later. Other pre-emptors, such as George
Mitchell, Pompey Jackson, John Cairns, Thomas Williams, and Armstead
Buckner, followed a similar pattern, using the first claim as a spring-
board for obtaining better land, which they went on to improve and
purchase.[16] For these settlers, pre-emption abandonment represented
flexibility rather than failure.

Joseph Akerman also shared with some of his island neighbours a
more strategic use of land abandonment. A number of settlers, including
Akerman's eldest son, Michael Gyves, Joseph King, and Henry Sampson,
held land in a pre-emption claim, unimproved and not paid for, for many
years. After they abandoned their claim, it was immediately pre-empted
by their son or son-in-law.[17] Similar land-transference strategies can be
found in other unimproved lands. A number of pre-emptors died after
living several years on their unimproved pre-emptions, leaving the land
to be improved and purchased by their widows. Most of these widows,
probably short of both cash and labour, were content to preserve their
pre-emptions without improvement, as all waited for re-marriage before
improving and purchasing their claims.[18]

Other pre-emptors used the system as an inexpensive vehicle for holding lands until they could pay for them. Take, for example, the case of Theodore Trage. Trage took up hundreds of acres in the Beaver Point area in the first three decades of settlement, much of it with his partner Henry (Heinrich) Spikerman. Both carefully used the pre-emption system to accumulate lands gradually, pre-empting and purchasing a number of times. Claim abandonment was one of their strategies: when Trage took up a pre-emption in 1884, and abandoned in it 1887, it was immediately purchased by Spikerman. Once the land was abandoned, pre-emption regulations allowed Trage to pre-empt more land, which he immediately did.[19] Similarly, Arthur Walter accumulated almost a thousand acres of land with a strategy of pre-emption abandonment and outright purchases. On one occasion, for example, he pre-empted one hundred acres in the Ganges area in 1884, and then abandoned and immediately purchased it in 1885.[20] Others may have been attempting a similar strategy of holding lands until they decided, or were able, to purchase them, but had their pre-emption claims scooped by other pre-emptors first. F.L. Lakin, William McAfee, and Henry Sampson took up lands, abandoned them, and then quickly purchased them after the subsequent pre-emptors in turn abandoned their claims a few years later.[21]

While some pre-emptors were clearly holding the land for future gains, others may have been reaping some of the other economic advantages of unimproved lands. Richard Maxwell and his brother David, for example, each pre-empted well-timbered lands around Mount Maxwell in the mid-1880s, at the beginning of their logging careers. David had abandoned his land by 1894, but Richard held onto his claim until 1925, when he abandoned and immediately purchased it. The land, useless for farming, once again held good stands of timber by that date.[22] Although new regulations in the late nineteenth century sought to prevent people from taking up pre-emption claims just to log off the best timber, a number of landowners used them as a source of salable timber and as woodlots.[23] Clearly, claim abandonment provided these settlers one more strategy in increasing their usable landholdings, for both themselves and their families.

Although the Maxwells, Akermans, and Trages seem to have been using claim abandonment as part of a strategy that would eventually turn land or its products into a commodity, the use of pre-empted but unimproved lands was not limited to commercial or speculative purposes. Almost a third of those who abandoned their claims lived on them for more than five years before leaving.[24] Most simply walked away from the land they had a right to use but not exchange, in very much the same way as a long-term lessee walks away from a secure rental property. The only significant difference was that, unlike renters,

Cordwood stacked at Beaver Point awaiting shipment. The wood was used to fuel boilers generating steam for heat and power and was also exported off the island for household use. (SSIA)

pre-emptors paid almost nothing for their occupation of the land. For these people, pre-emption was not so much an investment in land as a stage in life. As we will see in chapter 6, landholding on Saltspring Island provided a wide variety of economic alternatives for those who were only intermittently willing or able to turn their land into commercially viable farms. For many of these settlers, claim abandonment seems to have been part of a low-cost and flexible solution to the problem of where and how to live.

To suggest that claim abandonment represented a failure of the pre-emption system is to suggest that the goal of pre-emptors was always to improve and purchase their lands. Evidence presented here suggests that some pre-emptors had other uses for the lands they took up. Although some settlers were driven off lands they wanted to purchase by pre-emption regulations and the difficulties of pioneer life, others used claim abandonment for deferring, or putting off altogether, the necessity of paying for the land. Between the time they pre-empted and the time they abandoned their land, however, some settlers used it to great advantage. A few used land as part of a short-term accumulation strategy; others held it for the sake of future goals that may in some cases have been obscure even to them; some just used it as a place to live.

IMPROVEMENT, PURCHASE,
AND "SUCCESSFUL" PRE-EMPTORS

When we turn our attention to those who improved and then either traded or purchased their lands, we are seeing those who, in policy-makers' terms, proved the success of the pre-emption system. This system provided the opportunity for over a hundred settlers on the island to turn "useless" lands into the improved holdings necessary to create viable farms, and a further forty-two pre-emptions were traded after improvements had been made.[25] While a portion of both non-landowners and pre-emptors made up a steady stream of people taking up land and leaving Saltspring Island within a year, a solid core were permanent settlers who stayed longer than ten years. Figure 5.2 confirms this trend, and suggests, not surprisingly, that persistence was mediated by the decisions that pre-emptors made about their land. In spite of the flexible and varied uses of abandoned lands noted above, those who abandoned their claims stayed the least amount of time on the island, and those who purchased their claims stayed the longest.

Those who improved and purchased their land stayed a very long time on Saltspring Island: an average of twenty-six years, as opposed to the nine years that claim abandoners remained. A number of these pre-emptors had created thriving farms by the 1890s; farmers like Joseph Akerman, Theodore Trage, John Maxwell, John Cairns, Alexander McLennan, John Norton, and Henry Ruckle were growing and selling a variety of agricultural produce to Victoria, Vancouver, and the mining communities of Nanaimo and Ladysmith by the 1890s.

The behaviour of purchasers, however, resembled that of abandoners in one important way: most showed a surprising reluctance to turn their land into a commodity or themselves into full-time petty commodity producers.[26] This reluctance, visible in the state of agricultural development discussed in chapter 4, as well as in the high number of abandoned claims, is also reflected in the length of time it took pre-emptors to improve and purchase their claims. Those who pre-empted land in the 1860s and went on to purchase their claims waited, on average, ten years before registering improvements on their land. They waited another eight years, on average, before paying for it. Those pre-empting in the 1870s and 1880s waited an average of just under seven and six years, respectively, before registering improvements on their land, and another two before obtaining crown grants. We have looked in some detail at some reasons why pre-emptors might take so long to improve and purchase their lands: the physical difficulties in clearing land and building houses and fences were often formidable; bureaucratic processes were often cumbersome; transportation and communication were

Figure 5.2
Persistence by Pre-emption History

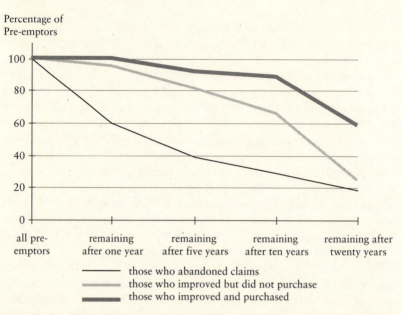

Source: British Columbia Department of Land and Works, Pre-Emption Records, Vancouver and Gulf Islands, GR 766 BCA; British Columbia Department of Land and Works, Certificates of Improvement, Vancouver Island and the Gulf Islands, GR 765, BCA; Land Register for Saltspring Island, Surveyor General's Office, Victoria. British Columbia Department of Finance, Surveyor of Taxes, 1892 Assessment Roll, Roll B 443, Gulf Islands Assessment District; Saltspring Island Database.

limited; and most settlers lacked the financial resources that, as Peter Russell has demonstrated, made so much difference to rates of land improvement in frontier areas.[27]

In spite of these impediments, one group of island pre-emptors managed to circumvent their impact more effectively and improve their lands more quickly than others: those who improved land and then transferred it without purchasing it. The behaviour of this small group is interesting because it differs significantly from those who improved and purchased their lands. As such, it extends our understanding of the range of possible behaviours for island landowners, particularly those who were able and willing to make the investments necessary to improve their lands. Table 5.2 examines the behaviours of that minority of pre-emptors who improved their lands. As the table suggests, most of those who transferred their lands – that is, those who improved but did not go on to purchase their pre-emptions – did so before 1882.

Table 5.2
Differences Between Purchasing and Transferring Pre-emption Claims, Saltspring Island, 1860–91

	No. of pre-emptions purchased (% of all claims)	Average time (years) between pre-emption and improvement: Lots purchased	No. of pre-emptions improved and transferred (% of all claims)	Average time (years) between pre-emption and improvement: Lots transferred
1860–71	13 (11%)	10.4	25 (21%)	3.7
1871–81	35 (41%)	6.8	13 (15%)	4.4
1882–91	75 (41%)	5.5	3 (2%)	0.7

Source: British Columbia Department of Land and Works, Pre-Emption Records, Vancouver and Gulf Islands, GR 766 BCA; British Columbia Department of Land and Works, Certificates of Improvement, Vancouver Island and the Gulf Islands, GR 765, BCA; Land Register for Saltspring Island, Surveyor General's Office, Victoria; British Columbia Department of Finance, Surveyor of Taxes, 1892 Assessment Roll, Roll B 443, Gulf Islands Assessment District; Saltspring Island Database.

Those transferring their lands took about half as long to improve their claims as did their counterparts who purchased.

The length of time between taking up and improving a claim speaks directly to the settlers' desire to turn their land into a tradable commodity on the one hand or a working farm on the other. Evidence presented in chapter 4 suggests that most farmers on the island did not turn their land into commercial farming operations. Evidence presented in this chapter suggests that those who improved their land, traded it, and left the island were different from those farmers, whose patience often verged on torpor, who purchased their lands.

Why did one group of "farmers" work so much harder and faster than all the others at improving their lands, and why did the most enterprising farmers then leave the island? Three explanations seem possible. First, those who quickly improved their lands and moved may have been wealthy enough to complete what their neighbours could only dream of, by hiring the necessary labour. Particularly for the years before 1881 (when most of the transfers occurred), we have no sources that could document this type of inequality; we simply don't know whether this group of farmers was wealthier. The evidence provided in chapter 4, however, seems to support broadly based poverty throughout the island. Second, the serious, commercially oriented farmers may have soon realized the island's limited agricultural potential and moved elsewhere to better pursue their agricultural aspirations. Third, they may have wished to make money out of their land, and did so by making improvements rapidly. In any case, the net result was that the motivated, hard-working

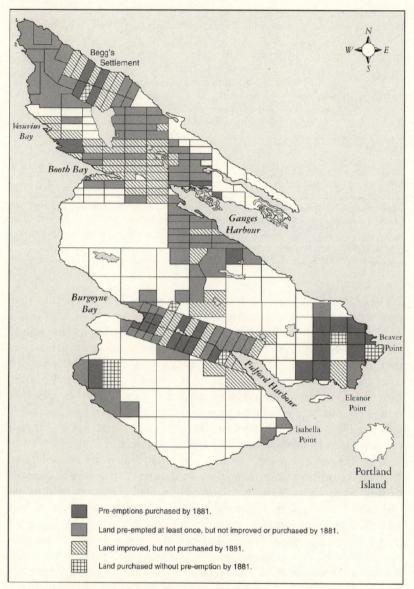

Begg's
Settlement

*Vesuvius
Bay*

Booth Bay

*Ganges
Harbour*

*Burgoyne
Bay*

Fulford Harbour

Beaver
Point

Eleanor
Point

Isabella
Point

Portland
Island

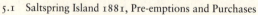

■ Pre-emptions purchased by 1881.

▨ Land pre-empted at least once, but not improved or purchased by 1881.

▨ Land improved, but not purchased by 1881.

▦ Land purchased without pre-emption by 1881.

5.1   Saltspring Island 1881, Pre-emptions and Purchases

individuals like Jonathan Begg left the island, leaving their slow-working companions behind to purchase their claims at their leisure. The behaviour of those who improved and transferred their land was, however, anomalous in a system that seemed otherwise to function primarily to maximize low-cost, low-risk, and unproductive tenure on the land.

The limited commodity value of land can be seen in another way. Although pre-emption was the primary method of land acquisition on Saltspring Island, the straightforward ownership of land – the possession of a crown grant and freehold title – remained unusual in these early years. This ambiguity can be seen clearly by looking at Map 5.1, which provides an overview of all the lands that had been pre-empted, improved, and purchased by 1881. As the map illustrates, by this date, little of the island had been improved, and even less purchased.

This characteristic of island landholding can also be seen in the 1881 and 1891 censuses, cross-linked with land records, as summarized in Figure 5.3. Of the fifty-five household heads who "owned" land in 1881, fewer than a quarter (twelve) had obtained a crown grant for some or all of their land by that date. A further 20 per cent in 1881, and 12 per cent in 1891, were living on pre-emptions for which they had obtained certificates of improvement that gave them provisional ownership rights only.

More than half the landowners (twenty-nine out of fifty-five) in 1881 were in possession of pre-empted lands, with no certificate of improvement. By 1891 more than a third of landowning household heads on the island were still in this situation.[28] Throughout most of the period under study, then, most landowners did not own their land.

THE MULTIPLE MEANINGS OF RURAL LANDS

Evidence presented in chapter 4 suggests that most pre-emptors were not just slow at improving their lands: a great many seem to have simply stopped improving them when a certain minimum amount had been cleared, fenced, and built on. A homogeneous community of commercial farmers on the island did not emerge. In speculating on the motivations behind the surprisingly unprogressive – and un-colonial – behaviours that characterized the rural experience for so many on the island, it is difficult to suppress the idea that many were not participating in commercial agriculture because they were not interested in doing so. If the temptation to lump all non-Native settlers into one homogeneous group, and then ascribe to them a particular colonial ideology of progress and development, is resisted, it is possible to find in the evidence presented here a different ideology of rural life being acted out on Saltspring Island.[29]

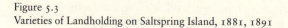

Figure 5.3
Varieties of Landholding on Saltspring Island, 1881, 1891

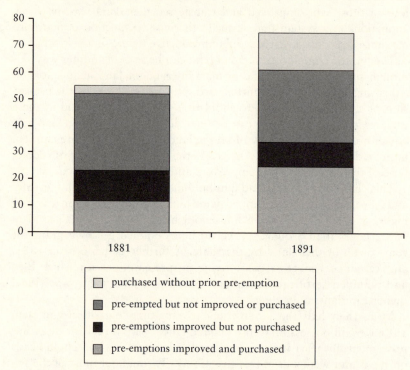

Source: British Columbia Department of Land and Works, Pre-Emption Records, Vancouver and Gulf Islands, GR 766 BCA; British Columbia Department of Land and Works, Certificates of Improvement, Vancouver Island and the Gulf Islands, GR 765, BCA; Land Register for Saltspring Island, Surveyor General's Office, Victoria. British Columbia Department of Finance, Surveyor of Taxes, 1892 Assessment Roll, Roll B 443, Gulf Islands Assessment District; Census of Canada, 1881, District no. 191, Vancouver, Cowichan and Saltspring Island, Schedule no. 1 – Nominal; Census of Canada, 1891, District no. 3, Vancouver, M2 – S.D. 14, Saltspring Island, Schedule no. 1 – Nominal; Saltspring Island Database.

Evidence of an alternative ideology of rural life acted out in rural practice is compelling. An examination of claim abandonment indicates that
a number of Saltspring Island pre-emptors made little investment of either labour or capital in their lands; instead, many were using the system
as a method of putting off altogether payment for inhabited and exploited lands. Most of those who pre-empted land were slow to turn
their land into a commodifiable investment, even if they did end up improving and purchasing it. Assessment rolls, available for Saltspring Island for the early 1890s, also indicate that landowners were reluctant to
part with cash to support their lands: one out of every four landowners

neglected to pay taxes in these years.[30] And, as we have just seen, the group of pre-emptors who were quickest to improve their lands were those who transferred their lands and left the island.

If land had little value to most settlers as a commodity, it did have some other valuable attributes. Although pre-emptors were not able to speculate on their land until purchase, they were able to live on their land with no obligation to pay for it until it was surveyed, at which time the applicant could apply and pay for their crown grant. Indeed, it was impossible to purchase claims at the discounted pre-emption price until improvements had been registered and the survey paid for. The government was increasingly concerned about problems associated with unsurveyed lands and encouraged and coerced pre-emptors, especially those who had received certificates of improvement, to have their lands surveyed.[31] Although the Land Ordinance of 1861 had specified two years as the minimum amount of time a pre-emptor must reside on the land prior to applying for the right to purchase it at the rate of $1 an acre, little attention was given to the maximum amount of time that could elapse between pre-emption and purchase; nineteenth-century legislators were much more interested in getting settlers onto the land than in compelling payment, at least in these early days. Thus, Joseph Trutch complained in 1868: "as it is found that the Government has no power under the Land Ordinance to compel payment by pre-emptors of the upset price of such pre-empted and surveyed lands, these lands must continue in this anomalous condition until the payment of the price thereof be enforced under penalty of forfeiture of all pre-emptive rights."[32]

Before the 1870s the government showed little inclination to pressure pre-emptors to fulfill the official directive to improve and purchase their lands within two years. None of the 317 pre-emptions taken out on Saltspring Island before 1876 had been purchased by that date.[33] By 1873 the government was growing concerned that throughout the province lands that had been purchased outright had not been paid for; a land return tabled by Robert Beaven in 1873 indicated that 75 per cent of land in the province was being purchased by deferred payment, and, of that, only 14 per cent had actually been paid for.[34] By the late 1870s pre-emptors were being encouraged to make payments by installment within four years of improvement, but legislation regulating the amount of time between pre-emption and improvement was not clarified before the 1884 land act.[35] After that date, increasing pressure was put on pre-emptors, first by threats to remove settlers from their lands if certificates of improvement were not obtained, and later by charging interest on unpaid amounts.[36] Pre-emptors obtaining their crown grants from the mid-1890s onward commonly had the price of a survey added to the price of their land, apparently paid to the

Surveyor General and recorded in the Land Register. Throughout this period, as the figures above suggest, enforcement of regulations surrounding payment for lands remained extremely lax, the result of large distances and administrative ennui.[37]

While pre-emptors were on their land, whatever their particular stage in the pre-emption system, they enjoyed secure tenure, with all the rights accorded to landowners except the right to trade, mortgage, or sell. They were generally unmolested by government officials. The low profile of government officials may help to account for the absence of squatters on the island.[38] Not only stability of tenure but also political voice was conferred by a pre-emptor's landholding status: most voters on the land gained their right to vote not by their education but by means of pre-empting land. Without either owning their pre-emptions or turning their lands into commercial agricultural enterprises, landholders occupied a privileged position in the island society and, in their own way, in the island economy.

CONCLUSION

A detailed examination of individual and aggregate land-related practices on the island provides some important answers to the question of why people were taking up land, and why they were staying on it for so long, in an area where commercial agricultural success remained elusive for the majority of "farmers." There can be little doubt that they were taking up land: the cross-linking of census and land records of 1881 and 1891 confirms what the land records alone suggest: the pre-emption system provided most settlers with their access to land. Furthermore, there can be little doubt that land acquisition in turn formed the basis of settlement on the island. In both 1881 and 1891 more than three-quarters of all household heads were landowners; of these, the vast majority had obtained their land by pre-empting it.[39] In each of the census years only two landowners had not pre-empted any land by the census date. By 1891 most landowners (81 per cent) were still living on land they had pre-empted; almost half of these were still living on pre-emptions for which they had not yet paid.[40]

While islanders did not generally achieve the goals normalized within the dominant discourse, this detailed study of land-related behaviours demonstrates that they succeeded in other ways, manipulating the terms of the pre-emption system to maximize their access to free land. Many pre-emptors on Saltspring Island did follow the letter of pre-emption law, but they found ingenious ways of getting around its spirit. Living on lands that were, at least provisionally, free, and in an environment that provided free access to a wide variety of foods and building materials, the "farmers" of Saltspring Island balked at the constraints involved in setting up and running a commercially viable family farm. For, after arriving on the island, settlers quickly discovered in the combination of the pre-emption system and a generous natural environment many advantages lying outside the benefits attendant on the improvement and purchase of land. Evidence concerning land acquisition and abandonment suggests that it was the economic flexibility offered by these provisional forms of landownership, and not the creation of a commercially viable farm, that appealed to many settlers. So it is easy to see why, as islanders grew accustomed to the advantages of free land, the ideal of the commercialized family farm lost its lustre. In chapters 6, 7, and 8, I will look in more detail at the particular benefits – social, economic and political – that low-cost land, flexible terms, and secure residence offered pre-emptors of country lands in nineteenth-century British Columbia.

6

Political Economy and Household Structure on Saltspring Island

Robert Brown, a British horticulturist leading an expedition through-out British Columbia in 1862, was an early visitor to Saltspring Island. After visiting the island and other areas of coastal Vancouver Island, he noted in his diary the following evaluation of rural British Columbia life in general, and Saltspring Island in particular:

Though not a pleasant topic, I cannot help noticing the want of confidence in the stability of the Colony manifested by most of the settlers, and a "Waiting for something to turn up" Micawber sort of disposition. This is more or less the way in all countries ... But though this is every day more and more decreasing owing to the recent discoveries of the expedition, yet it is preeminently so among a large portion of the Cowichan, Chemainis [sic] Saltspring and Comox settlers whose only ambition (it is no use mincing matters by refined language) seems to be "a log shanty, a pig, a potato patch, Kloomchman (Indian woman) and a clam bed"! This is easily accounted for, most of the Settlers being either men with no business and totally unacquainted with farming: Men who came here attracted by the gold-fever and got their eyes jaundiced by their Cariboo failures, prodigal sons who are just waiting to get reconciled to their families, or to go home having mistaken their vocation. The few who have been really bred to farming are the men who are doing most.[1]

Brown sums up, albeit in negative terms, the salient features of Saltspring Island's political economy: the marginality of commercial agriculture and the centrality of self-provisioning, household-based activities.[2] Brown saw these activities in racialized terms, believing that settlers' reliance on activities other than commercial agricultural pursuits was part of the same cluster of cultural values that made it acceptable to live with an Aboriginal woman. In his mind's eye, both were measured against the "civilized" and civilizing backdrop of the family farm, and both were found wanting. As Adele Perry has argued, many nineteenth-century observers found it "hard to reconcile an over-whelmingly male, racially diverse settler society living among a much larger First Nations population with mid-nineteenth century dreams of sober, hard-working men, virtuous women and respectable families."[3] Taking up life with a First Nations woman spoke to the same mistaken, fecklessness of these rural settlers as did their failure to make "proper" use of their lands and, indeed, their identity as farmers.

Brown's criticisms of islanders bespeak the various kinds of determinism – economic, geographic, cultural, and social – common in his day, that made him "read" country lands in a particular way. Less than a century later, however, a much more flexible approach to settlement practices was developed by James C. Malin, in his microhistorical examinations of the process of resettlement of the American grasslands in the late nineteenth and early twentieth century. Malin observed that resettlement would successfully occur when people were able to change both their culture and the new environment. With time to learn how to adapt to, and how to change, the environment, and with a certain cultural flexibility, people could, he believed, successfully settle any kind of place.[4] In this chapter, I look in more detail at the ways that settlers worked out their own economy, society, and culture on Saltspring Island. I approach the difference between discourse and practice, between a deterministic colonial vision and a more fluid local experience, by asking two related questions. First, if the farmers of Saltspring Island were not relying on agricultural production or land speculation to make money, then what were they doing to make a living? Second, if the narrative that associates rural life with farming and farming with commercial production does not explain the behaviours of Saltspring Islanders, in what context can we understand their political economy? What were the terms on which they built up their society, economy, and culture in the Gulf Islands environment of the late nineteenth century?

OCCUPATION

"Occupation" is a troublesome concept for rural historians. Defined as "one's habitual employment, profession, craft, or trade,"[5] it is one of the most common routinely generated formal categories of information available for the population on Saltspring Island. It appears consistently in such sources as voters' lists, parish records, assessment rolls, censuses, and business directories. But among these sources, only the Dominion Census is explicit about what occupation means. The 1891 *Instructions to Officers* advised enumerators on the subject as follows: "the profession, trade or occupation must be entered in full, as given to the enumerator. When two of these are united in one person, both may or may not be given; the point being decided by the importance attached to the fact by the person himself."[6]

While occupation seems at first to provide a sensible enough description of what people did to make a living, I soon discovered, as I began this study, some tension between the concept of "occupation" and the behaviours of Saltspring Island residents. The discourse of bureaucratic liberalism placed some well-defined limitations on this category of experience, most particularly with its assumption that people had a single and clearly definable "occupation" by which they made a living. The limitations of the term "occupation" are perhaps most apparent in definitions of women's work. In spite of numerous indications that Saltspring Island women were an important part of an economy rooted in the farm and household,[7] information on women's contributions to the island economy is very difficult to find. The silence that defines women's work in the primary sources can, in part, be attributed to women's legal status regarding land. More than 80 per cent of the information about Saltspring Island residents lies in documents relating in some way to landownership. In nineteenth-century British Columbia, where most women were prevented by law from participating in the most common form of land acquisition on the island – pre-emption – their relative obscurity in routinely generated sources is not surprising.[8] As figure 6.1 indicates, while women and children together made up 60 per cent of the population of the island in the census years of 1881 and 1891, together they generated fewer than 15 per cent of the records.[9]

When adult women *did* appear, however, as they did in the decennial census, the cultural constructions of "occupation" usually did not include their work. In 1891 enumerators were explicitly instructed not to list occupations for women and children "unless they have a definite occupation besides their share in the work of the family or household."[10] Housekeeping only became an occupation "for such persons as receive wages or salary for their services."[11] This decision speaks to much broader issues concerning the ways that society assigns significance to particular activities. In 1881 only two women out of fifty-eight who were fifteen and older (3 per cent) were listed with an occupation: one a widowed "farmer" and the other a forty-one-year-old "house servant." Nine young women over fourteen years of age and living with their parents listed no occupation. A further thirty-eight women were married to farmers but also listed no occupation. This is in stark contrast to the portrayal of men in this source: all those fifteen and over were listed with an occupation in 1881, including nine young men listed as farmer's sons.[12] Two fourteen-year-old boys also listed themselves as "farmer's sons."

Figure 6.1
Information from a Variety of Sources, Saltspring Island, 1877–91

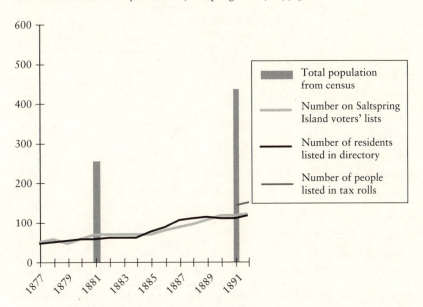

In 1891 more women – twelve of the ninety-two, or 13 per cent of all adult women – were listed as having occupations. Most of these women were single: three were nuns, one was working as a domestic, and three were farmers.[13] Four married women also listed occupations in 1891: two farmers, a baker, and an "unemployed teacher."[14] Nevertheless, occupational status for women remained unusual, subsumed in their traditional roles as wives, mothers, and daughters.[15] In the struggle to find out about women's work on Saltspring Island, I discovered the selectivity of both nineteenth-century bureaucrats and modern historians. The types of activities performed by women – self-provisioning, usually unwaged household-centred tasks, or irregular and part-time waged work – find little resonance within historical descriptions of British Columbia or any other developed region where work is commonly identified with earning money, most particularly wages.[16]

At first glance, recognition of men's economic role seems to be borne out by their classification, unlike that of their wives and daughters, within the occupational category of "farmer." Out of the 2,400 records containing information about occupation on Saltspring Island, over 70 per cent describe men as farmers.[17] As Table 6.1 indicates, almost 80 per cent of those declaring an occupation on the 1881 census were farmers or farmer's sons, and this occupational group accounted for 83 per cent of household heads.

Table 6.1
Saltspring Island: Occupation and Family Structure, 1881 Census

Occupation	No.	Average age	No. of families with children	Average no. of children	No. of landholders	No. of women
Farmer	65	47.1	30	3.5	47	1
Farmer's son	9	16.2	0	n/a	0	0
Farm labourer	2	20.5	0	n/a	0	0
Labourer	10	28.2	1	3	1	0
Storekeeper*	2	43	2	7	2	0
House-servant	3	21.7	0	n/a	0	3
Schoolteacher	2	39.5	0	n/a	0	0
Boatman	1	46	1	4	1	0
Fisherman	1	40	1	3	1	0
Postmaster	1	74	0	n/a	1	0
Baptist minister	1	57	0	na	1	0
Total	95		35		54	4

Source: British Columbia Department of Land and Works, Pre-Emption Records, Vancouver and Gulf Islands, GR 766, BCA; British Columbia Department of Land and Works, Certificates of Improvement, Vancouver Island and the Gulf Islands, GR 765, BCA; Land Register for Saltspring Island, Surveyor General's Office, Victoria; Census of Canada, 1881, District no. 191, Vancouver, Cowichan and Saltspring Island; Saltspring Island Database.

Note: *One of the two storekeepers is also listed as a farmer; therefore, he is listed twice. Only two women over 15 are listed as having occupations: Mrs Anderson, widow, as a farmer; and another woman as a house-servant (the other two women house-servants were under 15). Two of the 14-year-olds, and all of the men over 15 years of age were listed as having occupations. Sylvia Stark declared no occupation, but owned land.

As Table 6.2 indicates, in 1891 farmers and farmer's sons made up a full 90 per cent of those declaring occupations, and three-quarters of all household heads. By cross-linking the 1891 census with the 1892 assessment roll listing all the property owners on Saltspring Island, we can see that about 70 per cent of farmers owned land in 1891, leaving about 30 per cent of "farmers" without land. Of the nineteen household heads who did not own land, ten were on the island only briefly. Four of the others show up in directories and land records for the island for a span of twenty years or more, and had owned land either before or after 1891. In 1891, therefore, these men were not so much landless as "between land holdings." Four other non-landowning "farmers" soon took up lands on neighbouring islands. Only one, Jeremiah Chivers, remained a landless farmer for the duration of his stay on the island. As his sister was wife to Arthur Walter, a wealthy

Table 6.2
Saltspring Island: Occupation and Family Structure, 1891 Census

Occupation	No.	Average age	No. of families with children	Average no. of children	No. of landholders	No. of women
Farmer	90	41.2	35	4.1	66	6
Merchant & farmer	4	51.5	4	5.5	4	0
Farmer & fisherman	2	51.5	1	7	0	0
Blacksmith & farmer	1	47	1	2	1	0
Farmer's son*	14	16.6	0		0	1
Farm labourer	3	44	1	1	2	0
Gardener	2	68.5	0		0	0
Hunter	1	26	0		0	0
Logger	9	22.8	2	2.5	3	0
Labourer	6	25.2	1	2	1	0
Millwright	1	68	0		1	0
Miner	1	50	0		0	0
Painter	2	27.5	0		0	0
Carpenter	3	45.3	0		0	0
Engineer	2	48.5	1	5	2	0
Cook	4	25	0		0	0
Baker	2	35.5	1	1	1	1
House-servant	1	22	0	0	0	1
Schoolteacher	4	33.8	0		1	1
Sailor	1	47	1	3	0	0
Sealer	2	29	2	4	1	0
Fisherman	4	28	1	1	0	0
Shepherd	1	23	0			0
Dressmaker	1	23	1	2	0	1
Priest	1	39	0			0
Nun	3	37.9	0			3
Clergyman	1	59	1	4 ·	1	0
Total	124					

Source: British Columbia Department of Land and Works, Pre-Emption Records, Vancouver and Gulf Islands, GR 766 BCA; British Columbia Department of Land and Works, Certificates of Improvement, Vancouver Island and the Gulf Islands, GR 765, BCA; Land Register for Saltspring Island, Surveyor General's Office, Victoria; British Columbia Department of Finance, Surveyor of Taxes, 1892 Assessment Roll, Roll B 443, Gulf Islands Assessment District; Census of Canada, 1881, District no. 191, Vancouver, Cowichan and Saltspring Island, Schedule no. 1 – Nominal; Census of Canada, 1891, District no. 3, Vancouver, M2 – S.D. 14, Saltspring Island, Schedule no. 1 – Nominal; Saltspring Island Database.
Note: * The 1891 census does not designate men as "farmer's sons." In keeping with the 1881 census, where there are no "farmers" under 20, and all "farmer's sons" are sons of the household head under 20, this chart lists all "farmers" under 20 years of age as "sons" or in one case daughter, of the household head, as "farmer's sons." Re occupation: in 1891, there 14 women are listed as having occupations and only one woman is under 20. Sylvia Stark declared no occupation, but owned land.

Justice of the Peace and substantial landowner on the island, it is likely that this landless farmer was helping out on his sister and brother-in-law's lands, particularly when their children were young throughout the 1890s.[18]

Evidence about island men and women suggests that "farmer" was a broad and inclusive term. While a number of families on the island clearly supported the household, at least in part, by selling agricultural products, most men were not full-time farmers in any sense: few of them attained the status of commercial agriculturalist that we tend to identify with the term. A closer look suggests that the vast majority of men, like women, spent most of their time engaged in a wide variety of paid and unpaid labour that had more to do with the support of the land-based household than with the exigencies of either commercial agriculture or wage labour.

WORK

Occupational plurality has emerged as an important aspect of rural society and culture throughout nineteenth-century Canada,[19] and it provides a good descriptive framework for exploring the varied and intermittent kinds of work carried on by most Saltspring Island residents who remained on the island to eke out a living under the rubric of "farming." In addition to working on their "farms" as the exigencies of rural life required, most Saltspring Island men worked for wages at a variety of tasks at some points throughout the year. A few examples concerning island farmers will suffice here. William Lumley, who shows up receiving Managers' Drafts from ABC Packers in Canoe Pass in the 1890s, appears as a farmer, a fisherman, and a police constable in nineteenth-century directories and voters' lists, and as a farmer on the 1901 census.[20] A photograph entitled "building the Vesuvius Bay wharf" shows Benjamin Lundy and Alfred Raines wearing the customary garb of the logger: cork boots and sleeveless vests.[21] Between 1877 and 1901 Joseph King alternated between calling himself a farmer, a fisherman, and a boatman. William McFadden is described as a farmer in directories and voters' lists in the 1880s and 1890s, but in the 1891 census he, like two or three other men on the island, is listed as a sealer.[22] Richard Brinn owned land on Saltspring, and his wife and family shared a house and farmed the land there with his business partner's family, while he worked at his store in Nanaimo.[23] Nels Nelson always called himself a farmer, but he worked as a labourer for the provincial government from time to time throughout the 1890s and, like Lumley and King, was one of the many islanders who spent several weeks every year fishing commercially in a variety of locations up the coast.[24]

Logging, like fishing, played an important and variable role in the economic activity on the island. Because most of the crown land on Saltspring had been pre-empted or purchased by the time logging was established as a bona fide industry in the 1890s, logging was not done on the basis of crown grants to large companies. Instead, it usually took place as an informal arrangement, often between those wanting logs and those wanting pasture.[25] As a result, no formal records of nineteenth-century employment attest to the forestry industry on Saltspring Island. Only a tiny portion of those who listed an occupation on the island described themselves as loggers (zero in 1881, 4 per cent in 1891). Evidence presented in chapter 5 suggests that some families may have been using their unimproved pre-emptions as sources of harvestable timber. Concern that settlers were logging, and then abandoning their pre-emptions was reflected in the 1884 legislation that attempted to designate certain lands as "forested lands" unsuitable for farming, but there was little enforcement of this legislation.[26]

The informal and intermittent nature of logging on Saltspring was particularly obvious in the case of tie mills. Small, portable mills were established all over British Columbia in the second decade of the twentieth century to provide ties for the expansion of international railways, particularly in the Asian sub-continent. The oral history record for Saltspring in the 1920s is full of references to the role of tie mills in household economies on the island.[27] Like many aspects of this fluid and varied economy, logging waxed and waned on a seasonal basis, and in relation to international as well as local demand for the product.

The importance of trees to the household economy was not limited to providing waged labour or lumber sales, however, as the oral history record, personal correspondence, and published memoirs indicate. Islanders used the trees to construct their homes, barns, outbuildings, and boats. They used them to build the fences required by the pre-emption system regulations. Uncleared lands were used as woodlots, and provided the fuel burned in fireplaces and stoves. Some people made a business out of cutting the huge trees into "stove lengths" for other households on the island, as the use of stoves for cooking grew in the late nineteenth century.

The provincial government provided another important, though characteristically fluctuating, source of work for many people on the island. The most usual type of employment generated in this way was roadwork, which became almost the only kind of waged earning for islanders during the Depression of the 1930s.[28] But island men were paid for a surprising variety of tasks by the provincial government in the late 1880s and 1890s. In 1889, for example, thirty-seven Saltspring Island men were paid by the provincial government. Joseph Malcolm worked

Many island men worked for the provincial government for a few days a year, sometimes with their horse teams, helping to build the island roads while earning a precious cash income. This road crew is working on a bridge across Cusheon Creek. (SSIA)

as a blacksmith repairing tools for $9.32. George Sheppard spent two days working as a constable, serving summonses at nearby Portland Island for $11 (including transportation). Joel Broadwell worked as a judge at the court of revision on the island for one day for $5. Thomas Mansell, Alexander Wilson, and Alexander McLennan were paid $40 each for "incidental expenses" as school trustees. Four teachers were paid that year by the provincial government, with James Dougan and Raffles Purdy receiving $50 per month for six months. W.L. Levigne lasted one month at $50 per month before being replaced for the final five months of the school year by F.C. Fraser, also at $50 per month. Assessor and tax collector Samuel Maxwell earned a 10 per cent commission ($22.75) for the taxes he was able to collect. Most men (nineteen altogether) worked as labourers on the Beaver Point and Burgoyne Bay roads, working from one to thirty-five days at $2 per day. A few, such as Joseph Akerman, Alex Wilson, and Henry Rogers, worked with their teams of oxen or horses and a wagon, and were paid between $2.50 and $6 per day. Henry Ruckle, working as a foreman for twenty days, was paid $3 per day.[29] David Maxwell and Joseph Akerman each earned a dollar transporting the school inspector on and

Table 6.3
Work for the Provincial Government by Saltspring Island Residents, 1890–1901

Year	No. of islanders paid wages by the provincial government	Average yearly wage from this employer
1891	52	$98
1892		
1893	58	$90
1894	41	$105
1895	26	$31
1896	68	$77
1897	68	$81
1898	67	$80
1899	67	$79
1900	60	$82

Source: British Columbia Public Accounts, 1891–1900, *British Columbia Sessional Papers*, Victoria, 1892–1901.

off the island. Government wages could be picked up in a variety of other ways, including working at elections, helping in the conveyance of prisoners, or testifying at inquests.

As Table 6.3 illustrates, the average wage earned by Saltspring Island men per year from the province varied between $70 and $80 dollars. Most of the men averaged about a month's full-time work per year, working at a rate of $2 per day.[30] Teachers and the provincial tax collector earned the largest and most regular incomes, but about a third of the male population over fourteen years of age obtained some wages from this source in 1891, the only year for which this information exists.[31]

It is difficult to assess precisely how important these sums paid to island workers as wages were to the cash needs of Saltspring Island households.[32] General statistics on income were not kept for the populations in British Columbia in the nineteenth century, as the population's income was not routinely taxed. The daily wages of the Saltspring labourers were not, however, significantly less than the lower end of miners' wages in nearby Vancouver Island in the 1890s; and miners, as John Belshaw has argued, were well paid by comparison with other working-class men in British Columbia, Nova Scotia, Britain, and Australia. White miners had a starting pay of between $2 and $2.50 per day, and could hope to reach a maximum of about $90 per month.[33] Boys and "non-white" Chinese and Japanese workers were paid significantly less, at about $1 per day. Miners, like those working for the provincial government on Saltspring Island, could not, however, expect to work either a full day or a full working week.[34] If miners' work was not always better paid than that of labourers with the provincial government, their reputation as well-paid workers was significantly affected by the greater regularity of their waged employment compared to those in other areas of work across the country. The 1901 census is one of the only sources that asked household heads how much money they earned annually in this era. The average earnings of under $400 per household per annum on Saltspring Island – a low figure compared to $561 and $552 for Victoria and Vancouver respectively – provide us with some indication of the relative importance of the seemingly small amounts earned in the government's employ on the island, at a time and in a place where full-time waged employment was a rarity.[35]

There is little evidence that women participated actively in waged work during these years, either intermittently or consistently. And, as we have seen, there is little evidence that commercial farming was a full-time, household supporting activity for men or women in most "farm" families on the island. Men were more likely to engage in waged activities than women, but women participated in some cash-producing activities from time to time. The oral history record indicates that women worked seasonally in the fields for wages, and as domestic workers in a later period.[36] Like their husbands, fathers, and sons, women participated in some of the petty commodity production taking place on the island. Women probably cared for the 4,200 hens and chickens on the island in 1891 (the only year for which records are available) as well as for the 300 ducks and geese. They probably milked the 265 cows and made the 11,651 pounds of homemade butter produced in 1891.[37] Women also worked preserving food, foraging for wild fruits, tending orchards, and growing extensive vegetable gardens. For example, in the 1880s Mrs Gyves, a Cowichan Native, was picking fruit when she went into premature labour. The family maintained that she had miscarried on other occasions because of hard physical labour on the farm. When Mary Reanny died of puerperal fever in 1891, local residents suspected that the difficult labour was exacerbated by heavy work in the fields.[38] Even though anecdotal evidence suggests that some of the women's produce made its way to local markets or was exported off the island – in one of the two diaries available for the island during these years, John Beddis notes the sales of eggs to the store once or twice a week[39] – most of the labour performed by women, like that performed by most of the men most of the time, was not directed towards the creation and sale of marketable surpluses.[40]

Many islanders, such as Sylvia and Louis Starks'
two sons Willis and John, shown here, relied on
hunting for a significant part of their weekly diet.
(SSIA)

Saltspring Island was not exceptional in the varied economic activities performed by its residents. By 1890 the increased access to markets and the existence of some established farms on the island marked the island's transition from pioneer settlement to established farm community. Nevertheless, for most Saltspring Island men and women, and for many nineteenth- and twentieth-century Canadians, cash income was still not a regular, dependable, or exclusive foundation of the household economy.[41] Notwithstanding the normalization of full-time and permanent employment in the twentieth century, historians have noted that seasonal labour and intermittent unemployment remained characteristics of rural populations and urban working classes across Canada until World War II.[42] Fortunately, cash was not the only means of economic support available. In addition to petty commodity production and intermittent waged labour, self-provisioning provided a third, extra-commercial strategy, one of considerable importance within the varied economic activities that constituted making a living or "getting by" for island households.

With their largely non-productive farms and limited reliance on waged labour, island residents were obliged to provide for their own support in a variety of ways. In trying to understand the political economy of nineteenth-century settlers on Saltspring Island, it is important to remember that these settlers, just like their Aboriginal neighbours and relatives, found themselves in one of the richest areas in the world for providing food. Coastal British Columbia's hospitable climate and abundance of natural resources for food and shelter have long been identified as the key variables in sustaining both the large Native populations and the complex cultures that characterized the Pacific Northwest.[43] The richness of the environment helps to explain why Saltspring Island households were able to "get by" with limited commitment to both waged labour and commodity sales. Men, women, and children were actively involved in self-provisioning, throughout the entire nineteenth century.[44] The natural bounty of the island and its importance to early settlers is summed up most eloquently in an 1861 newspaper report: "Game abounds; some of the deer are noble looking animals, the mountain grouse very comeatable [sic] ... The shoals of fish are prodigious; standing upon the beach you rake in the smelts with a common hayrake by the bushel; salmon, rock cod and that delicious fish when properly cooked, the red mullet, abound, the oyster, also that shell fish that has been a by-word expressive of poverty, vociferated by disappointed gold-seekers during the excitement of '58, the Royal Clam."[45]

Marriage to a Native woman brought with it some clear economic benefits in this regard. If, as Malin has argued, the success of human settlement in any area is based on the population's ability to make a fit between their culture and the environment,[46] evidence suggests that Aboriginal women played a key role in transmitting the kinds of knowledge that settlers needed to both manipulate and adapt to their new environment successfully.[47] More than a quarter of the married couples on the island in both 1881 and 1891 were Aboriginal women and their non-Native husbands.[48] In spite of the pejorative rendering of these relationships by Robert Brown and others, the Aboriginal women on Saltspring Island played an important role in teaching their non-Native husbands, families, and neighbours about the environment of Saltspring Island. Memoirs of the early resettlement days note that Native women taught non-Native newcomers to find and prepare the foods and medicinal herbs that sustained generations of their families in the area.[49] Native men and women also traded to settlers the foodstuffs that they had hunted or gathered.

Women's important role in transmitting Aboriginal economic practices is particularly visible in the fishing industry. Through their Native

Fishing provided not only sport for island men, but, like hunting, an important part of islanders' food. (SSIA)

wives, a number of Saltspring Island men were welcomed into Aboriginal kinship networks, gaining access to the traditional fishing grounds enjoyed by their Native extended families. Some women actually taught their non-Native husbands how to fish.[50] Homer Stevens, whose family (on his grandmother's side) fished on the coast for centuries, writes of his grandparents, who were early settlers on Saltspring Island in the 1880s. His grandmother was a Cowichan and his father a Greek: "Emma was more interested in telling about the time when she and my grandfather were living on the farm on Saltspring Island and coming over to fish salmon on the Fraser ... Later on, when they had a family, my grandmother would usually stay on the farm on Saltspring Island, taking care of the kids while he went fishing, but in the early years, she'd come across and fish with him during the salmon season. I gather that she taught him a lot about how to catch salmon."[51]

Notwithstanding its obscurity at the level of government documentation, scattered sources indicate that the work of both Native and non-Native women was also central to the self-provisioning that was the basic support of Saltspring households well into the twentieth century. In addition to caring for children, growing vegetables and fruits in the household garden, and preparing food, women would help provision the family with at least some of the wild venison, grouse, clams, fish, and ducks that were an important part of people's diet. Primary sources concerning food are notoriously hard to find, but the importance of both wild game and household labour to the diets of Saltspring Island residents can be glimpsed in a variety of documents. When widower James McFadden ate a breakfast of "the heart and liver of a deer and a part of rabbit [and] a basin of wine" in 1868, it was prepared and placed on the table, like the (allegedly poisoned) coffee he drank and the under-cooked bread he ate, by his thirteen-year-old daughter. When William Robinson was murdered, he was just sitting down to a dinner of salmon and potatoes.[52] Bishop George Hills was particularly impressed by seeing Mrs Lineker "at the water's edge *raking* in smelts. We had some for dinner and capital they were, delicious."[53] As Richard Mackie notes in his study of an early non-Native Comox settler, access to the wealth of the coastal environment remained important to settlers throughout the nineteenth century: "The Gulf of Georgia was famed for its inter-tidal abundance of clams, mussels and other shellfish, which attracted settlers and gave rise to local expressions like 'when the tide's out the table is set'".[54]

The native fauna and flora that provided for so many of the dietary needs of early settlers also provided for livestock. Hogs and cattle were able to feed on the rich fern roots that covered significant portions of the island. As Bishop Hills noted in the early 1860s, the pigs belonging to the early settlers "live and thrive upon what can be obtained in the bush. Pigs root up 'pig nuts' and the camas."[55] Sheep were grazed in the large open rocky areas that were particularly prevalent at the island's southern end. Cows, too, often wandered freely, feeding on the grassy verges at the side of the dirt roads, or at the edges of fields.[56] They could wander some distance from their homes: after Armstead Buckner died in 1888, it took a neighbour two days to round up the three cows that he had been caring for. It took somewhat longer to retrieve the tools that neighbours had borrowed. As Joel Broadwell, Justice of the Peace on the island and executor of Buckner's estate, noted as he was trying to settle the probate file almost a year after Buckner's death, "I have been informed that there is some tools belonging to the Buckner Estate round amongst the neighbours. I took the liberty to stick up some notices calling them in."[57] Borrowing should probably be added to the list of self-provisioning strategies that households used to "get by."

Within the mixed economies of island households, children's work assumed great importance. Describing Edna Matthews Clifton, one of the children of a western "pioneer" family in the American west, Elliott West writes "she remembered happy family celebrations and the good times of play and school, but crowding these memories aside were images of a different sort – washing, mopping, soapmaking, and gardening, cutting wood, weeding, harvesting, gathering and hunting. It would be difficult, in fact, to name any part of the family's labour that this young girl had not done. 'It was instilled in us that *work was necessary.* Everybody worked. It was a part of life, for there was no life without it.'"[58] Although the identification of childhood with work has faded from contemporary historical consciousness, a wide historical literature confirms Edna's insistence on the importance of children's work in rural society.[59] The richest source on this type of informal and unrecorded work of children (as indeed the informal and unpaid work of adults) is the oral history record. Although not available for this early period, the island's oral history record from the 1920–1935 period is filled with descriptions of physical labour that children were expected to perform in the course of a day – chopping and stacking cord wood, carrying water, caring for younger children, hunting, gathering clams, picking stones in the rocky island soil, harvesting and preserving fruits and vegetables, caring for livestock, working for wages for a neighbour, and weeding the vegetable garden.[60] As Viviana Zelizer has pointed out, it was not until the later nineteenth century that the Western world began to identify children's work as a threat; before that, it not only helped to define children's lives but also was a measure of children's love, respect, and membership in both the family and society.[61]

Although children's work is rarely visible in routinely generated sources, glimpses do appear. Two twelve-year-old children show up on the 1881 census as "house-servants" and two others are listed as "farmer's sons." In 1891 two ten-year-old children are listed as "domestics," meaning, we can assume, that they were working for either pay or room and board for their unrelated employers. Thirteen-year-old Mary Anne McFadden was making breakfast for her father and complaining of overwork in her motherless household when she tried to poison her father.[62] When Babbington Sparrow was accidentally shot at fourteen, he and some friends were out hunting deer.[63] When

George Purser killed himself, his young son was out working at a neighbour's house.[64] When Mr Sampson's thirteen-year-old daughter eloped, she was living with and working for the local storekeeper, Mr Bittancourt.[65] Because children's work, like that of their parents, was so often of unpaid, variable, and erratic, it is also difficult to quantify.

Thus, although most adult males are identified as farmers, this occupational category does not describe the wide variety of work carried out by men, women, and children to support their families on a daily, seasonal, or life-long basis. Work, albeit often informal and unregimented, defined most people's lives most of the time. Men's work typically involved some waged work off the "farm" or off the island. Men were away from home for days or even weeks at a time, working in the resource industries that were growing up around Saltspring Island in the later nineteenth century. Many of these men undoubtedly showed up elsewhere in British Columbia as young – and not so young – migrant labourers "whose remittances from temporary wage work" as Gordon Darroch points out in the case of Ontario landholders, often "served to underwrite the economies of family farms."[66] When they appeared on Saltspring Island records, those who lived in landowning families appear most consistently as stable, land-based farmers, no matter what range of activities they drew on to make a living. While the men were away, women and children ensured the support of their families and "farms" on a daily basis. By remaining on the land, they ensured that they conformed to the residency requirement of the pre-emption system. In this way, as in so many others, the "work" of island inhabitants was a household affair.

HOUSEHOLD STRUCTURE AND COMPOSITION

In chapters 3, 4, and 5 I have argued that the resettlement of Saltspring Island was characterized by two divergent patterns. One group of settlers conformed to the image of "pioneer" British Columbia as a place characterized by high rates of geographic mobility associated with the modern, industrial, and largely male frontier.[67] This population stayed for only a short time before realizing that the island did not meet their requirements for rural life. In the second pattern a small percentage of settlers stayed for a very long time, raising families and "getting by." A closer examination of household size, composition, and wealth on the island gives us some clearer indications of the contours of their daily lives and some more hints about why they might have chosen to stay.

Evidence suggests that little money was earned through crop sales or waged labour on Saltspring Island, but the combination of cheap or free land, a bountiful environment, and a family provided island residents with a broadly based system of economic support that was both stable and flexible relative to other options available to people with limited capital.[68] The pre-emption system allowed most residents to acquire a secure land base, relatively untroubled for many years from the worry of high land payments, demanding landlords, or intractable employers. Securely rooted on the land, household members were able to draw on a wide range of activities – self-provisioning, intermittent waged employment, occasional sales of produce – that provided the economic support needed to keep their family on the land, albeit at a minimal level. A growing literature on working-class and settler history suggests that it was this mix of stability and flexibility, unattainable by most landless, urban, waged workers in the nineteenth century, that so many found so appealing about rural life.[69] What Gordon Darroch and Lee Soltow found in rural Ontario of the 1870s was also manifested on Saltspring Island in the late nineteenth century: "although the economy was undergoing fundamental transitions, the ownership of small property, primarily in the form of land, remained the foundation of many family economies and, in this sense, of the economy as a whole."[70] Household was the foundation of economic life.

As Gérard Bouchard has argued, communities in which individual households provided the epicentre of economic, cultural, and political life were typical of settlement in "new" rural areas of North America. High rates of fertility ensured that a labour force would be available to support the household-based economy on which the family relied, creating what were, Bouchard argues, "fundamentally peasant communities" in the backwoods of North America.[71] Unlike peasants, however, families in new rural areas who typify Bouchard's model either owned or had *de facto* ownership of their own land. Saltspring Island families meet these two criteria. A third characteristic of new rural communities identified by Bouchard was not common on Saltspring Island or in some other western North American settlements: island families did not typically pass their lands on to their offspring.[72]

As Table 6.4 indicates, Saltspring Island had a population of 257 in 1881 and 435 in 1891. Households had an average of 3.5 people in 1881, a figure that rose to an average of 4.5 in 1891. These households were smaller than those in other communities on the "western frontier," where household size hovered around five to six people per household, and they were also smaller than households in Ontario in 1871, where the average size of male-headed households was 5.9 persons.[73] A number of factors might help to explain these numbers. Buildings were cheap to build and materials were readily available on Saltspring Island, unlike in many parts of the North American West or Ontario, making it more economically feasible for people to live in

Table 6.4
Household Size, Saltspring Island, 1881, 1891

	1881 census				1891 census		
Household size	No. of households	No. of people	% of population	Household size	No. of households	No. of people	% of population
1 person	18	18	7	1 person	18	18	4
2	17	34	13	2	15	30	6
3 to 5	21	85	33	3 to 5	30	122	28
6 to 9	13	100	39	6 to 9	28	208	49
10 or more	2	20	8	10 or more	5	57	13
Total	71	257	100		96	435	100

Source: Census of Canada, 1881, District no. 191, Vancouver, Cowichan and Saltspring Island, Schedule no. 1 – Nominal; Census of Canada, 1891, District no. 3, Vancouver, M2 – S.D. 14, Saltspring Island, Schedule no. 1 – Nominal.

separate dwellings, even when they were in some sense living with another family. This was probably the case with George Dukes and George Watkins, both of whom are listed as living in separate households from Henry Ruckle, but with no household head. They are listed as "lodger" and "employee" respectively of the Ruckle family in 1891. In 1881 Josephine Edgar is similarly listed as a separate household from Daniel Fredison and his wife, but she and her two children are given a separate household number and listed as "lodgers" with the Fredison family. Low average numbers of household members may also have been distorted by the large number of single-person households. If the eighteen men living by themselves in 1881 and 1891 are removed from the calculations, the average household size for 1881 is 4.5, and in 1891 it rises to 5.3.

Seventeen households in 1881 and fifteen households in 1891 comprised two people. Eleven of the seventeen in 1881 comprised married couples without children; two comprised two unrelated single men; and four were single parent families, one of which was headed by a woman. In 1891 most two-person households were married couples, but four comprised two siblings and two were unrelated males (see Table 6.5). In 1881 80 per cent of people lived in families of three or more people. In 1891 this figure had risen to 90 per cent. Most of these households revolved around the nuclear family.

Saltspring Island had its share of British Columbia's single-resource-worker households. Altogether, in the population over sixteen,[74] thirty-one were single people, only six of whom were women. In 1881

Table 6.5
Household Structure, Saltspring Island, 1881, 1891

	No. of households	Single man	Couples without children	Nuclear households with children	With co-resident kin	With lodgers, unrelated	With servants or employees	With lodgers/ servants under 15
1881	71	18	11	30	5	8	3	2
1891	94	18	14	46	11	22	9	9

Source: Census of Canada, 1881, District no. 191, Vancouver, Cowichan and Saltspring Island, Schedule no. 1 – Nominal; Census of Canada, 1891, District no. 3, Vancouver, M2 – s.d. 14, Saltspring Island, Schedule no. 1 – Nominal.

ninety-one married people, two widows, three widowers, and nine men whose marital status is unknown were living on the island. In 1891 the number of single people had risen to eighty, of whom only about one-fifth (seventeen) were women; the number of married people had grown to 137; there were three widows and seven widowers; and there were seventeen men whose marital status is unclear. The island also had a higher proportion of married families with children than did neighbouring British Columbia communities.[75] In 1881 forty-three of the seventy-one household heads, or 60 per cent, were married, and thirty had children. In 1891 almost two-thirds of the ninety-six families listed on the census were headed by a married couple, and forty-six had children living at home. The nuclear family formation, therefore, where a married couple lived alone or with dependent children, was the most common household formation in both census years.

These families had very high fertility rates, as the strong presence of children on the island indicates. While the large number of children within the community was unusual in British Columbia in 1881 and 1891, the high rates of fertility conform to the pattern for "new" rural areas of North America in the nineteenth century identified by Gérard Bouchard. As Tables 6.6 and 6.7 illustrate, people under twenty years of age made up almost half of the population in both census years. In 1881 more than 40 per cent of the island's population was under fifteen, considerably higher than the provincial average and the 34.5 per cent for the under-fifteen cohort in the nearby mining community of Nanaimo.[76] In spite of an increase in the number of children on the island, their proportion of the population fell to just over 25 per cent in 1891, as young men flooded into the island and British Columbia generally.[77]

To estimate fertility rates from census data, historians general find the average number of co-resident children per married couple in which

Table 6.6
Ages of the Population, Saltspring Island, 1881

	Total	Males		Females	
		#	%	#	%
0–9	72	37	51	35	49
10–19	57	29	51	28	49
20–29	27	11	41	16	59
30–39	25	11	44	14	56
40–49	33	23	70	10	30
50–59	25	23	92	2	8
60–69	14	6	43	8	57
over 70	4	4	100	0	0
Total	257	144	56	113	44

Source: Gulf Islands Assessment District; Census of Canada, 1881, District no. 191, Vancouver, Cowichan and Saltspring Island, Schedule no. 1 – Nominal; Census of Canada, 1891, District no. 3, Vancouver, M2 – S.D. 14, Saltspring Island, Schedule no. 1 – Nominal.

Table 6.7
Ages of the Population, Saltspring Island, 1891

	Total	Males		Females	
		#	%	#	%
0–9	122	66	54	56	46
10–19	94	57	61	37	39
20–29	80	46	58	34	42
30–39	50	33	66	17	34
40–49	33	20	61	13	39
50–59	34	24	71	10	29
60–69	13	11	85	2	15
over 70	10	7	70	3	30
Total	436	264	61	172	29

Source: Gulf Islands Assessment District; Census of Canada, 1881, District no. 191, Vancouver, Cowichan and Saltspring Island, Schedule no. 1 – Nominal; Census of Canada, 1891, District no. 3, Vancouver, M2 – S.D. 14, Saltspring Island, Schedule no. 1 – Nominal.

the woman was between fifteen and forty-five. Using this formula, the rates for Saltspring Island were 4.1 in 1881 and 4.4 in 1891, as compared to 2.9 in the nearby mining community of Nanaimo and 3.9 for the rest of Canada in 1871.[78] Children seem to have been under-enumerated on Saltspring Island censuses for a number of reasons. In some of the larger families, many of the older children had left before the younger ones were born. A number of families sent their children to live with other families and, if they lived off the island, they did not appear in the Saltspring census. More visible in my records are the twenty-odd girls who went to live in the Sisters of St Anne's orphanage in Victoria.[79]

For the twenty-three families whose entire reproductive lives can be traced, the average number of children per household is 7.4. This pattern, where seven children per family on average live to adulthood, falls within the hyper-fertility identified by Bouchard as an important characteristic of settlement in new rural areas.[80] These rates were supported by early marriage. Using the clumsy tool of subtracting the date of birth for the first child listed on the census from the mother's date of birth (if she was under forty-five years of age), it is possible to determine an approximate age of marriage. In 1881 the average age of the mother at the birth of the first child was just over nineteen; fathers were almost twelve years older. We can estimate the age of marriage for these women at one year earlier, or just over eighteen. In 1891 the average age for mothers at the birth of their first child had risen to twenty-one, and fathers' had fallen to twenty-seven, giving the mothers an age at marriage of about twenty. The average age of marriage for the twenty-three families for which family reconstitution was possible was just over nineteen years.[81] Note the decline of the large age gaps between spouses observable in the early years of the settlement, particularly between non-Native men and Native women who were, on average, about thirteen years younger than their husbands.

Families with children, then, were a dominant feature of rural life in this British Columbia community. Cross-linking census data with other sources about household heads' arrival on the island indicates that more than two-thirds of the families with children in the two census years had arrived on the island after the birth of at least one child, when the household head was, on average, just under thirty-nine years of age, and his wife was, on average, just under thirty-two years of age.[82] These fifty-one families (out of the total of seventy-two appearing in the 1881 and 1891 censuses) who had children before arriving on the island had, on average, 2.9 children before their arrival.[83] As Bouchard has argued with specific reference to families in "new" rural areas, children represented a real advantage within an economy based on household labour, but the "life cycle squeeze," when children were too young to work, tended to put serious constraints on the amount of productive work that could be carried out within the household in the early years of married life. The strategy of arriving with children was, therefore, a good one for rural families.[84] In the families arriving with children, the eldest child was just over nine years old, on average, suggesting that many families were arriving on the island with some children, at least, who were able to contribute to the household economy. This would have represented an important advantage over those beginning their families after settling on the land. Entire families, then, and not simply young single men, were on the move in British Columbia in the late nineteenth century.[85]

If we assume that geographical persistence can be used to indicate how well settler culture fitted with the opportunities offered by the local environment, the families with both land and children were able to make the most of what the island had to offer. As we will see in more detail below, those with children tended to stay longer on the island than those without, and they were more likely to own land.[86] Landowning families with children had the highest rates of persistence on the island. Of all the families showing up in the 1881 and 1891 censuses, the fifty-nine landowners with children had an overall persistence rate of thirty years compared with twenty-four years for the forty-four landowners who had no children. The thirteen families that had children but no land stayed an average of twelve years. The twenty household heads who never had children and never owned land stayed an average of just under four years. The tendency of landholders with children to stay longer on the island than those without land and/or children points, on the one hand, to the difficulty of raising a family without a secure land base on the island when neither waged work nor commercially viable farming was widely available. More positively, it points to the economic advantages that might accrue to landholding families with children.

Most people living on the island in 1881 and 1891 lived in families headed by a married couple: 70 per cent of the population in 1881 and over 80 per cent in 1891.[87] If most people lived in nuclear households on the island in 1881 and 1891, in 1881 only about half of these met the criteria for "normal" nuclear families – married parents living with their own dependent children under eighteen – a figure that fell to a third by 1891.

Many households opened their doors to a variety of people during their tenure on the island. Eleven families (15 per cent) in 1881, and thirty-one (33 per cent) in 1891 took in "extra" members. In 1881 eight married couples with children, or about one quarter of all families with children,

A number of island families lived in households that included relatives and lodgers. The Stevens were unusual in running a more formal guest house that accommodated some of the wealthier bachelors who arrived on the island. Mr Cooke, schoolteacher on the island for many years, reclines in the foreground. (SSIA)

had extra members; three of the thirteen married couples without children lived with extra members, all non-related people.[88] In 1891 married couples with no children were particularly likely to have extra members in their family: just under 50 per cent of fourteen childless couples, with four childless couples having a lodger or employee, and two having a relative living with them. Only 30 per cent of married couples with children had extra members living with the family. In 1891 fifteen of the forty-nine households with children had extra family members, seven having a relative of the family living with them, most commonly a brother or brother-in-law; and two had fathers- or mothers-in-law living with the household. Thirteen had lodgers who were unrelated to the family, and six of the households headed by a married couple and with children had servants, three of whom were under fifteen years of age. Henry Ruckle had Charles Olsen working as a hired hand and living with his family in 1881, and Fred Foord had a young fellow-Englishman of sixteen living with him and working as a labourer. Henry Stevens and his wife had the schoolteacher Raffles Purdy staying with them as a lodger in their boarding house in 1891. It is not quite clear whether John Smith, listed as a seventy-year-old gardener on the census, who was also living with the Stevens family, was there as an employee, a paying lodger, or an elderly relative.

Some historians have understood the tendency of households to take in extra members as a crisis strategy.[89] Taking in boarders or moving in with another family provided families with a way of dealing with the "life cycle squeeze," that time when the house contained a number of children who were too young to contribute to the household economy. On Saltspring Island this does not seem to be the case. By 1891 families with children were less likely, not more likely, than childless couples to have either kin or lodgers living with the household. It seems more likely that those taking in boarders and lodgers, and in some case child servants, were doing so as a form of community aid. In an area without any institutional help for orphans, lunatics, indigents, or those down on their luck, households provided the only support.

The census provides a window on this particular role of households on Saltspring Island.[90] It is likely, for example, that some of the two children in 1881 and nine children in 1891 under fifteen (one was as young as two) who were listed as servants or lodgers were recipients of charity from friends or relations. Elizabeth Booth, wife of the Island's MLA, who was famous for her generosity and hospitality and had one child of her own, took in a number of children over the years, some of whom may have been related, and whom she listed as "servants" or "lodgers."[91] In 1891 Henry Ruckle had his six-year-old niece Bertha Brethour, who was living with his wife and four children, listed as a lodger, and Alex King, the ten-year-old son of the nextdoor neighbours living with him as a "domestic." John Willey, a thirty-year-old employee also lived with them, to help with his extensive farming operation. Theodore Trage headed one of three families that listed a child as "adopted" in 1881. The six-year-old "adopted Indian girl" living with his wife and children was perhaps a relative of his Aboriginal wife; she does not appear on the 1891 census. Jacob Crane and his wife, a childless couple in their early sixties, shared their house with an adopted nine-year-old daughter. Henry Shore, an African-American in his late forties, who had lived on the island since the 1860s, supported ten-year-old Sylvia Isaac, his "adopted daughter" in 1881. She may have been the daughter of his friend William Isaac, an African-American whose pre-emption Shore had obtained some years previously.[92] We will never know whether he adopted as an act of charity or because he needed the help of a young girl about the house and land.

For many island families responsibilities clearly overlapped with economic imperatives. This was not only reflected in the number of families taking in children as lodgers or servants. Two families in 1881 and 1891 had a mother- or father-in-law living with the family. Others took in siblings or adult children with families: Alfred Raynes took in his sister and her young children in 1891, and this may have been the case with Josephine Edgar and her two young children, who were living with the elderly Daniel Fredison and his wife. In 1891 Theodore Trage and his family were sharing their home with the elderly Henry Spikerman. Trage and Spikerman had come over from Germany to Saltspring Island in 1860 and had lived as neighbours ever since.

Many families provided residence for family members as a way of "getting them started" in a new life. Ontario-born blacksmith and businessman Joseph Malcolm had his sister living with him until she married his business partner in 1892 and moved to a new home on the island. In 1891 six families had unmarried brothers or brothers-in-law living with the family. In the late 1880s and early 1890s, when a growing number of young men were moving to the island, many simply moved in for a time with relatives or friends with children. Adult children tended to stay with parents until they had their own land, if they were men, or until they were married if they were women. As the community aged – as land became less available and waged work more available – there was a corresponding increase, from 7 to 11 per cent of households, of (mostly non-landowning) adult children living with their parents.[93] These flexible family formations, like the complex economic patterns on the island, increased the number of alternatives open to Saltspring Island families in their search for economic support. As Gordon Darroch and Michael Ornstein discovered in their study of Ontario families in 1871, a "large number of older children in the families may have been part of a strategy of "maximizing sources of sustenance and income."[94] While most adult sons had left their families, and indeed the island, by the time they started their own families, the tendency was for adult children to remain on their parents' land, contributing to the household economy throughout their twenties.

What of the young and single resource workers who figure so largely in the provincial historiography? The censuses for Saltspring Island in 1881 and particularly 1891 certainly contain single young men working as loggers, labourers, and (in one case) a miner. They indicate that this group made up less than a quarter of the adult population in 1881 and less than a third in 1891.[95] By 1891, as more young men arrived on the island to take advantage of the opportunities offered by secure land tenure and waged work in this resource-rich environment, the census recorded that in childless households the household head was almost as likely to be living with other men as with a wife.[96] With its high proportion of male households, Saltspring Island comes closest to the portrait of nineteenth-century British Columbia as an adult male frontier. Nevertheless, the ratio of one adult woman to two adult men in 1891 was still a far cry from the ratios of more than one to twenty in other up-country areas of the province in the nineteenth century.[97]

Table 6.8
Arrival Age for Household Heads Appearing in the 1881 and 1891 Censuses

Arrival age	No. of household heads in the 1881 census	No. of household heads in the 1891 census
< 15	1	3
15–19	3	6
20–29	15	26
30–39	21	31
40–49	16	14
50–59	12	10
>59	3	5
Total	71	95

Source: Saltspring Island Database.

By cross-linking census information, which contains the ages of all residents, with other information about individuals in the database, it is possible to estimate the earliest date, and hence the age, at which household heads who appear in the census first arrived on the island. These linkages suggest that household heads appearing on the 1881 census arrived on the island at an average age of thirty-eight. This average fell to thirty-four by 1891, mainly because of the large influx of younger men in the twenty-to-thirty range, as Table 6.8 suggests. This change reflects the increasing opportunities, including waged work in logging and fishing, available for young men on and off the island in these years.

Young men were by no means transitory migrants, however. Of those listed on the census who had arrived between the ages of sixteen and thirty, most were landowners by the time of the 1881 and 1891 censuses. Calculations of geographical persistence indicate that their average total length of stay on the island was over twenty-five years.[98] While only a small minority of those arriving in their late teens and twenties arrived with families, by the census years more than half of this group had established families and had their first child.[99] While these conclusions do not preclude the existence of a highly mobile group of people who stayed only briefly on the island, once again we see a pattern, even for single young men, where high transience co-existed with considerable geographical stability. Young men and landless men were more likely to define themselves as "labourers" or "loggers," although those living with landowning parents most often defined themselves as "farmer" or "farmer's son."[100] Once men became landowners, however, the status conferred seems to have translated into the occupational category of farmer, while the range of their economic activity in any given year seems to have increased, rather than decreased.

Two characteristics of Saltspring Island families are worth highlighting as unusual in the context of "frontier" settlement in North America. The first is the high number of "blended" families. In almost 30 per cent of families on Saltspring Island in 1881 the two parents were not both parents of all the children, a figure that fell to 10 per cent in 1891.[101] The number of step-parent and "blended" families is difficult to determine from routinely generated records. Microhistorical research suggests that they may not have been unusual in nineteenth-century Canada. Maternal mortality, disease, and accidents left many children without one or both parents. Within a household-based economy, one-parent families were at a distinct disadvantage, and remarriage was common.[102] On Saltspring Island, death, divorce, and separation took their toll. The significance of these blended families will be explored in more detail in chapter 8.

A second unusual trend is the high number of "mixed-race" marriages on the island. As we have seen, in more than a quarter of all households on Saltspring Island in both 1881 and 1891 the husband and wife were of different ethnic backgrounds. Children from these marriages made up almost 50 per cent of the children on the island in 1881 and just under 30 per cent in 1891.[103] These high rates of exogamous marriages became more unusual in rural British Columbia towards the end of the nineteenth century, as a number of historians have noted.[104] Comparisons with households in Quebec, Ontario, and the Maritime provinces in the later nineteenth century suggest, however, that rates of exogamy were exceptionally high throughout the settlement period in British Columbia in general.[105] "Mixed-race" marriage, therefore, distinguishes British Columbia nineteenth-century households from those in central and eastern Canada. As we have already seen, Aboriginal women had a significant impact on the culture and economy of resettlement on Saltspring Island.

An examination of families on Saltspring Island confirms their centrality in island society and economy. Households differed from those in most British Columbia communities in the late nineteenth century by having more families and more children than was typical at the time. We have seen that families on Saltspring Island, unlike settlers in new areas of central Canada and the United States, did not tend to provide land for their sons in a consistent way. In spite of the reluctance or inability of parents to hold the family together with a patrimony, however, family members worked together, and in an important sense for each other, to ensure the continuation of their lives on the island. Is there any evidence that suggests that this reliance "worked"?

WEALTH

In a series of articles concerning the society and culture of the populations involved in agri-forestry in the Saguenay region of Quebec, Gérard Bouchard explores different types of subsistence-based and market-oriented economic activity within the conceptual framework of "cointégration."[106] He argues that an analysis of economic change can only come from a broad understanding of the co-integration of economic and cultural imperatives at both the economic and household levels. On this basis, he argues that in the Saguenay region evidence of entrenched underdevelopment is not clear. He uses family reconstitution to argue that, in Quebec and New Brunswick, seasonal labour in the forests complemented and stabilized – it did not undermine or negate – work on the farm.[107] Bouchard maintains that the rural population continued to develop and change, without becoming proletarianized or stagnantly "under-developed," into the early twentieth century. Assumptions about the appropriate directions for change in rural society – towards greater market orientation on the one hand or proletarianization on the other – obscure the complexity of rural life revealed by these detailed studies.

This co-integration model, with its emphasis on local experience and its respect for the decisions of those living in rural areas, has some important advantages for understanding the behaviours of Saltspring Island residents. As we have seen, most landowners on the island failed to accumulate capital through land speculation or commercial agriculture, living out lives of considerable poverty. The high rates of geographical persistence, however, suggest some level of satisfaction with island life. An examination of the correlation between the number of children and the wealth in land, animals, and personal property suggests that choosing to have a family on the island was a rational decision. While poverty defined the daily lives of most residents on the island, those with children were able to accumulate wealth in the form of land and livestock. These "assets," although they did not easily translate into movable wealth, did provide a secure foundation on which to raise a family.

Families seem to have done a good job of supporting themselves. While it is impossible to document the amount of work done by children, its importance to the households of Saltspring Island can be inferred from aggregate information gleaned from cross-linking information on the assessment rolls for 1892 and the census of 1891. Having more children meant more mouths to feed, but the correlation between land, personal property, and children outlined in Table 6.9 suggests that children were contributing to, as well as consuming, the

Table 6.9
Families and Wealth of Household Heads, Saltspring Island, 1891

No. of children in house- hold	No. of house- holds	No. of land- owners	Average no. of acres	Average value of land	No. and percentage of families with livestock	No. and percentage of families taxed on personal property	Average length of stay to 1891
0	33	33	199.4	$777.58	22 (66%)	4 (12%)	10.5
1-2	11	11	280.7	$954.55	5 (46%)	2 (18%)	9.8
3-5	18	17	379.1	$1579.41	11 (61%)	9 (50%)	14.2
5+	13	13	797.1	$1361.54	11 (85%)	8 (62%)	15.1
Total	75						

Source: Saltspring Island Database.

wealth of the family. Families with more than five children in 1891 had almost four times as much land as those with no children. The average assessed price of land per acre was lower than it was for those without children, reflecting the fact that those with children had more reasons to take up mediocre and unimproved land than those without. For, as we have seen, land could yield families a multitude of advantages over and above planting crops and selling them. In spite of the lower assessed price per acre, those with more than five children held lands with an average value twice that of the lands of households without children; and twice as many were wealthy enough to declare personal property to be taxed. Even those families with one to two children were better off than those with no children in most regards.

Differences between those with and without children were not simply the result of the length of time that household heads had been on the island, as Table 6.9 demonstrates; nor were they a function of the age of the household head. Figures 6.2 and 6.3 provide profiles of the average acreages and the percentage of household heads owning personal property and livestock, distinguishing between those with children (Figure 6.2) and those without (Figure 6.3), by the age of the household head. Those in their forties or sixties with children owned between two and four times as much land as those in the same age cohort who had no children. Between two and three times as many of those with children owned personal property as those without. This suggests that children were one more important component in the complex island economy.

Figure 6.2
Wealth of Landowning Household Heads with Children, by Age, 1891

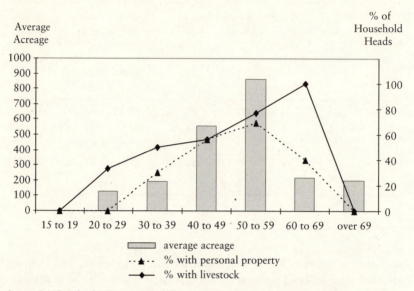

Source: British Columbia Department of Finance, Surveyor of Taxes, 1892 Assessment Roll, Roll B
443, Gulf Islands Assessment District; Census of Canada, 1891, District no. 3, Vancouver, M2 –
S.D. 14, Saltspring Island, Schedule no. 1 – Nominal; Saltspring Island Database.
Note: Figures for the 1892 Assessment Roll were gathered in 1891.

CONCLUSION:
PEASANT ECONOMICS IN BRITISH COLUMBIA?

This chapter opened with Robert Brown's negative evaluation of the
"farmers" he encountered during his expedition. For Brown, occupational plurality was but one more facet, along with co-habitation with
Native women, a reliance on hunting and gathering, and a paucity of
cleared land, that identified the farmers of British Columbia as feckless
failures. Other visitors shared this evaluation. George Blair, visiting
John Sparrow in the early 1860s, was not impressed with the abilities
or habits of his host: "like many others he thought he had the head if
only he had the means to carry on extensive business in the farm line.
He thought himself very clean but never used a dish cloth but his British flag."[108] Ashdown Green laconically noted that he, "saw a speci-
men of Saltspring Island farmer. A garden of one quarter acre and a
clam bed."[109] The relaxed attitude to economic activity hinted at by
these observers finds further support in the words of the island's elected

Figure 6.3
Wealth of Landowning Household Heads with no Children, by Age, 1891

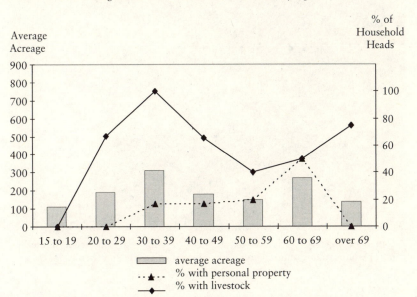

Source: British Columbia Department of Finance, Surveyor of Taxes, 1892 Assessment Roll, Roll B
443, Gulf Islands Assessment District; Census of Canada, 1891, District no. 3, Vancouver, M2 –
s.d. 14, Saltspring Island, Schedule no. 1 – Nominal; Saltspring Island Database.
Note: Figures for the 1892 Assessment Roll were gathered in 1891.

provincial representative, who, in 1875, though an islander himself, described his constituents as "a mob of drunken rowdies."[110]

The type of rural life disparaged by observers like Brown – characterized by a disrespect for industrious farming practices and an intermittent recourse to off-farm work – was either ignored or castigated by
government officials. Department of Agriculture statistics reflect a narrow concern with commercial agricultural production, and make no
mention of the complex economies of island households. The absence
of information concerning self-provisioning and the importance of off-
farm work found its counterpoint in the complaints that members of
the Department of Agriculture made about the rural population in general. In 1891, determined to gather the statistics on agricultural production "indispensably necessary in order to note the progress made
from year to year,"[111] bureaucrats in the Department of Agriculture
were compelled to reassure farmers throughout the province that "it is
a mistaken notion to suppose that these returns are of an inquisitorial

A Canadian trope: A Native couple call at Fernwood (Begg's Settlement) in their canoe, perhaps to buy and sell goods or to visit with family and friends. (SSIA)

nature."[112] In spite of these reassurances, officers seeking information about agricultural production were often met with "indifference and suspicion of the object of the enquiries."[113] By 1894 the Department complained that it "found it impossible to arouse the interest of the farming population sufficiently to furnish the required data through the medium of the circular enquiries."[114] These rural dwellers had little of the respect for the principles of order, regularity, and scientific management that increasingly defined appropriate practices in country and city alike in the nineteenth century. Rural society in this British Columbia community was clearly a contested space in which beliefs about appropriate behaviour were being negotiated.[115]

Economists have not been much kinder than nineteenth-century urban observers in their evaluation of the self-provisioning, occupational plurality, seasonal work, and failure to accumulate capital that characterized life in so many rural communities. In 1776 Adam Smith argued that the tendency of rural people to work at a variety of occupations did not bode well for the efficiency and productivity of their endeavours: "A man commonly saunters a little in turning his hand from one sort of employment to another ... The habit of sauntering and indolent careless application, which is naturally or rather necessarily acquired by every country workman who is obliged to change his work and his tools every half hour, and to apply his hand in twenty different ways almost every day of his life, renders him almost always slothful and lazy, and incapable of any vigorous application even on the most pressing occasions."[116]

Smith's intellectual descendants in the field of economics have generally supported him in this evaluation. Although rural populations in the industrial period have been largely ignored by social historians until recently, since the 1970s the theory of proto-industrialization has, in the European context, added complexity to our understanding of groups outside towns and cities. It has identified occupational plurality, intermittent and poorly paid wage labour, and the predominance of small, unsuccessful farms, as characteristics revealing the exploitation and under-development of rural areas of marginal agricultural production. Being unable to reap the benefits of high agricultural sales, because of poor land quality or distance from markets, and unable to sell their labour at a competitive, urban price, the rural poor are defined as dependent on the combination of wages that are insufficient to support a family and a farm that is incapable of accumulating capital. Trapped in the countryside, these "semi-proletarians" are unable to fulfill the destiny laid out for them by the terms of modern capitalism: to become fully fledged urban proletarians on the one hand, or owners of successful agri-businesses on the other.[117] For many island residents, life was one of considerable poverty, and most eked out an existence from the land on the margins of modern capitalist activity.

Does the failure model adopted by contemporary observers like Brown, or its more sophisticated articulation in theories of underdevelopment, provide an adequate framework for understanding the rural population of Saltspring Island? Neither of these interpretations takes into account the possibility that these island residents, like many Canadian rural populations, were making far more varied and complicated demands on their lands, with a much different end in view, than was commensurate with the more familiar Euro-American discourse of rural lands.[118]

In his study of rural populations in late nineteenth-century France, James Lehning explores a curious dissonance that he found between the behaviours of a small nineteenth-century rural population he was studying and the bureaucratic discourses through which it was represented. Descriptions of the population castigated peasants for their household-based economies and their unprogressive attitudes towards farming practices and market activities. He argues that the terms of market culture, developed around the discourse of economic liberalism, had become so widespread by the end of the century that it was "increasingly difficult to find language to describe non-market aspects of the workplace."[119] The discourse of agricultural improvement privileged rural producers who were motivated by the maximization of profit and "small rural producers who oriented their production towards family goals of subsistence found no place."[120] The increasing bureaucratic emphasis on particular types of activity served a two-fold purpose: by defining "normal" rural activity as market centred and rational, it marginalized rural populations at the same time that it reinforced the identity and the power of urban dwellers as responsible, progressive, and cultured people. Hal Barron, Daniel Samson, and Bruce Curtis have, in different ways, made similar arguments in the North American context. They have suggested that this liberal discourse, articulated so clearly in the literature surrounding rural improvement and development, has played an important role in constructing the independent, rational, and profit-maximizing individuals needed to sustain the relations of power within the modern state.[121]

Lehning sees great significance in the failure of nineteenth- and twentieth-century urban observers to understand the large numbers of people who refused to adopt new and improved methods of farming and the increased profits that they brought. "This refusal is worth pondering," he argues, as "the logic of nineteenth- and twentieth-century Western culture makes little sense of people who refuse economic development." Lehning adds that "portraying these people as, at best, 'peasants' isolated from the benefits of modern science serves only to reinforce the premises of the nineteenth-century discourse as it constructed 'peasants.' Rather, we need to understand this behaviour as a practice in which these country dwellers represented their own identities."[122]

The parallels with this study are obvious. While the material lives of Lehning's French peasants differed from those of Saltspring Island residents in some respects, the dissonance between representation and practice is similar. The colonial, bureaucratic, and popular discourse of rural life in British Columbia articulated in earlier chapters found little resonance in the lives of most island dwellers. And, as Lehning suggests, in trying to understand why a rural population lived as it did, it is simply not enough to articulate the discourses to which they did not conform. How can we reach beyond the liberal and colonial discourses that consign most of their rural behaviours to the "figurative dustbin?"[123] how do we do so? More specifically, if rural people were not maximizing production and accumulating capital, perhaps it is time to evaluate what Saltspring Island families *were* accomplishing; to look beyond the Euro-Canadian discourse of colonialism, beyond island farmers' failure to act out its ideological foundations; and to find in island behaviours the terms on which island residents understood their own lives. For, notwithstanding the Euro-centric discourse that attempted to frame Saltspring Island as a colonial society, the political economy of the island suggests that the assimilative process was significantly more successful in another way: the occupational pluralism, the limited success of commercial agriculture, the continued reliance on hunting, gathering, and other subsistence activities, and the high rates of Native-non-Native marriages suggest that Europeans were being successfully integrated into Aboriginal economic structures, rather than the other way around. More accurately, the people of Saltspring Island, like the Aboriginal peoples of neighbouring coastal areas, were living in an emerging economy where waged labour and commercial sales were but two strategies in a new economy. In spite of links to international capitalism and, in some ways, *because* of these links, the people of Saltspring Island were able to remain rooted in the land, where household labour and the rich environmental bounty of the Pacific Northwest provided a minimal, but relatively secure, living.

How can we understand the economies of Saltspring Island? Were the people of Saltspring Island "Peasants on the Coast"? These people conformed to many of the characteristics of rural as defined by Allan Greer: they were small-scale agricultural producers, they worked economically as a family, they were self-sufficient to varying degrees, and they possessed – or at least had secure legal access to – the means of production, their land.[124] Like peasants elsewhere in the nineteenth century, they were an "awkward class" in a modernizing world.[125] The people of Saltspring Island were constrained by poverty, but enjoyed some benefits that eluded both peasants and proletarians: although this was not an egalitarian society, evidence that landholders were systematically dominated or exploited by any privileged class or group is strikingly absent. These people may not have been peasants, but neither were they capitalists or proletarians. They sit awkwardly on the margins of historical representation, not fully the idealized self-sufficient, "traditional" peoples of the European imagination, nor the successful yeomen farmers of the American imagination, nor yet members of a proletarian or "under-developed" class imagined by a more contemporary sociology. I have suggested in this chapter that the failure of this rural population to conform to "normal" categories of economic behaviour is intimately tied to their invisibility in the historical record. Canadian historians have had little experience dealing with populations that refuse definition as capitalists, proletarians, or farmers.

The picture that is emerging from a close examination of economic practices on Saltspring Island suggests that the economy was based on a wide variety of work, carried on by most family members. Though the earliest settlers enthusiastically embraced the ideal of commercial agricultural production for the first few years, this enthusiasm waned as the years progressed. By 1891 most families did not have enough land cleared to rely exclusively on commercial agricultural activity.

Wages, lower than those in Victoria and Vancouver, were probably not sufficient to provide exclusive support to families throughout most of the year. The economic foundation of most households, therefore, was a wide variety of activities, including waged work, commodity sales, and self-provisioning, all of which engaged all family members capable of work. Central to this economy and society was secure tenure on cheap or practically free land. Like the rural populations that Mick Reed describes in nineteenth-century Britain, "the behaviour of the great majority was precisely the opposite of entrepreneurial, in that most producers actively sought to avoid risk, and were primarily concerned with earning a living, rather than maximizing profit. Whether producing for direct consumption or exchange, their main interest was subsistence."[126] As we have seen in this chapter, this household-based and land-centred economy had some unusual characteristics, particularly in terms of the high rates of marriage across ethnic divides. As we will see in the chapters 7 and 8, it also lacked the bucolic harmony so often associated with rural.

The African-American Murders: Violence, Racism, and Community on Saltspring Island, 1859–1871[1]

Between August 1867 and December 1868 the tiny community of Vesuvius Bay on Saltspring Island, populated by about twenty-five families, was the scene of three brutal murders. All the victims were members of the island's African-American population, and coastal Natives were widely believed to be guilty of all three murders. A Native man, Tschuanahusset, was convicted in the only case that was brought to trial. Within the provincial historiography, these murders, and the outcry they gave rise to, have helped to define the racialized context of life on the coast during the colonial period. In the scattered published histories of the island, these murders have, furthermore, provided a platform for contrasting brutal racism, attributed to the Natives, with peaceable frontier egalitarianism, generally attributed to other groups on Saltspring Island.

My goals in this chapter are twofold. On one level, I will re-examine the African-American murders that shook the island in the late 1860s. Focusing particularly on the murder of William Robinson, I will examine the evidence used to convict the accused murderer, and find it wanting. On another level, I hope to reach beyond the kinds of evidence that may be used to find a murderer (and prove him or her guilty), to ask the broader questions about context and meaning that historians use to puzzle out human relations. This microhistorical study within a microhistorical study – this narrow focus on murder in one tiny community inside a two-year period – reveals ambiguities about identity, racism, and community on Saltspring Island.

In recent years some scholars have shied away from using the concept of "race" to explore social relations. They have argued that "race" is not a coherent descriptive category that makes meaningful distinctions among people. Instead, it speaks to historically contingent and socially constructed meanings arbitrarily attached to particular kinds of observable difference. While people often distinguish themselves, and are distinguished by others, on the basis of ethnic (or cultural) differences, there is no biological basis to so-called "racial" differences because the latter, unlike the former, do not inherently go together.[2] For example, the important blood type differences among people, which assuredly are biological, do not correlate with any of the standard criteria that have been used to identify "races," such as skin and hair colour or skull and lip shape. On the other hand, sets of ethnic attributes used to distinguish people, such as cuisine, marriage practices, and death rituals, often do hang together, for obvious, though historically contingent, reasons.

Paradoxically, "race" has re-emerged in historical studies as one of the most significant categories of analysis. Historians frequently find themselves in the uncomfortable position of recognizing that the people they are studying held beliefs that we know to be false and that these beliefs had material consequences. But human behaviour is not determined by "race," however much it has sometimes been determined by racist beliefs. I acknowledge that by the late 1880s "race," though a historically contingent and socially constructed category of analysis and description, was beginning to shape the way that Canadians were understanding their social, economic, and political world. But untangling its role is even more complicated at the microhistorical level. While racist categories clearly influenced some social and economic relations, they had shifting and indeterminate meanings on the island, coalescing occasionally as very significant social and economic phenomena and fading away at other times. By examining social relations through the lens of the African-American murders I discovered a point of entry for generally re-assessing the influence of racism in the dynamics of that pioneer community in the 1860s. As such, this chapter supports Giovanni Levi's contention that "the unifying principle of all microhistorical research is that microscopic observation will reveal factors previously unobserved."[3] After exploring the role that these murders have played in narratives of British Columbia history, I will explore how the evidence thrown up by the murders conflicts with published narratives of events in some important ways. I will conclude, not by solving the murders, but by describing the variability of social and economic relations revealed by this investigation. This part of my research has, more than any other, brought home the overwhelming importance of local detail in interpreting the complex interactions of power and place that comprise the context of society.

Table 7.1
Place of Birth of Saltspring Island Residents, by Gender, 1881

Place of Birth	No. males	No. females	Total	% of population
B.C.	62	69	131	51
Ontario	3	2	5	2
Total Canadian			136	53
England	29	14	43	17
Ireland	7	1	8	3
Scotland	6	1	7	2
Wales	1	1	2	1
Total British			60	23
Norway	2	1	3	1
Sweden	1	0	1	.5
France	0	1	1	.5
Germany	2	0	2	1
Azores	2	0	2	1
Turkey	1	0	1	.5
Prussia	1	0	1	.5
Denmark	1	0	1	.5
Total Europe and Scandinavia			12	5
U.S.A.	16	22	38	15
Hawaii	7	1	8	3
Australia	1	0	1	.5
Bermuda	1	0	1	.5
Mauritius	1	0	1	.5
Total Other			49	19
Total	144	113	257	100

Source: Census of Canada, 1881, District no. 191, Vancouver, Cowichan and Saltspring Island, Schedule no. 1 – Nominal.

Table 7.2
Place of Birth of Saltspring Island Residents, by Gender, 1891

Place of Birth	No. males	No. females	Total	% of population
B.C.	106	107	213	49
Ontario	7	10	17	2
Quebec	1	3	4	–
Other Candian	3	4	7	.5
Total Canadian			241	55
England	44	13	57	13
Ireland	21	6	27	6
Scotland	10	5	15	3
Wales	0	1	1	–
Total British			100	23
Norway	1	1	2	
Sweden	2	0	2	
France	0	0	0	
Germany	5	0	5	
Belgium	1	0	1	
Switzerland	0	1	1	
Greece	1	0	1	
Portugal	3	0	3	
Denmark	1	0	1	
Total Europe and Scandinavia			16	4
U.S.A.	35	18	53	12
Hawaii	5	0	5	
Argentina	3	0	3	
India	1	0	1	
Japan	1	0	1	
China	12	3	15	3
Total Other			78	18
Total	263	172	435	100

Source: Census of Canada, 1891, District no. 3, Vancouver, M2 – S.D. 14, Saltspring Island, Schedule no. 1 – Nominal.

DISCOURSES OF "RACE": RELATIONS BETWEEN AFRICAN AMERICANS AND NON-AFRICAN AMERICANS ON SALTSPRING ISLAND

How were racialized social, political, and economic relations realized in the daily lives of island residents? Saltspring Island was a remarkably international community in the nineteenth century. As Tables 7.1 and 7.2 indicate, people born in British Columbia dominated the population in both censuses, but more than three-quarters of the native-born population were under fifteen years of age in 1881 and 1891.[4] Amongst adults, British-born people, particularly those from England, dominated in both census years. People had moved to Saltspring Island from Hawaii (still called the Sandwich Islands by census takers), a number of European countries, Japan, China, India, Scandinavia, the United States, Bermuda, the Argentine Republic, the Azores Islands, and Mauritius.[5] The population included Hawaiians, African-Americans, Americans (who were not listed as such if they were African-American), Europeans, Scandinavians, and Aboriginal peoples, in addition to the English, Scots, Irish, and Welsh. The African-Americans on the island census were listed as "EB" which means, I assume, "English Black."

Saltspring Island was unusual in having among its first settlers a contingent of African-American families. These families, including the Starks, the Robinsons, the Harrisons, and the Copelands, as well as a number of single men, had been living in California at the time of the Dred Scott decision of 1857 and the March 1858 California Assembly Bill 339. At the same time, James Douglas, Governor of Vancouver Island, was looking for settlers for his recently established British colony, where Natives still far outnumbered non-Natives. Douglas persuaded a group of African-Americans of the economic and civil rights advantages of life in the new British colony.[6] In April 1858 about sixty-five of them left San Francisco for Victoria, just after gold had been discovered on the Fraser River in the mainland British Columbia colony. Although many settled in and around Victoria and Saanich, others chose to take up land on Saltspring Island. By 1863 these African-Americans made up an important portion of settlers on the island. Maps 7.1 and 7.2 illustrate the settlement patterns of household heads, by ethnic origin, in 1881 and 1891. Figures 7.1 and 7.2 provide a breakdown of the Saltspring Island population by ethnicity and gender.

In the published histories of Saltspring Island, the harmonious relations recorded between African-Americans and whites fit well with a literature that emphasizes the bucolic nature of rural life on the island. Bea Hamilton, long-time resident and author of a book-length history of Saltspring Island, maintains "there was no problem of integration on the Island. The Negro people joined in all the community projects

Figure 7.1
Gender and Ethnicity on Saltspring Island, 1881

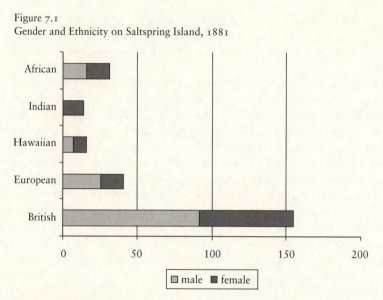

Source: Census of Canada, 1881, District no. 191, Vancouver, Cowichan and Saltspring Island, Schedule no. 1 – Nominal.

Figure 7.2
Gender and Ethnicity on Saltspring Island, 1891

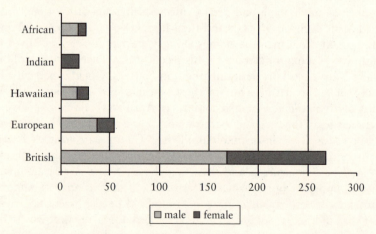

Source: Census of Canada, 1891, District no. 3, Vancouver, M2 – S.D. 14, Saltspring Island, Schedule no. 1 – Nominal.

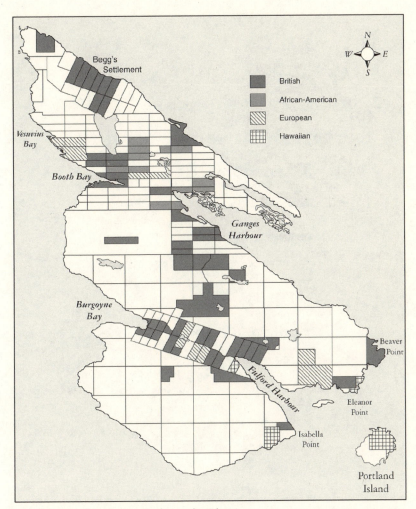

7.1   Saltspring Island 1881, Settlement by Ethnicity

over the years, working side by side with the white people."[7] James Pilton also notes the absence of racial problems on the island: "most of
the settlers were far too busy working their lands to be concerned
about complexional [sic] differences."[8] Crawford Kilian agrees with
Pilton and Hamilton's evaluation of race relations, concluding that the
Saltspring Island experience was unusual even in the Vancouver Island
context. The "lack of racial hostility was no doubt grounded in
the same circumstances as in the gold fields. Confronted with a rich
but dangerous country, African-Americans and Whites could not afford to be bigoted; prejudice was a luxury of Victoria's comfortable

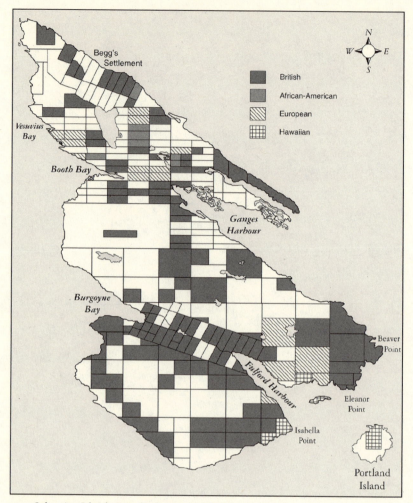

British

African-American

European

Hawaiian

Vesuvius Bay

Begg's Settlement

Booth Bay

Ganges Harbour

Burgoyne Bay

Fulford Harbour

Beaver Point

Eleanor Point

Isabella Point

Portland Island

7.2   Saltspring Island 1891, Settlement by Ethnicity

bourgeoisie. When a neighbour's help meant the margin of survival, it scarcely mattered whether he were African-American, White, Indian, Hawaiian or Mauri [sic]."[9]

The frontier egalitarianism of the Saltspring Island community, these writers suggest, helps explain why no separate, let alone segregated, African-American community emerged on the island. This point is explicitly addressed by historian Charles Irby, who traces the unusual ethnic homogeneity of the Saltspring Island community to a different cause. Drawing on the memoirs of African-American settlers, particularly Mrs Stark, he argues that "the major event, in the sequence of events leading up to the occupancy of the land, was Governor Douglas'

This mural was painted on the wall of an island pub by an
unknown artist. It celebrates the life and work of John
Craven Jones, an African-American and graduate of
Oberlin College, Ohio, who was the first schoolteacher on
the island. (SSIA)

disallowance of a African American [sic] segregated colony. This event
determined the character which distinguished Saltspring Island from
other African American settlements in British North America and
Canada."[10]

Finding no evidence of ethnic clustering or other indications of ethnic conflict, historians have concentrated on the important role that
African-American men occupied within the community. As well as having pride of first place in the resettlement of the island, people like
Abraham Copeland, William Robinson, and Henry Robinson participated in civic affairs, helping to establish school boards and municipal
governments throughout the 1860s and 1870s.[11] The first teacher, John
C. Jones, was an African-American from Ohio who had obtained a
university degree from Oberlin College. One of the first island constables, Jim Anderson, was also African-American. Members of this ethnic group then, "held responsible positions in all organizations ... and
were very much a part of the island community life."[12] By 1863 the
African-American population consisted of about twelve families, with
other ethnicities accounting for another thirty or so. As Crawford
Kilian argues, although "most of the African Americans were eventually to leave," this was not the result of discrimination. Instead, as "agriculture developed in the Fraser Valley and Okanagan, farming
became only marginally profitable. For economic reasons, the children
and grandchildren of the African American pioneers moved to Victoria,
Vancouver, or even the United States."[13] The end of the civil war in

Jennie Kahana and her children were among the Hawaiian
settlers living in the Isabella Point area of the island who married
Aboriginal and European peoples. (SSIA)

the United States in the late 1860s certainly provided an incentive, or
removed a disincentive, for African-Americans to return to the United
States. It was around this time, the late 1860s and early 1870s, that so
many African-Americans left the island.

From the 1870s onward a small number of Hawaiian families moved
north after leaving the employ of the Hudson's Bay Company, taking
up land on southern Saltspring Island and the small islands immediately to the south. Many of the Hawaiian men who arrived married
Aboriginal women, taking up land around the Isabella Point area that
historian Tom Koppel identifies as "Little Hawaii."[14] Average land size
for the fourteen Kanaka landholders was 133 acres, less than the

Naukana was born in Hawaii in the early nineteenth
century and worked for the Hudson's Bay Company in
Oregon. He moved to Saltspring Island in the early 1870s,
when the San Juan Islands became part of the United States
and people of colour were prohibited from owning land
there. A lively Hawaiian community was established on the
south end of the island. (SSIA)

146 acre average of white landholders, and more than the African-
American average of 124 acres. This community remained quite isolated, culturally and economically, from nearby settlers at Beaver Point
and Fulford Harbour. Community and familial ties were sustained
much more rigorously with neighbouring Aboriginal communities.[15]
As Tom Koppel argues, in spite of clear evidence of ethnic clustering
amongst the Hawaiian population, racial relations between Hawaiians
and whites, as among African-Americans and whites, were generally
deemed peaceful and not unfriendly.

DISCOURSES OF "RACE": NATIVE-SETTLER
RELATIONS ON SALTSPRING ISLAND

While the relations between African-Americans and whites are invariably portrayed as typical of the harmonious social relations on the island, other inter-racial relations were not so trouble-free. The question of permanent Aboriginal settlement on Saltspring Island in the late 1850s has been the subject of some debate. Archeological digs indicate that permanent villages existed in at least two locations on the island between 1,700 and 2,400 years ago, and shell middens attest to the importance of the area as a seasonal resource location for centuries.[16] Mention is made of at least one abandoned Native village in the 1850s, but there is little evidence of regular seasonal use of the island at this time.[17] As we have seen, in spite of attempts by Douglas to extinguish Native title to colonial lands in the late 1850s, particularly those on which the first agricultural settlers were taking up lands, Native peoples of the area had not relinquished title to their lands before the settlers arrived on Saltspring Island.[18]

According to the *New Westminster Times* of 1859, issues surrounding Native land ownership were apparent from the earliest days of non-Native settlement, and continued to worry settlers. As the newspaper noted about the Saltspring settlement in 1859: "we have to urge upon the Government the necessity of some immediate measures being adopted to settle the Indians' claims, if any exist, upon these Islands, as the settlers are subjected to constant annoyance and insult from these claimants, more especially by the Penalichar tribe who boldly tell the settlers that the Island is theirs, and that Governor Douglas has "cap-swallowed" it, which, in the elegant Chinook jargon (we believe) means stolen it."[19]

In the 1850s and early 1860s Douglas had hoped that Native populations would be assimilated into the new European society of the Pacific Northwest through their access to land, made available on the same terms as it was to be made available to whites. This "Douglas System" was never implemented in a coherent way and after 1866 Aboriginal peoples were no longer allowed to pre-empt land. Instead, they were obliged to live on Reserve lands given to them by the government. Although a number of Aboriginal pre-emption claims were taken out before that date in both the Lower Fraser Valley and the Okanagan,[20] there are no indications that any Native people tried to pre-empt land on Saltspring Island before the policy was officially rescinded by Joseph Trutch in 1866.[21] The only land-related information available about Aboriginal people on Saltspring Island in the period under study indicates that in 1876 a small group of ten Aboriginal adults were living with five children and some livestock on the newly created Indian Reserve at Fulford Harbour.[22]

Inter-tribal fighting between Aboriginal peoples on the coast was frequently remarked in the colonial press. From the earliest days of settlement on Saltspring Island, relations between Natives and non-Natives were seen as analogous to such reputed inter-tribal violence. Readers of Victoria's *British Colonist* were introduced to what would become the standard portrayal of Native-settler relations on the coast early in 1860, when the paper re-printed a letter sent by a Saltspring settler to Governor Douglas, describing a bloody massacre that had occurred near his home on Ganges Harbour. He reported that rival Haida and Cowichan tribes, in the company of a white trader, had landed in Ganges Harbour and waged a bloody battle on the shore, leaving many from both tribes dead and settlers badly frightened. The newspaper coverage of this incident, which includes the letter sent by Lineker to the Governor, nicely summarizes the issues that helped to define relations between Natives and non-Natives in colonial British Columbia.[23]

BRITISH COLONIST, 12 July 1860

An Indian War – Saltspring Island Settlers in Danger

A gentleman who arrived from Saltspring Island gives us an account of the killing of two Cowichan Indians by Fort Rupert Indians, a few days ago. Our informant was in a schooner, not far from Saltspring Island and a canoe containing two Indians was observed about two hundred yards from the shore; near the canoe was a whale boat, in which were two white men. The Indians were engaged in fishing, when around a point of land a short distance off, came several canoes filled with Fort Rupert Indians, making directly for the Cowichan canoe. The latter made for the boat containing the white men, and got into it, evidently seeking protection, and deserting their canoe, which went adrift. The Fort Ruperts soon came alongside and, seizing the unhappy redskins, five or six knives were buried in each, their heads cut off, and their bodies thrown to the fishes. No violence was offered to the white men, who of course were much alarmed at the terrible sight. The Fort Ruperts, after accomplishing the bloody deed, continued on their course, taking the heads of the victims with them. The next day, one of the heads, divested of its scalp, was found stuck on a tall pole on a small island near Saltsprings [sic].

Much alarm is felt at Saltspring Island, and government aid is loudly called for. The settlers only number about seventy souls, and they are scattered over a large tract of country, and in case of an attack, could afford but little protection to each other.

In addition to the above information we have been handed the following letter, received by a gentleman of this city, for the island, which gives an account of another massacre, and represents the urgent necessity for a military force near that point:

Admiralty Bay [Ganges Harbour]
Saltspring Island, 8 July 1860

Mr Chas Gowan, Victoria

Dear Sir: – We have had very exciting times here since I last wrote. On Wednesday morning, 4th July, an Indian canoe came into here with nine men, two boys and three women of the Bella-Bella tribe. They were conveying to this side a person by the name of McCawley, who had business here. At the time of their arrival, there were about 50 Indians, of the Cowichan tribe, encamped here, who appeared friendly to them. However, while McCawley was up at my house, we were startled at the sound of firearms on the beach. The Indians by this time had got into a regular fight, which lasted about an hour, and terminated in the Cowichans killing eight men and plundering the canoe, which they carried off with the women and boys, whom they took as prisoners. This occurred close to the beach. They fired some 200 shots, some of the bullets flying close by our heads. I sent my wife and children through the woods, to the other side, for safety. Some of the settlers came over from there at night. One of the Bella-Bellas, who had escaped, came to my house. As I could not give him shelter without danger to myself, I passed him on to the other side of the island. I hope he escaped. He had two bullets in him – one in the cheek, and the other through the arm. The Cowichans did not, I believe, lose a man. It was a treacherous affair on the part of the Cowichans, who had all the position and numbers, and professed friendship which misled the Bella-Bellas. All the Indians have now left the Bay, anticipating, I suppose, an attack from the Northern Indians.

I intend addressing the Governor on the subject, soliciting some protection from these savages, for, should they come here and find the Cowichans had left, and learn the defenceless position we are in on this Island, who can tell what they may attempt here, after the troubles in Victoria. Surely the Government will see the necessity of affording us protection to meet the emergency.

Yours etc.

W.F. Lineker

For historians, this act of violence on the island provided one of the first in a long line of incidents that show, according to one early chronicler, John T. Walbran, "how precarious life was among Indians on this Coast up to a comparatively recent period."[24] Sylvia Stark, a freed African-American slave who arrived with her family on Saltspring in 1860, describes in her memoirs a violent altercation between the Haida and the Cowichan tribes as the first thing that occurred after she had arrived on the island.[25] Incidents of theft from homes and gardens on Saltspring by Natives were reported on various occasions throughout the early 1860s, and Natives were allegedly involved in larger scale "cattle-rustling" on the island.[26] As Barry Gough and Chris Arnett have detailed, gunboats were called in on a number of occasions to control the behaviour of Natives, and to inhibit retaliatory acts.[27] Altercations between settlers and Natives weren't limited to thefts, however; throughout the early 1860s, Natives from a variety of tribes were implicated in a number of brutal murders around the Gulf Islands.

The first in a bloody series of documented cases involving Native violence against non-Native victims near Saltspring Island occurred in 1863. In May of that year, four Natives had visited William Brady on or near Saltspring, and returned later that evening to murder him. Three Native men and one Native woman were caught and hanged for this crime.[28] In April of the same year, the murder of Mr Marks and his daughter on an island near Saltspring, allegedly by some visiting Natives, sparked the shelling of an Indian village just north of Saltspring as the officials in Victoria sought the murderers.[29] Two Native men were eventually caught, tried and executed. In September 1864 two Aboriginal men, an Aboriginal woman married to Samuel Smith of Saltspring, and their child were murdered on the island. Two members of the Cowichan tribe were executed, after one confessed that "I have been shot at by Indians going backwards and forwards from the North ... and did it out of revenge."[30] In October 1866 a Hawaiian who was working at the whale fishery in Shawnigan was murdered by a Mr Phillips on Saltspring Island. Here too Natives were implicated because they were, according to the newspaper, sheltering the Hawaiian, who had stolen kegs of brandy and a "a quantity of provisions from the whaling station." Phillips was acquitted, as the jury agreed that he had killed the Hawaiian in self-defence while trying to retrieve the stolen goods.[31]

Within British Columbia historiography, such acts of violence define settler-Native relations on the Coast in the 1860s. As Robin Fisher has argued, while both fur traders and Natives benefited in many ways from the pre-settlement, fur trade-based contact of the 1840s and 50s, this symbiosis was altered when Europeans began to settle on agricultural lands throughout the province after 1858. Both settlers and Natives tended to "select land for the same reasons; they both wanted land that was fertile and productive."[32] Fisher argues that relations became strained and then increasingly violent as the scale of settlement increased. This competition for land was exacerbated by cultural differences surrounding land use, and by Europeans' evolutionist convictions about their own superior traditions of land use. This competition removed Aboriginal peoples from their lands, deprived them of traditional occupations, decimated them by disease and, as Barry Gough and Chris Arnett have demonstrated, resulted in bloody attacks by armed agents of the state.[33]

A SYNTHESIS IN RACIST RELATIONS: THE SALTSPRING ISLAND MURDERS

The three murders of African-American settlers between 1867 and 1869 were quickly absorbed into the discourse of violent Native-settler conflict established by newspapers and government officials in the early 1860s. Historians have accepted this interpretation with little question. The first African-American murder victim on Saltspring was never identified, and the murder attracted very little attention in the press. The *British Colonist* reported that a dead man, partially buried after being shot, was discovered in the old stone quarry in August 1867.[34] An inquest was apparently held, but the culprit, like the identity of the victim, was never discovered. The only other mention of this murder appeared in late December, when the same newspaper noted that "the remains of the colored man found murdered at the stone quarry ... have never been interred, and ... the bones lie there bleaching on the ground. What shocking inhumanity!"[35]

The murder of William Robinson at the Vesuvius Bay settlement a few months later attracted considerably more attention. His body was discovered in his secluded cabin in March 1868 by a neighbour, several days after his murder. He had apparently been shot while he was eating dinner, by someone sitting on his hearth at the time. A "good double shot gun, some clothes and the man's books were found to be missing."[36] No direct evidence linked this murder to Natives, but the newspaper speculated that it was an act of revenge for the recent arrest of a Native man. Although the date of death was unclear, the newspaper noted the "suspicious" presence of Natives in the area of the murder. The history of problematic relations with Natives in the past was put before the *Colonist* readers in lieu of any specific evidence.[37]

Although the newspapers had expressed shock and horror about the second murder, when the third murder occurred in December 1868, the diatribe against the "Indian menace" on the coast reached a fever pitch. The third victim was Giles Curtis, an African-American who had been working on the island for another African-American, Howard Estes, when he was shot. Like Robinson and the first unidentified man, he was alone in his house when he was murdered.[38] The only evidence that linked this murder to a Native was provided by Mr Norton, a Portuguese who lived on a neighbouring claim. He reported to officials that he had been approached and threatened by two Native men the evening before the murder. Further investigation by the commander of the gunboat *Sparrowhawk*, who was sent out to investigate, failed to substantiate this allegation.[39] Notwithstanding the lack of evidence, particularly of the theft that was usually identified with Native murders, the press had little doubt who was responsible for the crime: "the perpetrators were believed to have been Indians, who must have been alarmed at some noise and fled before they had had time to plunder the premises."[40]

These three murders created considerable fear among settlers in the Vesuvius Settlement. After Robinson's murder, the *Colonist* had reported that "many of the coloured men have their wives and families there, and

The murder scene: William Robinson's original property, showing the Bittancourt house. (SSIA)

they hardly dare leave for a day alone."[41] In the wake of the second murder, settlers banded together to demand from the colonial government "the appointment of a resident Justice of the Peace to take cognizance of offences as they may arise, and bring the culprits to justice":

They add that, unless adequate protection be supplied, they will be compelled either to emigrate, or to organise a vigilante Committee and inflict swift punishment upon evildoers. We have frequently directed attention to the frequent occurrences of murders and outrages on Saltspring Island and its vicinity, but so far as we can learn, little exertion has been used to bring the perpetrators to justice or to adopt measures against their recurrence. We hope, now that the state of things has been brought directly to the notice of the Executive by the sufferers themselves, an effort will be made to purge the East coast of assassins and robbers, and render the fairest portion of this beautiful Island habitable, which it really is not now.[42]

In January, as public pressure to find the murderers increased, the issue of the unsolved murders was raised in the Legislature in Victoria and better policing of the island recommended.[43] In early March a Saltspring family returning home narrowly missed being shot by an unknown assailant[44] whose race, however, was established by the *Colonist* without doubt: "These East Coast Indians are about the worst on the Island. They have been a pestilent nuisance from its earliest settlement to the present time, and have destroyed more whites than all the other tribes on the coast put together."[45] As we have seen, Louis Stark requested a new pre-emption, in 1868, because of his fear of the "Indiens."[46]

Except for a lone article from early January noting evidence from witnesses that a white man, and not a Native, was responsible for Giles Curtis's death,[47] the newspapers continued to report the murders as problems relating to the "Indian menace" and the absence of sufficient law and order to subdue it. As the *Colonist* reported in April 1869, "[l]et the ships save their powder and shot unless utilised by destroying the Indian camps and in every case let examples be made of these un-civilised wretches, that people may be protected who desire to be law-abiding and industrious. Several of the settlers have already left the Island ... But what are fine farms and fertile land where life and prop-erty are in such peril?[48] Articles in March and April kept readers re-minded of the "series of shocking murders on the east coast"[49] which, by mid-April had escalated to "three or four" murders that were now being portrayed as elements in a long and unceasing program of wan-ton violence against the Saltspring settlers. As the *Colonist* saw the sit-uation, "a tribe of Indians are located on the Island, who, failing any other kind of excitement murder a settler now and then by way of a change, and carry off his property to the bush where it is secreted till the little puff of a sensation is passed; that booty is then brought out and duly divided ... It is well known that the perpetrators of all the robberies and murders ... are at large on the Island, and could be had if proper means were adopted for their capture."[50]

On April 10 the *Colonist* was able to report that an arrest had finally been made in the murder of William Robinson. "Through the exertions of John Morley, J.P." in Cowichan, a Native had confessed to being with Tschuanahusset, who had shot and killed Robinson fifteen months previously.[51] Tschuanahusset was arrested and brought for trial in Victoria. Not surprisingly, on the basis of a confession and the testi-mony of a fellow Native, he was found guilty of the murder of William Robinson and was hanged in July 1869.

THE MURDER EVIDENCE RE-EXAMINED

The murders of William Robinson and Giles Curtis have been incorpo-rated without question by historians into the fabric of Native-settler ra-cial relations on the coast. Within the provincial historiography, the murders of the late 1860s have merged with those of the early years to reinforce the violent conflicts between settlers and Natives. Within the local historiography, the murders have acted as a violent backdrop against which the harmony of "the settlers" shows up in sharp relief.[52] As Charles Irby describes it, "the society was composed of a mosaic of persons who were inextricably linked by the real and imagined realities of their existence. The Native American's threat of violence, against property and person, was a causal link in the process of developing varying amounts of social cohesion. Regardless of genealogy, a neighbor was considered an asset. Proximity provided both protection against the enemy and a vehicle for social relationships."[53] Community, in other words, was defined on Saltspring Island in terms of the peaceful frontier egalitarianism of non-Native groups and sustained by the exclusion of conflict between Natives and non-Natives from definitions of the island's identity. A closer look at Saltspring Island murders suggests the need for a more complex and fluid reading, one that takes into account more of the tensions, accommodations, and ambiguities of racialized social relations on the island.

Racialized tensions can be seen in the events leading up to the trial of Tschuanahusset for the murder of William Robinson. Although a Native man had confessed to witnessing the murder and the theft that allegedly motivated the murder, the Attorney General's office was perturbed by the lack of evidence in the case. If the only motive for the murder had been theft, surely there should be some evidence, other than the confession of the witness, that a theft had occurred? John Norton, who had searched Tschuanahusset's house in Cowichan after Indian Dick's confession, declared that he had found William Robinson's auger during his search of the house, but, unfortunately, it had been lost overboard on the trip back to Saltspring Island.[54] Henry Crease wrote on the back of one of the statements, "Would it not be well to make a specific effort to get the dead man's gun or coat and trace some special article which can be produced in court into the prisoner's possession after the murder."[55]

When special constable Hambro Rinner was sent by the magistrate to search Tschuanahusset's house again in response to this request, he made what was, under the circumstances, a surprising discovery. He found an axe that allegedly belonged to William Robinson, "in the Prisoner's house laying down in a corner plain to be seen."[56] It had, inexplicably, been missed during the first search. This axe provided the pivotal piece of evidence at the trial. Even though two of the five witnesses believed that the axe was not stolen from Robinson at all, but instead belonged to the accused, other evidence convinced the jury that the axe had indeed been the property of William Robinson, and that its theft had provided the motive for this otherwise inexplicable murder.

The verdict seemed improbable to some of those witnessing the trial. Erstwhile Saltspring Island resident and future premier of the province William Smithe attended the trial, and wrote to the *Colonist* two days after Tschuanahusset was convicted of murdering William Robinson. Smithe, who had "mixed with more and had a more extensive knowledge of both Indians and white people in the agricultural districts than perhaps any other settler on the Islands," argued that the jury members were not "thoroughly conversant with Indians." Because they "were not men versed in such matters," he argues, they "were in consequence quite unable to apply properly material facts that were brought out in evidence." Smithe added that "the result arrived at was not warranted by the evidence adduced"; he drew on specific evidence from the trial to argue that Tschuanahusset could not have wielded the murder weapon to create the wound that killed Robinson.[57]

Smithe was not the only one challenging the verdict. At the end of June a large delegation of Songhees "waited on the Administrator of the government ... to petition for a commutation of the sentence of death passed on Tschuanahusset."[58] A few days later Mr Ring, the condemned man's lawyer, "waited on the Chief Justice and submitted the statements of several Chemainus Indians, which went to establish an alibi on behalf of his prisoner." The Chief Justice "regretted that the statements were not made at the time of the trial," and Tschuanahusset was hanged later that month.[59]

RE-EVALUATING THE CONTEXT: NATIVE-SETTLER RELATIONS RE-EXAMINED

As Smithe hinted, the most convincing evidence offered against Tschuanahusset was a set of discursive assumptions about Native-settler relations on the island during that decade. Notwithstanding the newspaper reports of the time, historians of the late twentieth century, like Smithe in 1869, question the simplistic interpretation of race relations on the coast. Looking beyond gunboats and sensational violence, their work is revealing a complexity of racial relations that has been obscured by an intense focus on this one indicator. Historians have recently been looking for and finding evidence that "beyond the realm of government dictates and official wrangling, there existed a relationship that was predicated upon confrontation, negotiation and conciliation."[60]

Evidence from Saltspring supports this more complex reading of Native-settler relations. Letters and reminiscences of some of the earliest settlers provide glimpses of different kinds of interactions between Natives and settlers than the conflict-ridden relations that have become so familiar to British Columbia historians. There are numerous indications, for example, that Native men were important to settlers during the early years, both in providing food and labour and in fostering commerce. As the first storekeeper on the island, Jonathan Begg, reported in an 1860 letter, "it is very cheap living here as the Indians who are very useful and very good to white men bringing us large quantities of the best the water, woods and forest can produce for a mere song."[61] Begg's tone, which smacks of gloating avarice, leaves little doubt that he was happy to extract such beneficial terms from the Natives with whom he was trading; the type of negotiation going on here is a far cry from the thefts and murders used in the *Colonist* to characterize Native-settler relations.

The continuing importance of Natives to the trade and commerce of the island is supported by the memoirs of early residents such as Margaret Shaw Walters. She arrived as a child on the Gulf Islands in 1877. Her memoirs noted that Natives were their "kind and considerate neighbours."[62] She also insisted on the important role of the Natives in transportation and commerce on the island.[63] Bea Hamilton's history also comments on the positive role of the Natives in the early years, when settlers depended on them for transportation and food items for trade.[64] Evidence of Native workers being hired on the island by surveyors, farmers, and the government supports historian John Lutz's contention that the Native presence in trade and industry did not disappear with the arrival of settlers on the coast in the 1860s.[65] These relationships, and the power structures they contained, need to be noted and examined before their dynamics can be defined.

Although scattered evidence indicates that Natives played an important role in the early settler economy through trade, Native contact with many settlers went far beyond such intermittent and business-like interactions. When Native women rather than Native men are seen as representative of inter-racial relations, the pattern of Native-settler interaction becomes dominated by co-habitation and the raising of families. Bishop Hills and Ebenezer Robinson, ministers visiting the island in 1860 and 1861 respectively, were struck by the fact that "nearly all" of the first settlers in Begg's Settlement were "living with Indian women."[66] Whereas Sylvia Van Kirk portrays Native-white relations in the post-fur-trade era as temporary or short-lived, the mixed-race families on Saltspring Island were an important part of the community at that time. According to the 1881 census, more than a quarter of marriages (27 per cent) on the island were between Native women and non-Native men. These families were among the most persistent of all island families, staying for an average of twenty-nine years, seven more than non-mixed-race families.[67] Families of mixed ethnicity, such as the Maxwells, Trages, and Gyves, went on to be among the largest landholders on the island by the 1890s, owning more than twice as much land as the average householder.[68] By the 1890s they constituted what could be considered the Establishment of the south end of the island, with fathers and sons serving on school boards and working as jurors and municipal councillors.

As we have seen, Native influences, transferred largely through marriage between Natives and non-Natives, played a significant role in shaping the cultural and economic practices that emerged in nineteenth-century Saltspring Island society. The economic rhythms of Saltspring Island life bore a closer resemblance to the hunting and gathering Aboriginal societies of coastal British Columbia than they did to the farms and factories of central Canada, or indeed to the rural ideologies and colonial discourse of policy makers and journalists. Although much more work needs to be done to explore the power relations within these "mixed-race" households, the evidence offered here suggests the need to expand categories of analysis that have limited inter-ethnic relations to same-sex violence and government oppression. The racialized boundaries by which historians construct race were blurred in rural nineteenth-century British Columbia. By the late 1860s the majority of Natives on Saltspring were settlers, married to white men and living in a complex and largely unexamined position of relative economic and political inferiority and partnership defined by their gender as much as by their ethnicity. They were not violent marauders.

One final point needs to be made about violence as a defining characteristic of relations between Natives and non-Natives in the late 1860s. By this time, the terrible smallpox and measles epidemics of the early 1860s had both depopulated and demoralized Native communities, and may have contributed to a notable decline in the kinds of violent altercations that helped to define relationships between the two groups a decade earlier. When William Robinson was murdered in 1868, there had been no violence by Aboriginal peoples against settlers on the island for almost five years, with the single exception of a cattle-rustling incident in 1867. This non-violent trend was interrupted only by the African-American murders.[69] Even Chris Arnett, who argues in *The Terror of the Coast: Land Alienation and and Colonial War on Vancouver Island and the Gulf Islands, 1849–1863* that violence defined relations between Native and non-Natives in south western British Columbia in the 1850s, ends his study in 1863. This revised profile of Native-settler relations on Saltspring Island, when seen in the broad context of dramatically decreased violence in the later 1860s and in the narrow context of the weak legal case against Tschuanahusset, suggests that it might be fruitful to look for other sources of tension when trying to understand conflict within the community.

RE-EVALUATING THE CONTEXT: A LOOK AT VESUVIUS BAY

If a discourse of generalized violence between Natives and settlers at this particular time and place does not provide a completely convincing motive for the murders, perhaps it is time to ask, in the great tradition of murder investigation, *Cui Bono?*, or Who Benefited from these violent acts? In a time and place where land was the main form of wealth and the primary means of both security and support, the definitions of "benefit," like relations of power on the island, can reasonably be sought for in landownership. William Robinson was the only African-American murder victim who had pre-empted land, but a close study of who benefited from his death points to some very interesting trends in African-American landownership, relations of power, and definitions of community on the island. A detailed look at landownership by ethnicity suggests a very different view of relations between African-Americans and whites than the positive representations in the newspapers, colonial correspondence, published histories, and Sylvia Stark's memoirs.

Although William Robinson's murder appeared to newspaper writers in Victoria as one more event in the ongoing struggles between Natives and settlers in British Columbia, it was perceived by some members of the island community in quite a different light. As some "concerned citizens" wrote to the Justice of the Peace in January 1869, Robinson died leaving "one of the most valuable pieces of property on this island, being the only place where the mail steamer can call on this side of the Island. Aside from this, the land is worth four or five hundred dollars to anyone wishing to obtain a farm."[70] These citizens were expressing their concern that "although we have reason to believe that Mr. Robinson's heirs have not been contacted about the property, it has never been offered at public sale; nor has it been advertised, nor would the executor give out information to potential purchasers."[71] The property had, in short, passed into the hands of another African-American man, Fred Lester, without being offered to island residents in general. As Mr Booth, a well-off settler from Britain explained, "an uneasy feeling [has] been created in this community in consequence."[72]

Whoever killed William Robinson had taken an important step towards bringing this valuable property onto the market. Not only was section 9, range 2, west located on Vesuvius Bay, the only place where a steamer could dock on that part of the island, but by 1868 Vesuvius Bay provided the only steamer dock for the entire north end of Saltspring; a petition by Begg's Settlement residents to maintain steamer service to their (exclusively British) locale on the east side of the island had been turned down.[73] The Vesuvius property, furthermore, was in the ambiguous legal position of having been granted a certificate of improvement, but having not yet received a crown grant.[74]

What happened to this piece of land after Robinson's death? Its history in the late 1860s and early 70s is complex and puzzling. After Robinson's murder, the land was apparently auctioned rather quietly to Lester. Lester then disappeared from the island record after improving, but not purchasing, a neighbouring property. He purchased neither of his claims.[75] At this point, the ownership seems to pass to another African-American, Abraham Copeland. Copeland was not in possession of this land for long, however, because just after his negotiations surrounding the building of a wharf, the Bittancourt brothers start insisting on their right to this particular piece of land.

The Bittancourt family is shown here on the porch of their large house, which doubled as a store. Estalon Bittancourt eventually ended up owning William Robinson's land. (SSIA)

Antoine Bittancourt had come to Saltspring around 1863 from the Azores Islands, taking up land near St Mary's Lake, perhaps because he was acquainted with the other Portuguese settler, John Norton, who had taken up land nearby. In 1866 Bittancourt had tried to "jump" a valuable claim on Ganges Harbour belonging to absentee owner Henry Lineker, but was dispossessed when Lineker made a complaint.[76] In November 1872 Antoine's brother Estalon José Bittancourt had his Victoria lawyers write to the Department of Land and Works, informing Mr Morley that Mr Copeland had no legal claim to the Vesuvius wharf property. The letter was accompanied by a certificate signed by J.P. Booth, a member of the Legislative Assembly, and his brother, declaring that the land in question had not been taken up, but was open for pre-emption.[77] The lawyer's threat of legal action was apparently taken seriously, as Estalon Bittancourt is registered as the pre-emptor of the property in 1874.[78] He did not rest easy on his claim until he had his lawyers negotiate two more altercations: one involving the re-issue of his pre-emption *without* the one acre exemption for a public wharf (which was denied); and the second resisting his brother Antoine's attempt to oust him from the claim.[79] Antoine maintained that he, and not Estalon, was the first to take up the property, upon which he cleared land and built a house. The courts settled the matter, giving Estalon the north half of the property (containing the dock) and Antoine the south.[80]

Although Antoine appears on voters' lists on the island throughout the 1870s, no other details of his life on the island are forthcoming after 1874. In 1880, however, he shows up for the last time as being arrested for arson in connection with a fire in Victoria and committed to the lunatic asylum in New Westminster.[81] By 1891 Estalon had taken over the entire property.[82] In a similarly macabre twist of fate, the owner of another neighbouring property, Moses Mahaffey, was arrested on an unknown charge in 1877 and died in 1878.[83] His probate file reveals that shortly before he died he contracted a debt with Estalon Bittancourt, and died owing him an amount of money equal to value of his property. Bittancourt agreed to take his land in lieu of cash. As the probate file noted, "The said deceased left a widow who is a half breed Indian woman, and totally incapable to manage the estate of the said deceased, being without education and having had no experience in matters of that kind."[84]

Bittancourt did very well from his investments in land. He built what became a successful hotel and store in Vesuvius Bay, taking full advantage of the steamer trade to support his business. Although his personal life was marred by his estrangement from his wife, and her subsequent suicide, assessment rolls indicate that by the 1890s he was among the wealthiest men on the island.[85] When he died in 1917, he left an estate valued at almost $20,000, a considerable fortune in those days.[86] A study of the fate of the land that Robinson pre-empted demonstrates that the ultimate beneficiary of the murder was Estalon Bittancourt.

Clearly, this does not establish guilt. Unlike a detective, the historian is not able to interrogate a suspect to find out whether "benefit" can be traced backwards to intention or culpability. Answering the question of who benefited, however, highlights the negotiations of power that were worked out around land on the island. Bittancourt gained from his association with the property in question just as surely as Robinson, Copeland, and Mahaffey lost out. To find out whether these negotiations of power were part of larger racialized context of social and community relations, however, it is expedient to look a little more closely at land, ethnicity, and community relations on the island, to see whether the problems around section 9, range 2 west find an echo in any other discordant notes in the inter-ethnic harmony on the island.

RETHINKING ETHNIC RELATIONS: A LOOK AT LAND, ETHNICITY, AND COMMUNITY

Notwithstanding Charles Irby's contention that there was no African-American community *per se* on Saltspring, land records, as summarized in Map 7.3, provide clear evidence of the role of ethnicity in the geography of land settlement throughout the 1860s. Although only twenty-three out of 232 pre-emptions before 1868 (about 10 per cent)

Melvin Estes, son of William Estes. Three generations of the Estes family arrived on the island in the early 1860s. (SSIA)

were taken out by African-Americans, the African-American population appears considerably more significant. They made up seventeen out of ninety-five pre-emptors, or just under a fifth of pre-emptors residing on their land before 1868.[87] Their numerical dominance in the total population is further emphasized by their regional dominance in the north-west part of the island. As Map 7.3 illustrates, by 1868 African-Americans owned most of the land in the fertile valleys stretching between Ganges Harbour and Vesuvius Bay and an African-American had control over the north end's only transportation and communication link with the rest of coastal British Columbia. If there were an African-American community on Saltspring in 1868, it was certainly in an advantageous position *vis a vis* the white community in Begg's Settlement.

But was there a African-American community on the island? As the portrait of harmonious racial relations on the island outlined above would suggest, local historians have resisted the notion of a separate African-American community and historians of the African-American experience in British Columbia have concurred. Charles Irby argues that African-Americans on Saltspring were simply individualistic pioneers: "Island communication and economic cohesiveness were stifled because of distances and no adequate infrastructure."[88] To those visiting the island during the 1860s, however, the coherence of the African-American community attracted notice. Ebenezer Robson noted in his diary of his visit to the island in February 1861, "There are in the settlement 21 houses on the same number of claims. 4 of the houses are inhabited by white people, and the remainder by coloured people. I preached in the house of a coloured man in the evening to about 20 persons, all coloured except 3 and one of them is married to a coloured man."[89]

Evidence from other sources also supports the existence of a separate African-American community on Saltspring. Map 7.3 shows clear evidence of ethnic clustering and pre-emption records indicate that this clustering survived the arrival and departure of many African-Americans. An examination of land transactions shows that of the thirty-seven involving African-American settlers, where we know the previous and subsequent pre-emptor or purchaser, twenty-four (about two-thirds) were other African-Americans.[90] Similarly, in the neighbouring community of Begg's Settlement, before 1868 all land transactions involved whites buying from and selling to whites.

Evidence from parish records indicates a similar pattern. Although, as Bea Hamilton noted, African-American men occupied positions of status in local government, parish registers suggest that family relations were dominated by associations with others of the same ethnicity.[91] Marriages between African-Americans and whites did occur, as we saw in the case of John Norton, whose in-laws were African-American Henry Robinson and his Irish Catholic wife, but parish registers and censuses reveal that this was unusual.[92]

Narrative accounts suggest that the existence of a coherent African-American community was accompanied by tensions between African-Americans and whites. When the African-American Clark Whims tried to elope with the constable's thirteen-year-old daughter in 1881, both Sampson and the schoolmaster, who appeared to side with Sampson, were accused of racism. We can infer, therefore, that racial tensions existed on the island and that they were contested by a number of residents. The complaint made by Mr Walter in 1885, warning that the settlers would not tolerate the hiring of an African-American constable, also speaks to these tensions.[93]

Emma Stark was one of the children of Sylvia
and Louis Stark. She became a schoolteacher in
Nanaimo. After Louis left his wife, he lived with
Emma. He died under suspicious circumstances
in the late nineteenth century. (SSIA)

to Hon. Mr Smithe, Premier,
B.C. April 28, 1885; Vesuvius Bay, SSI

Sir,

I am somewhat diffident as to whether it may not be beyond my province to
address you on a particular subject, still as being an interested party both from
my official position and as a settler here, I venture to do so.

The subject that I allude to is the appointment of Mr. W. Anderson as Constable, which is considered by many people here as decidedly hazardous and
more likely to lead to breaches of the peace than serve the cause of order.

Personally, I am by no means prejudiced with regard to colour but I do think
that to set a coloured man to preserve order and make arrests amongst a large
number of whites is very risky and likely to lead to serious results.

This feeling is shared by others here and I was informed today that the men
threaten not to allow a coloured man to arrest any of their number.

This doubtless to a certain extent may be bombast but not unlikely to be fulfilled should the men be in liquor at the time.

Of course there can be little doubt that should any trouble be brought along it will prove detrimental to the Island which has only in the last year or so shown itself to be as well appreciated by settlers as it deserves to be.

Hoping you will consider this worthy of some attention.

I remain, your obedient servant,

A Walter.

I wish this communication to be considered strictly private.

Narrative accounts are few, and the portrait of ethnic relations that they provide is far from conclusive about the nature and extent of tensions between different ethnic communities on the island. Aggregate data provides a much more damning account of racism on the island. If, as this evidence suggests, an African-American community existed on the island before 1868, Table 7.3 illustrates that this community was as seriously disrupted after 1868 as it was privileged before that date. Evidence suggests that eleven of the fifteen African-American landowners in the Vesuvius area left in the three years following the murders. Only one new African-American family came to the island after 1868; other new pre-emptions were taken up by children of original African-American settlers.

One of the clearest indications of differences between the African-American and white communities can be found in the size of lands owned by individuals in these different ethnic groups. As Table 7.4 shows, African-Americans took up lots similar in size to those of whites when they first arrived on the island in the 1860s. Their early arrival gave them, like other early pioneers, some clear advantages in finding and settling on good land. After 1868, however, African-Americans' first pre-emptions were becoming ever smaller. As Table 7.4 indicates, although all pre-emptions on average fell in size, African-Americans' fell about twice as much as others – a 38 per cent drop from pre-1868 levels as opposed to the 18 per cent drop for whites.

As these charts suggest, while African-Americans stayed longer on the island than whites, they did so in relatively smaller numbers, and under increasingly disadvantaged conditions. This "disadvantaging" after 1868 also shows up in the assessment rolls of the early 1890s. Whereas white settlers such as Trage, Booth, Maxwell, and Gyves, who took up lands in the early 1860s, were among the wealthiest residents of the island by the 1890s, African-Americans arriving at the same time fared very differently. By 1891 many African-Americans had left the island, and the average value of the land of those remaining was only about 60 per cent of that of their white neighbours. Although about one in five Saltspring residents in 1891 had some "personal property," none of these was African-American.[94] Whether they left the island, or

Table 7.3
Pre-emption Profile by Ethnicity, Before and After 1868

	No. of pre-emptions	No. occupied ≥1yr	Average acreage	No. of pre-emptors	Average length of stay	% >5 years	% >10 years
WHITES							
before 1868	232	92	163.9	78	12	45	28
after 1867	191	159	140.2	118	22.1	84	75
Total	423	251	146.3	182*	17.1	66	54
AFRICAN-AMERICANS							
before 1868	23	22	152.3	17	15.9	77	59
after 1867	23	23	103.4	16	26.8	94	81
Total	46	45	123.5	26*	20.4	81	69
HAWAIIANS							
before 1868	0	0	0	0	0	0	0
after 1867	14	12	133.4	11	21.5	75	66
Total	14	12	133.4	11	21.5	75	66
TOTAL	483	308	142.3	219*	17.8	69	57

Source: Saltspring Island Database.
*Average stay figures relate to individual pre-emptors; I have avoided counting the same individual twice. These figures are based on my Saltspring Island Database, which calculates the first and last dates for which information is available for those living on the island.

Table 7.4
Acreages in First Pre-emptions, by Ethnicity

First Pre-emption	No. of African-Americans	Average Acreage for African-Americans	No. of Whites	Average Acreage for Whites
Before 1868	16	164.9	78	176.9
After 1867	10	102.5	104	144.2
		38% drop after 1867		18% drop after 1867

Source: Saltspring Island Database.

just their valuable lands in the Vesuvius Bay area, African-Americans were deprived of the advantages of their early arrival. By 1881 the wealth and success promised by early settlement on valuable lands had not materialized, and the African-American community was frag-mented. Relations between African-Americans and whites on the Island were clearly more complex than has been assumed. From this vantage point, however, the answer to the question of who benefited from William Robinson's murder is clearly the white community.

CONCLUSION

What conclusions can be drawn from this microhistorical study? Were the murders of three African-American men in rapid succession the re-sult of a deliberate attempt by a group of whites to destroy, or lash out against, a coherent African-American community? Or, as other histori-ans have suggested, was Native racism against African-Americans to blame? Or can historians glean a different message from the incidents of violence described here?

I suggest that the murder of William Robinson has a lot to tell us about the ways people perceived and related to each other on the is-land. Violent altercations between Natives and settlers had subsided by 1864, and by 1868 relations between the two groups were being nego-tiated in a variety of ways, including marriage and trade as well as con-flicts over land.[95] The institutionalized racism against Native peoples that was increasingly defining relations between Natives and non-Natives on the coast after mid-century can be seen in the trial of Cow-ichan Native Tschuanahusset. If, as I have shown here, Aboriginal peoples had nuanced and complex dealings with non-Natives in the later nineteenth century, these were seldom characterized by the domi-nance of Natives in relation to land or any other formalized systems of power.[96] Between 1859 and 1867 the African-American community on Saltspring Island was, by contrast, positioned very advantageously to reap the benefits usually accruing to early pioneers in Canada, in the form of good land, advantageously placed. Not only did African-American individuals benefit from the larger land holdings that tended to characterize early arrivals, but their community had a coherence that may have translated into a powerful control over who was able to take up land in this privileged area. On Saltspring Island in 1868, these ad-vantages were held by African-Americans at the expense of both their white and their Aboriginal neighbours.

These advantages were dissipated by the dissolution of the African-American community that followed the murders of 1868. We know that African-American settlers such as Louis Stark left because he was afraid of being murdered, as Robinson and Curtis had been before him. Ironically, Stark's move did not save him; he was murdered several years later near Nanaimo on Vancouver Island.[97] We cannot know for certain what role the Saltspring Island murders had in the decisions of the many other African-Americans who left around this time. Were the murders the result of racist hatred and economic calculus, carried out with the explicit purpose of driving the African-Americans off their valuable lands? Was this slaughter of over 10 per cent of the adult male population in the community the work of a single deranged individual? I would suggest that whoever the culprit or culprits were, or whatever their *reasons* were, the *effect* of the murders was to tip the balance for many African-American settlers, providing an important incentive for them to leave their valuable but dangerous Vesuvius Bay lands. In this way, they lost the advantages that they had gained from early settlement at just the time when settlement in their native United States became much more attractive with the end of the Civil War.

Whatever the causes, the result was that African-American settlers were replaced by non-African-Americans on some of the most valuable lands on Saltspring Island. As Map 7.3 shows, by 1881 the African-American community had decreased in size, and no longer had a coherent centre in some of the most valuable lands on the island. By 1891 the African-American community had all but disappeared. Those who remained carried on in an increasingly disadvantaged position relative to their non-African-American neighbours. Whoever did murder Robinson and Curtis markedly improved conditions for non-African-American settlers on the island, at the expense of the African-Americans.

The question "Who killed William Robinson?" has not yielded a detective story ending. It has done much more, helping me to tease out the complexity of racialized relations on the island. William Robinson's story by no means exhausts the history of racism on the island. Racism also structured inequality on Saltspring Island in some formal, though strikingly arbitrary ways. As we have seen, African-Americans and Hawaiians, though unable to own land in the United States, were able to pre-empt land north of the border after 1858. But the larger context of late nineteenth-century racism is visible in colonial and provincial land policies that explicitly restricted landownership. Aboriginal men lost the legal right to pre-empt land in 1866, but there are few indications that they used their right in colonial British Columbia before that date, and no evidence that any tried on Saltspring Island. Men identified as "Orientals," the other specific victims of legal racism, were also prohibited from pre-empting land.[98] These legal prohibitions ensured that Asian and Aboriginal men were disadvantaged relative to other members of the community and ensured that they, like most women and

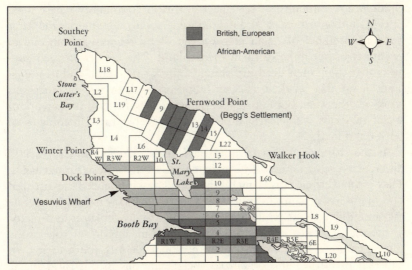

7.3a Ethnicity on North Saltspring Island, 1868

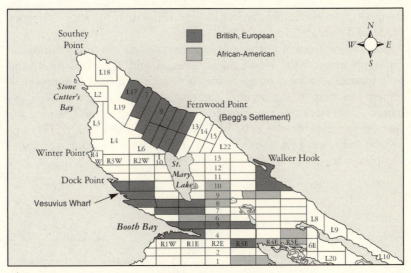

7.3b Ethnicity on North Saltspring Island, 1881

children, are difficult to "see" in a historical community where most information is provided about landholders only. In the decade after 1891 the number of Asian men on the island increased from one to twenty-two, but none of them owned land. The census of 1901 suggests that these men lived in fishing camps at the south end of the island. A number worked as farm labourers and, in two instances, as cooks for the wealthier families on the island.[99] The legal framework of social relations was clearly influenced by deeply racist ideologies of power and land.

As the story of William Robinson reveals, perceptions of "racial" difference also structured interpersonal relations in less formal ways. They created ethnic clustering on the island and influenced the distribution of landownership. In spite of islanders' inclination today to define racism reductively as white-black, and then to downplay it as a factor in the island's history, racism clearly played an important role in the ways that some people constructed personal identity (both their own and that of others) and organized social relations in this rural space. On the island "race" was a category of difference that organized *some* households and *some* aspects of society on Saltspring Island in the nineteenth century. But evidence suggests that "race" held variable meanings – from acutely divisive to practically invisible – as a category of social difference in island life.

A study of these murders raises important ethical and ontological questions about how a community creates and organizes itself, and how it sustains a view of itself through its history. Most important, it reminds us that to get beyond generalized assumptions of social dynamics, historians need to look to the geographically and historically specific contexts of the lives and behaviours under study. This approach may not solve a murder, but it can open the door to a more complex, varied, and challenging view of the past.[100]

Cohesion and Fracture
in Saltspring Island Society

In 1866 thirteen-year-old Mary Anne McFadden was accused of trying to poison her father by putting strychnine in his breakfast coffee. She confessed to the attempt shortly after her arrest. James McFadden had become ill immediately after drinking a cup that she had prepared for him. Mary Anne Sampson, the fifteen-year-old wife of Constable Henry Sampson (McFadden's closest neighbour), was charged with being an accessory in the case. McFadden seems to have been living apart from his daughter for at least some of the time, perhaps since his wife died some years previously. He had left her in the care of Mrs Brinn, who lived with the Sampsons.[1] Lawyers were nevertheless careful to question Mary Anne closely about any possible physical abuse by her father. His daughter denied any such charges, confessing that the murder attempt had been prompted by Mrs Sampson's promise that if the father were dead, the daughter would be free to "go away anywhere [she] wanted."[2] The fact that the daughter had confessed to the crime after being threatened with a whipping by her father raised some questions in her lawyer's mind about whether the confession was admissible evidence. But, as McFadden explained to the court, while he did threaten a whipping and while she did confess immediately after that threat, "I did not whip her. She was not influenced by my natural authority over her as her father."[3]

The jury was apparently swayed by medical evidence that stated conclusively that Mary Anne could not have poisoned her father because the amount of strychnine she claimed to have administered would have killed the intended victim in minutes. The doctor providing evidence in the case attributed McFadden's sickness instead to an overindulgence in both food and wine at breakfast (much to the amusement of the court). Perhaps, like the newspaper reporter covering the trial, they also were moved by that fact that the "misguided creature" was a "bright eyed girl," who "seems to have lacked the careful moral training of a good mother."[4]

No such compassion moved the jury that convicted, or the judge that sentenced, Mrs Sampson. The judge stated as he sentenced her to two years of hard labour, "a more horrible crime could scarcely be conceived" than her attempts to use her "evil influence [to persuade] a child to poison her own father."[5] As the Victoria *Colonist* noted, the jury's verdict was one of the strangest on record: "the jury that a few hours previously had acquitted the principal, actually convicted the accessory of instigating the commission of a crime that they had just before found had not been committed."[6] Before the end of March the Attorney General had overturned Mrs Sampson's conviction and given her a full pardon.[7] Under the circumstances, it is perhaps not surprising that she never returned to the husband who had arrested her, but returned to the mainland, where she began living with another man.[8]

These trials highlight some of the tensions that mediated social relations on Saltspring Island. Clearly some conflicts arose around control and power in parent-child relations. The fact that Henry Sampson's wife was Aboriginal may have influenced the proceedings, but marital status, rather than age or ethnicity seems to have played a greater role. For both judge and jury, this life-course difference enabled them to distinguish the relative culpability of two young women, both of whom were of the same age and had one Native parent.[9] Gender tensions, apparent in the daughter's desire to escape her father's authority, can also be glimpsed in the relationship between Sampson and his wife.[10] The case also draws attention to the larger relationships between family, local community, and the state on Saltspring Island. In some ways, the personal conflicts within and between households are less surprising – particularly given the jury's conclusion that no crime had been committed – than McFadden's decision to call in the local constabulary to deal with the alleged crime. Why did he insist on dealing with the situation in this way?

In this chapter, I will examine how distinctions based on religion, life-course, gender, and class influenced the ways that people interacted with each other on the island. And finally, I will critically examine the role of formal political and state-sanctioned structures. How did the nascent state co-exist with other, less structured, social and political relations on the island? Can we find in this rural population evidence that the liberal state, and the political subjectivity on which theorists have argued it was premised, was transforming Saltspring Islanders into modern citizens? How did people make distinctions amongst themselves? What united people in this rural space? What divided them? In this chapter, I explore the lines of cohesion and the points of fracture within household and society, in an attempt to articulate some aspects of the "bounded rationality" by which people on the island constructed their identities and, perhaps, a community.

RELIGION

Saltspring Island had a remarkably international population in the years under study.[11] Differences in religious affiliation tended to follow ethnic divisions: the African-Americans were mostly Methodists or Baptists; the English and Irish Anglicans; the Scots Presbyterians; and the Hawaiians and Natives Catholic.[12] As Table 8.1 indicates, by 1891 the great majority of families were Church of England, reflecting the increased immigration from England after the late 1870s. The strength of religious ties *per se*, like the force of religious difference, is difficult to trace in the years under study. No churches were established on the island before the mid-1880s, when an Anglican, a Methodist, and a Catholic church were built.[13] There were no resident clergy on the island until 1892, when The Reverend Wilson arrived to tend his Anglican flock. Methodist Ebenezer Robson, Anglican Bishop Hills, and Catholic Father Donckele visited the island periodically in the earlier decades, marrying and burying members of all denominations and giving sermons to people of all faiths who chose to attend.[14]

We can infer from scattered sources that religion and religious differences were important to some people. Twenty-one daughters of Saltspring Island families, including one of James McFadden's daughters, show up in the registers of the Sisters of St Ann's School and Orphanage in Cowichan throughout the decades under study here.[15] Although some young girls were clearly placed there to receive the Catholic education denied them by their remote location on the island, this was probably not the case with others, particularly those placed in the convent permanently, as orphans. For these children, poverty or other family problems were probably significant factors in the decision.[16]

Families of mixed religious composition were not unusual among island families, indicating that religious differences may not have been quite as important on Saltspring Island as they were in other parts of Canada and in the settlers' country of origin. In 1881 ten out of the forty-three married couples, or almost a quarter of households, did not have a common religion, a figure that fell to 20 per cent (twelve out of fifty-nine marriages) in 1891. This figure was high compared to those for other parts of nineteenth-century Canada.[17] Household heads were

Table 8.1
Religions of Saltspring Island Residents, 1881, 1891

1881: Religion	No.	%	1891: Religion	No.	%
Baptist	20	8	Baptist	2	.5
Catholic	70	27	Catholic	105	24
Church of England	97	38	Church of England	192	44
Lutheran	9	3	Lutheran	10	2
Methodist	33	13	Methodist	73	17
Presbyterian	18	7	Presbyterian	43	10
Other Christian	10	4	Other Christian	4	1
Non-Christian	0	0	Non-Christian	6	1.5
Total	257	100	Total	435	100

Source: Census of Canada, 1881, District no. 191, Vancouver, Cowichan and Saltspring Island,
Schedule no. 1 – Nominal; Census of Canada, 1891, District no. 3, Vancouver, M2 – S.D. 14,
Saltspring Island, Schedule no. 1 – Nominal.

more likely to marry someone of a different ethnicity than someone of
a different religion: there were more than twice as many "mixed-race"
marriages as those of mixed-religion, suggesting that religion played a
role in the cultural life of the island, although the paucity of sources
and the absence of established churches makes its difficult to assess its
extent in this first generation of settlement.[18]

Differences in wealth can be observed among the various religious
groups in 1891, the only year for which this comparative data is available. As Table 8.2 indicates, Presbyterians demonstrated the lowest rate
of landownership, slightly lower than the 80 per cent for the members of
other religious groups.[19] The size of landholdings varied among the four
groups, with Anglicans holding the most land and Catholics holding the
least. The assessed value of land per acre was surprisingly similar, rang-
ing from $4.09 per acre for Presbyterians to $4.59 for Catholics, reflecting the unimproved condition of most island land. These prices were a
far cry from the $50 to $125 per acre that cleared land cost in 1891.[20] By
the early twentieth century, religious, ethnic, and political distinctions
had crystallized on the island, with British Anglican Conservatives creating one community and American Methodist Liberals another. Members
of these two groups demonstrated their political, religious, and social al-
legiances by shopping at only one of the two general stores on the island:
Mouat's or the Island Trading store.

Table 8.2
Wealth by Religion of Saltspring Island Household Heads, 1891

Religion of Household Heads	No. and percentage of Household Heads	No. and percentage of Landowners	Average Acreage	Average Assessed Price of Land	Average Persistence to 1891, in years	No. and percentage Taxed on Personal Property	No. and percentage of HH with Children	Average No. of Children per HH
Baptist	2 (2)	2 (100)	100	$500	22.5	0	0	0
Catholic	20 (21)	15 (75)	206	$915.40	11	3 (15)	15 (75)	3.7
Church of England	35 (37)	28 (80)	563	$1338.30	8.7	11 (31)	20 (57)	4.3
Lutheran	7 (7)	7 (100)	191	$671.40	15	2 (29)	3 (43)	5.3
Methodist	15 (16)	12 (80)	191	$866.70	9	3 (20)	6 (40)	4
Presbyterian	15 (16)	11 (73)	306	$1263.60	9.9	4 (27)	8 (53)	3.5
Other Christian	1 (1)	0	–	–	6	0	–	–
Non-Christian	0	–	–	–	–	–	–	–
Total	95 (100%)	75 (79%)	355.5	$1090.70	11.7	23 (24%)	52 (53%)	4.2

Source: Census of Canada, 1891, District no. 3, Vancouver, M2 – S.D. 14, Saltspring Island, Schedule no. 1 – Nominal; British Columbia Department of Finance, Surveyor of Taxes, 1892 Assessment Roll, Roll B 443, Gulf Islands Assessment District.

Table 8.3
Wealth by Ethnicity of Saltspring Island Household Heads, 1891

Ethnicity of Household Heads	No. and percentage of Household Heads	No. and percentage of Landowners	Average Acreage	Average Assessed Price of Land	Average Persistence to 1891, in years	No. and percentage Taxed on Personal Property	No. and percentage HH with Children	Average No. of Children per HH
English	33 (35)	26 (79)	338	$1346.50	7.2	9 (27)	19 (58)	3.7
Irish	16 (17)	13 (81)	812	$1238.50	12.6	4 (25)	9	3.4
European	14 (15)	10 (71)	250	$1030.00	11.9	4 (29)	6 (43)	6.8
Scotch	10 (11)	8 (80)	288	$1287.50	9.5	5 (50)	5 (50)	4.8
Hawaiian	8 (8)	7 (100)	156	$585.70	12.8	0 (0)	7 (88)	2.9
African	7 (6)	6 (100)	102	$458.30	17.6	1 (14)	3 (43)	3.3
American	6 (6)	4 (67)	154	$537.50	4.8	0 (0)	2 (33)	4.5
Aboriginal	1 (1)	1 (100)	190	$500.00	14	0 (0)	1	3
Total	95	75 (80)	355.5	$1090.70	11.9	23 (24)	52	4.1

Source: Saltspring Island, Schedule no. 1 – Nominal; British Columbia Department of Finance, Surveyor of Taxes, 1892 Assessment Roll, Roll B 443; Gulf Islands Assessment District.

Children such as Betty and Steven Dunnell, shown here milking, provided important labour for island households. (SSIA)

In the nineteenth century, however, the inequalities of wealth that can be seen in the data in terms of religious affiliation can be explained more coherently in terms of ethnic differences, as outlined in Table 8.3. By 1891 a number of wealthy British settlers had moved onto the island, bringing with them money to invest in land, and this can be seen particularly in the Irish and English figures from Table 8.3. At the other end of the economic spectrum were the Hawaiians and other Catholics, many of them married to Native wives, none of whom declared the personal wealth of the English and Irish. As we saw in chapter 7, by the later nineteenth century, ethnic differences that were not obvious in the first twenty years of settlement were being translated into differences of wealth and status on the island.

AGE AND LIFE-COURSE

Landownership on Saltspring Island, as in other rural communities in Canada, represented the most important form of wealth and economic stability, and it correlated with age and life-course characteristics.[21] Landowners were, on average, about eight years older than those who did not own land, and those in their forties and fifties were much more likely to own land than those in their twenties. Those who were older, married, and had more children usually had more land and livestock than those who were single, young, and had none. Most men tended to take up land just after they were married and were starting families.[22]

Figure 8.1
Landownership on Saltspring Island, 1881, 1891

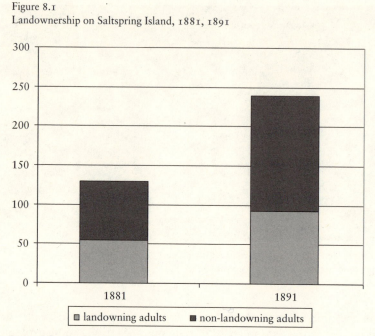

Source: Saltspring Island Database.

Landowners made up the majority of household heads, as Figure 8.1 illustrates, but only about 40 per cent of the entire adult population in both census years.[23] If wealth and status centred on the extent of land-ownership, then the most significant inequalities throughout this entire period can be measured not among landowners, but between landowners and those who did not own land. Most adult men owned land, while the vast majority of adult women did not. Because of the high proportion of landowning household heads on Saltspring Island, therefore, the greatest inequalities were not manifested *between* households as often as they were expressed *within* them. Notwithstanding the importance of the household and family to island life, therefore, households were defined by significant inequalities, particularly regarding access to land, based on patriarchal structures of age and gender.

Age was an important factor in organizing social relations. In both 1881 and 1891 children outnumbered landowning adults by about two to one.[24] Children were introduced early into the family economy via the world of work, but as Chad Gaffield summarizes, "within the patriarchal family, children, youth and adults did not simply share the interests or experience family life in undifferentiated ways."[25] Evidence indicates that children held a special status increasingly accorded by the

This boy seems to be enjoying his task of herding a bull, though his success does not seem assured. (SSIA)

state and by their parents in the nineteenth century by attending school.[26] The 1881 census indicates that of the fifty-three children on Saltspring Island who were between six and thirteen, thirty-nine (three-quarters) attended school. Only one of the nine fourteen-year-olds, and none of the eleven fifteen- and sixteen-year-olds are so listed.[27] The 1891 census did not ask whether children attended school, but Department of Education statistics for the island indicate that most children between five and sixteen attended school, even though attendance on the island, as in other rural areas of the province, often proved irregular. The figures indicate that between 65 and 100 per cent of eligible children were attending school, although absentee rates hovered around the 20 per cent throughout the period.[28] As we will see in greater detail, teachers complained about poor attendance throughout rural areas of British Columbia, but these complaints did little to discourage parents from keeping daughters at home to care for younger children or all children at home to help with a wide variety of tasks as needed.[29] Unfortunately, few records exist from this time to document the experience of children attending school.

By the age of fourteen children seem to have transcended their childhood identity in at least one regard, as their school participation ended abruptly. As we have seen, most youths who remained on the island continued to live with adults until their late twenties. Most lived with parents, but a number lived with relatives, or as lodgers with other families. By 1891 a growing number took the latter course, living in households with other adults until they married or left the island.[30] Young women tended to marry and leave the house of their parents earlier than young men, entering the world of full adulthood at a younger age.[31] Women tended to marry in their late teens or early twenties and usually began their own families in their own separate households.[32]

Even though the household was at the centre of the island economy, its economic influence on Saltspring Island did not usually extend to settling adult children on family lands. In other parts of Canada in the nineteenth century, families who moved to "new" rural areas with older children tended to do so as part of a strategy for providing children with the land to start their own farms. These areas provided the opportunity for buying up cheap lands for adult sons that was often impossible in more settled areas, where land was usually considerably more expensive.[33] But Saltspring Island farmers generally did not do so, even though, as we saw in chapter 6, most families arrived on the island with children, and those with children in the two census years had considerably more land than those without.

That so few island landholders were able to pass on "extra" land to their children may have been an unintended consequence of the pre-emption system. Linkages between pre-emption and census records confirm that most landholders in the time under study were living on pre-empted lands. Of the seventy-two such people in 1891, only thirty (40 per cent) had purchased their land by 1891, and a further eleven people had received a certificate of improvement.[34] Notwithstanding the benefits that the pre-emption system brought to island residents, it did not work well for the transmission of wealth to younger generations, at least not as the system was utilized by island residents. The only way that unimproved lands could be transferred to a son or daughter was by cancelling an existing claim and immediately registering it in the name of a son old enough to register a claim. As we saw in chapter 5, some landholders used the pre-emption system in this way to pass on lands without legal title to their children, but most adult children apparently decided to take their chances elsewhere and disappeared from the island.

The economic importance of children on Saltspring Island, as we saw in chapter 6, is visible in diaries, inquests, and the public accounts of the provincial government. Children and youths worked at a wide variety of paid employment – working for neighbours, logging, fishing, farming, and "on the roads" for the provincial government – and at an even wider range of non-waged occupations that contributed to the well-being of the family.[35] The diary of John Beddis, aged sixteen in

1890, outlines the daily activities on the Beddis farm, where he worked at a wide variety of tasks, including fence building, egg-gathering, and weeding.[36] Memoirs and the oral history record available for the later period suggest both that children and youths worked a lot harder than they liked in the service of the household economy, and that many gained considerable self-respect and social identity from doing so.[37]

It is more difficult to assess the relationships that existed between younger children and their parents, between the young and the old. Historians have used occupational endogamy as one empirical indicator of continuity between the generations, and, by implication, of the cohesiveness of the family as an economic and social unit.[38] On Saltspring Island, young men generally listed themselves as having an occupation from the age of fifteen onward, and most shared an occupation with their father. Of the ten adult sons living with their parents in 1881, and the thirty-four adult sons doing so in 1891, almost all listed the same occupation as their father, reinforcing the supposition that the farm was an important locus of household support.[39] David Gagan's work on rural Ontario has demonstrated some of the problems that could accompany such intergenerational co-residence, particularly in cases where fathers were reluctant to give up control of their lands to their adult sons and their families. No evidence exists on Saltspring Island of this particular type of troubled family relations. Perhaps the skilful use of the pre-emption system helped to ease the pressure on land that Gagan associates with these troubled father-son dynamics.[40]

But relations between adults and children, so central both to families and social hierarchies on the island, were not free from conflict. As we have just seen, Saltspring Island children were occasionally placed in the Sisters of St Ann's School in Cowichan because of family problems, often the death or disappearance of a parent. The following story of child abandonment recounted by one of the Sisters of St Ann speaks to the poverty and desperation that could accompany such a decision:

One evening Father Danckele was canoeing homewards among the uninhabited, wooded Gulf Islands when he heard the wailing of a young child. Listening, he got his proper bearings and came upon a little girl, lying in all the desperation of abandonment upon the beach. He put her in his canoe and listened to her, as between sobs she told him that her father and a woman had brought her on a boat ride. When they got off on that place they had said, "Go there among the trees for berries and flowers." She thought she was gone a little while but when she came back they had gone away and she could see them paddling very fast. The poor child who had been left to die of fright and hunger on that unfrequented island and that by her own father, a kanaka [Hawaiian] and a Vancouver Island native woman. She grew up in the orphanage. [By the time she grew up] her father, who lived on Salt Spring Island had come to understand his heartless deed towards her. He invited her to his house and tried to make amends, but when he claimed his parentage, Elizabeth declared, "The sisters are everything to me."[41]

Children also, on occasion, brought trouble on their families themselves by their refusal to accept parental authority. Two occasions stand out in the historical record, both involving girls, and indeed both involving Constable Sampson's immediate family. We saw in the introduction to this chapter Henry Sampson's young wife accused of aiding and abetting the neighbour's daughter, Mary Anne McFadden, in poisoning her father. During the trial, evidence was given that McFadden's son William "does not like to live with his father because he whips him and he would like to see his father die."[42] In 1881 the thirteen-year-old daughter of Sampson and his new partner, Lucy, was also in trouble with the law for challenging parental authority. It was not his daughter Ann Maria, but Clark Whims and William Anderson who were charged, however, with "unlawfully taking, or causing to be taken an unmarried girl under fourteen years of age out of the possession and against the will of her father and mother." Ann Maria was living with the Bittancourt family at the time, as Bittancourt had "agreed with Mr Sampson to treat her as one of my own and give her six dollars a month as long as she liked to stay."[43]

It is quite clear from the statements of Ann Maria and her older sister (who was married to Whims' brother and helped to arrange the "abduction") that what had taken place was an elopement, even though the marriage between the thirty-year-old Clark Whims and Ann Maria was not, apparently, deemed legal. When Ann Maria was asked, "Did you on the night Mr Whyms [sic] came for you go with him of your own free will?" she answered, "Yes I did. I was all ready [sic] prepared knowing he would come that evening. I met him not far from the house up by the Barn. I had arranged with him to come for me. I went of my own free will." On further cross-examination, she said, "I had made up my mind to go with him about a week [before]. My father and mother always treated me well. I think Mr Bitancourt [sic] treated me kindly. I had no reason for leaving because of unkindness by anyone."[44] While Ann Maria might have been confident about what she wanted, the courts did not agree. Anderson and Whims were indicted and the relationship ended.[45]

It is difficult to know what conclusions to draw from such cases. Clearly, they were unusual within the community, as the legal proceedings they instigated suggest. Nevertheless, these children challenged parental authority and the parents resorted to the legal system in their attempts to discipline their children, suggesting that the kind of parental authority normally associated with the nineteenth century was, at the very least, under some strain.[46] When we turn to gender relations, we see some indications of a similar pattern.

GENDER

Gender, like age and life-course, was important in defining people's identity in the family and the wider society. Gender differences helped to determine the types of work carried out on the island and the roles that people played in all aspects of their lives. Glenda Riley has argued in the context of pioneer America that women's work in rural areas was closely focused on the household and family, and domestic tasks were often carried out in isolation from other adults.[47] Such household-based work characterized women's lives on Saltspring Island, and similar patterns have been observed in other parts of pioneer British Columbia.[48] Both men and women participated in a wide variety of self-provisioning activities, but men's work was more likely to involve more social interaction – through fishing, logging, working on the roads – than was women's. Similarly, leisure activities seem to have been divided along gender lines. Church services, a traditional extra-household activity of women, were not regularly available to men or women during these years, and many of the events that they spawned, including the very popular church picnics, were not established until the 1890s. The arrival of the steamer three or four times a week was often greeted as a welcome excuse to socialize, hinting at the dearth of other social occasions. Evidence suggests that women seldom participated in the alcohol consumption and hunting that were favoured recreational activities of island men.[49]

Violence and drunkenness tended to characterize homosocial relations among men. Drinking and a gambling debt were probably involved in the accidental shooting of Charles Bird in 1896. Drinking was certainly involved in the 1907 murder of Alfred Douglas, who was killed in a drunken brawl, and in the murder of Mr Brown by his drunken wife and her lover in 1891.[50] Leonard Tolson, a cultured Englishman who would go on to start a private school on the island, describes his first contact with the island's drinking culture. Landing at Vesuvius Bay in 1887, "Charlie collected two gallons of scotch, Scovel two gallons of rum and Mansell two gallons of rye, all of which had been ordered for Christmas. These three took a shot of each all the way to Ganges ... It was a most curious experience for me as I was a teetotaler at the time. On entering the ward room, we were served sherry and bitters and dinner consisted of bottled bass (ale) so you can imagine the results!"[51]

Relations between men were not limited to drinking and violence, however.[52] Men on Saltspring Island forged important bonds with each other that were marked by co-operation and strong emotional ties. John Maxwell and James Lunney arrived together from Ireland in the early 1860s, taking up land together and living as neighbours for their entire lives on the island. Similarly, Theodore Trage and Heinrich Spikerman, arriving together from Germany at about the same time as Maxwell and Lunney, took up land together. Trage, like Maxwell, married a Native woman and raised a family. Spikerman lived with Trage and his family as he grew old. Through the words of E.H. Cartwright, an Englishman who lived on Saltspring Island in the early twentieth century, we can see that a variety of relationships were tolerated between men on the island:

Jack [Scovell] was a bachelor, and with him lived a strange character, Hugo Robershaw. Hugo had come to the Island with Ross Mahon, a wealthy Irishman, who owned the land at the head of an inlet running parallel to Ganges, Long Harbour. Ross Mahon had, by way of transport, a small steam vessel named *The Mist*, and he had brought Hugo out from Ireland to run her. Ross was drowned when bathing at Long Harbour and Jack Scovell, who understood Hugo, gave him a home. Hugo was a man of great strength and a small squeaky voice, a eunuch we always supposed, a good gardener, a splendid cook, and a very willing hairdresser who knew how to sharpen his own scissors. His devotion to and dependence on Jack was almost pathetic. Fortunately, perhaps, he died of pneumonia just at the time when Jack himself was going into hospital for his last illness.[53]

Gender not only determined patterns of work, leisure, and sociability but also played an important role in allocating who had access to the land, the foundation of wealth and power in this rural society. As Christopher Clarkson and Paulette Falcon have argued, government policies regarding property in nineteenth-century British Columbia were profoundly influenced by patriarchal assumptions and were designed to maintain patriarchal authority.[54] Prior to the Married Women's Property Act of 1873 British Columbia women had very few rights to property. The 1865 Homestead Protection Act allowed deserted wives protection from creditors to the extent that the family home was protected, but this was only at her husband's discretion. The same act, however, allowed a widow to hold the homestead for the duration of the children's minority, or until she remarried, making British Columbia women the first in the Dominion to have dower rights. As we have seen, a number of Saltspring Island widows took advantage of this law to live on their deceased husbands' pre-emptions.[55] In 1873 single women were briefly allowed to pre-empt land, a right that was rescinded the following year. After that, only widows with dependent children were allowed to do so. Only two women on Saltspring Island seem to have taken out land in this capacity in the years under study. The 1873 Married Women's Property Act allowed women to hold property in their own name, but they were prohibited from conveying land until 1887.[56]

As Carol Pateman has argued, such gender distinctions were fundamental to the creation of the modern state. The limitations on women's civil rights evidenced in property regulations and enfranchisement laws were closely tied to liberal notions of the hierarchical division of family and state: "the fraternal social contract creates a new, modern patriarchal order that is presented as divided into two spheres: civil society or the universal sphere of freedom, equality, individualism, reason, contract and impartial law – the realm of men or 'individuals'; and the private world of particularity, natural subjection, ties of blood, emotion, love, and sexual passion – the world of women, in which men also rule."[57] The exclusion of women and the family from civic identity removed them from definition as individuals in the liberal sense, bolstering patriarchal structures in the process. Such exclusion also allowed the family its key role within the state as a bulwark against capitalism, providing the stability and extra-capitalist values needed to protect the capitalist state from itself.[58]

On Saltspring Island, women made up the majority of those adults who did not own land.[59] Women's meagre presence in the land records confirms their marginal status within the liberal state. Unable to pre-empt land independently, rural women were limited in their opportunities for economic activity outside their relations to men, as daughters, wives, or mothers. Most landless women also lacked political voice: none voted in provincial or federal elections or participated in the nascent government bureaucracy by occupying positions on the local boards or councils.[60] Only the widows granted landowning status by the Homestead Exemption Act were able to vote municipally in the period under study, a political advantage limited by the short-lived nature of municipal government on the island and the tendency of widows to remarry. Outside their municipal vote, women expressed their political voice in the community only once: in 1891 a number appended their names to a petition requesting the implementation of provincial liquor laws on the island, as municipal ones were not being enforced. This public forum was exceptional in a community where, until the 1890s, women's lives were usually excluded from the formal structures of power.[61]

Women's circumscribed civil identity in rural society limited their opportunities outside marriage and is reflected in their poverty relative to

men: in the assessment roll of 1891 only four women owned land, and
only one woman, Mary Broadwell, declared personal property.[62] She
alone is listed in business directories as a businesswoman, the propri-
etor of the family store.[63] Poverty translated into dependence or at least
co-residency: women did not live alone on the island, but with a husband, parent, or, more unusually, an employer.[64]

The predominance of male-headed single parent households hints at
the difficulties for women living outside their families. A combination
of poor economic opportunities outside marriage, isolation, hard
work, and the difficulties of childbirth contributed to the reluctance of
women to stay in rural areas without a husband. The prevalence of
male, single-parent households also suggests high mortality rates
among child-bearing women.[65] After the one-armed Dr Hogg died under mysterious circumstances in 1866, there was no doctor living on
the island until 1898, when Dr Baker, aided by an annual provincial
grant of $161, began his practice there.[66] Before that time, women re-
lied on other women to help them with illnesses and childbirth. A number of women seem to have specialized in helping with childbirth,
including Mrs Beddis and "Granny Gyves," of Cowichan descent.[67]
Parish records from the 1880s onward suggest that death during childbirth was not uncommon; estimates are, however, difficult to make because of poor registration of births and deaths throughout the
nineteenth century.[68]

The difficulties of settler life on the island were exacerbated by the
violence within this island society, as the case of William Robinson illustrates. At least seven murders occurred within this tiny population in
the years under study.[69] No documentation is available to allow us to
measure the extent to which women's lives were affected by the informal structures of power contained in personal violence. But personal
violence surely did affect women, even though men were the victims of
most of the murders on the island. In 1864 a Mrs Smith and her son
were murdered on the island and the murderer was never found.[70] In
1866 Mrs Robinson accused one of her neighbours of attacking and attempting to rape her. He was charged and convicted of indecent as-
sault.[71] When Mary Reanney died in childbirth in 1891, the neighbours
who attended during her difficult confinement suspected the husband
of spousal abuse. Demonstrating considerable solidarity with this
Native woman, Mrs Beddis and Mrs Broadwell were apparently responsible for taking the unusual step of insisting on an inquest for
an otherwise unremarkable case of puerperal fever. At the inquest,
Mr Reanney was compelled to swear, under oath, that "it is not true
that on the 3 March or any day between that and the 13 of April my
wife was drawing oxen or assisting me in drawing oxen. There was

always plenty of food in the house and the deceased had always the full run of the house. I swear that I never had any words with the deceased nor acted in any way violently towards her. Deceased never complained to me of having bruised her leg by falling down the step."[72] The cause of death was confirmed as childbed fever. Mary Haumea died in childbirth, along with her twin babies, in 1892. According to local folklore, their deaths were the result of a beating by her violent husband, which explains why her ghost walked through the orchard on the property for so many years after her death.[73]

The bureaucratic and legal structures within which women lived in rural society, like the exigencies of an isolated and often violent society, imposed immeasurable restrictions on women's economic options and their social relations within the household. Nevertheless, as we have seen throughout this study, considerable distance existed between formal and administrative structures on the one hand and their application to the lives of Saltspring Island residents on the other. It is worth considering whether the disjuncture between liberalism and Saltspring Island experience, between the narratives of appropriate behaviour and the gendered practices of everyday life, might have offered some benefits for island women relative to men. Some intriguing hints in the historical record suggest that it did.

There is certainly considerable evidence that the liberalism that Pateman identifies as particularly limiting for women in the modern world was constrained on the island. The civic or public sphere that she associates so closely with male privilege in the modern state was being seriously contested on the island, particularly in the 1880s. As we will see by the end of this chapter, though men were able to vote, their involvement with formal political and bureaucratic structures remained limited in practice. Furthermore, some of the gendered economic inequalities usually associated with liberal, capitalist societies were disrupted on the island. Men were not the breadwinners in the ordinary sense of providing the sole wage for the family. Instead, men's participation in the world of waged work was intermittent, part time, temporary, and in some senses marginal to the economy of the household. Subsistence activities and the sale of small-scale agricultural produce (especially eggs, chickens, and butter) were probably equally important, and they were also performed by women and children.

Was patriarchal privilege limited as a result of the relative economic and political symmetry between men and women? If, as Jeanne Boydston has argued, women's inferior position within the liberal, capitalist household has been sustained by a discourse that privileged waged work, women on Saltspring Island may have been in a advantageous position relative to both their urban sisters and their rural husbands.[74]

And the system of landholding on the island, while it explicitly excluded women, included men in a relationship with property that resembled, in some respects, the relationship between women and property in nineteenth-century Canada. Although only men were given the right to own land under most circumstances, most men, like women, had their relation to land mediated not by ownership, but by use-rights that were contingent on specific behaviours. A woman's relation to the land was based on her legal and personal relations with her husband and was negotiated through the husband's provisional land rights. Her husband's provisional rights were negotiated through the state, but both differed from the normal relations of power associated with property ownership in a modern, liberal society. The removal, in practice, of the patriarchal privilege of land commodification may have had repercussions for the balance of power within the household.

How can we assess the effect that these issues had in practice on the gendered hierarchies within island households and society? The high rate of "mixed-race" marriages distinctive to nineteenth-century settlement in western Canada in general, and Saltspring Island in particular, may provide some clues.[75] As Adele Perry has argued, the phenomenon of ethnic mixing in British Columbia tended to be constructed in the nineteenth century as evidence of cultural breakdown and/or the sexual servitude and exploitation of women. In the twenty-first century, these relations tend to be read as colonial domination, a byword for the oppression of both women and Natives.[76] On Saltspring Island the meaning of inter-ethnic relations is not quite so clear. As we saw in chapter 7, marriages between Native women and non-Native men occurred within the families that were the most geographically persistent and among the wealthiest in terms of landholding. By marrying non-Native men, these women were not conforming to social and cultural patterns acceptable in Native society, but marriage brought some decided material advantages to both Native women and non-Native men, at least relative to many other island households.

Sylvia Van Kirk and Adele Perry have argued that "mixed-race" marriages became increasingly unacceptable in settler society as non-Natives and same-ethnicity marriages came to define the population of British Columbia in the later nineteenth century.[77] Can we "read" Saltspring Island society's relaxed attitude to the social rules that regulated women's behaviour in more urbane centres as evidence of resistance against the more confining aspects of being a woman at that time? Whether this phenomenon resulted in greater gender equality on a day-to-day basis is, unfortunately, impossible to say. As writers on "mixed-race" unions have argued, the relaxation of social constraints that made such unions an option for white men might have held very different meanings and implied very different relations of power for Native women.[78] We cannot assume that freedom from social constraints about marriage had an equal impact on women and men. The most important indicator of gender inequality is, unfortunately, not available for the island: it is impossible to assess the relative access that women had to resources inside the household.[79] Mary Reanney's inquest suggests that some people, at least, believed that women should have equitable access to household resources, but the inquest also suggests that such access was not always provided.[80]

One pattern of behaviour among island women does suggest that women had a different relationship to patriarchy than was common in other parts of the country: women showed some tendency to leave their husbands and sometimes their children. This trend is visible in the high rates of "blended" families, where, as we saw in chapter 6, the children were clearly were not the offspring of both parents. Whether women changed husbands as a result of death or abandonment, or to escape an intolerable life, or to find a preferable one, is not clear. One of the early settlers on the island, Margaret Shaw Walters, identifies the tendency to leave husbands as something peculiar to marriages between Natives and non-Natives:

These native wives – often so without benefit of clergy as Kipling puts it, adapted themselves in a surprising degree to the white man's ways – learning also to speak English more or less. One thing seemed curious in this direction. The mothers often spoke to the children in her own tongue, but the youngsters invariably answered in English – at least those we knew did. And while these wives might be docile, this did not mean subservient. Should conditions become too uncomfortable there was always the tribal ancestry to fall back on, and hubby had to choose between seeking them there or having his domestic arrangements put out of gear. This used to amuse my mother, who thought they were more independent in various ways than their white sisters ... As time went on they might be moved, or persuaded to marry legally, and one of such events we knew of, took place when the father and mother were married, and their grandchild christened on the same day.[81]

We have glimpsed in these pages a number of such "independent" women, both Native and non-Native. The first Mrs Sampson left her husband after he put her in prison for aiding and abetting the alleged poisoner next door. She apparently "refused to return to her husband preferring to live with another man somewhere on the mainland of British Columbia."[82] Mrs Purser left her husband and some of her children in favour of another, healthier man, after Mr Purser had a debilitating stroke.[83] Like his wife's family, William Harrison was part of the

African-American contingent that had arrived in the colony in 1858. When Harrison died in 1878 in nearby Victoria, he left all of his property and much of the little wealth he had to his brother-in-law, who was had been caring for him during his last illness, leaving only a residue "if any" to his wife, who was living at the time in Oberlin, Ohio.[84] After his death, his widow Harriet Harrison returned to Saltspring Island, taking up her husband's unimproved pre-emption as the law allowed. The land could not, after all, be transferred to her brother as her husband had requested before his death, because it had not yet been improved.[85] By 1881 Harriet had married a young Englishman some fifteen years her junior, and they were living together on her first husband's pre-emption.

Mrs Akerman, in her old age, demonstrated a similar determination to live apart from a troublesome husband. She had come over on the "bride ship" from England to Victoria as Martha Clay in the early 1860s and married Joseph shortly thereafter. The Akermans had obtained substantial landholdings by the 1890s. By 1901, however, Mrs Akerman had left her husband, who was reputed to be a bad-tempered man, and was living with one of her sons and his wife.[86] Julia Sheppard had left her husband, and she appeared with her young daughter as a lodger on the 1891 census.[87] Sylvia Stark had asked her husband to leave by 1879, when he moved to Nanaimo. After he died under suspicious circumstances in 1895,[88] his will noted that he left his wife "1 dollar in lieu of dower because she has some years since without cause left my bed and board consequently she is not entitled to any of my property." He left everything to his youngest daughter, Louisa Stark.[89] Mrs Brown was probably too drunk to know exactly what happened on 18 December 1891, but the jurors at the inquest formed their own ideas when a neighbour found her the next morning in bed with one Mr Darlington, and Mr Brown dead on the living-room floor.[90]

As we have seen, while the island society differed from the discourse of rural life articulated in urban Britain and Canada, it shared a variety of cultural, social, and economic patterns with other rural societies, particularly in newly settled areas of western Canada and the United States in the late nineteenth century. Families tended to be large, economies tended to be household centred, and the nuclear family was the norm.[91] But some evidence suggests that gender relations were a little more flexible on Saltspring Island than they seem to have been in many areas of nineteenth-century Canada. Is the tendency of women to leave their husbands a distinguishing characteristic of Saltspring Island society? If so, can this trend be traced to the island's marginal relation to liberal and commercial society? Unfortunately, comparative evidence is difficult to find. Other community studies might reveal similar ten-

Sylvia Stark, who arrived on the island in 1860 with her husband, father, and small children, lived to be well over 100 years old. To modern Canadian eyes her life was marked by poverty, but her memoirs reflect considerable satisfaction with her more than eight decades on Saltspring Island. (SSIA)

dencies that are simply not visible in formal, particularly legal, records. Without access to sources that speak more directly to women's understanding of their own experience, interpretations of women's lives reveal only tantalizing glimpses that the hard work of raising families, characteristic of women across Canada, might have been mediated by greater liberty and autonomy than that accorded their sisters.

CLASS

The issue of class has been conspicuously absent both from the list of inequalities discussed in these chapters and from discussions of how meaning and identity were formed on Saltspring Island. Class is a concept that has come under considerable attack in recent years. The importance of the means of production as an empirical measure of class relations has been seriously undermined by the influential work of E.P. Thompson, which defines class in experiential rather than materialist terms.[92] At the same time, as William Reddy has argued, historians have failed to establish any simple correspondence between ideology, political identity, and class interest, limiting its usefulness as an analytical tool.[93] A number of rural historians have been particularly cognizant of the difficulties involved in trying to reconcile the inequalities of rural society within the framework of class, a category of analysis that, despite its vagaries, is better suited to examining inequalities of power generated within urban and industrial rather than rural settings.[94] The society of Saltspring Island presents similar problems, not because inequalities did not exist but because it is difficult to explain or even describe them within the terms of class analysis.[95]

The most vexing aspect of islanders' class position is their problematic relation to the means of production. The provisional forms of landholding challenge any normal interpretations of ownership and land usages on the island challenge normal ideas of production. Furthermore, if, as has been argued here, the provisional forms of landholding in the pre-emption system provided the measure of inequality, then the most important inequalities did not occur between households in this land-based community, but within them. As a number of theorists have argued, it is very difficult to incorporate gender and the internal dynamics of the household into class analysis for many reasons. The most compelling are offered by feminist critiques of liberal or Marxist economic theory. Within this framework, critics argue, women's independent economic status is either collapsed into their husbands', by means of the joint utility function, or erased entirely by a discourse that fails to recognize the significance of the economic activities carried on by women within the household.[96]

If formal class structures did not exist on Saltspring Island in 1891, economic inequalities were apparent. Gender, age, ethnicity, and life-course marked the differences by which people organized themselves and each other, and were visible in differences in landholding, political voice, and personal property. But by 1891, in spite of these inequalities, structures of power had not solidified in such a way as to consistently funnel power within Saltspring Island society to one particular group: no local elite had, by that time, emerged to dominate the island's economy, society, or politics. The final part of this chapter turns to the formal structures of political and state power to see how the people of Saltspring Island negotiated the growing relationship between the household, the community, and the state.

THE LIMITS OF MODERNITY: THE NASCENT
LIBERAL STATE ON SALTSPRING ISLAND

By the 1870s a small elite could be discerned on the island, defined by gender and ethnicity, and measured by land size and wealth. At that time, the elite began to mobilize its power through the institutions of formal politics and state-building on the island. How did the rural culture and economy of Saltspring Island that has been outlined in earlier chapters – household based, influenced by Aboriginal economic and cultural practices, and sheltered from the full brunt of proletarianization, from complete reliance on petty commodity production, and from the exigencies of the harsh Canadian climate – respond to the growth of the modern bureaucratic state? I will argue here that in spite of the clearly articulated discourse of modernity, governmentality, and state-building that began to emerge on the island in the second decade of resettlement, the power that the elite was able to wield within island society was limited in practice by the fragility, or marginality, of liberal political and economic structures.

At first glance, and when viewed exclusively through government-generated records, people on Saltspring Island, like those in rural areas across North America in the nineteenth century, can be seen actively creating community by developing the institutions characteristic of the new bureaucratic state. Many behaved as if the new regularized bureaucratic processes and institutions of the state building era would benefit both themselves as individuals and the wider community. Men generally followed the letter of the law as they made use of the pre-emption system to take up land. They went to considerable trouble to organize voting in their first colonial election early in 1860. Islanders began petitioning for better mail service and better transportation both on and to the island in the 1860s.[97] Concerned about an alarming number of thefts and murders in the area throughout the 1860s, settlers also petitioned the government in Victoria to provide a Justice of the Peace for the island.[98] Although an official resident police officer was not appointed to Saltspring until the formation of the provincial police force in the late 1890s, special constables were appointed on numerous occasions from the 1860s onward. Public education provided another platform for community sponsorship of state bureaucracies, and throughout the 1860s and 1870s settlers petitioned for new schools for the rapidly growing population.[99]

By the 1870s the entry of British Columbia into Confederation and the influx of public monies it generated had stimulated further bureaucratic activity on Saltspring Island. Post offices, which not only facilitated trade but also provided a money-order service essential for business, were established.[100] In 1873 the island set up its first municipal government and by 1874 a regularly paid constable had been installed. By the late 1880s lines of communication and transportation had improved dramatically from the pre-railway boom years. Steamers had replaced the canoe and sailboat as the most important type of transportation, and were stopping at three locations on the island, providing mail four times a week to Vancouver Island.[101] By 1891 schools were established at Burgoyne Bay, Beaver Point, Begg's Settlement and Vesuvius Bay.

Records kept by the Public Accounts Department of the British Columbia government, by detailing the steady increase in public monies being spent on Saltspring Island, provide the most visible index of growing state involvement in the area. Money from provincial investments in roads, schools, and the judicial system provided an important economic contribution to most of the cash-strapped islanders throughout the later nineteenth century. The oral history record, in which proud grandchildren of early settlers inevitably recite the official positions held by their forebears, confirms the prestige, status, and power these positions represented for families, at least retrospectively.[102] Their importance can also be glimpsed in the surviving government correspondence.[103]

Published local histories also portray the history of community through the development of government forms, community institutions, and increasingly regularized behaviours.[104] Formal social organizations were being established, and two churches were opened on the island in the 1880s. Landowners were those most frequently called on for the nascent state-building functions on the island, filling government posts, signing petitions, performing temporary assignments, and reaping the associated financial and social benefits.

Those who filled the most prestigious and lucrative positions offered by the provincial government – Justice of the Peace, jury member, school trustee, foreman in a road-building crew, special constable, and postmaster – were a more select group. These were the landowners who demonstrated, through their well-regulated economic activities and general sobriety, the desire to accept as their own some of the most important tenets of liberalism. Men from the same eleven families – that 10 per cent of households whose agricultural production made up most of the island's commercial produce, whose land was valued at twice the average, and who possessed the vast majority of the island's personal wealth – appeared most frequently in these most honorific positions. It was not a coincidence that when the first municipal elections were held in 1873, members of this economic elite were elected, thereby demonstrating their ability to turn conformity with the new subjectivity required by the modern state into political power.[105] State power appeared on Saltspring Island through nascent state bureaucracies that succeeded, as they did in so many rural communities across Canada, in funnelling power to local elites.[106]

This type of state building has been closely monitored by historians throughout rural North America and has been seen as an important feature – a hallmark, even – of the modernization of rural societies. This transition has provided a way of tracking the progress of rural society towards a rationalized, organized, efficient society, closely resembling urban areas and imperial centres of power. In his book *Those Who Were Left Behind: Rural Society in Nineteenth Century New England*, Hal Barron was one of the first rural historians in North America to reach beyond this whiggish and progressive interpretation of state building. He provided a critical edge to his analysis of rural modernization, arguing that New England witnessed a significant "divergence of urban and rural culture during the second half of the nineteenth century." Urbanites exhibited a "growing commitment to social science and professionalization, which epitomized the elusive search for order by the new urban middle class."[107] This was manifested in their growing criticism of the disorganization and inefficiency of rural areas. Barron suggests that this organization of knowledge created asymmetries of power that had a negative effect on rural society in New England.

Recently, historians such as Bruce Curtis and Daniel Samson have argued in the Canadian context that what Hal Barron identified as the "search for order" was in fact evidence of the hegemony of the modern state. They argue that while the new state structures tended to reinforce asymmetries of power between urban and rural society, these inequalities cannot be explained simply by the desire of an elite to control a powerless rural population through the bureaucratic institutions of the modern state. Instead, following Foucault, they suggest that modernization "works" through the creation of a particular type of individual – rational, individualistic, and sober – who willingly consents to being governed.[108] Curtis has argued that this was the role of public education: "educational reform in mid-nineteenth century Upper Canada sought to reconstruct political rule in society by reconstructing the political subjectivity of the population."[109] The system of public education, Curtis argues, played a pivotal role by reinforcing in practice the civic ideal constructed by the ruling elites. Samson argues, in the context of rural Nova Scotia, that political legitimacy was increasingly linked to the creation of men who, through their "independence, respectability, propriety and later sobriety" demonstrated their right to be represented and governed, as well as to rule, within the burgeoning democratic state.[110] Like Curtis, he emphasizes that rural areas were much slower than urban centres to absorb these new ideals of citizenship, and he charts the complex political and economic reasons for the loosely structured rural resistance to the modern state.

Tina Loo has examined a similar process in up-country British Columbia, describing the important and contested role that the legal system played in promulgating the liberal discourse, with its emphasis on constructing independent, rational, profit-maximizing individuals, throughout the nineteenth century.[111] The legal system was central to the process of amalgamation between subjectivity and the demands of the state because it worked to construct "certainty in social relations, but also ... a degree of predictability in them that benefits the calculating individual."[112] This was particularly important in British Columbia, Loo argues, where social relations were not mediated by the traditional or cultural patterns evident in more settled and culturally cohesive locales, and "the bonds of community were not sufficiently developed ... to allow for the informal settlement of disputes."[113]

As Barron, Curtis, Samson, and Loo would concur, the modern state not only created new bureaucracies but its emphasis on efficient and regular practices privileged particular people (the elite and white classes) and particular areas (urban centres). According to J.I. Little these new structures served to formalize and consolidate the privileges of local elites into political power.[114] How were these two processes – increased regulation of self and increased regulation of the community – manifested on Saltspring Island?

A closer look at the society suggests that the people of Saltspring Island resisted both modernization and the structures of power that it privileged. The behaviours of most members of the island community suggest that the official rural discourse – where modernity and civic responsibility coalesced – were identified not with freedom and individualism, but with structures of domination that most settlers wished to avoid. The difficulty that island residents had in internalizing and exhibiting the values of the new liberal society – rationality, sobriety, respectability – are documented in a number of sources. Department of Education reports, post office inspectors' reports, and government correspondence chart the progress that Saltspring Island residents were making (or in many cases, *not* making) towards the ideal of civic responsibility contained within the liberal discourse of improvement and nation-building. Governor Douglas had complained in 1861 that he could find no one on the island to perform the function of Justice of the Peace, "none of the resident settlers ... having either the status or intelligence to serve the public with advantage in the capacity of local justices."[115] Twenty years later, officials were still not impressed with the calibre of the locals. Postal Inspector Fletcher advised against making

This log schoolhouse at Central Settlement (near Ganges) was one of the earliest schools on the island. In 1894 oxen, which could negotiate rougher terrain than horses, were still being used to draw wagons. (SSIA)

the Burgoyne Bay Post Office a money-order office in 1887, because the postmaster "is not in my opinion able to carry on the duties appertaining to the money order office ... I doubt whether he could understand the system."[116] Justice of the Peace Fred Foord had to be asked several times, and finally threatened with the termination of his employment, before he would send the returns of convictions and other matters to Victoria.[117] In 1882, while he was the appointed postmaster of Vesuvius Bay Post Office, he "refused to render his accounts in accordance with the regulations of the Department."[118] In 1872 Henry Sampson had to be removed from his office as constable because of his failure to marry his long-time partner, a Native woman. This marked a departure from a new policy which "apart from all the moral considerations, it is necessary to enforce for the sake of maintaining the respectability of the Public Service."[119] Saltspring Island residents also showed considerable resistance to accepting the authority of state-appointed officials, at least when that official was W. D. Anderson, a long-term resident of African-American descent.[120] Sampson, the police constable, was exceptional in the Saltspring Island community in his assiduity in applying the rule of law, but his field of operation was not large: two of the three cases where island residents were brought to trial between 1860 and 1881 involved members of his immediate family.[121]

Were Saltspring Island residents simply unable to conform to the rigorous standards imposed by the modern state, or were they disinclined to do so? The interactions between the Department of Education and Saltspring Island residents shed more light on this question by highlighting the expectations and behaviours that frequently polarized Saltspring Island residents and agents of the modern state. British Columbia educational historians have noted that teachers and superintendents consistently complained about the failure of rural parents and children to conform to the rules of efficiency and responsible behaviour advocated by the new urban Boards of Education.[122] Some Saltspring Island residents were eager, as one of the first petitions requesting a school stated, "to express ... our strong attachment to the throne of our illustrious and beloved Sovereign Nation" through the extension of services like public education.[123] But school inspectors complained about the abilities of teachers to teach, of pupils to learn, and of the island population to maintain acceptable standards of punctuality and regularity, which, as Bruce Curtis argues, were key characteristics of the good citizen. Quarrels between teachers and parents were common. Many of the complaints made by the educational bureaucracy focused on the low rates of school attendance: "the people with children growing up around them have repeatedly jeopardized the existence of the school by apathetic carelessness about attendance."[124] In 1882, amidst accusations of racism and political squabbling, the trustees fired the schoolteacher and closed the school entirely for a number of months, forcing the third closure since 1875.[125] As the school inspector complained on this occasion, "[h]aving been notified by the trustees that they had dismissed the teacher, and intended to close the school until there was a prospect of better attendance, I visited the school for the purpose of examining it before it closed. Although the teacher's services might have been utilized for a month after the notice of his dismissal was given him, the children ceased attending as soon as the fact became known."[126] Neither parents nor children were, in other words, properly appreciative of the advantages provided by a system of public education.

Conflict, largely unmediated by the salve of governmentality or other accoutrements of a liberal democratic society, seems to have been endemic throughout this community, emerging whenever families had much to do with each other in any capacity. Schools provided a focus for bickering and squabbling within the broader school community as well. The schools were closed entirely for months at a time on a number of occasions throughout the 1870s and 1880s, not just as a result of disagreements between parents and teachers but also because of quarrels between families.[127] The Cairns family, for example, complained about the fights that their children got into at school, but the teacher was unable to resolve the problem, as Mrs Cairns and "her husband are at loggerheads with nearly the whole community."[128] Mr Stark had little success in co-operating with his neighbours to build a road that would link several of the houses with each other, and to the main road. In 1870 Stark first asked the Department of Land and Works to intervene in the road-building process on Saltspring Island to ensure that his neighbours would help build the road. He then complained that all of his neighbours had conspired to work while he was observing the Sabbath. As a result, they had diverted a common road away from his property and directly toward a neighbour's barn.[129]

Rifts within the community were readily apparent in one of the few formal social organizations to have emerged on the island before 1891, the Hope of Saltspring Lodge.[130] The lodge was a branch of the Independent Order of Good Templars, a temperance organization, and bi-weekly meetings were held to confirm faith in God, promote sociability, stimulate debate on the important matters of the day, and advertise the virtues of sobriety. Almost from the first meeting of February 1886, however, relations within the lodge were marked by discord, acrimony, and suspicion.[131] At meetings throughout 1887 and 1888, brief periods of harmony were broken by squabbles over money and supplies. Increasingly, accusations of impropriety were levelled against lodge members by other members for such things as refusing to pay dues, violating constitutional procedures, or using profane language.[132] Investigations of suspected misdemeanours took up an increasing amount of the members' time and energy. By the time the society closed in September 1888 – "in view of the want of harmony displayed at several meetings of this Lodge displacing the fraternal feeling that should prevail" – ten out of a total of forty-nine members had resigned, two had been expelled, and thirteen had been suspended.[133] Not all episodes of conflict ended so benignly. Some fractures within the island community were marked by extreme violence. Violent episodes – in which heavy drinking usually played a role – were frequently recorded and at least seven murders were prosecuted within this tiny population in the thirty years under study.[134]

These incidents suggest that Saltspring Island residents were actively and passively resisting both the self-discipline and the external authority needed for the creation of modern political sensibilities and the smooth running of the modern bureaucratic state. Their resistance to the growth of the modern state and to the increasing power that it channelled to the island's nascent elite, was formalized in their rejection of municipal government on the island in the mid 1880s.[135]

Politics had always been a contentious affair on Saltspring Island. The first colonial election was held just a few months after the first settlers arrived in January 1860. Setting the tone for political activity for years to come, those dissatisfied with the results alleged that the returning officer, Jonathan Begg, had failed to give proper notice of the election. By nailing the notice of the on a tree in the midst of the trackless wilderness, they maintained, Begg had kept away opponents, thereby fraudulently securing the election of the candidate that he favoured.[136] A similar fracas occurred in 1863 when a Court of Revision, called at the request of suspicious voters, was attended by none of the voters, because of the remote location of the court proceedings. Two years later, after the elected representative had declared bankruptcy, a similar court served to disqualify the subsequently elected member of council from the list of eligible voters for the island, thereby removing him from office.[137]

After confederation with Canada in 1871, British Columbia passed legislation allowing the formation of municipal governments, but on Saltspring Island attempts to sustain this level of government fared badly. In 1873 a petition requesting that letters patent be granted to the Municipality of Saltspring Island was accepted by the legislature. Almost immediately, an anonymous letter to the Victoria *Colonist* maintained that the petition had been obtained by fraudulent means, as many of those whose signatures appeared on the petition were in fact illiterate, and therefore unaware of what they were signing.[138] Later that year a number of island residents charged the municipal councillors with violating the Municipal Act in a number of ways, including by being in receipt of unlawful monies.[139]

The hostility to municipal government grew until, following the 1881 election, a number of settlers on the island brought a suit against three of the councillors, accusing them of inappropriate behaviour during the election. The accusation was not disputed, and one of the officers was charged with the costs.[140] A month later, a petition was brought to the Lieutenant-Governor in Council, condemning the behaviour of the Saltspring Island councillors, and claiming that they were running municipal affairs entirely for their own purposes and without any accountability, financial or otherwise. Further instances of election irregularities were cited. No action was taken at that time, but a year later, when Reeve Booth was accused of retaining his position without holding an election, community members pressured the government to pass an act in the Provincial Legislature to "annul the Letters Patent establishing a Municipality on Saltspring Island."[141] Although councillor Foord may have been correct in accusing island settlers of rejecting municipal government to avoid taxation,[142] the rejection had the practical effect of limiting the power flowing to the emerging elite on the island.

In rejecting municipal government, the people of Saltspring Island were cementing their independence from larger forms of bureaucratic power. Although poor, islanders were not exclusively dependent on the opportunities for either waged work or commercial activity controlled by the nascent elite. By owning their own land, and pursuing their own complex forms of economic survival, most island landowners were sheltered from, and thus able to resist both actively and passively, the kinds of power that defined social, economic, and political relations in other areas of the country. In rejecting municipal government, island voters eliminated the only means by which the island's most wealthy and powerful residents could, in the absence of economic control, consistently regulate their behaviour. And with this rejection they also rejected much of the modern, bureaucratic, state-building apparatus on which it rested, in favour of a more unstructured, less regulated, and untaxed government function.

CONCLUSION

Although Saltspring Island was characterized by widespread landownership, not all members of the community had equal access to the advantages of landholding. Religion, age, life-course, and gender, as well as ethnicity, were important categories by which people on the island constructed their identities; they also provided the axes along which access to wealth and other relations of power were negotiated. If these categories provided the framework for identity and community, however, they were often resisted, challenged, and transgressed. It is impossible to say whether island residents were more unruly and violent than other rural communities in British Columbia or Canada, but the boundaries of acceptable (and even legal) behaviour were at times stretched to the limit. Families negotiated internal relations of power in a variety of ways. At times, children challenged parents, parents rejected children, and a number of island women left offending husbands for better, or at least different, partners. As a society, residents demonstrated a notable antipathy to the more formal kinds of social organization usually identified with the growth of community and state in the nineteenth century, including the growth of state-run institutions such as municipal government and schools.

If their active antipathy towards formal social structures and modern institutions was *made possible* by settlers' relative economic independence, it was *rendered desirable*, I would argue, by the existence of a distinct rural culture on the island. This culture was characterized by high levels of social disorganization and conflict, which sometimes exploded into violence. It was also characterized by a flexible and household-based economy, the relative openness of household formation, intimate contact with cultures having different customs and practices, and a bountiful and benign environment. Above all, a stable and cheap land base provided considerable independence from employers or land-lords. Rejecting the status and identity of either full-time wage labour-ers or full-time commercial farmers, and without either the incentive or (if we can believe their critics) the social skills to pull together and re-ally "work" as a community, island residents were slow to develop the personal characteristics – punctuality, obedience, regularity of personal habits – that would mark them as respectable modern citizens. If resi-dents showed a deep ambivalence towards the social organization and formal structures embodied in the modern state, their rejection of mu-nicipal government in 1883, ten years after its initial acceptance, was a successful bid to block local elites from consolidating their power. By rejecting municipal government, islanders limited the influence of pow-erful individuals within their society, and muted the role of the liberal state in their lives. In the process, they confirmed their identity as a dis-parate collection of independent households that never quite succeeded in coalescing into a community.

Conclusion

Reflecting late in his life on his vast studies of resettlement in the grass-lands of the western United States, James Malin generalized that successful human occupation of any place depends on making use of available natural resources to the best advantage. Whatever environment people live in, we should expect both environment and culture to change in response to new settlement, for, as Malin put it, "each and every place and time is unique and change is continuous, irreversible and indeterminate."[1] Arguing against both economic and environmental determinism, he maintained that very few places are unlivable for human beings, provided people take the time to learn how to fit their culture into the natural givens of their environment.[2] What is valuable here is the way Malin shifted the point of argument so flexibly away from the old focus on land availability, which rested on deterministic assumptions about what people should do, to the process of learning land use as the key to understanding the social history of settlement. Nobody, in other words, should prejudge for the settlers how their relationship to the environment and culture would evolve.

Rural societies in nineteenth-century Canada have usually been understood within the dual framework of the staples thesis and a generalized theory of progress that starts with pioneer settlements and ends with either intensive and specialized commercial agriculture or urban industrialization. The tendency of British Columbians to define the province in terms of resource extraction, rather than agricultural production, has encouraged historians to understand rural British Columbia as a resource or industrial frontier.[3] A more recent historiography has contrasted this vision of settler society with the "other" rural society in the province, a land-based Aboriginal society and culture, organized according to kinship and non-market relations, that provides the "red shadow" of white colonization.[4]

I have suggested that an agricultural vision played a more important role in the resettlement of the province than historians have generally allowed. In the first years a dominant discourse identified rural with the commercially viable family farm and became a significant force in shaping reformist policies. The discourse of agricultural success that mobilized land policies and coloured the literature about the island succeeded in bringing settlers to Saltspring and provided a foundation for a land-based and household-centred rural society. This vision of rural life was reflected in the behaviours of some Saltspring Island families. Most pre-emptors in the years under study, however, neither improved nor paid for their land, and they showed little interest in developing successful family farms. Most seemed to have economic ambitions that reached no further than the stability offered to householders by a resource-rich environment with cheap land on very easy terms. It is as if, once settlers were on the island for some time, they discovered the other, more agreeable compromises that could be struck between culture and environment.

Nineteenth-century commentators tended to construct rural society in general as an enclave where petty-commodity production on the family farm would provide the stability and wealth required by the more dynamic and aggressively capitalist urban centres. When it became difficult for contemporaries to define Saltspring Island in terms of agricultural success, it was evaluated as a failed agricultural enterprise. The dominant discourse in nineteenth-century British Columbia shared with the frontier thesis and contemporary theories of under-development the tendency to evaluate this type of economy, culture, and society as a failure. Poor soil, distance from markets, the deleterious effect of "mixed-race" marriages, or incompetent farmers were held up by way of explanation for the otherwise incomprehensible distance between the island society and the normalizing rural discourse. Present evaluations urge that similar societies, when they are considered at all, be understood as products of the cultural breakdown characteristic of the isolation and abundant land of the frontier and/or as the victims of the financial vulnerability characteristic of economically marginal areas.[5]

I have argued here that a study of rural behaviours, of rural practice, provides grounds for a re-evaluation of the dominant rural and colonial discourses, for the people of Saltspring Island were not in any simple sense acting out a pre-determined pattern of "white" settlement. A close examination of land settlement and community formation reveals high rates of geographical persistence, a mixture of ethnic groups, a variety of land-related strategies, and the relative economic stability of households. Saltspring Islanders were not failing to achieve universal (European) goals articulated by policy makers; instead, they were using

The Akerman Family, Burgoyne Valley, circa 1890 (SSIA)

the pre-emption system and the rich local environment to facilitate their own household-centred goals and non-profit-maximizing aspirations. Pre-empted land provided most families with the economic "edge" – both the flexibility and the stability – that allowed them to participate intermittently as proletarians, petty-commodity producers, and self-provisioners, while concentrating on their main goals in life: raising their families and staying on their land.

This study reveals the crucial importance of specific land-related and household-related strategies to the creation of a "new" society. It reminds the reader of the contingent nature of historical knowledge. For much of the evidence on which this study is based was created by people describing and prescribing a world that they were looking in on from the outside. It also argues that it is possible to look at rural settler societies from the inside, through the daily practices by which the population defined their own lives. The rural dwellers of Saltspring Island had their own ideas of how to live, but they borrowed ideas and practices from a variety of sources, from Native as well as non-Native family and friends. They held on to them when the particular ideas and practices "worked" to mediate between culture and environment on acceptable terms. Many of those hoping to make a life on the island left it within a few months, unable to make a successful link between cultural practice and the exigencies of the economic and ecological environment. For those who wanted to make a lot of money, or have a commercially successful farm, or buy a lot of goods, or live in a close-knit community, Saltspring Island was a poor choice. But for those who were content to work at a variety of jobs, whose desire for material wealth was offset by an appreciation of a more leisurely pace of life, and who appreciated their relative freedom from demanding landlords or employers, Saltspring Island was a good choice. And from time to time, Saltspring Islanders defended their choice by rejecting formal (and expensive) government by the local elite or resisting control by school officials. In the process, they were reacting against the constraints of dominant social and cultural formations in the larger society. These alternative world views, and the resistance that they sometimes embodied, are invisible if historians elide discourse and practice.

Although Saltspring Island differed in many ways from the mobile, urban, and wage-dependent social formations generally associated with British Columbia, there is little evidence to support the contention (raised independently by a number of my colleagues) that it was the quality of "islandness" that created or sustained this community's identity. First, the people of nineteenth-century British Columbia depended on water to provide the best type of transportation, minimizing the insularity usually identified with island life. Even after the Cariboo Wagon Road was built, the ease of transportation offered by water meant that those living on Saltspring Island in the years under study were much closer to both the economic advantages and the normalizing effects of urban society, than were the people of the Interior, or northern Vancouver Island, for example. Furthermore, many islanders participated in a wide variety of seasonal work off the island – fishing, logging, and selling agricultural produce – and so were not entirely isolated from the influences of other areas.

Second, although the society on Saltspring Island differed in some important ways from representations of urban life and the official discourse of rural, it differed in many of the *same* ways that other rural populations did. The particular combination of occupational plurality, political disorganization, and resistance to the "governmentality" of the modern state that has been described on Saltspring Island has also been discovered in many areas outside towns and cities throughout Canada; and like many "new" rural areas, it was marked by a household-centred, peasant-type economy, and high fertility rates.[6] Saltspring Island was not the only nineteenth-century society where people were more interested in getting by than in getting rich. As Daniel Samson has summarized in the context of rural Atlantic Canada, "what marked life for country people – and defined it as 'rural life' – was their ability to exploit the land or the sea, to produce for themselves a major part of their subsistence either directly (as food, shelter, or clothing) or indirectly through exchange, and their ability to obtain some measure of independence – derived from either their own resources or resources from which access was not restricted in this way – at least deferring full dependence on wage labour."[7] The qualities that have been used here to distinguish Saltspring Island from an urban-centred discourse of rural in British Columbia were not, therefore, specific to this island or to island life in general.

On the other hand, high rates of inter-ethnic marriage, violence, and an antipathy to formal social and political organization may indicate that a number of people found in the island a kind of free zone, disconnected from the more orderly urban societies springing up around them.[8] Were these characteristics caused by the agglomeration of individuals who were drawn by the island's rural culture? Or did they instead mark the effects of living in a remote society that was prepared to encourage, or at least willing to tolerate, the levels of social disorganization evident on the island? Or did these characteristics, particularly the rich ethnic mix on the island, reflect the deep humanitarianism of mid-nineteenth century colonialism?[9] Generalized constructions of "islandness" as isolation provide only blunt tools of description and analysis for answering such questions, for they cannot explain the important differences occurring *among* isolated areas in general or islands in particular. Most islands – including Saltspring Island in the twentieth century – were *not* characterized by inter-ethnic marriage, the failure of municipal government, or high levels of violence.[10] In sum, isolation, or "islandness," is better suited to measuring the distance from the discursive centres of the dominant historiography than to explaining different rural practices.

The case of Saltspring Island raises important cautions about microhistory itself. While microhistory has the advantage of illuminating previously unknown behaviours and beliefs, and putting them into new focus, the problem of context legitimately worries those who want to know just how, exactly, the society under study relates to other places or other times. Is it typical, or is it unusual? Does it "fit" within the bigger picture of history and, if so, how? I suggest that although the specific challenges that Saltspring Islanders made (and make) to the ideas of a coherent white settler society and a regular progression over time (from self-sufficient pioneer household to modern commercial society) were (are) unique to that island, such rural transgressions in Canada's master narrative are not limited to this one community. A variety of recent rural studies in Canada suggest the need to revise our understanding of nineteenth- and twentieth-century society to accommodate the kinds of rural communities emerging from recent microhistorical research. Microhistorians are, curiously, revealing a new, common pattern.

Research is confirming that in rural Canada, the household remained an important locus of the economy well into the "modern" era. While the continuing role of the farm household is marginalized within the master narrative of Canadian history, historians have found it almost impossible to describe any particular rural economy or society in Canada without placing the family at its centre.[11] Most rural families maintained characteristics that are clearly identifiable as a-liberal (i.e., not exclusively about capitalism, or maximizing the individual's self-interest); for example, they continued to rely to some extent on subsistence-oriented activities into the twentieth century.[12] More surprising are the diverse ways in which older patterns of self-provisioning, or production through kinship systems, were integrated – as on Saltspring Island – into modern patterns of international trade or into the new bureaucracies of the welfare state.[13] Although it is possible to construct the behaviours observed on Saltspring Island as unusual anomalies in an otherwise coherent system of capitalism, individualism, and the growth of the modern state, this study, among many others, suggests that it may be time to re-evaluate the hegemony of liberalism and to question the utility of its companion discourse of modernization, in our attempts to understand nineteenth-century Canada.[14]

I have stopped short of presenting the Saltspring Island community as engaged in self-conscious resistance to urban capitalism, the modern world, and the discourse of liberalism. There is little evidence, aside from the sustained protest against municipal government in the early 1880s, that islanders developed the organized political consciousness usually associated with resistance or revolt. The decisions that people made about their lives occurred in the context of a wide variety of factors: family composition, ethnicity, gender, geographical persistence, date of arrival, the rich and temperate environment of the Pacific northwest, and, most particularly, access to land. Those who stayed on Saltspring Island did so because the society, economy, and culture of the island supported them in what they wanted out of life – or what they were prepared to settle for: the economic stability needed to raise a family or to just get by.

Geographical isolation from centres of trade and political power probably muted their exposure to the bureaucratic gaze of Victoria and may have supported patterns of marriage, family life, and economic activity that were variable and sometimes unorthodox. But specific responses to particular elements within this rural place, not a generalized response to being either rural or isolated, provided the contexts of people's lives and directed their choices. The economic independence of landowners, no matter how marginal their activities seemed to those at the capitalist centre, was a primary component in these decisions.

Landownership sheltered them from the more familiar structures of power within capitalist society. Land, situated in the rich environment of the Pacific coast, provided the modest, but secure and flexible economic base on which rural practice was built during these years. Their secure land tenure allowed families a marked indifference to the modern, liberal discourse and the structures of power it proposed to define and discipline rural society.

This study has not determined whether the marginality of farming and waged work to the households on Saltspring Island will prove typical of rural nineteenth-century British Columbia, nor whether such land-based, family-centred economies will emerge as the norm. But it has shown, I suggest, that until we start looking outside towns and cities and examine more critically the sources and concepts that we use to construct the country's history, we will not be able to observe the varieties of practice, much less the differences between discourse and practice, that have shaped rural societies. As historians of Aboriginal peoples in British Columbia have eloquently argued, until we look beyond the discourse of dominant populations and through the "transparency" of primary sources, too many voices will remain unheard on the margins of our history.

Notes

ABBREVIATIONS

BCA   British Columbia Archives
BCSP British Columbia Sessional Papers
NAC   National Archives of Canada
SSIA Saltspring Island Archives

PREFACE

1 Ian McKay, "The Liberal Order."
2 Dorothy Dodds, 1990 interview, Saltspring Island Archives (hereafter SSIA).
3 Ian McKay, "The Liberal Order," 630.
4 Ibid., 624.
5 Ibid., 630.
6 Ibid.

INTRODUCTION

1 The term "resettlement" was coined by Harris, *The Resettlement of British Columbia*.
2 Harris, "Voices of Disaster;" Boyd, "Smallpox in the Pacific Northwest."
3 These problems are described in detail in chapters 1 and 3.
4 An important exception to this is the microhistorical study by Thomson, "A History of the Okanagan." For a review of rural history in British Columbia, see Sandwell, "Finding Rural British Columbia," in Sandwell, ed. *Beyond the City Limits*, 3–14.
5 See for example Fisher, *Contact and Conflict: Indian-European Relations in British Columbia*; Harris, *Making Native Space*; and Tennant, *Aboriginal Peoples and Politics*.

6 Lutz, "Work, Wages and Welfare."

7 If the Douglas System, which sought to include Native peoples as farmers and was originally proposed by Governor Douglas (himself a person of mixed parentage), had been followed, it is just conceivable that British Columbia would have continued as the same mixed community it was in the 1850 and 60s. For a discussion of the Douglas System, see Harris, *Making Native Space*, 17–44. For a discussion of British Columbia in the colonial period see Perry, *On the Edge of Empire*; and Barman, *The West Beyond the West*. For a discussion of the continuation of mixed-race families in British Columbia in the twentieth century, see Barman, "Invisible Women and Mixed-Race Daughters in Rural British Columbia" in Sandwell, ed., *Beyond the City Limits*; and Lutz, "Work, Wages and Welfare."

8 Measurable rates of illiteracy were a little higher on Saltspring Island (16 per cent of adults over fourteen in 1891, the only year that the census asked the question "can you read English"), than in Ontario in 1861 (under 10 per cent). But a distinction is being made here between those who were able to write and those who used the written word to understand and constitute their identity. Saltspring Islanders left few written records. Letters and documents delivered to government officials suggest that most settlers were unaccustomed to writing and, before the 1890s, few references, in sources such as wills, inquests, and probate files, are made to the possession of reading materials. Many of those who were absolutely unable to read and write English on Saltspring Island were Hawaiian, Native, or eastern European. For a discussion of the extent and significance of literacy in rural society, see Darroch and Soltow, *Property and Inequality in Victorian Ontario*, 112–60. For a wider discussion on the meaning of literacy in the nineteenth century, see Vincent, *Literacy and Popular Culture in England, 1750–1914*; and Anderson, *Imagined Communities*.

9 Dirks, Eley, and Ortner, "Introduction" to Dirks, Eley, and Ortner, eds., *Culture, Power, History*, 25.

10 Ibid., 27.

11 Gaffield, "Historical Thinking," 11.

12 Levi, "On Microhistory," in Burke, ed., *New Perspectives on Historical Writing*, 94.

13 Ibid., 107.

14 Michel de Certeau, *The Practice of Everyday Life*, xiv.

15 For a detailed critique of discourse analysis, see Palmer, *Descent into Discourse*.

16 For an introductory exploration of this contention for historians, see Cornell, "Early American History in a Postmodern Age."

17 Levi, "On Microhistory," 107.

18 Ibid., 98.

19 Samson, "Introduction," in Samson, ed., *Contested Countryside*, 1.

20 See for example Harris, *The Re-Settlement of British Columbia*; and Furniss, *The Burden of History*.

21 As Joan Scott has noted, statistical representations are not free from normative structures that inform narrative representations. Scott, "A Statistical Representation of Work," in Scott, *Gender and the Politics of History*, 113–38. As Pierre Bordieu argues, however, a study of historical practice reads beyond the intentions of those who gathered the statistics, looking for evidence to help us understand the systems of meaning by which a population, or part of a population, organized their experience: "Systems of classification which reproduce, in their own specific logic, the objective classes, i.e., the divisions by sex, age, or position in the relations of production, make their specific contribution to the reproduction of the power relations of which they are the product, by securing the misrecognition, and hence the recognition, of the arbitrariness on which they are based." Bordieu, *Outline of a Theory of Practice*, 164.

22 As Grant McCracken argues, "Cultural categories are the fundamental coordinates of meaning. They represent the basic distinctions with which a culture divides up the phenomenal world ... Cultural categories of time, space, nature and person create the vast body of categories. Together they create a system of distinctions that organizes the phenomenal world. It is thus that each culture establishes its own special vision of the world and thus that it renders the understandings and rules appropriate to one cultural context and preposterously inappropriate in the next." McCracken, *Culture and Consumption*, 73. For a critique of the imperialism of anthropologists' traditional uses of cultural formation, see Pratt, *Imperial Eyes*; and Dirks et al., "Introduction," 1–6.

CHAPTER ONE

1 Marie Albertina Wallace (née Stark), "1867–1966, Salt Spring Island, B.C." Xerox of typescript, Add. Mss. 91, British Columbia Archives.

2 Jonathan Begg, Correspondence to William and Margaret Chisholm, 1858–1862, Saltspring Island Archives (hereafter SSIA).

3 For a history of Aboriginal peoples on the coast, including their complex relations to land and sea, see Carlson, McHalsie, and Perrier, *A Sto:lo Coast Salish Historical Atlas*; Duff, *The Indian History of British Columbia*; and Clayton, *Islands of Truth*.

4 Harris, *Making Native Space*, 46–57.

5 Harris with David Demeritt, "Farming and Rural Life" in Harris, *The Re-settlement of British Columbia*, 219.

6 Harris, *Making Native Space*, 17.

7 Ibid., 17–44; Tennant, *Aboriginal Peoples and Politics*, 26–38.

8 Harris, *Making Native Space*, 17.

9 For an overview of these battles, see Tennant, *Aboriginal Peoples and Politics*; and Asch, *Aboriginal and Treaty Rights in Canada*.

10 Mackie, "The Colonization of Vancouver Island, 1849–1858"; and Cail, *Land, Man and the Law*.

11 For an overview of the Wakefield system, see Loo, *Making Law, Order and Authority*, 39–40; and Little, "The Foundations of Government." Ged Martin has recently questioned the practical impact of Wakefield's influence on colonial settlement policy, arguing that his theories of colonization were not taken seriously by his contemporaries. Martin, *Edward Gibbon Wakefield*.

12 Cail, *Land, Man and the Law*, xiii, 13–14. Harris, *Making Native Space*, 30–44.

13 For a review of the goals and problems of early land legislation, see Cail, *Land, Man and the Law*, chapter 1; Hendrickson, "The Constitutional Development of Colonial Vancouver Island and British Columbia"; and Harris, *Making Native Space*, 45–72.

14 Cail, *Land, Man and the Law*, 6–8.

15 See for example Lytton to Douglas, 14 August 1858, no. 8. Great Britain, Colonial Office, Papers Relative to the Affairs of British Columbia, presented to both houses of Parliament by command of Her Majesty, 1859–1862, 48–52, cited in Cail, *Land, Man and the Law*, 5–7.

16 "Proclamation Enclosure in No. 51," Papers Relative to British Columbia, cited in Cail, *Land, Man and the Law*, 11.

17 Cail, *Land, Man and the Law*, 11.

18 Cail, *Land, Man and the Law*, 9–10.

19 *British Colonist*, 13 June 1859.

20 Jonathan Begg to William and Margaret Chisholm, 10 March 1860, Begg File, SSIA.

21 Jonathan Begg to William and Margaret Chisholm, 2 February 1858 and 10 March 1860, Begg File, SSIA.

22 Begg to William and Margaret Chisholm, 10 March 1860, Begg File, SSIA.

23 *British Colonist*, "Land Reform Meeting," 24 June 1859. Jonathan Begg appears as one of those drawing up resolutions for the petition.

24 *British Colonist*, 4 July 1859.

25 *British Colonist*, 4 July 1859.

26 *British Colonist*, 4 July 1859. Although Cail suggests in *Land, Man and the Law*, xi, that Douglas invented the pre-emption system of land acquisition before any other examples, such as the 1862 American Homestead Act, were available, this is not so. The terms outlined by de Cosmos and the other petitioners closely follow the Donation Land Claim Act, established by Oregon's provisional government in 1850. Under the terms of this act, every white male citizen over eighteen could take up 320 acres of land if single; if married, his wife could hold an additional 320 acres in her own

right. Personal residence for four years and the cultivation of some of the land were the only stipulations. African-Americans and Hawaiians were excluded from this system. Schwantes, *The Pacific Northwest*, 103.

27 *British Colonist*, 8 July 1859.

28 *British Colonist*, 8 July 1859.

29 See Flucke, "Early Days on Saltspring Island."

30 *British Colonist*, 11 July 1859. The concept of land "improvement" is a profoundly cultural construction, one that was implicated in differences between Native and non-Native definitions of "beneficial use." See, for example, Stadfeld, "Manifestations of Power"; and Fisher, *Contact and Conflict*, chapter 5.

31 *British Colonist*, 13 July 1859.

32 *British Colonist*, 4 July 1859.

33 *Victoria Gazette*, 14 July 1859.

34 *Victoria Gazette*, 14 July 1859.

35 *British Colonist*, 27 July 1859.

36 Jonathan Begg to William and Margaret Chisholm, 10 March 1860, Begg File, SSIA.

37 Jonathan Begg to William and Margaret Chisholm, 10 March 1860, Begg File, SSIA.

38 Joseph Pemberton to John Copland, 26 July 1859, Correspondence Outward, Department of Land and Works, CAA30.7J1, BCA.

39 Pemberton to Copland, 26 July 1859.

40 Flucke, "Early Days on Saltspring Island," 15.

41 See, for example, Barman, *The West Beyond the West*, 87; and Cail, *Land, Man and the Law*, 12–15.

42 Joseph Trutch to Governor, 12 August 1868, File 953, Correspondence of the Department of Land and Works, BCA, 19; Cail, *Land, Man and the Law*, 12–13.

43 *Victoria Gazette*, 30 July 1859.

44 See Barman, *The West Beyond the West*, 87, where she cites 1860 as the date of the first pre-emptions in the Fraser Valley. F.W. Laing, Secretary to the Minister of Agriculture, notes 1858 as the time of the first application for farmland, at Hope, but he too notes that pre-emptions were not granted until 1860. Laing, "Early Agriculture in British Columbia," BCA.

45 *British Colonist*, 19 August 1859; Joseph Pemberton to Mssrs Manly, Sparrow, and Wright, 30 July 1859, Correspondence Outward, Department of Land and Works, CAA30.7J1, BCA.

46 Copland to Pemberton, enclosed in Pemberton to Copland, 19 Sept. 1859, Correspondence Outward, Department of Land and Works, CAA30.7J1, BCA.

47 See also Pemberton to Copland, 19 September and 8 December 1859, Correspondence Outward, Department of Land and Works, BCA.

48 Pemberton to Douglas, 12 December 1859, Correspondence Outward, Department of Land and Works, BCA. In this letter Pemberton outlines an early version of the pre-emption system that is to pertain to Vancouver Island and give pre-emptive rights to single men for 100 acres of land and 200 acres to married men.

49 Hendrickson, *Journals of the Colonial Legislatures*, 1 March 1860.

50 Cail, *Land, Man and the Law*, 15. Flucke also notes this discrepancy, but provides no explanation, "Early Days on Saltspring Island," 170–3.

51 Harris, *Making Native Space*, 36.

52 The Douglas System is outlined by Tennant, *Aboriginal Peoples and Politics*, 26–38, and by Harris, *Making Native Space*, 17–44. Hendrickson, *Journals of the Colonial Legislatures*, 21 January 1864, quoted in Harris, *Making Native Space*, 35.

53 Hendrickson, *Journals of the Colonial Legislatures*, 1 March 1860; Tennant, *Aboriginal Peoples and Politics*, 21.

54 "The Pre-emption Ordinance," 1866; "An Ordinance to Amend and Consolidate the Laws Affecting Crown Lands in British Columbia," 1 June 1870. For detailed discussions, and differing views about the problems that Aboriginal land claims caused early settlers, see Stadfeld, "Manifestations of Power," and Lutz, "Relating to the Country," both in Sandwell, ed., *Beyond the City Limits*, 1–46.

55 Hendrickson, *Journals of the Colonial Legislatures*, 4 October 1859.

56 Flucke, "Early Days on Saltspring Island," 171–72; See also British Columbia, Attorney General; file 96/72, GR 419, BCA for copies of the documents on this incident, preserved in the file of W.K. Brown, whose 1859 claim was tied up in a dispute stemming from this altercation.

57 *New Westminster Times*, 24 September 1859.

58 Henry Sampson, George Sampson, George Mills, James McFadden, and Edward Walker were among Begg's Settlement settlers who had worked with the Hudson's Bay Company. Family Files, SSIA.

59 Hills, Diaries, 11 September 1860.

60 Hills, Diaries, 11 September 1860.

61 As W.K. Brown noted in a letter to the colonial surveyor in March 1860, "After arriving on the said land, I immediately with the others went to work making a main road several miles long on the Island." file 96/72, British Columbia Attorney General, GR 419, BCA. Louis Stark wrote complaining that a number of complications arose around the construction of a road near his property, when other settlers created a detour leading directly to a neighbour's barn, and away from Stark's property. Stark to Trutch, 22 November 1870, British Columbia Surveyor General, Correspondence Inward from Louis Stark, 1869,1870, C/G/30.71k/s+2, BCA.

62 *New Westminster Times*, 10 December 1859.

63 *Daily Press* (Victoria), 23 April 1861.

64 Joseph Trutch to Governor Frederick Seymour, 12 August 1868, File 953, Correspondence of the Department of Land and Works, BCA, 9–17.

65 African-Americans, Natives (before 1866), and Hawaiians were able to pre-empt lands, as long as they swore an oath of allegiance to the British crown, whereas Chinese were not.

66 Cail, *Land, Man and the Law*, 15.

67 Cail, *Land, Man and the Law*, 17–18.

68 Cail, *Land, Man and the Law*, 30–2.

69 Cail, *Land, Man and the Law*, 33.

70 There is no indication on Saltspring that lands acquired after these dates were being classified in this way in practice. See Cail, *Land, Man and the Law*, chapter 3, for a closer look at these pieces of legislation.

71 *Victoria Gazette*, 30 July 1859.

72 For personalized views of the appeal of this agricultural ideal, see Mackie, *The Wilderness Profound*, and Ormsby, ed., *A Pioneer Gentlewoman in British Columbia*.

73 *Weekly British Colonist*, 12 May 1860.

74 *Weekly British Colonist*, 14 January 1860. Richard White argues that failure of governments to recognize the sustainability of logging or other non-agricultural land practices had severe environmental and social consequences; he maintains that "at the root of these land problems [in the American West] was the supposition that agriculture was the highest use for all lands." White, *It's Your Misfortune and None of My Own*, 148.

75 Hendrickson, ed., *Journals of the Colonial Legislatures*, vol. V, appendix A, "Confederation Debates," 470.

76 Marshall, "An Early Rural Revolt." *Beyond the City Limits*, 47–61.

77 *British Columbia as a Field for Emigration and Investment*, 15.

78 *Handbook of British Columbia*, 3.

79 *Handbook of British Columbia*, 4–5.

80 *Province of British Columbia, Canada: Its Climate and Resources*, 82.

81 See for example *British Columbia as a Field for Emigration and Investment*; and the First Report of the Department of Agriculture of the Province of British Columbia, 1891, *British Columbia Sessional Papers* (hereafter BCSP), 1892, 733.

82 Sandwell, "The Limits of Liberalism."

83 *Province of British Columbia, Canada: Its Climate and Resources*, 101.

84 Wilson, *Salt Spring Island, 1895*, 11.

85 Phillips, *Salt Spring Island, 1902*. For the significance of British middle-class immigrants to British Columbia, see Barman, *Growing up British in British Columbia*; Koroscil, "Resettlement in Canada's British Garden of Eden"; and Bennett, "The True Elixir of Life."

86 These ideas are explored in Meek, *Social Science and the Ignoble Savage*.

87 Cruikshank, "The Invention of Anthropology"; see also Pratt, *Imperial Eyes*; and Anderson, *Vancouver's Chinatown*.

88 Perry, *On the Edge of Empire*, 3.

89 Mallandaine, *First Victoria Directory*, 15. For a discussion of this point, see Fisher, *Contact and Conflict*, 104–5; and Cruikshank "Invention of Anthropology," 29.

90 R. Cole Harris and Robert Galois have argued that the 1881 census both reflected and helped to construct historically specific categories of social and political understanding. From this perspective, the census of 1881 provides a view of how "the human geography of the Strait of Georgia had been remade in approximately European terms. It had become a place of towns, 'pioneer' countrysides, and industrial work camps, all broadly controlled by the infrastructure of the state and the cultural assumptions of its English-speaking inhabitants." Galois and Harris, "Recalibrating Society." See also Lutz, "Relating to the Country."

91 Harris, *Making Native Space*, 48.

92 Lutz's research indicates that capitalist domestic manufacturing existed along with resource extractive industries in the nineteenth century. John Lutz, "Losing Steam."

93 Clarkson, "Property Law and Family Regulation." For a fuller discussion of these issues, see Clarkson, "Liberalism, Nation Building and Family Regulation."

94 For a review of the extra-capitalist position accorded to the family farm in the North American discourse of rural, see Sandwell, "Rural Reconstruction," 15–19.

95 Adele Perry, "I'm Just Sick of the Faces of Men."

96 Clarkson, "Property Law and Family Regulation," 391.

97 Clarkson, "Property Law and Family Regulation," 391–2.

98 Clarkson, "Property Law and Family Regulation," 392.

99 Cail, *Land, Man and the Law*, xi.

100 Zeller, *Inventing Canada*, explores the ways in which the zeal for scientific information influenced nineteenth-century Canada. Zeller does not, unfortunately, mention British Columbia in her otherwise excellent book.

101 Fourth Report of the Department of Agriculture, British Columbia, 1894 (BCSP, 1895), 1009.

102 In the 1894 report the author quotes the rave reviews that published excerpts from the Report of Agriculture are finding in the immigration literature: "This useful report should be in the hands of everyone who contemplates settling in British Columbia, as it contains a vast amount of detailed and reliable information on the nature of the soil, stock raising, sheep farming, agriculture and fruit growing in the several districts of the Province." Fourth Report of the Department of Agriculture, British Columbia, 1894 (BCSP, 1895), 828.

103 First Report of the Department of Agriculture, British Columbia, 1891 (BCSP, 1892), 734.

104 As Joan Scott has argued, "statistical reports are neither totally neutral collections of fact, nor simply ideological impositions. Rather they are ways of establishing the authority of certain visions of social order, of organizing perceptions of experience." Scott, "The Statistical Representation of Work," 115.

105 See, for example, Wilson and Stortz, "May the Lord Have Mercy on You," Carlisle, "Early Agricultural Education in British Columbia"; Jones, "The Zeitgeist of Western Settlement," 71–89; Wells, "Making Health Contagious"; and Koroscil, "Soldiers, Settlement and Development in British Columbia, 1915–1930," stresses the perceived benefits of rural life in solving the problems of soldiers returning after the Great War.

106 *Agriculture of British Columbia, Canada, Bulletin No. 8,* 13.

107 Laing, "Colonial Farm Settlers on the Mainland of British Columbia, 1859–1871," documents the registering of 3,000 pre-emptions on the mainland before 1872. The total population of whites (Asians and Natives were prohibited from pre-empting land) in 1871 was 8,576. Barman, *The West Beyond the West,* Table 5, 363.

108 See Cail, *Land, Man and the Law,* appendix B, table 1. A total of 33,784 pre-emptions were listed between 1873 and 1913.

109 MacPherson, "Creating Stability in a Marginal Industry," 5.

110 The number of farms in British Columbia increased from 2,743 in 1881 to 26,079 in 1931. *Census of Canada, 1931,* vol. 8, table 1.

111 *Daily Province* (Vancouver), 15 July 1927, 6.

CHAPTER TWO

1 Begg to William and Margaret Chisholm, March 1860, SSIA.

2 Begg to William and Margaret Chisholm, 28 November 1862, SSIA.

3 For a detailed examination of the narrative of settlement in the American West, see Kerwin Klein, *Frontiers of Historical Imagination.*

4 For an excellent overview and comprehensive synthesis of the North American literature see Bouchard, "Family Reproduction in New Rural Areas."

5 Begg to William and Margaret Chisholm, 28 November 1862, SSIA.

6 *Daily Press* (Victoria), 11 November 1861.

7 *New Westminster Times,* 24 September 1859.

8 Ibid.

9 *New Westminster Times,* 23 December 1859.

10 *New Westminster Times,* 10 December 1859; *New Westminster Times,* 23 December 1859.

11 Henry Sampson, George Sampson, George Mills, James McFadden, and Edward Walker were among Begg's Settlement settlers who had worked with the Hudson's Bay Company. Family Files, SSIA.

12 Hills, Diaries, 6 September 1860.

13 *Daily Press* (Victoria), 23 April 1861.

14 *British Colonist*, 8 May 1860.

15 Begg to William and Margaret Chisholm, 23 November 1862, SSIA.

16 Personal correspondence with Bruce Watson, whom I thank for sharing with me his encyclopedic research into Hudson's Bay Company men.

17 Henry Sampson and George Baker to Colonial Surveyor, 11 January 1862, contained in Sampson file, Vancouver Island Colonial Surveyor; Office of the Land Recorder for Saltspring Island, Copy of the Pre-Emption Register to 17 October 1862; CAA/30.71/Sa3.1, BCA.

18 *British Colonist*, 7 June 1864, 3.

19 Mallandaine, *Guide to the Province of British Columbia for 1877–78*, 27.

20 *British Colonist*, 9 March 1865.

21 Chapter 8 explores the geography of settlement by ethnicity.

22 For a history of this migration, see Kilian, *Go Do Some Great Thing*, especially chapters 1–4; and Pilton, "Salt Spring Island." In chapter 6 I look at the role of ethnicity on Saltspring Island in detail.

23 *Daily Press* (Victoria), 25 July 1861.

24 Robson, Diaries, 13 October 1861, BCA.

25 Louis Stark, Pre-emption No. 1492, 16 March 1874. British Columbia Department of Land and Works, Pre-Emption Records, Vancouver and Gulf Islands, GR 766, BCA. For a detailed look at the murders, see chapter 8. Tennant, *Aboriginal People and Politics*, 21–5.

26 John Craven Jones, Pre-emption, 1861 (no number); Improvement Certificate No. 154, 2 January 1872, British Columbia Department of Land and Works, Pre-Emption Records, Vancouver and Gulf Islands, GR 765, BCA.

27 To Colonial Secretary from Fred Lester, May 1874, file F988-1, GR 1372, BCA; Superintendent's Report on Saltspring Island, First Annual Report on the Public Schools of British Columbia, for the year ending 31 July 1872, *British Columbia Sessional Papers*, 1872.

28 *Daily Chronicle* (Victoria), 28 February 1866.

29 Between 1859 and 1866, 247 pre-emptions were taken out on the island in total, and 214 or 87 per cent of these were abandoned. Of the 247 pre-emptions, 127 pre-emptors left no other evidence that they had any connection with the island and probably never took up their land.

30 *Daily Chronicle* (Victoria), 28 February 1866.

31 Green, Diary, BCA.

32 Of the forty-two people taking up land in the south end between 1859 and 1881, sixteen left after a year or less on the island, four left after two to five years, and twenty-two stayed longer than ten years. At the north end of the

island, by contrast, forty-two of the ninety-six people pre-empting lands left after a year or less on the island, eighteen stayed for two to five years, nine stayed for six to ten years, and twenty-seven stayed for more than ten years.

33 Fewer south Saltspring Island families had children (seventeen of thirty-nine) than north-end families (twenty out of thirty-two), but they had a greater number, on average: 4.5 per household as opposed to 2.8 for north-end families. It is difficult to assess why this would be so. The average age of the household heads in the north end was slightly higher (47.8 for north-end households, 45.9 for south-end), and north-end household heads had been on the island longer by the time census data is available in 1881: an average of 10.3 years as opposed to 7.3 years for south-end household heads. Both of these factors would suggest higher birth rates at the north-end. Cultural factors may be responsible; south-end families included more Hawaiians and Native women, who tended to have larger families than British women.

34 See Gyves family file, SSIA. For a detailed popular history of the San Juan boundary dispute and the Pig War, see Richardson, *Pig War Islands*.

35 Pre-emption no. 908, British Columbia Department of Land and Works, Pre-Emption Records, Vancouver and Gulf Islands, GR 766, BCA. Gyves took eighteen years to obtain the certificate of improvement, obtaining it in 1884, and purchasing the land from the crown the following year.

36 Norcross, *The Warm Land*, 116–17; *British Colonist*, 27 March 1867.

37 Green, Diary, 29 August 1874, BCA.

38 Blair, Diary, 1862, 124, BCA.

39 Ovanin, *Island Heritage Buildings*, 86.

40 Pedlow, *Ruckle Provincial Park*.

41 Hamilton, *Salt Spring Island*, 43, 93, 94, 96–7. See also entry under Ruckle, in Claydon and Melanson, eds and comps, *Vancouver Voters, 1886*, 619–20; and Pedlow, *Ruckle Provincial Park*.

42 Koppel, "Little Hawaii," in *Kanaka: The Untold Story*, 105–14.

43 Green, Diary, BCA.

44 University of Toronto, *Dictionary of Canadian Biography*, vol. XIII, 761–2.

45 Akerman Family File, SSIA; Joseph Akerman, Pre-emption no. 494, 1863, British Columbia Department of Land and Works, Pre-emption Records, Vancouver and Gulf Islands, GR 766, BCA; Toynbee, S*napshots of Early Saltspring*, 43.

46 Russell, "Emily Township"; and Little, *Crofters and Habitants*, 134–55.

47 Walbran, *British Columbia Place Names*, 520– 1.

48 "Edward Mallandaine's Reminiscences," BCA, 91.

49 For information on the stone quarry, see *New Westminster Times*, 3 March 1860; *Daily Press* (Victoria), 23 November 1861; *British Colonist*, 13 September 1885, *British Colonist*, 25 March 1863, 16 April 1863; *Chronicle*,

26 February 1866. On the *Industry*'s role in carrying wood, see *British Colonist*, 8 September 1863.

50 William Isaacs, Saltspring Island Correspondence and By-Laws, 1871–1882, B.C. Provincial Secretary's Correspondence, box 1, file 2; GR 1707, BCA.

51 *Saltspring Island Parish and Home*, February 1896.

52 British Columbia Department of Finance, Surveyor of Taxes, 1892, Assessment Roll B 443, Gulf Islands Assessment District, BCA.

53 Gyves family file, SSIA.

54 Trage, "Vertical File," reel 144, frame 0036, BCA.

55 Hills, Diaries, 11 September 1860.

56 See Drushka, *Working in the Woods*; Morton, *The Enterprising Mr. Moody*; and Lamb, "Early Lumbering on Vancouver Island." On Saltspring Island itself, The Reverend Wilson, for example, does not mention logging as an industry on the island in his 1895 pamphlet, nor are trees mentioned as anything but a nuisance in Department of Agriculture reports of the nineteenth century. Wilson, *Salt Spring Island, 1895*, SSIA.

57 *Daily Press* (Victoria), 11 November 1861. The same theme is forwarded in the *Colonist*, 13 September 1885.

58 It was not until the late 1870s that a longer-headed, double-bitted axe was developed in Seattle. The cross-cut saw, used in Europe since the fifteenth century, was not used on the coast, and the two-man cross-cut saw specially developed for harvesting the trees of the Pacific Northwest was not in common use until the 1880s. Drushka, *Working in the Woods*, 32–3.

59 Elliott, *Mayne Island and the Gulf Islands*, 5. Charlie Horel and Johnny Bennett talk about these methods of land clearing. Interviews, 1990, SSIA.

60 Walters, *Early Days Among the Gulf Islands*, 16.

61 Hills, Diaries, 6 September 1860.

62 Blair, Diary, 1862, 124, BCA.

63 Begg to William and Mary Chisholm, 16 July 1860, SSIA.

64 Data is difficult to obtain about this aspect of island life. Some documentation suggests that these items were commonly purchased. See Pedlow, *Ruckle Park*, 127, for evidence from a later period (1900–14).

65 On 15 April 1861, for example, the *British Colonist* reported that the island was thriving and "will be enabled to supply our market with considerable produce throughout the coming season"; nevertheless "great complaint is made of the want of proper communication with Nanaimo, a week sometimes elapsing without communication being had with the latter place." In 1862, Begg speculated that the loss of a third of the Saltspring Island population after the unusually cold winter of 1862 was probably "owing to the Government providing no mail communication." *British Colonist*, 5 May 1862.

66 *British Colonist*, 9 March 1865.

67 Fred Foord and Thos. H. Williams to Mr Roscoe, 24 March 1877, Divisional Inspectors' Reports, National Post Office of Canada, British

Columbia, 1877–1880, RG3, Series 6, vol. 2, Reel c7225, file no. 304, National Archives of Canada (hereafter NAC).

68 William Smithe, Minister of Agriculture, to Post Master General, Ottawa, 17 July 1877, Divisional Inspectors' Reports, National Post Office of Canada, reel c7227, file 304, NAC.

69 Begg to William and Mary Chisholm, 3 June 1860, SSIA.

70 *Daily Press* (Victoria), 10 November 1861.

71 Hills, Diaries, 6 September 1861.

72 Barman, *The West Beyond the West*; and McDonald, *Making Vancouver.*

73 Flucke, "Early Days on Saltspring Island," 163.

74 A total of 388 pre-emptions were taken out from 1860 to 1891, 47.6 per cent of which were taken out between 1882 and 1891. In this last decade under study, 24,204 of the total 50,442 acres pre-empted were taken up; 34 per cent (17,175 acres) were pre-empted from 1884 to 1888.

75 8,954 acres of pre-empted land was purchased from 1882 to 1891, by sixty-two pre-emptors. Before 1882, fifteen people purchased pre emptions of 2,286 acres.

76 778 acres were purchased outright between 1876 and 1881; none before that time. Between 1882 and 1891, 15,465 acres of land were purchased outright.

77 Figures from 1881 and 1891 come from a cross-linkage of land records with the 1881 nominal census, and from 1891 from the Assessment Roll of 1892 for Saltspring Island. Aggregate information from the assessment roll indicates that by 1891 37,784 acres of land was under some form of ownership, whether pre-empted or purchased. Census of Canada, 1881, District no. 191, Vancouver, Cowichan and Saltspring Island, Schedule no. 1 – Nominal; Census of Canada, 1891, District no. 3, Vancouver, M2 – S.D. 14, Saltspring Island, Schedule no. 1 – Nominal; British Columbia Department of Finance, Surveyor of Taxes, 1892, Assessment Roll B 443, Gulf Islands Assessment District, BCA.

78 Correspondence from Acting Superintendent to Divisional Inspector, 16 February 1884, Divisional Inspectors' Reports, National Post Office of (Canada), British Columbia 1882–1884, RG3, Series 6, vol. 4, Reel 7226, no. 13, NAC.

79 See the example of the Cowichan Valley in Norcross, *The Warm Land*; and Wright, "A Study of the Social and Economic Development of the District of North Cowichan."

80 Begg to William and Margaret Chisholm, 3 June 1860, SSIA.

81 First Report of the Department of Agriculture of the Province of British Columbia, 1891 (BCSP, 1892), 804.

82 See Department of Agriculture Reports, 1891 (BCSP, 1892), 804–6; 1892 (BCSP, 1893), 866–70; 1894 (BCSP, 1895), 1017–20; and statistical returns for the island in 1895–96 Report (BCSP, 1897), 1137–47.

83 Second Report of The Department of Agriculture of the Province of British Columbia, 1892 (BCSP, 1893), 866.

84 Williams, *British Columbia Directory*, 187.

85 The figures are 13,739 apple trees, 1,161 pear trees, 1,689 plum and prune trees, 474 cherry trees, and 279 other fruit trees; "Recapitulation of General Returns from Vancouver Island and Adjacent Islands," Fourth Report of the Department of Agriculture of the Province of British Columbia, 1894 (BCSP, 1895). 1050–51.

86 Report on Agriculture, 1891 (BCSP, 1892), 805.

87 Fifth Report of the Department of Agriculture for the Province of British Columbia, 1895–96 (BCSP, 1896), 1072.

88 See Stratton, "Agriculture: Farms, Farmers and Farming." See also Cartwright, *A Late Summer*, especially 13–15; and Wilson, *Salt Spring Island, 1895*.

89 Source: *Fourth Dominion Census of Canada 1891*, Table XVI, 244; and Table II, 8.

90 *British Colonist*, 13 September 1885; *Henderson's British Columbia Gazetteer and Directory* (1889), 275, 276, 348.

91 Topping, "Research Report," SSIA. For a discussion on the importance of the money-order business, see, for example, Fletcher to National Post Office, June 1887, file 723, and August 1887, file 768. Divisional Inspectors' Reports, National Post Office of Canada, source RG3, reel C7227, NAC.

92 Mr Fletcher to Post Master General, 20 May 1887, Post Office Inspectors' Reports, British Columbia, 1886–87, RG3, series 6, vol. 8, reel C7227, file no. 696, NAC.

93 Aitken, Diary, 16 February 1892, SSIA.

94 Aitken, Diary, 1891, SSIA.

95 See, for example, Hamilton, *Saltspring Island*; Flucke "Early Days on Saltspring Island"; and especially Wilson, *Salt Spring Island, 1895*.

96 All the men, but only two women over fifteen listed occupations. Nine of the men were listed as farmers' sons, and one was listed as a farmer and storekeeper. Census of Canada, 1881, District no. 191, Vancouver, Cowichan and Saltspring Island, Schedule no. 1 – Nominal.

97 Census of Canada, 1891, District no. 3, Vancouver, M2 – S.D. 14, Saltspring Island, Schedule no. 1 – Nominal.

CHAPTER THREE

1 In 1881, husbands were on average about nine years older than their wives, but fifteen (almost a third) of the forty-six married couples had an age gap of more than fifteen years. By 1891 the average husband-wife difference had fallen to eight years, and fewer than one in five marriages (eleven out of sixty-two) had an age gap of more than fifteen years.

2 Lots 8 and 9, Land Register, Saltspring Island.

3 British Columbia Department of Finance, Surveyor of Taxes, 1892 Assessment Roll, Roll B 443, Gulf Islands Assessment District, SSIA.

4 Twelfth Annual Report on The Public Schools of the Province of British Columbia, 1882–83, BC Sessional Papers, 1883; and Thirteenth Annual Report on The Public Schools of the Province of British Columbia, 1883–84, BC Sessional Papers, 1884.

5 File 158, British Columbia, Supreme Court, (Victoria), Probates 1859–4974; GR 1304, BCA.

6 The land registers for Saltspring Island, which detail land transactions before the granting of land title, are located in the Surveyor General's Office. Most of the pre-emption records are contained in British Columbia Department of Land and Works, Pre-Emption Records, Vancouver and Gulf Islands, GR 0766; and British Columbia Department of Land and Works, Certificates of Improvement, Vancouver Island and the Gulf Islands, GR 765, BCA. The land registers for North and South Saltspring Island, which list properties up to and including purchase from the crown, are housed at the Surveyor General's Office in Victoria. The Land Office in Victoria contains the records of land dealings after the issuing of the crown grant, but these were not used in this study. Information was also gleaned from Census of Canada, 1881, District no. 191, Vancouver, Cowichan, and Saltspring Island, Schedule no. 1 – Nominal; Census of Canada, 1891, District no. 3, Vancouver, M2 – S.D. 14, Saltspring Island, Schedule no. 1 – Nominal; and British Columbia Department of Finance, Surveyor of Taxes, 1892–4 Assessment Roll, Roll B 443, Gulf Islands Assessment District, BCA.

7 Cail, *Land, Man and the Law*, and, more recently, Tennant's *Aboriginal Peoples and Politics*, are the only two book-length studies of land in British Columbia. Both of these historians have largely limited their discussion of land to policy development rather than the practices of land acquisition and use.

8 I would like to thank Keith Ralston for explaining the theory behind the inaccessibility of land records in British Columbia, and the Land Titles Office for demonstrating it in practice.

9 Between 1859 and 1870, 271 pre-emption claims were taken out on Saltspring Island, encompassing 14,260 acres of land. Only fifteen of these claims (5.5 per cent) were ever purchased by the pre-emptors. (2,296 acres, or 16 per cent of the pre-empted land). From 1871 to 1891 a further 269 pre-emption claims were registered, covering 34,931 acres, of which 110 claims (41 per cent) with 14,933 acres (43 per cent of the land) were eventually purchased. Between 1876 and 1891, a further 16,243 acres were purchased outright, with no pre-emptions; the vast majority of these purchases were made by three individuals between 1884 and 1886. Out of 541 pieces of land pre-empted between 1859 and 1891, 224, or 42 per cent were pre-empted more than once. Of these, 143, or almost two-thirds (64 per cent) were pre-empted three or more times.

10 Registers for Saltspring Island are reliable from 1871 onward, providing a comprehensive source that is well supplemented by a variety of pre-emption records.

11 These records include landownership documents relating specifically to transactions such as pre-emptions, transfers, and land purchases (690 records), and other information directly concerning their relation with the land, such as leaves of absence from pre-emption claims, witnesses to land transactions, and secondary legal matters (593 records). Business directories (464 listings) and voters' lists (683 listings) were not, in theory, limited to listing landowners, but in practice this group overwhelmingly dominated both lists. Any person of substance (including most landowners) appeared in business directories, but inclusion in the voters' lists was more formalized; voters did not have to own property, as an educational provision allowed people with a university education to vote in addition to property owners. In practice, comparisons of voters' lists and directories show considerable similarities: for example, in 1882 the voters' list contained sixty-six names and the directory of the same year contained fifty-nine; forty-five of these names were the same. The database linking the 1881 manuscript census to landownership documents indicates that of the fifty-five landowners on the island in 1881, forty-seven had lived there for more than a year.

12 Between 1882 and 1891 pre-emptions included 23,526 acres and outright purchases included 15,838 acres, or 40 per cent of all the land acquired. 8,601 acres were taken up by three individuals, Robert Holburn, William Robertson, and Edward Musgrave, in 1885 and 1886. Two of these were absentee landowners, and the third, Musgrave, stayed on the island for only two years. Altogether, thirty-three people purchased land outright on the land in the years under study.

13 See "Mr. Morley's Old Book, Land Records and List of Squatters," British Columbia Department of Land and Works, GR 514, BCA, which contains listings of thirty-nine Saltspring pre-emptions from the colonial period.

14 The 387 pre-emption claims between 1860 and 1891 were taken out by only 271 individuals. As the table below suggests, the proportion of first claims taken out by individuals arriving on the island declined as the years passed.

	% of First Pre-emptions	% of Subsequent Pre-emptions	Average Acres in First Pre-emptions	Average Acres in Subsequent Pre-Emptions
1860–70	80	20	148	120
1871–81	77	23	143	125
1882–91	61	39	139	124

In the first decade of settlement, 80 per cent of claims were first claims by individuals. By the 1880s almost a third of claims were taken out by people who already held pre-emptions. At the same time that first pre-emptions were declining in size, therefore, the proportion of subsequent claims was increasing slightly, a factor that contributed to the declining average acreages pre-empted over the first thirty years of settlement. See chapter 5 for more details about patterns of land acquisition and abandonment.

15 Many of those taking up pre-emptions abandoned them before taking up additional lands. Cross-linkages with the assessment roll, available for the first time in 1891, indicate that, of those landowners arriving on the island before 1871, more than half (54 per cent) owned more than 200 acres; of those arriving between 1871 and 1881, 45 per cent owned more than 200 acres; of those arriving after 1882, only 27 per cent owned more than 200 acres. British Columbia Department of Finance, Surveyor of Taxes, 1892 Assessment Roll, Roll B 443, Gulf Islands Assessment District, BCA.

16 Joseph Trutch to the Colonial Secretary, 12 August 1868, file 953, 4, Department of Land and Works, Colonial Correspondence, BCA. See also Cail, *Land, Man and the Law*, 15.

17 Memorandum, no date, Estalon Jose Bittancourt's 1874 pre-emption, no. 1485, and Daniel Fredison, who pre-empted sections 5 and 6, range 4 east in 1881. British Columbia Department of Land and Works, Pre-Emption Records, Vancouver and Gulf Islands, GR 766, BCA. In 1888 the land register for the neighbouring property, section 7, range 5 east, notes that Fredison "was allowed to purchase the above 2 acres, to include his improvements placed on them."

18 For example, see listings for T. Edwin Johnson and Robert Layzell, Island Colonial Surveyor; Office of the Land Recorder for Saltspring Island, Copy of the Pre-Emption Register to Oct. 17, 1862, CAA/30.71/sa3.1, BCA; Henry Sampson, Pre-emption no. 760, October 1864; Manuel Bittancourt, Pre-emption no. 918; William Meiss, Pre-emption no. 104; George Booth (no number) 1868; William Smith, no. 408; Louis Stark (no number), 1871; David Overton, no. 651; Jacob Crane (no number), 1871. British Columbia Department of Land and Works, Pre-Emption Records, Vancouver and Gulf Islands, GR 765, BCA and Saltspring Island Database. Clerical error seems to be the case in lands pre-empted by John C. Jones in 1860. Both David Overton and John Moore are listed in some records as pre-empting the same land that Jones was occupying, and in other records their addresses are different. Robert Layzell and T. Edwin Johnson are similarly listed with the same address, but records provide no indication that these conflicting claims ever created serious problems, and the historian can assume that these were clerical errors. See John C. Jones's pre-emption, 1860, Saltspring Island database, for an overview of the confusion about this claim, and also John Moore, Vancouver Island Colonial Surveyor; Office of the Land Recorder for Saltspring Island, Copy of the Pre-Emption Register to 17 October 1862. This contrasts with his address given in the *British Colonist*, May 1861, which is that of John C. Jones. Just to make things more complicated, Moore writes to the Surveyor General in 1861 to complain that both his

name and his address have been recorded inaccurately, see "Vancouver Island Colonial Surveyor, Correspondence and Papers re Settlers on Saltspring Is, 1859, '61, '62, '66", CAA/30.71/Sa3.1, BCA.

19 Report of the Chief Commissioner of Lands and Works of the Province of British Columbia for 1 December 1873 to 31 December 1874 (BCSP, 1875), 148–9.

20 See, for example, Fry, "Field Notes"; and Aldous, "Regarding the S.E. Quarter of Section 52." Many pieces of island property were missed by Green in the first comprehensive survey of the island and, although the government required surveys before purchase, island residents were slow to pay for and hence survey their claims.

21 See chapter 3 for more details on Maxwell's farming endeavours. See also Hamilton, *Salt Spring Island*, 51.

22 Enclosed in Pre-emption no. 84, John Maxwell, British Columbia Department of Land and Works, Pre-Emption Records, Vancouver and Gulf Islands, GR 766, BCA.

23 Pre-emption no. 84, British Columbia Department of Land and Works, Pre-Emption Records, Vancouver and Gulf Islands, GR 766, BCA.

24 That is, Michael Gyves and James Lunney, Certificate 244, British Columbia Department of Land and Works, Certificates of Improvement, Vancouver Island and the Gulf Islands, GR 765, BCA.

25 The recording of pre-emption improvements became sloppier in the 1880s and 1890s, with many land records listing only the pre-emption date and the date of the crown grant. In these cases, in the Saltspring Island database, the purchase date and improvement date are listed as being the same, in lieu of evidence to the contrary. The data may be exaggerating the reduced time between improvement and purchase in these years.

26 For those taking out pre-emptions between 1860 and 1870, the average length of time between pre-emption and purchase was 18.7 years; this decreased to 8.6 years for those pre-empting lands between 1871 and 1881; and 8.2 years for those pre-empting land between 1882 and 1891.

27 Sparrow is mentioned in Blair, Diary, 1862.

28 John C. Sparrow, Certificate of Improvement no. 56, 1866, British Columbia Department of Land and Works. Certificates of Improvement, Vancouver Island and the Gulf Islands, GR 765, BCA. After 1871 applications for certificates of improvement, like pre-emption applications, became more standardized. Certificates of improvement contained less information as time went on. The disorganized holdings of these certificates by BCA in GR 765 trail off after the colonial period, although they continue to be recorded in the land register for Saltspring. Only sixteen of the ninety-one certificates of improvement issued on Saltspring before 1887 provide details of improvements. Witnesses had to be "bona fide settlers," and were almost always residents of neighbouring claims. The names that appear on these various signed docu-

ments have been an important supplement to pre-emption records in establishing who lived in what part of the island and for how long, particularly in the early years of settlement when other sources are scarce.

29 Between 1860 and 1891, 271 people took out pre-emption claims. One hundred and ninety-nine took out one claim, forty-nine took out two claims, seventeen took out three claims, and six others took out more than three claims. Those who took out more than one claim, not surprisingly, stayed longer, on average, than those who took out only one. The average length of stay on the island was 12.3 years for those who took out one claim, 21.9 for those taking out two, and 25.2 years for those taking out three.

30 Of the 171 pre-emptions taken out between 1859 and 1891 that were improved, 126 (73.7 per cent) were purchased and the remainder were traded or deserted.

31 Pre-emption no. 916; Vancouver Island Colonial Surveyor; Office of the Land Recorder for Salt Spring Island, Copy of the Pre-Emption Register to 17 October 1862, CAA/30.71/Sa3.1, BCA.

32 Saltspring Island Database, John Booth, especially under "census summary," 1881.

33 As Joseph Trutch argued in a letter to the Colonial Secretary, 12 August 1868, the "evil results" of selling land by auction could be observed around New Westminster and Victoria, where "large tracts of land purchased at auction for purely speculative purposes remain still in the same primitive condition as when they were sold – not a tree felled, not an acre ploughed up – totally unproductive to the owners and retarding the general progress of the Country." Trutch to Colonial Secretary, 12 August 1868, 8, file 953–4, Department of Land and Works, Colonial Correspondence, GR 1440, BCA.

34 Correspondence of the Land and Works Department, file 953–4, 7–9, Joseph Trutch to the Colonial Secretary, 12 August 1868, GR 1440, BCA. Trutch maintains that the occupation of the pre-emptor on his land is a positive requirement of the pre-emption system in the Vancouver Island colony, as distinguished from the mainland colony, where anyone can stand in for the pre-emptor by residing on the pre-empted land.

35 Correspondence of the Land and Works Department, file 953–4, 5. Joseph Trutch to the Colonial Secretary, 12 August 1868, GR 1440, BCA.

36 See, for example, Voisey, *Vulcan*; Dick, *Farmers Making Good*; and Parr, "Hired Men." For an overview of the importance of "off-farm work" to rural areas in Canada throughout the nineteenth and twentieth centuries, see Sandwell, "Rural Reconstruction," 13–15.

37 W.K. Brown to Pearse, 16 March 1860; file 96/72, British Columbia Attorney General, GR 419, BCA.

38 "Our client has no claim whatever to the land, as he failed to carry out his settlement duties and that the installment of 11.4.0 paid on the 16 April

1860 was forfeited to the crown." Correspondence from Chief Commissioner of Land and Works, 12 August 1896, file 96/72; British Columbia Attorney General, GR 419, BCA. The Land Proclamation of 1861 was quite clear about this: as section XX put it, "all deposits paid in respect of such forfeited claims, and all improvements, buildings and erection thereon shall ... be absolutely forfeited."

39 Letter from James Shaw, Vancouver Island Colonial Surveyor; Correspondence and Papers re Settlers on Saltspring Is., 1859, '61, '62, '66, BCA.

40 Correspondence re James Shaw, Vancouver Island Colonial Surveyor, Correspondence and Papers re Settlers on Saltspring Is., 1859, '61, '62, '66, BCA.

41 Francis wrote to Pearse in 1864, demanding that his land be returned to him. He accused the new pre-emptor of "jumping other people's improvements, his name having before appeared as a pre-emptor of land on Saltspring Island to which he had no right whatever, and it was certainly never the intention of the proclamation to encourage such practice and will never be sanctioned by you." In spite of this vague threat of legal action, Pearse did not relent and Francis lost the land. Francis to Pearse, 11 May 1864, Jacob Francis, Pre-emption no. 574, 1863, Pre-Emption Records, Vancouver and Gulf Islands, GR 766, BCA.

42 Mr Lineker twice left his land, and twice found that his claim had been "jumped" by another settler in the mid-1860s. Because he had followed proper procedures in registering his leave, Mr Lineker was able to evict the interlopers and get his land back. Vancouver Island Colonial Surveyor; Correspondence and Papers re Settlers on Saltspring Is., 1859, '61, '62, '66, and British Columbia Department of Land and Works, Pre-emption Records, Vancouver and Gulf Islands, Pre-emption no. 918, BCA.

43 Vancouver Island Land Proclamation, 1862. B.C. Statutes, 1873, 36 Vict., no. 1, quoted in Cail, *Land, Man and the Law*, 24. Recognizing the continued need of settlers to work outside their land, the 1873 Land Act Amendment allowed pre-emptors to be absent from their claims for up to six months each year, "provided the land be cultivated" up to the specified twenty acres. B.C. Statutes, 1873, 36 Vict., no. 1, quoted in Cail, *Land, Man and the Law*, 24. Unfortunately, records documenting leaves of absence, like records of paid employment, are far from complete, making it impossible to gauge the rhythms of off-island employment in these years. Thirty-three leaves of absence have been found for the island, most from the colonial period. Some documentation shows up as a notation in the margin of colonial and provincial pre-emption records, and a few letters requesting leaves are included in the pre-emption files. A few more notices appear scribbled under certain land descriptions in the land register for Saltspring: "Leave of absence 3 months, 3/12/84." The only single collection of the actual documentation to be found so far is filed, without any organization, amongst a miscellaneous collection entitled "Miners Certificates and Leaves of

Absence", British Columbia Department of Lands, "Misc. Mining Receipts and Leaves Of Absence," box 4, GR 1057, BCA.

44 Other claims resolved on the basis of residency were Francis Jacob, no. 574 1863; Manuel Antone, no. 918, 1866; Edward Mallandaine, no. 422, 1859; and Henry Sampson, no. 750, 1864; British Columbia Department of Land and Works, Pre-Emption Records, Vancouver and Gulf Islands, GR 766, BCA. See also Vancouver Island Colonial Surveyor, Correspondence and Papers re Settlers on Saltspring Is., 1859, '61, '62, '66, CAA/30.71/Sa3.1, BCA, for overview of conflicting claims.

45 The tendency of settlers to police the land-related behaviours of their neighbours was not always used to make way for legitimate landholding practices. Squatting – living on lands without gaining legal title to do so – is notoriously difficult to document, in large part because squatters are usually committed to avoiding the attention of anyone wanting to record their land-related activities. In only one case on the island during this time do I seriously suspect squatting. William Hutson, a forty-year-old Englishman first shows up on the island in 1864, signing a petition to the Surveyor General stating that Richard Brinn, neighbour and business partner of co-signer Henry Sampson, has not been residing on his pre-emption. Brinn was forced to give up his land, but rather strangely that land was not taken up again for almost 20 years. (Pre-emption #749, 1864, Richard Brinn, Saltspring Island Land Register). It seems likely that Hutson was squatting on this land until 1878, when he purchased a piece of neighbouring land outright.

46 Pre-emption records indicate that all but one of these had obtained their land, and hence their suffrage, by pre-emption. See List of Voters, 30 January 1862, District of Saltspring Island and Chemeynes; Poll Book of the Saltspring Is. and Chemainus District, 27 July 1863; List of Voters, 29 January 1866, District of Saltspring Island and Chemainus Sheriff's Office, GR 1666, BCA.

47 Voters' lists appeared in the British Columbia *Sessional Papers* in the year following each election.

48 Census takers in 1881 were instructed to include in their household listings everyone normally residing in their district, even if they were temporarily absent.

49 Other sources indicate that two of those missing from the 1881 census (Abraham Copeland and Alexander McLennan) were on the island around 1881, although the census taker did not record their presence. Of the remaining six, there is no record that one, Charles Hooper, ever owned land on Saltspring. Of the remaining five who appear on the voters' list but not on the census, three (Mills, Pimbury, Pollard) had obtained crown grants around 1881, and were not, therefore, absent from their pre-emption claims, although they may have been absentee landowners. Census of

Canada, 1881, District no. 191, Vancouver, Cowichan and Saltspring Island, Schedule no. 1 – Nominal.

50 While eight people who are not on the census show up on the voters' list, five who do not appear on the voters' list show on the census, in spite of evidence from land records indicating that they were in fact landowners in that year. The inadequacies in the printed records for the island underline the advantages of using a variety of sources in the database.

51 The information was gathered in 1891, and taxes imposed in 1892. Non-residents were listed as such in this year's listings. British Columbia Department of Finance, Surveyor of Taxes, 1892 Assessment Roll, Roll B 443, Gulf Islands Assessment District, BCA.

52 Twenty-two of these non-residents (three-quarters) had crown grants for their land, while a further seven were pre-emptors who did not. As analyses of household heads later in this chapter, in chapter 2 and in chapter 6, suggest, the great majority of those living on Saltspring Island for more than a year were landowners, and tenancy, when it occurred, seems to have been of short duration, at least for household heads.

53 Non-residency is difficult to trace. Thirty-seven were clearly identified as being non-residents through cross-linkages. A further 133 individuals only appeared in the island's records once, while staking their claim, indicating that they probably did not take up their land.

54 Of the 170 non-residents taking up land in the years before 1892, 95 per cent abandoned their claims without purchasing them and 86 per cent did so within a year of staking their claims. Residency was established by cross-linking all records about an individual to find an indication that they lived on the island. A number of people sometimes did and sometimes did not live there; only if there was no evidence of residency was someone declared a non-resident.

55 Of the 272 pre-emptors who took up land between 1860 and 1891, eighty-six stayed for a year or less, twenty-eight stayed from two to five years, twenty-three stayed from six to ten years, forty-five stayed for eleven to twenty years, and ninety stayed longer than twenty years. The average length of stay for all those who stayed for more than a year was 22.3 years; for all those who pre-empted land, it was 15.3 years.

56 The average stay for those first pre-empting land in 1860–1871 was 9.9 years; for 1872–1881, the figure is sixteen years; and for 1882–1891, it is 19.2 years.

57 Belshaw, *Colonization and Community*, 158–60.

58 Pre-emption no. 114, 1861, British Columbia Department of Land and Works, Pre-emption Records, Vancouver and Gulf Islands, GR 766, BCA.

59 Flucke provides a detailed account of Cusheon's misadventures with Saltspring land in "Early Days on Saltspring Island," 170–1.

60 See, for example, section 3, range 1 east and 1 west, Ganges, which was pre-empted six times between 1861 and 1888; section 8, range 1 east, Ganges was pre-empted at least eight times between 1860 and 1898; section 12, range 1 north, was pre-empted eight times between 1860 and 1879, and was finally purchased in 1891.

61 In 1881, 109 of 257 residents (42 per cent) were younger than fifteen; in 1891 171 of 436 (39 per cent) fell into this category.

62 In 1881 fifty-eight women and ninety men were fifteen and over; in 1891 ninety women and 175 men were fifteen and over; in 1881 forty-four out of seventy-one household heads were married and thirty-seven had children; in 1891 fifty-one out of ninety-four families had children and fifty-nine of ninety-four household heads were married.

63 In 1881, thirty-four (76 per cent) of the forty-five married men over seventeen years of age owned land, while only twelve (52 per cent) of the twenty-three single men did so. In 1891 fifty (74 per cent) of sixty-seven married men owned land, while only twenty-eight out of sixty, or 47 per cent, of single men did so. Thirty-nine out of forty-nine, or 80 per cent, of married men with children owned land in 1891, while 47 per cent of single men did so (twenty-eight of sixty). These figures are not intended to connote causality; as later chapters suggest, landownership correlated very closely with age, which in turn relates closely to both marital and landowning status.

64 In 1881 fifty-five (76 per cent) of seventy-one household heads were landowners, a figure that rises to seventy-five (80 per cent) of ninety-four in 1891. Of the island's 258 people, 201 lived on land owned by the household head in 1881; 347 out of 436 did so in 1891. Landownership, as we will see in greater detail in chapter 5, was a complex concept in the period under study: it included land that had been pre-empted but not improved; land that was improved but not yet purchased; and land for which a crown grant had been obtained.

CHAPTER FOUR

1 Land Register, Saltspring Island.

2 Flucke, "Early Days on Saltspring Island."

3 British Columbia Department of Finance, Surveyor of Taxes, 1892 Assessment Roll, Roll B 443, Gulf Islands Assessment District.

4 Wilson, *Salt Spring Island 1895*.

5 Only twenty-seven out of 124 landowners were taxed on their personal property. British Columbia Department of Finance, Surveyor of Taxes, 1892 Assessment Roll, Roll B 443, Gulf Islands Assessment District.

6 British Columbia, *Public Accounts for the half year ended 31 December, 1889*, Victoria: R. Wolfenden, 1890 and to 1899.

7 Mr Trage reported in 1891 that "Labour is very scarce; only white men are working here. Wages, $1 per day." First Report of the Department of Agriculture of the Province of British Columbia, 1891 (BCSP,1892), 805. In 1894 Trage reported that Japanese and whites were being employed at the same rate of $1 per day, but "they are not easily procured." Fourth Report of the Department of Agriculture of the Province of British Columbia, 1894 (BCSP, 1895), 1017.

8 Russell, "Emily Township."

9 Begg wrote that labourers' wages varied from $24 to $40 per month, and "a man and his wife can get $50 readily." Begg to William and Margaret Chisholm, 16 July 1866, SSIA.

10 Mr McLennan of Saltspring Island reported in 1891 that farmers were bothered by "a few rats and blue jays." First Report of the Department of Agriculture of the Province of British Columbia, 1891 (BCSP, 1892), 804.

11 British Columbia Royal Commission on Agriculture, 1912, testimony given at Ganges Harbour, 10 April 1912; box 1/4, GR324, BCA.

12 As F.M. Phillips notes in his overview of Saltspring Island in 1902, "The felling of timber ... is done in winter and the trees being left to dry through the summer, a fire is run over them in the fall; the logs that remain being cut up, piled and burnt, the land is then seeded down to grass or broken up for a first crop of potatoes." Phillips, *Salt Spring Island*, 8–9, SSIA. For a lengthy discussion of the problems of land clearances for farmers, see "Clearing Land" in the Fifth Report of the Department of Agriculture of the Province of British Columbia, 1895–96 (BCSP, 1897), 1156–67.

13 Fourth Report of the Department of Agriculture of the Province of British Columbia, 1894 (BCSP, 1895), 1017.

14 See particularly interview with Mary England, Charles Horel, 1990, SSIA.

15 "The people generally seemed to approve," he wrote, "thinking it would help to bring settlers to the island." Wilson, "Our Life on Saltspring Island, B.C.," unpublished manuscript, 151, SSIA.

16 Wilson, *Salt Spring Island 1895*, 11. This pamphlet was republished in 1994, and has sold briskly to the tourists flocking to Saltspring Island.

17 Wilson, *Salt Spring Island 1895*, 11.

18 A cross-linkage between the 1881 census and land records indicates that the average size of landholdings on the island was 166.9 acres, with more than half the landowners (thirty-two out of fifty-three) owning between one and two hundred acres. Twelve people owned under a hundred acres and three owned more than 300. With the railway boom in the mid-1880s, speculators became part of island life, and took up large tracts of mostly uninhabitable land. Greater disparities among settlers can be discerned: the 1892 assessment roll indicates, for example, that about a third of the island's landowners owned more than 300 acres and almost one in five lived on fewer than 100 acres; and the 1894 assessment roll indicates that three

landowners owned almost 30 per cent of the island. Census of Canada, 1881, District no. 191, Vancouver, Cowichan and Saltspring Island, Schedule no. 1 – Nominal; and Census of Canada, 1891, District no. 3, Vancouver, M2 – S.D. 14, Saltspring Island, Schedule no. 1 – Nominal; British Columbia Department of Finance, Surveyor of Taxes, Assessment Rolls 1892–94, Roll B 443, Gulf Islands Assessment District, BCA.

19 About a third of those appearing on both the assessment roll and the census (thirty-four people out of the ninety-six appearing on both lists) owned more than two hundred acres, and about two-thirds (sixty-two people) owned less, with most (thirty-seven people) owning between one hundred and two hundred acres. An examination of the assessment roll of 1892 (collected in 1891) cross-linked with other information in the Saltspring Island database and looking at all resident landowners, indicates that the ninety-six on the island in 1891 had been there an average of 12.2 years; 74 per cent for more than five years and 44 for longer than ten years. British Columbia Department of Finance, Surveyor of Taxes Assessment Roll for 1892, Gulf Islands Assessment District, Saltspring Division, Roll B 444, BCA; Census of Canada, 1891, District no. 3, Vancouver, M2 – S.D. 14, Saltspring Island, Schedule no. 1 – Nominal.

20 For example, Squire Henry Bullock, the Mahon brothers, the Tolson brothers – family files, SSIA.

21 Begg to William and Margaret Chisholm, 3 June 1860, SSIA.

22 For an overview of criticisms of new world farming practices, see Whitney, *From Coastal Wilderness to Fruited Plain*, 228–30.

23 Begg to William and Margaret Chisholm, 3 June 1860, SSIA.

24 Cited from a letter of an early Saltspring Island pioneer in Koppel, *Kanaka*, 107.

25 Province of British Columbia Public Schools Report, 1877 (BCSP, 1878), 19.

26 Henry W. Robinson, Chairman of the Trustee Board, Saltspring Island, to C.C. McKenzie, Superintendent of Education, Saltspring Island, 4 August 1879, in British Columbia Superintendent of Education, Inward Correspondence, GR 1445, BCA. Thanks to Jean Barman for drawing this source to my attention.

27 Green, "Diary," July 25, 28, 1874, BCA.

28 George Stainburn, teacher at Burgoyne Bay, to C.C. McKenzie, Superintendent of Education, Burgoyne Bay, 11 January 1882, in British Columbia Superintendent of Education, Inward Correspondence, GR 1445, BCA.

29 Stainburn to McKenzie, 11 January 1882, British Columbia Superintendent of Education, Inward Correspondence, GR 1445, BCA.

30 Stainburn to McKenzie, 11 January 1882, British Columbia Superintendent of Education, Inward Correspondence, GR 1445, BCA.

31 Inquest of George Purser's Death, file 18-1886, British Columbia Attorney General, Inquisitions, 1872–1937, GR 1327, BCA.

32 Stainburn to Mackenzie, 2 March 1882, in British Columbia Superintendent of Education, Inward Correspondence, GR 1445, BCA.

33 Evidence of Henry Sampson, trial of Tom for the murder of William Robinson, 2 June 1869; Vancouver Island, Supreme Court of Civil Justice, Bench
Books of Criminal Cases Heard Before Judge Joseph Needham, 1867–
1869, GR 2030, BCA.

34 William Robinson, probate file 13 (1868), British Columbia, Supreme
Court (Victoria), Probates 1859–1974, GR 1304, BCA.

35 Armstead Buckner, probate file 1902 (1889), British Columbia, Supreme
Court (Victoria), Probates 1859–1974, GR 1304, BCA.

36 Darroch and Soltow, *Property and Inequality in Victorian Ontario*, 4.

37 Stratton, "Agriculture: Farms, Farmers and Farming," typescript, SSIA.

38 Russell, "Emily Township," 317.

39 Environment Canada, *Saltspring Island: A Landscape Analysis*, 1.

40 Agriculture Canada, Research Branch, *Soils of the Gulf Islands of British
Columbia*, 103–5.

41 Green, "Diary," 18 June 1874, BCA.

42 Green, "Diary," 20 August 1874, BCA.

43 Green, "Diary," 24 August 1874, BCA.

44 Cail, *Land, Man and the Law*, xiii.

45 The 1873 Land Act Amendment was the first to specify that a set number
of acres (twenty) be cleared to obtain a certificate of improvement but, like
so many provisions, it was not enforced. See Cail, *Land Man and the Law*,
24, 29–30, 36–8.

46 Legislation requiring the identification of wildlands as distinguished from
agricultural lands emerged in the 1890s, affecting land taxation on
Saltspring Island after this date. See Cail, *Land, Man and the Law*, 35–8.
See also British Columbia Department of Finance, Surveyor of Taxes, Assessment Rolls 1892–94, Roll B 443, Gulf Islands Assessment District, BCA.

47 Fourth Report of the Department of Agriculture, 1894 (BCSP, 1895), 1018.
In 1894 an estimate of the total value of improvements (buildings, fences,
and other improvements) on the island was given as $77,710. Fourth Re-
port of the Department of Agriculture, 1894 (BCSP, 1894), 1019.

48 18,526 of the 49,192 acres had been improved.

49 For $13 per acre, see Michael Gyves, pre-emption no. 908; 1884; for those
closer to $50 per acre, see Theodore Trage, 1877 pre-emption no. 1066;
John Maxwell, 1875, no. 84; Ke-awe hou, no. 1082, n.d. British Columbia
Department of Land and Works, Pre-emption Records, Vancouver and Gulf
Islands, GR 766, BCA.

50 Russell suggests that most early settlers cleared between one and two acres,
although those on better lands cleared about three acres per farm per year.
Russell, "Forest into Farmland," 133, and Tables 1 and 2, 140.

51 John Maxwell, pre-emption number 84, 1861; Certificate of Improvement no. 244, British Columbia Department of Land and Works, Certificates of Improvement, Vancouver Island and the Gulf Islands, GR 765, BCA.

52 Green, "Diary," 15 July and 18 July 1875, BCA.

53 The probate file notes that his 100–acre claim was worth only $125. Mr Moss offered to purchase Buckner's land for $265 in October 1889. File 1902, British Columbia, Supreme Court (Victoria), Probates 1859–1974, GR 1304, BCA. *The Province of British Columbia, Canada: Its Climate and Resources, with Information for Immigrants* (1883) notes that unimproved, timbered land in Cowichan and Comox was selling for between $2.50 and $15 per acre. Buckner's land was finally auctioned off for $600, or $6 per acre, but not until after his creditors had lobbied for parliamentary intervention to speed up the process. See "Return … Concerning the intestate estate of the late Armstead Buckner, specifying therein the amount realized, the expenses incurred and what disposition has been made of the balance," (BCSP, 1891), 333. The Department of Land and Works had noted in 1875 that many pre-emptors were "absent, and the improvements under which they have obtained their certificates, years ago, having become obliterated." B.C., Department of Land and Works Annual Report, 1875 (BCSP, 1876), 531. Possibly Buckner cleared this land and then let it revert, but the question would still remain: why did he do so, rather than purchase the land for $1 per acre and sell it for the higher price that improved land could bring?

54 Dominion Bureau of Statistics, British Columbia Census of Agriculture, *7th Census of Canada*, Volume 8, 1931, 2.

55 Dominion Bureau of Statistics, British Columbia Census of Agriculture, *7th Census of Canada*, Volume 8, 1931, Table 1. Figures on the rural/urban split in population are not available until 1891.

56 Dominion Bureau of Statistics, *Third Census of Canada*, 1891, Table XVI, 244–5. The figure 1,592 comes from totalling 804 acres on Saltspring, 619 acres on South Cowichan, and 179 acres on North Cowichan.

57 Cail, *Land, Man and the Law*, 36, and chapter 8, "The Railway Belt to 1884."

58 In 1901 the census reported that figures of "the present census refer only to lands of agricultural production and those of the former [year, 1891] to all occupied lands in the Province, including tracts of timber land; hence the greater number of occupiers and the larger area of occupied land in 1891 and 1901. Woodland and forest in the former year's returns included all unimproved land whereas in those of the latter the forest area is given separately but is also counted as part of the unimproved land." Bulletin XII, Census of Agriculture, British Columbia, *Fourth Census of Canada, 1901*, 3. Improved land is land under crops (excluding hay and some minor crops) plus areas in orchard and garden. In 1901 improved land included land

under hay, forage crops, flax, tobacco, and hops, excluded in 1891. As we will see below, 1881 figures were differently based again.

59 *Fourth Census of Canada, 1891*, Table XVI, 244–5. My own figures from the 1892 assessment roll for the island indicate that the number of occupied acres was 37,784, bringing to 3.4 per cent the proportion of improved lands. Much of the pasture land on the island was uncleared, rocky, treeless, and steep mountainside, suitable for grazing sheep but little else. British Columbia Department of Finance, Surveyor of Taxes Assessment Roll for 1892, Gulf Islands Assessment District, Saltspring Division, Roll B 444, BCA; Census of Canada, 1891, District no. 3, Vancouver, M2 – S.D. 14, Saltspring Island, Schedule no. 1 – Nominal.

60 First Report of the Department of Agriculture, 1891 (BCSP, 1892), 804.

61 Resident landowners are taken from the assessment roll for 1892, taken in 1891. Seventy-four of those listed as owning land were identified as household heads in the 1891 census, twenty-six were not. Thirteen of those listed as resident landowners in the 1892 assessment roll do not show up in the census, some apparently because they arrived between the time of the census and the assessment roll enumeration, some because the census enumerator simply missed them. British Columbia Department of Finance, Surveyor of Taxes Assessment Roll for 1892, Gulf Islands Assessment District, Saltspring Division, Roll B 444, BCA; Census of Canada, 1891, District no. 3, Vancouver, M2 – S.D. 14, Saltspring Island, Schedule no. 1.

62 As outlined in n10.

63 Russell, "Forest into Farm Land," 140.

64 Ibid.

65 Aggregate statistics for Saltspring Island are contained in two charts, "Recapitulation of General Returns from Vancouver Island and Adjacent Islands," 1050–1, and "Recapitulation of Returns of Products from Vancouver Island and Adjacent Islands," 1054–5; Fourth Report of the Department of Agriculture of the Province of British Columbia, 1894 (BCSP, 1895). Statistical data of this sort are not available before 1894. These were gathered by a number of correspondents on the island (Theodore Trage, Alexander Wilson, Estalon Bittancourt, Walter Dukes, Raffles Purdy, George Dukes, Alfred Raynes, the Beddis Brothers, and Alexander McLennan), who were asked for data on their own farms and for estimates of island totals. These estimates provided the statistics in the annual reports. See also British Columbia Department of Finance, Surveyor of Taxes Assessment Roll for 1894, Gulf Islands Assessment District, Saltspring Division, Roll B 444, BCA.

66 The Reverend Wilson's estimates on the nineteen people he mentions list their combined holdings as 14,974 acres compared with 15,324 acres. *Salt Spring Island 1895*.

67 British Columbia Department of Finance, Surveyor of Taxes, 1895 Assessment Roll Roll B 443, Gulf Islands Assessment District, BCA. The census, as the chart notes, lists 111 farmers in 1891.

68 The nineteen farmers mentioned by Wilson owned a total of 15,324 acres or 42 per cent of the owned land, while the remaining 109 landowners owned 21,418 acres or 58 per cent of the land. The nineteen farmers owned properties averaging 807 acres assessed at an average of $4,144, and sixteen of the nineteen declared personal property. The 109 not mentioned by Wilson averaged 197 acres valued at an average of $906, and only twelve of the 109 listed any personal property. See Wilson, *Salt Spring Island 1895*; British Columbia Department of Finance, Surveyor of Taxes Assessment Roll for 1894, Gulf Islands Assessment District, Saltspring Division, Roll B 444, BCA.

CHAPTER FIVE

1 See Table 3.1 for a detailed breakdown.

2 Belshaw, *Colonization and Community*, 158–60; and Johnston, "Native People, Settlers and Sojourners."

3 David Gagan found that more than half of those showing up in decennial censuses at mid-century were still in Peel County ten years later. Gagan, *Hopeful Travelers*, 114–20. J.I. Little, using a more comprehensive methodology, found more than 50 per cent of families persisted for two decades and a "remarkable forty-eight per cent" persisted over a thirty-year period. Little, *Crofters and Habitants*, 95, 93–104. Peter Russell found slightly higher persistence rates in Emily Township, Ontario. Russell, "Emily Township," 324–6. Lower persistence is found by Gérard Bouchard, in his study of Laterriere. He attributes high mobility to a transition point in the community, where mature families were leaving for frontier areas of Lac St Jean to settle their grown children on cheaper and more available lands. Bouchard, "Family Structures and Geographic Mobility."

4 For a discussion of this particular problem with local studies, see Gagan, *Hopeful Travelers*,14; and Russell, "Emily Township," 322–3. Bruce Elliott's study, which follows 775 families from Ireland to two different Canadian locations, over a number of generations, overcomes many of these problems. Elliott, *Irish Migrants in the Canadas*.

5 Between 1860 and 1881 fifty-three of the 204 pre-emption claimants show up only as pre-emption registrants, appearing in no other sources. In the 1881–1891 period fourteen of the 183 pre-emptors show up only at registration, abandoning their claims.

6 It may also reflect the increasingly strict regulations about registering a claim. The *British Colonist* of 18 May 1861 listed the names and addresses of those who had officially taken up land on Saltspring to that date, and

issued notice that those who did not comply with pre-emption regulations, including prompt payment for surveyed lands, would forfeit their claims. Land agent John Copland protested, and apparently won. Copland to Pemberton, 6 July 1861, Correspondence of the Land and Works Department, Colonial Correspondence, BCA. A history of this dispute can be found in the file of W.K. Brown, file 96/72, British Columbia Attorney General, GR 419, BCA.

7 Particularly the terrible winter of 1862. *British Colonist*, 2 May 1862.

8 See, for example, *British Colonist*, 3 June 1860, 5 May 1862, 9 April 1863, 9 March 1865; petition regarding postal service, 21 November 1868, "Petitions, 1868–1870," Colonial Correspondence, GR 1372, BCA.

9 *British Colonist*, 12 July 1860, 14 July 1860, 20 August 1860, 23 August 1860, 9 April 1861, 15 May 1861, 6 May 1863, 8 May 1863, 15 May 1863, 3 October 1866, 2 November 1866. See also Hollins to Wm. A. Young, Colonial Secretary, 24 February 1869, file 789/69; and petition protesting violence of Natives, f1354, Colonial Correspondence, GR 1372, BCA.

10 Louis Stark to Joseph Trutch, November 1869, C/B/30.71K/S+2, BCA.

11 Joseph Trutch to Louis Stark, 10 November 1860, C/B/30.71K/S+2, BCA.

12 Louis Stark, no pre-emption number, Vancouver Island Colonial Surveyor; Office of the Land Recorder for Saltspring Island, Copy of the Pre-Emption Register to 17 October 1862, CAA/30.71/Sa3.1, BCA.

13 Of 388 claims staked on the island between 1860 and 1891, 223 were abandoned by 156 pre-emptors. 113 abandoned their only claims, and over half of these (sixty-one) abandoned the island within a year. Thirty took up one other claim and a further thirteen took up more than two. From 1860 to 1871 those who abandoned their claims stayed on their claim an average of 3.1 years, a figure that fell to 2.4 years in the 1870–1881 period and increased again to 3.7 years in the 1882–1891 period. Abandonment dates were seldom recorded, and so dates are inferred here from the next date that the pre-emptor took up land (pre-emption regulations usually prohibited holding more than one claim), from the next date that the land was pre-empted or purchased, and from miscellaneous other routinely generated sources.

14 Of the 156 people who abandoned their first claim pre-empted between 1860 and 1891, ninety-three remained after one year, sixty-one remained after five years, forty-five remained after ten years, and thirty remained after twenty years.

15 The average was 9.3 years, while the average length of stay on a claim (taken out between 1860 and 1891) was 2.6 years.

16 Joseph Akerman, pre-emption no. 494, 1863, no address. According to Bob Akerman, his grandson, Joseph Akerman disliked the long shadows cast on his first pre-emption by Mount Maxwell, and chose a sunnier location second time round. Interview with Bob Akerman, 1989, SSIA. See also George Mitchell (pre-emption no. 960), who took up land in Begg's Settlement in

1862, and subsequently took up land in the south end; Pompey Jackson, who abandoned land pre-empted in 1863 to take up a more suitable claim in 1867; pre-emption no. 1008, British Columbia Department of Land and Works, Pre-Emption Records, Vancouver and Gulf Islands, GR766, BCA. Similarly, John Cairns took up land (pre-emption no. 1438) in 1873 and lived on it until 1878, when he abandoned it and purchased a neighbouring piece of land outright. Section 12, range 1, south, Saltspring Island Land Register. Thomas Williams first pre-empted land at range 1, section 9, Burgoyne Bay (no pre-emption no.) in 1866, and abandoned it when he took up section 6, range 1 in 1868 (pre-emption no. 108). When Armstead Buckner arrived on the island in 1859 he took out a pre-emption on section 3, range 1 east and west, but in 1863 he abandoned that claim to take out a second pre-emption, no. 619, on which he stayed until his death in 1888.

17 In 1878 Akerman pre-empted a further sixty acres of land in the Burgoyne Valley. He improved and purchased the north forty acres in 1885, but held onto the south portion, without improving it, until 1910. When he abandoned the claim at this time, his son William immediately took it up; Joseph Akerman, homestead pre-emption no. 9, 1878, Saltspring Island Database. Joseph Akerman's son, Joseph J. Akerman, followed a similar strategy, pre-empting land in 1885 and abandoning it without improvement until 1907, when his son Thomas pre-empted it (pre-emption no. 136). Joseph King pre-empted land in 1882, holding it without improvement until 1904, when he abandoned it, allowing his son to pre-empt it immediately thereafter; (pre-emption no. 35, 1882). Michael Gyves took out an additional pre-emption in 1885, abandoning it in 1914 when it was immediately taken up by his son (pre-emption no. 120). Similarly, Henry Sampson pre-empted land in section 15 in 1886 and abandoned it in 1891, at which point his son-in-law immediately pre-empted it (pre-emption no. 130, 1886).

18 Thomas Williams held his pre-emption for four years before dying and leaving his unimproved land to his son-in-law, George Furness, who resided with his wife and mother-in-law on the land until he in turn died and left it to his wife. See Thomas Williams, pre-emption no. 1083; Thomas Griffiths lived on his pre-emption from 1868 till his death in 1879, leaving it to his wife Elizabeth. Elizabeth finally purchased the land and moved onto it with her new husband in 1885. Thomas Foord (no. 907) left his unimproved land, pre-empted in 1866, to his wife Charlotte after holding it for a year. Charlotte improved and paid for her land in 1876, shortly after her marriage to William Morley (no. 955). William Harrison took up a claim in 1874 that he left to his wife when he died in 1878, with no record of improvement (no. 1499). Mrs Harrison, who left the island to live in Oberlin, Ohio, before William's death, returned with her new husband, Albert Staff, to live on this land, and paid for it in 1892. John Kelly took up his claim in 1881; it was transferred to his wife in 1883, presumably because he died in

this year; it was finally improved in 1898 (no. 30). George H. Anderson left his 1870 (no. 119) unimproved pre-emption to his wife, who improved it in 1890, after her marriage to Henry Robinson. British Columbia Department of Land and Works, Certificates of Improvement, Vancouver Island and the Gulf Islands, GR 765, BCA and Saltspring Island Database.

19 See pre-emption no. 83, 1884, Theodore Trage, British Columbia Department of Land and Works, Pre-emptions, Vancouver Island and the Gulf Islands, GR 766, BCA and Saltspring Island Database. Regulations placed limits on the number of acres and the number of pre-emption claims that could be held.

20 See pre-emption no. 21, Arthur Walter, 1884, British Columbia Department of Land and Works, Pre-emptions, Vancouver Island and the Gulf Islands, GR0766, BCA and Saltspring Island Database.

21 F.L. Lakin (pre-emption no. 160, 1886), William McAfee (pre-emption no. 2649, 1907), and Henry Sampson (pre-emption no. 750, 1864). British Columbia Department of Land and Works, Pre-emptions, Vancouver Island and the Gulf Islands, GR766, BCA and Saltspring Island Database.

22 Richard Maxwell, pre-emption no. 143, 160 acres, south-west quarter of section 80, 1885, and David Maxwell, pre-emption no. 223, 1888, eighty acres, south-east quarter section 80, Land Register for Saltspring Island.

23 Legislation passed in 1884 restricted the sale of timbered lands, but compliance was not enforced for twenty years. See Cail, *Land, Man and the Law*, 92. Joe Garner, an early resident and one of the early loggers on the island, discusses the logging of pre-emption claims by his family and others in the late nineteenth and early twentieth centuries. Garner, *Never Fly Over an Eagle's Nest*, 141–58. The temptation for loggers to take up pre-emptions, only to log off the lands and abandon them, became a significant general problem in the late nineteenth century. In the Lake States, for example, loggers have been described as using the pre-emption system as a "de-facto pattern of licensing private timber cutting on public lands." Hurst, "The Institutional Environment of the Logging Era in Wisconsin," 141.

24 Of the 156 pre-emptors who abandoned their claims, fifty-five spent more than five years on their claims.

25 124 pre-emptions were purchased on land pre-empted between 1860 and 1891.

26 Even in the years between 1875 and 1879, when, under the Homestead Act, pre-empted lands could be obtained free of charge, only six of the pre-emptors already on the island – John Cairns, Richard Brinn, Thomas Williams, Joseph Akerman, Richard Jackson, and Abel Douglas – used this provision to obtain land on what they assumed would be free lands, while another eight arrived on the island at this time to do so. Only John Cairns actually obtained the crown grant for his property before the law changed to restore the purchase price to $1 per acre in 1879, but the land register for

Saltspring indicates that the fourteen who obtained homestead pre-
emptions, and went on to improve and purchase their claims, were not required to pay this price when they eventually obtained their crown grants,
on average seven years later.

27 Russell, "Emily Township," 317.

28 Of the seventy-five landowning household heads in 1891, sixty-one had pre-
empted all or some of their land. Nine were living on land that they had improved and twenty-five had purchased their pre-emptions. A further fourteen
were living on land that they had purchased without a pre-emption.

29 See for example Harris, *Making Native Space*, 45–69. A more nuanced approach to settlers and colonial identity is provided in Perry, *On the Edge of
Empire*, especially 6–9.

30 On the 1892 assessment roll, thirty of 125 landowners (24 per cent) did not
pay their land taxes. This figure rose to 25 per cent in the following year. By
1894 30 per cent were not paying taxes. Further assessment rolls are missing until 1902, by which time the numbers not paying taxes had dropped
substantially, probably as the result of government threats in the late 1890s
to sell up the lands of delinquent taxpayers. British Columbia Department
of Finance, Surveyor of Taxes Assessment Roll for 1892–4, Gulf Islands Assessment District, Saltspring Division, Roll B 444, BCA.

31 See, for example, the warnings in the *British Columbia Gazette*, 20 March
1875.

32 Trutch to Colonial Secretary, 12 August 1868, 15–16, file 953–4, Land and
Works Department, Colonial Correspondence, GR 1440, BCA.

33 Only one was purchased in that year, with only fourteen pre-emptions purchased before 1882.

34 "Return of Government Reserves," *British Columbia Journals*, 1st Parl.
2nd sess; 1872–73, cited in Cail, *Land, Man and the Law*, 25.

35 This act raised the price of unsurveyed and surveyed land to $2.50 an acre,
and distinguished between agricultural and waste land, the latter of which
was still sold at $1 an acre. Land registers for Saltspring indicate that all
land was sold at the "waste land" price. The act allowed settlers two years
to register their improvements and another four to make annual installments on their land. Cail, *Land, Man and the Law*, 36–7.

36 Thirteen of those taking up lands before 1892 were being charged interest
on their unpaid installments beginning in the 1890s. The practice became
common for those taking up lands after 1891. See Land Register for
Saltspring Island, Surveyor General's Office, Victoria. For threats to confis-
cate unsurveyed lands, see the *British Columbia Gazette*, 20 March 1875.

37 Cail, *Land, Man and the Law*, xiii.

38 Squatters in many areas of North America successfully fought the legal establishment – and bona fide landowners – for these rights on a number of
occasions in the eighteenth and nineteenth centuries. See, for example,

Taylor, "A Kind of War;" and Pisani, "Squatter Law in California, 1850–1858." There is no conclusive evidence of squatters on Saltspring Island.

39 Out of seventy-one household heads, fifty-five (76 per cent) were landowners in 1881. Of these, 96 per cent had obtained some of their land through pre-emption and two-thirds (78 per cent) of landowners had obtained *all* of their land by pre-empting it. In 1891, seventy-five of ninety-four household heads (seventy-eight per cent) were landowners. In both 1881 and 1891 all but two landowners pre-empted land at some time. In 1891, sixty-one of the seventy-five household heads (80 per cent) who owned land were still living on land acquired through pre-emption. Census of Canada, 1881, District no. 191, Vancouver, Cowichan and Saltspring Island, Schedule no. 1 – Nominal; and Census of Canada, 1891, District no. 3, Vancouver, M2 – S.D. 14, Saltspring Island, Schedule no. 1 – Nominal.

40 By 1891 sixty-one of the seventy-five household heads who owned land had obtained at least some of it through pre-emption. Thirty-six of these had still not obtained crown grants for their land.

CHAPTER SIX

1 Hayman, ed., *Robert Brown and the Vancouver Island Exploring Expedition*, 122.

2 It is not clear that the phrase "political economy" is appropriate for this social formation. As we have seen, land policies formulated off the island were part of the wider discourse of political economy so dominant in the nineteenth century, but practices on the island reveal that the etymologically original household scale of "economy" prevailed.

3 Perry, *On the Edge of Empire*, 17; see chapter 2, "The Prevailing Vice: Mixed-Race Relationships," 48–78, for a detailed discussion of representations of First Nations women in the mid-nineteenth century.

4 Malin, *History and Ecology*, xxii. Malin's key arguments are summed up in Robert P. Swierenga's valuable editorial comments and introduction to this collection.

5 *Chambers English Dictionary* (1988), 993.

6 Canada, *Instructions to Officers*, 13.

7 See, for example, Hamilton, *Salt Spring Island*; and Flucke, "Early Days on Saltspring Island."

8 While nineteenth-century women could purchase land, they were prevented from pre-empting land unless widowed with dependent children. About 94 per cent of men owning land in 1881 had obtained it by pre-empting. Urban women were much more likely to own land. For a detailed discussion of women entrepreneurs and landowners in urban B.C., see Baskerville "She Has Already Hinted at Board," 205–9.

9 Women (females over fourteen) and children fourteen and under made up 65 per cent of the population (167 out of 258 people) in 1881, and 60 per cent (263 out of 436) in 1891. Census of Canada, 1881, District no. 191, Vancouver, Cowichan and Saltspring Island, Schedule no. 1 – Nominal; Census of Canada, 1891, District no. 3, Vancouver, M2 – S.D. 14, Saltspring Island, Schedule no. 1 – Nominal.

10 *Instructions to Officers*, 13.

11 *Instructions to Officers*, 15.

12 In 1881 all 90 males over fourteen declared an occupation. Census of Canada, 1881, District no. 191, Vancouver, Cowichan and Saltspring Island, Schedule no. 1 – Nominal. In 1891 sixteen young men fifteen to nineteen years of age declared no occupation, even though most of them (twelve of the fifteen) were sons of household heads listed as farmers.

13 One of the three unmarried women farmers was widowed, but the other two were sisters, age seventeen and twenty-three, who were single and living with their families. Their appearance as "farmers" is so anomalous that it seems more plausible that this is a clerical error. Census of Canada, 1881, District no. 191, Vancouver, Cowichan and Saltspring Island, Schedule no. 1 – Nominal.

14 Of two married women who listed themselves as farmers, one (we know from other sources) was separated from her husband. Mrs Stark is listed as married, but by 1891 her husband was living in Nanaimo; see Stark File, Attorney General's Office, GR 419, Box 67, BCA. Another married woman listed herself as a baker; like the dressmaker and the domestics, she was not a wife or daughter of the household head, but was listed as a lodger. Most unusual of all, a married woman with a large family listed herself as a teacher, even though "unemployed in the preceding month." Census of Canada, 1891, District no. 3, Vancouver, M2 – S.D. 14, Saltspring Island, Schedule no. 1 – Nominal.

15 Thirteen women who were over fourteen years of age and single listed no occupations, and a further forty-six women who were married to farmers listed no occupation in 1891. Census of Canada, 1891, District no. 3, Vancouver, M2 – S.D. 14, Saltspring Island, Schedule no. 1 – Nominal.

16 For a critique of this particular problem see Boydston, *Home and Work*. For further discussion of gender and the problems of liberal economic theory see Hart, "Imagined Unities," 129; and Wilk, *The Household Economy*.

17 Out of the 2,337 records containing information on occupation in my database – directories, voters' lists, censuses, parish records, and public accounts – 1,635 describe people as farmers.

18 John Mahaffey, William Hutson, Louis Peterson, and Clark Whims, all of whom show up on Saltspring Island voters' lists, directories, or land records over a span of twenty years or more, had either owned or would go on to

own land during their long residence on the island. W.J. Curran, Joseph Silvy, and Cortez Pandelli lived on neighbouring islands. *William's British Columbia Directory 1899*. Jeremiah Chivers shows up in directories as living on the island from about 1889 to 1902, but he does not show in the 1901 census. His sister was the wife of Arthur Walter who owned over 900 acres of land on the island in 1891, with two children under two years of age, fifty-five cattle, forty sheep, and five hogs.

19 For a review of the numerous rural histories documenting occupational plurality as a characteristic of rural Canada in the nineteenth and twentieth centuries, see Sandwell, "Rural Reconstruction," 1–32.

20 See ABC Packers, University of British Columbia Special Collections. See also Stevens and Knight, *Homer Stevens*, chapter 1.

21 Thanks to Bob and Diane Hele for providing the photograph of Bob's grandfather, Benjamin Lundy; and to Duncan Stacey for pointing out the significance of their clothing.

22 Census of Canada, 1891, District no. 3, Vancouver, M2 – S.D. 14, Saltspring Island, Schedule no. 1 – Nominal.

23 See Regina vs McFadden and Sampson, file 24–1866, Attorney General's Papers, GR 419, BCA.

24 See ABC Packers, interview with Bob Hele, 1990, SSIA.

25 See Land Register for Saltspring, Surveyor General's Office, Victoria. Most of the land had been taken up by 1890. For logging on the island, see Garner, *Never Fly Over an Eagle's Nest*; Charlie Horel, 1990 interview, SSIA. Ken Drushka explains that the combination of technology and terrain in B.C. particularly favoured the individual hand logger, who, "with only a few hand tools and a lot of determination" could obtain work. He contrasts this to Oregon and Washington, where the gentler terrain favoured the establishment of large-scale logging operations. Drushka, *Working in the Woods*, 40.

26 See chapter 5, n23.

27 In 1927 the bottom fell out of the market and farmers on Saltspring, as elsewhere, suffered from this sudden reduction in their resource options. See particularly the interviews with Bob Hele, Bob Dodds, and Charlie Horel, 1990, all of whom worked in the logging industry; Interviews, SSIA.

28 See Hele, 1990 interview, SSIA. See also the relief books for Saltspring Island, detailing payments towards taxes earned by working on the roads. Relief Books, 1931–36, SSIA. For 1885–91 evidence, see Province of British Columbia Public Accounts (BCSP) for these years.

29 *British Columbia Public Accounts for the half year ended 31 December, 1889.*

30 In 1888 thirty-one men worked for an average total pay of $94 for the year, a figure that declined to about $50 in 1889, 1890, and 1891, providing the men (at an average of $2 per day) about a month's work in most of the years under study.

31 The 1891 census lists 175 men over fourteen, in which year fifty-two work-ers (30 per cent) received wages averaging $62 per person. Information about the total number of men on the island in other years is not available. Census of Canada, 1891, District no. 3, Vancouver, M2 – S.D. 14, Saltspring Island, Schedule no. 1 – Nominal.

32 For a discussion of the cost of living on Vancouver Island at this time, see Belshaw, *Colonization and Community*, 99–109. Belshaw finds figures sug-gesting that a "basket containing a pound each of beef, sugar, coffee, and tea and one gallon of beer – cost about $2.90 in 1865, $2.00 in 1870 and $1.38 in 1891." As Belshaw notes, however, these prices fluctuated signifi-cantly from one community to another on Vancouver Island. Fruit and veg-etable prices were kept high by the cost of farm labour. The tendency of island residents to raise and gather a portion of their own meat, fruits, and vegetables makes it difficult to assess their cash needs.

33 Ibid., 97. If miners were working a forty-hour week, this works out to only $2.25 per day, but as Belshaw points out, miners seldom worked a full shift, nor did they work regularly throughout the year.

34 Ibid., 96–9.

35 I thank Dr Peter Baskerville, University of Victoria, for supplying the fig-ures from Victoria and Vancouver in 1901. Census of Canada, 1891, Dis-trict no. 3, Vancouver, M2 – S.D. 14, Saltspring Island, Schedule no. 1 – Nominal.

36 Interviews with Valentine Reynolds and Ellen Bennett, 1990, SSIA.

37 We know that about two-thirds of families (sixty out of ninety-six resident landowners) in 1891 had cows, sheep, pigs, or horses, and most kept poul-try. There were over 300 ducks and geese on the island, and well over 4,200 hens and chickens, whose care was traditionally part of farm women's work. *Third Dominion Census of Canada*, 1891, table III, Animals and An-imal Resources, 115–16. The Gyves family explicitly lists cattle as the women of the family's responsibility. Typescript, Gyves Family File, SSIA.

38 On the Gyves family, see typescript, Gyves Family File, SSIA; Mary Rean-ney, Inquest, File 52–1891, BC Attorney General, Inquisitions, 1872–1937, Roll B 2373, GR 1327; The Rev. Ebenezer Robson describes cows as women's concern. Robson, Diaries, 16 September 1861 to 27 March 1862; 13 October 1861, H/D/R57, R57.3, BCA.

39 Beddis, Diary, 1 January 1890 to 30 June 1890, SSIA.

40 Although clearly important to the economy of the island, self-provisioning activities, such as growing produce in the farm garden for household con-sumption, are regularly excluded from agricultural statistics on production. See, for example, Inwood and Irwin, "Canadian Regional Commodity In-come Differences."

41 For the importance of urban strategies that reached beyond commodity pro-duction and waged labour see, for example, Bradbury, *Working Families*;

and in the British twentieth-century urban context see Pahl, *Divisions of Labour*. In the Canadian rural context see Sandwell, "Rural Reconstruction." The importance of self-provisioning into the 1930s and 40s is clear in the oral history record for Saltspring Island. See, for example, interviews with Val Gyves, Johnny Bennett, and Charles Horel, SSIA.

42 See, for example, Baskerville and Sager, *Unwilling Idlers*; and Struthers, *No Fault of their Own*. As Kathryn McPherson notes in her review of Canadian working-class history, "studying workers by distinct occupation groups blinds us to one of the defining features of the work experience of both men and women of the past: mobility." McPherson, "Feminist Reflections," 187.

43 For an examination of aboriginal populations and their economic support, see, for example, "Variation in Habitat and Culture on the Northwest Coast," and "Coping with Abundance: Subsistence on the Northwest Coast," in Suttles, *Coast Salish Essays*, 15–66.

44 See Belshaw, *Colonization and Community*, 101–2, for a discussion of self-provisioning activities in the Vancouver Island coal communities, particularly during strikes.

45 *Daily Press* (Victoria), 11 November 1861.

46 Malin, *History and Ecology*, xxii.

47 For a discussion of the important role of Native women in the fur-trade period of Canadian history, see Van Kirk, "Women in Between"; Van Kirk, *Many Tender Ties*; and Brown, *Strangers in the Blood*.

48 In 1881 twenty of the forty-eight married couples, or almost 42 per cent, were made up of people of different races; thirteen of these, or 27 per cent of all marriages, were between Aboriginal women and non-Aboriginal men. Seven were between African-Americans and whites. In 1891 the proportion of mixed-race marriages declined to twenty of the sixty-nine married couples, 29 per cent of all marriages. Eighteen of these, or 26 per cent of all marriages, were between Native women and non-Native men.

49 Hamilton, *Salt Spring Island*, 53.

50 For the continued ties within mixed-race families, see Gyves, Family File, SSIA; and Barman, "The Worth of an Everyday Woman," unpublished paper.

51 Stevens and Knight, *Homer Stevens*, 4. Stevens goes on to write of the arguments his grandparents had deciding on whether the salmon fishing or the berry picking would get priority.

52 For evidence on diet from the 1930s, see especially Johnny Bennett, 1990 interview, SSIA, and Val Gyves, 1990 interview. These interviews are now available in audio form on line at the Saltspring Island Archives online site. R. v Mary Anne McFadden, File 24–1866, British Columbia Attorney General's Papers, GR 419, BCA; Murder of William Robinson, Trial of "Tom," testimony of John Norton, 2 June 1869, Benchbooks of Chief Justice Needham, BCA.

53 Hills, Diaries, 6 Sept. 1860.

54 Mackie, *The Wilderness Profound*.

55 Hills, Diaries, 7 September 1860. Camas is a plant that provided an important part of the Native diet. See also Blair, Diary, 123, BCA.

56 The tendency of island residents to let their cattle wander free to graze prompted councillors to pass the following resolution: "For the improvement of cattle, it shall not be lawful for any bull to run at large during the month of April, May or June." Saltspring Island Municipal By-Laws, Saltspring Island Correspondence and By-Laws, 1871–1882, British Columbia Provincial Secretary, box 1, file 2, GR 1707, BCA.

57 Joel Broadwell, 4 June 1889, Probate File 1902, Armstead Buckner, British Columbia, Supreme Court, (Victoria), Probates 1859–4974; GR 1304, BCA.

58 Edna Matthews Clifton, Reminiscences, I, 12 and passim. SWC/IT. West, *Growing Up With the Country*, 75.

59 Sutherland, *Growing Up*; Parr, *Labouring Children*; and Loewen, *Family, Church and Market*. Bettina Bradbury's research into Montreal families suggests that between a quarter and a half of children over sixteen in this urban area worked in paid employment in the 1861–91 period, while children's unpaid work within the family often made the difference between discomfort and absolute want. Bradbury, *Working Families*, table 4.4, 240, and especially 118–51.

60 Childhood is one subject that most people were happy to talk about at length. Especially good interviews were with Charles Horel (1990), Ted Brown (1990), Johnny Bennett and Mrs Lee (1990), and Bob Hele (1990). Interviews, SSIA.

61 Zelizer, *Pricing the Priceless Child*.

62 British Columbia, Attorney General, Documents, 1875–1966, file 24/66, box 6, GR 419, BCA.

63 British Columbia, Attorney General, Inquisitions, 1872–1937, file 73-1888, GR 1327, BCA.

64 British Columbia, Attorney General, Inquisitions, 1872–1937, file 18-1885, GR 1327, BCA.

65 British Columbia, Attorney General, file 1881–18, box 22, GR 419, BCA.

66 Darroch and Soltow, *Property and Inequality*, 9.

67 Harris, "Industry and the Good Life Around Idaho Peak," 315.

68 For a detailed examination of the importance of stability and independence for rural families, see Darroch and Soltow, *Property and Inequality*, 202–3. For a historiographic overview of the importance of stability and independence throughout rural Canada, see Sandwell, "Rural Reconstruction," 1–32.

69 A wide literature underlines the importance of a secure land base among the poor. In the English context, see Snell, *Annals of the Labouring Poor*, chapter 4; and Chase, *The People's Farm*. In the Canadian context, see, for example, Darroch and Soltow, *Property and Inequality*.

70 Darroch, "Scanty Fortunes and Rural Middle Class Formation," 621–2.

71 Bouchard, "Family Reproduction in New Rural Areas," 493.

72 Ibid. Bouchard points out that other community studies in North America have noted the reluctance of parents to settle their children on the land. Chad Gaffield sees a similar pattern and argues that parents may have replaced an inheritance of land with an inheritance of education as economic change affected the usefulness of land. Gaffield, *Language, Schooling and Cultural Conflict*. Voisey's *Vulcan* notes a similar trend, but attributes it to their desire to accumulate wealth. Bouchard discusses this phenomenon, 493.

73 May, *Three Frontiers*, 130. In the frontier communities in Oregon, Utah, and Idaho, studied by May, the average household size was 6.1, 5.7, and 5 respectively in 1881. For the Ontario figures, see Darroch and Ornstein, "Family and Household in Nineteenth Century Canada."

74 No married or widowed people under seventeen lived on the island in either census year.

75 In the Nanaimo area, for example, 40 per cent of the miners on Vancouver Island were married. Belshaw, *Colonization and Community*, 66. In a comparable resettlement community, Sublimity, Oregon, in the same period, 92 per cent of the ninety-seven households were headed by a married couple. May, *Three Frontiers*, 114–15.

76 Belshaw, *Colonization and Community*, 64–5.

77 In 1881 42 per cent, and in 1891 26 per cent of the population were under fifteen.

78 In the whole Vancouver Island district in 1881, married couples where the wife was under 45 years old had an average of 2.75 children. The miners had a slightly higher rate of 2.82 and 2.96 in 1881 and 1891 respectively. Belshaw, *Colonization and Community*, 69. Ontario, Nova Scotia, New Brunswick, and Quebec had an average fertility rate of 3.9.

79 RG II, S 36, box 1, St Ann's Cowichan Register; Sisters of St. Ann, Victoria, Archives. Register of First Arrivals at the school.

80 These twenty-three families have been reconstituted from censuses, parish records, and family records. They represent a third of the seventy families with children appearing altogether in the 1881 and/or 1891 censuses. Bouchard, "Family Reproduction," 486–7.

81 The average age at the birth of the first child for the twenty-three mothers was 20.6 years.

82 Fifty-one of the seventy-two families, or 71 per cent, who show up in the 1881 and 1891 census had children before arriving on the island. Of the forty-seven households in the 1881 and the 1891 censuses, where we know that the family had children before coming to the island and we know the mothers's birth date, the average age was 31.5 for women and 38.2 for men.

83 Of the thirty-seven families who were living with their children in 1881, twenty-two (60 per cent) had arrived on the island with at least one child.

In 1891 twenty-nine of the fifty-three of those with children (55 per cent) had come to the island with children. Cross-linking the families in the two censuses reveals that fifty-one of the seventy-two families who ever had children had arrived after the birth of at least one child.

84 For a discussion of the impact of the "life-cycle squeeze" on the life cycle of Canadian households, see Darroch and Ornstein, "Family Co-Residence in Canada in 1871," 54–5; Bradbury, "Women and Wage Labour in a Period of Transition"; and "Pigs, Cows and Boarders"; and "Gender at Work at Home."

85 Although marriage records that could document when or where most couples were married are not available, my database for the island does allow me to estimate whether or not household heads had children before they arrived on the island, by subtracting the date at which a household head shows up on the island from the birth date of the eldest child showing up on the 1881 or 1891 census. Belshaw finds a similar trend in the Nanaimo coalfields, which, as he notes, stood in contrast to the European immigrants to the eastern United States in the late nineteenth century, who tended to migrate as individuals. Of the fifty-one households that had children before they arrived, the average age of the eldest child was 9.3 years and of the household head was 39. The families would go on to have an average of 4.5 children.

86 Of the twenty-nine households with children on Saltspring Island in 1881, fifteen had children before coming to the island, and two more had families between the time they arrived and the time they pre-empted. Of the eight household heads who had no land in 1881, seven had children when they arrived. In 1891 forty-two landowning households had children; twenty-four of these brought their children with them to the island; and three had children between their arrival and the time they pre-empted land. In 1881 landowning household heads with children had their first child at thirty-two, and pre-empted their first claim at thirty-four years of age on average. In 1891 the average ages were thirty-four and thirty-six, respectively.

87 In 1881, 180 of the island's population of 257 (70 per cent) lived in families headed by a married couple. Two families consisted of a married couple and a live-in employee or servant. In 1891, 361 of the 436 people, or 83 per cent, lived in households headed by a married couple. Fifty of the couples showing up in the 1891 census had children; eight lived as a couple with no children or lodgers; but just under half headed by a married couple with no children (six of the fourteen households) had extra members – two were in-laws and four were lodgers or employees.

88 In 1881 eight married couples with children had extra household members; one of these had the mother-in-law, two had adopted children under fifteen, three had non-related lodgers, and two had servants.

89 See n82, particularly Darroch and Ornstein, "Family Co-Residence in Canada in 1871," 55.

90 Ibid. For a discussion of the help that families routinely gave to each other on the American frontier at this time, see May's *Three Frontiers*, 107–45.

91 Walters, *Early Days Among the Gulf Islands*, 24.

92 Pre-emption 1144, Saltspring Island.

93 In 1881 five households out of seventy-one had adult children – defined here as those over 18 – living with them (7 per cent). By 1891 the number of such households had increased to ten out of ninety-four (11 per cent).

94 Darroch and Ornstein, "Family Co-Residence in Canada in 1871," 55.

95 Single men between fifteen and thirty-five years of age made up less than a quarter of the adult males in 1881 (eleven out of ninety) and less than a third (fifty-four out of 183) in 1891; they made up about 1 per cent of the total population in 1881 and 12 per cent in 1891.

96 In 1881 only eighteen men were living alone, and only two were living with a single other person – in both cases what appears to be a non-related man. In 1891 eighteen household heads were still living alone, four were living with a single sibling, two with another unrelated man, and one in what seems to have been a logging or work camp with a group of unre-lated men.

97 This is especially true in 1891, when the proportion of adult men to adult women grew from 2:1 in 1881 to 3:1. For a discussion of the treatment of this imbalance, see Perry, "I'm Just Sick of the Faces of Men"; and Belshaw, "Cradle to Grave," 52–3.

98 Seventeen of the nineteen household heads who were between sixteen and thirty years old on arrival were landowners by 1881; thirty-one of the thirty-eight household heads who were between sixteen and thirty years of age on arrival were landowners by the time of the 1891 census. The aver-age total length of stay for those appearing as household heads on the 1881 census, and arriving between the ages of sixteen and thirty was thirty-three years; in 1891 the average was twenty-eight years in total for those arriving before age thirty. Average total persistence rates were lower for those arriving in their thirties: twenty-seven years for household heads in 1881 and nineteen years for household heads in the 1891 census.

99 Of the nineteen household heads in 1881 who had arrived between the ages of sixteen and thirty, birth dates of the children indicate that only three had had children before their arrival on the island. By 1881 ten of the nineteen had at least one child. Of the thirty-seven household heads in 1891 arriving between the ages of sixteen and thirty, seven had arrived with children, and eighteen, or just under half, had had their first child by 1891.

100 In 1881 twenty-four of the thirty-five landless males over fourteen defined themselves as farmers or farmer's sons. In 1891 most of these landless farmers (thirty-one) were under the age of thirty, and were sons or broth-ers of farmers. In 1881 landless farmers were older (nine were under thirty

and were sons or brothers of landowners, and fifteen were over thirty), but most had arrived within a year of the census date. Most landowners in both census years called themselves farmers: in 1881 forty-eight out of fifty-five; and in 1891 seventy out of eighty-five.

101 Eleven of the thirty-seven households with children, or 30 per cent, were blended families. Five of the fifty-five households with children in 1891 were blended families.

102 Gossage, "La maratre."

103 Sixty-four of the 130 children on the island, or 49 per cent, had parents of different races. Sixty-two of these had a Native or Hawaiian mother and a non-Native father or mixed-race father. In 1891, sixty-nine, or 32 per cent of the 218 offspring of island residents had parents of mixed race.

104 The tendency of men to marry women of their own race in the later nineteenth century has been noted by Van Kirk, *Many Tender Ties*; and Barman, "Invisible Women and Mixed-Race Daughters." For a critique of this interpretive framework, see Perry, "I'm Just Sick of the Faces of Men."

105 For a discussion of exogamy amongst coalminers, see Belshaw, *Colonization and Community*, 66–9. Belshaw argues that the British Columbia pattern amongst the non-mining population was closer to patterns of intermarriage in New Zealand, hovering around 50 per cent of all marriages in 1881.

106 Bouchard, "Co-intégration et Réproduction de la Sociétée Rurale."

107 Bouchard, "Introduction à l'étude de la société saguenayenne aux XIX et XXᵉ siècles." In his article "Mobile Populations, Stable Communities," Bouchard argues that family-based inter-regional migrations were central to the cohesiveness of rural society.

108 Blair, Diary, 125, BCA.

109 Green, Diary, 19 June 1875, BCA.

110 *British Colonist*, 22 April 1875, 3. The voters of Saltspring were apparently unperturbed by this characterization, as they returned Mr Booth to the Legislative Assembly almost every election until he died in 1902.

111 "Report of the Immigration Agency," 1883 (BCSP, 1884), 299.

112 Ibid., 300.

113 First Report of the Department of Agriculture, British Columbia 1891 (BCSP, 1892), 731.

114 Fourth Report of the Department of Agriculture, British Columbia, 1894 (BCSP, 1895), 827. An act was therefore passed in that year to hire people specifically to gather statistics.

115 Barron, *Those Who Stayed Behind*.

116 Smith, *The Wealth of Nations*, 114–15.

117 For one of the earlier outlines of the theory of proto-industrialization see Medick, "The Proto-Industrial Family Economy." For a summary of the

theory of proto-industrialization and its relevance to Canadian nineteenth-century rural history, see Sandwell, "Rural Reconstruction," 22–8.

118 For a discussion of the discord between rural practices and normative Euro-Canadian discourses of rural life see Sandwell, "The Limits of Liberalism," 423–50; and Sandwell, "Rural Reconstruction."

119 Lehning, *Peasant and French*, 81. This argument was first made by Reddy, *The Rise of Market Culture*.

120 Lehning, *Peasant and French*, 81.

121 Barron, *Those Who Stayed Behind*; Curtis, "Preconditions of the Canadian State"; Samson, "Industry and Improvement."

122 Lehning, *Peasant and French*, 87.

123 Lehning, *Peasant and French*, 87.

124 Greer, *Peasant, Lord and Merchant*, xi. For a broad-ranging discussion of modern peasants, see Shanin, ed., *Defining Peasants*.

125 Shanin, *The Awkward Class*.

126 Reed, "Gnawing it Out," 84.

CHAPTER SEVEN

1 For those interested in following the evidence presented in this chapter, and perhaps drawing your own conclusions, all the documents cited here are available on the website "Who Killed William Robinson?" created by John Lutz and myself: http://web.uvic.ca/history-robinson/

2 For a thoughtful discussion of race as a social construct, see Anderson, *Vancouver's Chinatown*, 8–33; and Carter, *Capturing Women*. With regard to Native and non-Native relations in British Columbia, see Harris, *Making Native Space*; and Perry, *On the Edge of Empire*.

3 Levi, "On Microhistory," 98.

4 Ninety-six, or 73 per cent, of the 131 people born in B.C. in 1881 were under fifteen years of age; in 1891, 171 (80 per cent) of the 213 born in B.C. were under 15 years of age.

5 Those born in India, the Argentine Republic, and a number of those born in China, were of English or Scottish descent, and were children of parents who, like the Musgraves and Robertsons, had travelled throughout the empire as missionaries or colonial officers. See Tables 8.1 and 8.2 for the place of birth of Saltspring Island residents in 1881 and 1882.

6 For a history of this migration, see Kilian, *Go Do Some Great Thing*, chapters 1–4; and Pilton, "Salt Spring Island," in "Negro Settlement," unpublished MA thesis.

7 Hamilton, *Salt Spring Island*, 16.

8 Pilton, "Negro Settlement," 135.

9 Kilian, *Go Do Some Great Thing*, 103.

10 Irby, "The Black Settlers," 371. Kilian and Hamilton also make reference to Douglas's decision, mentioned by Mrs Stark: "Sylvia Stark remembered that a delegation of colored people called on Governor Douglas requesting permission to form a colony of colored settlers on Saltspring Island about that time [1858], but he refused, saying it would be to the best interest of all to have a mixed settlement." Marie Albertina Wallace (Stark), 1867–1966, Saltspring Island, 18, BCA. I have not found any other reference to Douglas's statement.

11 See, for example, a letter from John C. Jones, William Robinson, and Frederick Lester requesting a school on the island. Jones, Robinson, Lester to Mr Kennedy, Governor, May 1864, file F988-1, Colonial Correspondence, GR 1372, BCA. For the important role of Henry Robinson in municipal politics, see British Columbia, Provincial Secretary, Saltspring Island Municipal By- Laws, Saltspring Island Correspondence and By-Laws, 1871–1882, box 1, file 2, GR 1707, BCA.

12 Hamilton, *Salt Spring Island*, 12.

13 Kilian, *Go Do Some Great Thing*, 115.

14 Koppel, *Kanaka*, 105–24. Cross-linked land records indicate that fourteen Hawaiian families took up land on South Saltspring, Russell, and Portland Islands between 1872 and 1891.

15 Barman, "The Worth of an Everyday Woman," unpublished manuscript.

16 For a summary of the archeological and ethnographic data, see Kahn, *The History of Salt Spring Island*, 16–26.

17 Bishop Hills notes that he walked through an abandoned Indian village on his arrival at Ganges Harbour. Hills, Diaries, 5 September 1860.

18 Harris, *Making Native Space*; and Tennant, *Aboriginal Peoples and Politics*.

19 *New Westminster Times*, 24 September 1859.

20 Tennant, *Aboriginal Peoples and Politics*; and Thomson, "The Response of Okanagan Indians to European Settlement."

21 See Tennant, *Aboriginal Peoples and Politics*, 34–40.

22 Indian Reserve Commission, Census of British Columbia Indians, 1876–77, RG 88 v 494 file, NAC. Thanks to John Lutz for drawing this source to my attention.

23 *British Colonist*, 12 July 1860. For original of letter, see Lineker to James Douglas, July 9, 1860; Correspondence, Department of Land and Works, F1000.0, GR 1372, BCA.

24 Walbran, *British Columbia Place Names*, 199, under "Ganges Harbour." This incident is reproduced in almost every history of the island. See Hamilton, *Salt Spring Island*, 17–20; Pilton, "Negro Settlement," 137–8; and Walters, *Early Days Among the Gulf Islands*, 29–31.

25 "The History of the Stark Family: Early Settlers Encounter Hostile Indians" *Gulf Islands Driftwood*, 12 December 1979, from the manuscript of Sylvia Stark's Memoirs, Wallace, Marie Albertina, 1867–1966, BCA.

26 See, for example, *British Colonist*, 15 May 1861 and 21 April 1863; see also Lillard, *Seven Shillings a Year*, 151. On cattle rustling, see *British Colonist*, 27 March 1867. A detailed (and romanticized) description of this incident appears in Hamilton, *Salt Spring Island*, 51–3. In the end it was whites who were arrested in the largest cattle-rustling incident.

27 Gough, *Gunboat Frontier*, 134–6; and Arnett, *The Terror of the Coast*.

28 *British Colonist*, 15 May 1863. For a fuller account, see Gough, *Gunboat Frontier*, 139.

29 Gough, *Gunboat Frontier*, 140–7.

30 Confession of Stashul, W. Hales Franklyn to William Wakeford, Acting Colonial Secretary, September 22 1864, Colonial Correspondence, file F595.13, Microfilm Reel B-1329, BCA.

31 *British Colonist*, 2 November 1866.

32 Fisher, *Contact and Conflict*, 105.

33 Gough, *Gunboat Frontier*; and Arnett, *The Terror of the Coast*.

34 *British Colonist*, 10 and 15 August 1867.

35 Ibid., 28 December 1867.

36 Ibid., 24 March 1868.

37 Ibid., 24 March 1868.

38 Ibid., 21 December 1868.

39 Correspondence of the Gunboat *Sparrowhawk*, from H.W. Mist, Commander, to Rear Admiral the Hon. George F. Hastings, 5 January 1869; copy in Saltspring Island Archives.

40 *British Colonist*, 21 December 1868.

41 *British Colonist*, 24 March 1868.

42 *British Colonist*, 25 December 1868. See the Petition from Saltspring Island settlers, 21 December 1868, Petitions, F1354, GR 1372, BCA.

43 *British Colonist*, 11 January 1869.

44 Hollins to Young, 24 February 1869, F780/1, GR 1372, BCA.

45 *British Colonist*, 13 April 1869. Mrs Stark's memoirs indicate that she believed that the attacks on African-Americans were intended for her husband, Louis; see "Stark Family Moves to Fruitvale," *Gulf Islands Driftwood*, 16 January 1979, 13.

46 Louis Stark to Mr Trutch, November 1869, B.C. Surveyor General, Correspondence Inwards, file C/B/30.71K/S+2, BCA.

47 *British Colonist*, 4 January 1869.

48 *British Colonist*, 13 April 1869.

49 *British Colonist*, 13 March 1869; 2 April 1869; 13 April 1869.

50 *British Colonist*, 13 April 1869.

51 *British Colonist*, 10 April 1869.

52 See, for example, Gough, *Gunboat Frontier*, 147; Pilton, "Negro Settlement," 142; Kilian, *Go Do Some Great Thing*, 109–15; Hamilton, *Salt*

Spring Island, 21–2; and Flucke, "Early Days on Saltspring Island," 186. See Fisher, *Contact and Conflict*, 91, for the racism of Natives against African-Americans, which is discounted by Kilian, 110.

53 Irby, "The Black Settlers," 373.

54 Testimonial of John Norton, 2 April 1869, sworn before J. Morley, File 1860/20, Attorney General, Documents, GR 419, BCA.

55 File 1860/20, Attorney General, Documents, GR 419, BCA.

56 2 June 1869, Tom, Indian Murder of William Robinson, Bench Books of Criminal Cases Heard Before Judge Joseph Needham, 1867–1868, Supreme Court of Civil Justice, GR 2030, BCA.

57 *British Colonist*, 5 June 1869.

58 Ibid., 30 June 1869.

59 Ibid., 3 July 1869.

60 Stadfeld, "Manifestations of Power," unpublished MA thesis, 1.

61 Begg to William and Margaret Chisholm, 10 March 1860, Begg File, SSIA.

62 Walters, *Early Days*, 8.

63 Walters, *Early Days*, 9, 24, 55.

64 Hamilton, *Salt Spring Island*, 53, for example.

65 Lutz, "Work, Wages and Welfare," unpublished PHD thesis. For Native employment on the island, see, for example, *British Columbia Public Accounts for the fiscal year ended 30 June 1891*, R. Wolfenden, Victoria, 1891, 56; Green, Diary, BCA.

66 Hills, Diaries, 11 September 1860. Ebenezer Robinson noted that "Of these 9 men, 5 are living with Indian women in a state of adultery. Some have families from such connexion. One man has commenced this degrading course since I was here last. He is a young man who was educated in [?] College, England, for the Bar and passed his examination for this profession. His father is an old and wealthy Methodist. His son, poor man, is far gone in the way to hell." Robson, Diaries, 25 March 1861, BCA.

67 Van Kirk, "Women in Between." Mixed-race families comprised twelve out of forty-four marriages and 35 per cent of those staying more than thirty years.

68 Michael Gyves, Theodore Trage, and John Maxwell, for example, owned an average of 684 acres each, according to the 1892 assessment roll for the island, in contrast to the 288 acre average. British Columbia Department of Finance, Surveyor of Taxes, 1892 Assessment Roll, Roll B 443, Gulf Islands Assessment District, BCA.

69 *British Colonist*, 27 March 1867.

70 John Booth to the Colonial Secretary, 2 January 1869, file F988-1, Colonial Correspondence, BCA.

71 John Booth to the Colonial Secretary, 2 January 1869, file F988-1, Colonial Correspondence, BCA.

72 Ibid.

73 Begg, who owned a store near the old steamer stop, had petitioned the government but failed to get service re-established in 1865. *British Colonist*, 9 and 14 March 1865.

74 Vancouver Island Colonial Surveyor, Office of the Land Recorder for Saltspring Island, Copy of the Pre-emption Register to 17 October 1862, BCA.

75 Pre-emption #606, August 1863, British Columbia Department of Land and Works, Pre-Emption Records, Vancouver and Gulf Islands, BCA. The 1868 listing of Lester's 1868 pre-emption and improvement certificate covers not section 9, but section 8, range 2 west and section 7, range 3 west. See pre-emption no. 1070, 28 November 1868.

76 Vancouver Island Colonial Surveyor, Correspondence and Papers re Settlers on Saltspring Is., 1859, '61, '62, '66, re lot 3, range 2 and 3 east, Ganges, BCA.

77 British Columbia Department of Land and Works, Pre-Emption Records, Vancouver and Gulf Islands in file #1485, January 1874; Letter of Nov. 1872 from lawyer to Mr Morley, Department of Land and Works.

78 Land Register, Saltspring Island, North Divison, Surveyor General's Office, Victoria, 464.

79 Letter from Robertson and Johnson, April 1872 to Department of Land and Works, file #1485, January 1874, British Columbia Department of Land and Works, Pre-Emption Records, Vancouver and Gulf Islands and reply, 13 April 1874 from Robert Beaur (same file).

80 File #1485, British Columbia Department of Land and Works, Pre-Emption Records, Vancouver and Gulf Islands, memorandum, no date; see also Land Register for Saltspring, North Division, 464.

81 *Daily Colonist*, 23 March 1880 and 26 March 1880. My thanks to Chris Hanna for finding this.

82 British Columbia Department of Finance, Surveyor of Taxes, 1892 Assessment Roll, Roll B 443, Gulf Islands Assessment District, BCA.

83 BCSP 1879, 109.

84 Moses Mahaffey, file 430, 1878, British Columbia, Supreme Court, Probates 1859–1974; GR 1304, BCA.

85 According to the 1892 assessment roll, his "personal property" was valued at over $800, with only three other landowners owning more. He owned almost twice as much land as the island average (550 acres compared to 299) and his land was worth $3,000, compared to the average of $1,500. Saltspring Island, Assessment Roll for 1892, BCA.

86 File 5043, British Columbia, Supreme Court, (Victoria), Probates 1859–4974; GR 1304, BCA. He had over $15,000 in personal property and $4,200 in real estate, much of which was loaned out in the form of mortgages to island residents.

87 The evidence on whether individuals actually took up their land was based on a cross-linking of voters' lists, directory listings, parish records, diaries, letters, and, most valuable for this period, pre-emption records and other land records containing witnesses to land transactions.

88 Irby, "The Black Settlers," 371.

89 Robson, Diaries, 21 February 1861, BCA.

90 Saltspring Island Database.

91 In a survey of 500 parish records, I could find no examples of a non-African-American witnessing an African-American birth or marriage, or vice-versa, except in the few cases where there was a racially mixed family.

92 Robinson, an African-American, was already married to his wife Margaret, an Irish Catholic, when they moved to the island. His daughter married Mr Norton, their nextdoor neighbour, at a very early age. Only three other marriages between African-Americans and non-African-Americans are documented. This is in stark contrast to the high rates of inter-marriage between other racial groups – particularly Hawaiians and Native women.

93 A. Walter to Premier Smithe, 28 April 1885, B.C. Premier's Office, Correspondence Inwards, Box 1, File 3, GR 441, BCA.

94 British Columbia Department of Finance, Surveyor of Taxes, 1892 Assessment Roll, Roll B 443, Gulf Islands Assessment District, reveals that the eight African-American landowners had only 124 acres, compared to the 300 acres that whites possessed on average. The value of African-American land was, on average, $675, as opposed to $1,018.27 for whites. In this year 18.9 per cent of whites declared personal property to be taxed but no African-Americans did.

95 For a discussion of different interpretations of relations between Natives and non-Natives during this time, see Stadfeld, "Manifestations of Power."

96 For the most thorough and thoughtful discussion of issues of power and place in British Columbia, see Harris, *Making Native Space*.

97 Louis Stark, Box 67, British Columbia, Attorney General's Office, GR 419, BCA.

98 For a discussion of Asians in British Columbia, see Roy, *A White Man's Province*; and *The Oriental Question*. A forthcoming volume will carry her study up to 1967. Women were barred by their gender and marital status, not their ethnicity, from owning land, see chapter 8. Aboriginal men, as we saw in chapter 1, lost the right to pre-empt land in 1866. Asian men were not offered the special status that African-Americans were to become "British subjects" and so were not allowed to pre-empt land.

99 Census of Canada, 1881, District no. 191, Vancouver, Cowichan and Saltspring Island, Schedule no. 1 – Nominal; Census of Canada, 1891, District no. 3, Vancouver, M2 – SD 14, Saltspring Island, Schedule no. 1 – Nominal; Census of Canada, 1901, District No. 3, Vancouver Electoral

District, Polling Sub-division Saltspring Island, Schedule no. 1 – Nominal. The diary of Alexander Aitken, a young shepherd who came to work at the Musgrave's farm at the south end of the island in 1891, contains a number of references to the Chinese domestic servant, with whom he shared lodgings. Alexander was astounded at the depth and dignity of Chinese culture that Young [sic] described to him in the summer of 1891 Aitken, Diary, July and August 1891, SSIA.

100 As microhistorian J. Revel has noted: "Why make things simple when one can make them complicated?" quoted in Levi, "On Microhistory," 110.

CHAPTER EIGHT

1 *Colonist*, 22 February 1867.

2 Regina vs Mary Anne McFadden and Mary Ann Sampson, file 24/66, British Columbia, Attorney General, Documents, 1857–1966, GR 419, BCA; also British Columbia, Colonial Correspondence, Franklyn to Colonial Secretary, 16 November 1866, file F 602.24, reel B 1329, BCA.

3 *Colonist*, 22 February 1867.

4 Ibid.

5 Ibid.

6 Ibid.

7 Henry Pellew Crease, Attorney General, to Colonial Secretary, 13 March 1867, and Frederick Seymour to Colonial Secretary, 15 March 1867, file F 68.16, reel B 1303, BCA.

8 Sampson took up with another Native woman, Lucy, after the first Mrs Sampson left. Because he was unable to get a divorce from the first Mrs Sampson, he was unable to marry his new partner. As a result, he was relieved from duty as a police constable when the provincial government tightened up on the moral behavior of its employees. He was dismissed, it is important to note, not for living with a Native woman, but for living with her without being married. The difficulties of his situation are explained to the Provincial Secretary by the local Member of the Legislative Assembly, John Booth, in 1872. Provincial Secretary, Correspondence Inward, from J.P. Booth to A.R. Robertson, 19 September 1872; file 602/72, GR 526, BCA.

9 While Mrs Sampson is identified as being of mixed race in the newspaper coverage and trial records, the fact that she ran away to her family in the Fraser River to avoid arrest suggests that she may have been a full-blooded Aboriginal woman, which descendant Rocky Sampson believes to be the case. Franklyn to Colonial Secretary, 11 December 1866, file F 602.24 reel B 1329, BCA.

10 Testimony of Mary Ann Sampson, December 17, 1866. File 24/66, GR 419, BCA.

11 See Tables 7.1 and 7.2.

12 In 1891 only three out of the sixteen Irish household heads were Catholic, and the rest were Protestant. Seven were Church of England, four were Presbyterian, and two were Methodist. Eight out of eleven household heads of Scottish origin were Presbyterian, one was Church of England, one was Methodist, and one was agnostic. Of the fourteen European household heads, seven were Lutheran, five were Catholic, one was Methodist, and one was agnostic. Of the seven household heads of African origin, four were Methodist, two were Baptist, and one was Church of England.

13 St Paul's Catholic Church was opened in 1885; the Burgoyne United Church was opened in 1887; and Saint Mark's Anglican Church was opened in 1892. The history of the two latter are contained in "Saint Mark's Centennial, 1892–1992, Parish of Saltspring Island," typescript, SSIA, and "The Little Church in the Valley: Burgoyne United Church, Fulford-Ganges Road, Saltspring Island, B.C. Researched and Written by Mary E. (McLennan) Davidson," 1987, typescript, SSIA; St Paul's Catholic Church was consecrated in 1885: "St Paul's 100 Year Celebration, May 10, 1980," pamphlet, SSIA.

14 Robson, Diaries. Hills, Diaries.

15 They contain the names of children of a number of well-known Saltspring Island families: Mary Anne McFadden, Elizabeth Whims, and a number of Sparrow, King, and Purser girls. St Ann's, Cowichan, Register of First Arrival at the school, Registers of First Communion, RG II, S36, box 1, Sisters of St Ann Archives, Victoria. My thanks to Dr Jean Barman for sharing this information with me.

16 This was the case of Sophie Purser, later Sophie King, who was placed there in the late 1890s as a young child, shortly after her father became ill; she never knew her parents. Interview with Mrs King, SSIA. Most of the twenty-one girls were placed there as children, not babies, a number of them in their early teens. Most stayed a number of years.

17 John Belshaw found high levels of exogamy among married couples with children in mining communities on Vancouver Island in this same period, and concludes that sectarian conflict was much more muted in the new country than it had been in the old. Thirty-one of the sixty-nine marriages in the Nanaimo area between 1874 and 1899 (45 per cent) were between couples with different religions. Belshaw, *Colonization and Community*, Table 23, 186. This pattern was not typical of the rest of Canada, however. For a contrasting situation, where few inter-religious marriages occurred despite geographical propinquity, see Little, *Crofters and Habitants*, 105–34, 180–218.

18 Ten of the forty-three married household heads married a woman of a different religion, while twenty-two married women of different ethnicity. In 1891 twelve of the fifty-nine married household heads had married women of a different religion and twenty had married women of a different ethnicity.

19 83 per cent of Anglican, 78 per cent of Catholic, and 80 per cent of Methodist household heads appearing on the census in 1881 also appeared on the assessment rolls as landowners. Methodists and Anglicans had been on the island ten years, on average, while the Presbyterians and Catholics had been there for about fifteen years.

20 Wilson, *Salt Spring Island, 1895*, 29.

21 For the importance of landownership and its correlation to age in nineteenth-century Ontario, see Darroch and Soltow, *Property and Inequality in Victorian Ontario*, 201–3.

22 In 1881 none of the household heads owned land before the age of twenty. Six of the eleven men in their twenties, five of the eleven men in their thirties, and forty-two of the fifty-six men over forty owned land. In 1891 twenty of the forty-eight men in their twenties, seventeen of the thirty-four men in their thirties, and thirty-five of the forty-five men over forty owned land.

23 In 1881 fifty-five landowners, representing 42 per cent of the 130 people over eighteen, lived on the island. All but two of these landowners were men. In 1891 landowners made up 39 per cent of the population, or ninety-three of the 239 people over eighteen years of age.

24 Records concerning children (defined here as people under fifteen) are limited to nominal census records (280 out of 378), a few scattered school records, and a small number of birth and death registry entries in the period under study. Only 378 of the 4,652 records in the database contain information about children under fifteen years of age.

25 Gaffield, "Children, Schooling and Family Reproduction."

26 For an overview of the changing role of childhood in Canadian society, see Sutherland, *Childhood in Canadian Society*; and Comacchio, *The Infinite Bonds of Family*.

27 No question about schooling was asked in the 1891 census. Census of Canada, 1881, District no. 191, Vancouver, Cowichan and Saltspring Island, Schedule no. 1 – Nominal; Census of Canada, 1891, District no. 3, Vancouver, M2 – S.D. 14, Saltspring Island, Schedule no. 1 – Nominal.

28 See Public School Reports (BCSP, 1872–91) for statistical breakdowns of the number of students between five and sixteen years of age. For some indication of typical attendance rates in the province, see Penelope Stephenson, "Mrs. Gibson Looked As If She Was Ready for the End of Term"; and Wilson and Stortz, "May the Lord Have Mercy on You."

29 Wilson, "Lottie Bowron and Rural Women Teachers"; and Wilson and Stortz, "May the Lord Have Mercy on You."

30 In 1881, of the twenty-four men from fifteen to thirty years of age, five were married household heads, and two were single households heads. Half (twelve) were sons, living with their family, five were lodgers who may have

been related to the women's side of the family. In 1891 eighty-eight men were between fifteen and thirty: almost half (thirty-four) were sons and a further six were brothers of the household head; seventeen were lodgers, twenty-one headed their own households, and nine of these were married. Three were married but lived in other households, as servants in one case, as in-laws in another. Census of Canada, 1881, District no. 191, Vancouver, Cowichan and Saltspring Island, Schedule no. 1 – Nominal; Census of Canada, 1891, District no. 3, Vancouver, M2 – S.D. 14, Saltspring Island, Schedule no. 1 – Nominal.

31 Of the forty-seven women between fifteen and thirty years of age on the island in 1891, thirty were married. Of the seventeen who were unmarried, twelve lived with their parents and six were lodgers. Census of Canada, 1881, District no. 191, Vancouver, Cowichan and Saltspring Island, Schedule no. 1 – Nominal.

32 In 1881, in sixteen of the twenty-three married couples the wife was younger than thirty-six. Assuming that women in this age group would not have children who had left home, the mother's average age at the birth of the first child was calculated by subtracting the age of the eldest child listed in the census from the mother's age. In 1881 that age was seventeen. In 1891 twenty-four household heads were married with children, and the average age at the birth of the first child for women thirty-five and under was nineteen. Census of Canada, 1881, District no. 191, Vancouver, Cowichan and Saltspring Island, Schedule no. 1 – Nominal.

33 See, for example, Bouchard, "Family Structure and Geographic Mobility at Laterriere," and "Family Reproduction in New Rural Areas," where the migration of whole families to frontier areas like Saltspring Island is explained in this way.

34 Eighty-nine of those showing up on the census had been assessed as landowners in 1891. Of these, seventy-two had obtained all or some of their land by pre-empting it. Only thirty had purchased their pre-empted lands by 1891, but cash sales, or purchases without pre-emption, had already begun to increase by the late 1890s, as chapter 3 explains.

35 File no. 18-1885, roll B2372, British Columbia Attorney General, Inquisitions, 1872–1937, GR 1327, BCA.

36 Beddis, Diary, SSIA.

37 This is particularly clear in the interview with the Dodds family, who arrived on the island just after 1914, and with Charlie Horel, whose mother ran a sawmill on the island in the 1920s and 30s. See interviews with Dorothy, Lassie, and Bob Dodds, 1990, and Charlie Horel, 1990, SSIA. This pride can be inferred in the diary of John Beddis, who carefully outlines the daily work he performs in the year after his father's death. Beddis, Diary, SSIA.

38 See, for example, Accampo's skilful use of this concept in her analysis of industrialization in *Industrialization, Family Life and Class Relations*.

39 Of the fourteen families with adult children in 1881, ten included fifteen adult sons. All except three of these were listed as farmers, just as their fathers (or in one case the widowed mother) were. In 1891 the twenty-six families with adult children included thirty-four adult sons; of these thirteen were listed with no occupation, twenty were the same as their fathers, and one was different – a thirty year-old painter living with his farmer father.

40 Gagan, *Hopeful Travellers*, 53–4.

41 St Ann's Cowichan School, Sisters of St Ann, Victoria, Archives, RG1 S27 Box S27, 50, dated 1939. This box contains writings by the various sisters in the order, organized by person; this is one of the boxes by Sister Mary Theodore. Many thanks to Jean Barman for drawing this source to my attention.

42 Testimony of Mary Ann Sampson, December 17 1866. File 24/66, GR 419.

43 Regina v Whyms [sic] and Anderson, December 21, 1881, file 1881–18, box 22, British Columbia, Attorney General, GR 419, BCA.

44 Regina v Whyms [sic] and Anderson, December 21, 1881, file 1881–18, box 22, British Columbia, Attorney General, GR 419, BCA.

45 Or maybe it didn't. Ann Maria does not appear on the island's census in 1891. Whims does, living with a six-year-old son called William, whose mother is listed as being born in B.C. In 1901 Ann Maria is listed as the wife of Benjamin Lundy (although they don't legally marry until 1902) with a fifteen-year-old son called William, and two daughters aged ten and six. While the two daughters seem to be Lundy's children, William does not. It is not possible to know from the available documentation whether or not William Lundy is the William Whims of the 1891 census.

46 Tamara Myers has documented the tendency of working-class parents to use the judicial system to discipline unruly children and adolescents in early twentieth-century Montreal, as occurred in these two trials involving Constable Sampson. Myers, "The Voluntary Delinquent."

47 Riley, *The Female Frontier*.

48 Ormsby, ed., *A Pioneer Gentlewoman*; and Cole Harris and Phillips, eds, *Letters from Windermere, 1912–1914*.

49 Evidence from inquests is particularly informative here. Charles Bird, file 84–1896, roll B2375; Alfred Douglas, file 18-1907, roll B2382, John Brown, file 5-1892, roll B2373, British Columbia Attorney General, Inquisitions, 1872–1937, GR 1327, BCA.

50 Inquests, File 15 or 18: 1907, GR 1327, BC Attorney General, Inquisitions, 1872–1937, roll B2382; file no. 5-1892, British Columbia Attorney General, Inquisitions, 1872–1937, GR 1327, BCA.

51 Tolson, "Memoirs," SSIA.

52 This point is emphasized by Perry, "Bachelors in the Backwoods."

53 Cartwright, *A Late Summer* 10, SSIA.

54 Falcon, "if the evil ever occurs," unpublished MA thesis. Clarkson, "Liberalism, Nation Building and Family Regulation," unpublished MA thesis; and Clarkson, "Property Law and Family Regulation."

55 In 1833 British women lost their right to dower. Clarkson, "Liberalism, Nation Building and Family Regulation," 42–9; for a discussion on pre-emption rights and landownership, 47, 81–2; for a discussion of the Homestead Exemption Act, see Clarkson, "Property Law and Family Regulation," 392–8.

56 Clarkson, "Liberalism, Nation Building and Family Regulation," 42–9, 81–2.

57 Pateman, *The Disorder of Women*, 43.

58 Clarkson maintains that women's position within liberal capitalism was, nevertheless, improved, as a side effect of new definitions of companionate marriage and responsible womanhood, a point of view that Pateman would not accept. She argues that the discourse of the liberal state is premised on the gendered division of personal and private, within which women are marginalized. Clarkson, "Liberalism, Nation Building and Family Regulation," 96–100; Pateman, *The Disorder of Women*, 44–53. For other arguments about the incompatibility of the liberal state and gender equality, see Gailey, *Kinship to Kingship*; Stewart, *Women, Work and the French State*; and Fraser, "Talking About Needs."

59 In 1881 two of the fifty-one women eighteen and over (4 per cent), and fifty-three of the eighty-one men (65 per cent) in the same age category were landowners. In 1891 only four of the eighty-three women eighteen and over (5 per cent) were landowners, as opposed to eighty-four of the 154 men over seventeen (55 per cent). Only two women took out pre-emptions in the years under study, although a number inherited them from their deceased husbands.

60 Single women in British Columbia were the first in the Dominion to be enfranchised at the municipal level. Single women got the municipal vote in 1873, if they met the property qualification and remained single. Clarkson, "Liberalism, Nation Building and Family Regulation," 100–8. Before 1876 men in the province needed to own land valued at over $250, or hold pre-emptions of more than 100 acres, in order to vote. After that date, universal male suffrage came into effect. Barman, *The West Beyond the West*, 101.

61 Petition Submitted to the Provincial Government by the People of Saltspring Island, 1890 (BCSP, 1891), 415. Similar petitions were made in this year by the Presbyterian Church of British Columbia and other groups. In an important exception to women's exclusion from public organizations women participated actively in the Order of Good Templars temperance organization of the 1880s. A number of women were also teachers on the island before the 1890s.

62 Harriet Staff, who obtained her property from the pre-emption of her late husband, Ernest Harrison, owned 150 acres valued at $1,000; Mary Broadwell,
wife of the merchant J.P. Joel Broadwell, owned 100 acres valued at $400,
which she had purchased outright. She also declared $500 worth of personal
property. She is listed in a business directory as "store-keeper" in 1887. Mallandaine, *British Columbia Directory*, 1887, 133. Sarah Caldwell, a widow
living with her son and his wife, owned 160 acres, valued at $400, which she
pre-empted. Sophia Kelly owned sixty-six acres, valued at $300, which she
had obtained from her husband's pre-emption. It is not clear whether he died
or simply left. British Columbia Department of Finance, Surveyor of Taxes,
1892 Assessment Roll, Roll B 443, Gulf Islands Assessment District, BCA.

63 Mallandaine, *British Columbia Directory*, 1887.

64 Forty-three of the fifty-eight women over fifteen (78 per cent) in 1881 were
listed as wives of the household head, although forty-five (78 per cent) said
they were married. In 1891 sixty-eight of the ninety-two women over fifteen and listed themselves as married (74 per cent), although only sixty-one
(6 per cent) were listed as wives of the household head. Of the women over
twenty, forty out of forty-nine in 1881 and sixty-five out of seventy-nine
in 1891 listed themselves as married. Census of Canada, 1881, District
no. 191, Vancouver, Cowichan and Saltspring Island, Schedule no. 1 –
Nominal; Census of Canada, 1891, District no. 3, Vancouver, M2 – S.D. 14,
Saltspring Island, Schedule no. 1 – Nominal.

65 In 1881 three women household heads were listed in the census: one
widow, one abandoned wife, and one unknown. In 1891 there were two:
one was a widow, the other's marital status is unknown. Census of Canada,
1881, District no. 191, Vancouver, Cowichan and Saltspring Island, Schedule no. 1 – Nominal; Census of Canada, 1891, District no. 3, Vancouver,
M2 – S.D. 14, Saltspring Island, Schedule no. 1 – Nominal.

66 For the account of Dr Hogg's alleged murder, we have only the evidence of
Sylvia Stark, who believed that he was murdered by the same Native Bad
Willie who, she maintained, was guilty of murdering William Robinson and
Giles Curtis. See Marie Albertina Wallace (nee Stark), 1867–1966, BCA.
The inquest declared that he died of natural causes; *British Colonist*, 17
September 1866. For information on Dr Baker, see British Columbia Public
Accounts for the fiscal year ended 30 June 1898 (BCSP, 1899).

67 "Granny Gyves" was known for this role, according to the family. Gyves
Family File, SSIA. The inquest of Mary Reanney contains numerous details
about Mrs Beddis's role in childbirth on the island. Inquest of Mary Reanney, 23 April 1891, Vesuvius Court House, file no. 52–1891, British Columbia Attorney General, Inquisitions, 1872–1937, GR 1327, BCA.

68 Parish records on the island are not kept until the 1880s, and are not reliable throughout the period under study. However, before 1900, when the
population of the island was between 250 and 450, seven babies are listed

as being buried in the Anglican and Methodist churchyards, and five women died in childbirth. [Anglican] Register of Burials, Diocese of British Columbia, and Burials on the Burgoyne Circuit, County of Victoria, Register of Burials, Methodist Church of Canada, SSIA.

69 For an overview of these, see "Who Killed William Robinson? Race, Justice and Settling the Land," a website created by Ruth Sandwell and John Lutz, http://web.uvic.ca/history-robinson/index.html. Typical rates of violence in rural communities are difficult to establish, but studies indicate that rural societies were not the havens from social and personal conflict that so many urban dwellers imagine. See, for example, Dubinsky, *Improper Advances*; Peterson del Mar, "*What Trouble I Have Seen*"; and Lewthwaite, "Violence, Law and Community in Rural Upper Canada."

70 Franklyn to Wakeford, 22 Sept. 1864, file 595/12–16, microfilm reel B1329, Colonial Correspondence, GR 1372, BCA.

71 British Columbia. Attorney General, file 1866/25, box 6, GR 419, BCA.

72 Inquest of Mary Reanney, April 23, 1891, Vesuvius Court House, file no. 52–1891, British Columbia Attorney General, Inquisitions, 1872–1937, GR 1327, BCA.

73 For an account of the incident, see "A Salt Spring Ghost Story," in Kahn, *The History of Salt Spring Island*, 105.

74 Boydston, "To Earn Her Daily Bread," 8–9, and *Home and Work*.

75 Carter, "First Nations Women of Prairie Canada," and "Categories and Terrains of Exclusion."

76 Adele Perry has done an excellent job of articulating the colonialist discourse that identified mixed-race marriage and unorthodox marriage patterns as destructive to civilization in British Columbia. Perry, "I'm Just Sick of the Faces of Men," 27–44, and *On the Edge of Empire*.
For a wider discussion of gender, race, and the colonialist discourse, see Jolly and MacIntyre, eds, *Family and Gender in the Pacific*; Strobel, *Gender, Sex, and Empire*; Young, *Colonial Desire*; and Stoler, *Race and the Education of Desire*. The relation between sexual/familial propriety and class and respectability has been more widely studied, particularly in the British literature. See, for example, Lewis, ed., *Labour and Love*; Poovey, *Uneven Developments*; and Levy, *Other Women*.

77 See, for example, Van Kirk, "Women in Between"; and "What if Mama is an Indian?"; and Perry, *At the Edge of Empire*.

78 Sylvia Van Kirk argues for the social restrictions imposed on colonial society, particularly for women, by the incursion of white women into mixed-race communities, a point re-inforced by Jean Barman. See Van Kirk, "Women in Between"; and Barman, "Invisible Women and Mixed-Race Daughters."

79 For the importance of access to resources, as well as to production, as a measure of inequality within the household, see Moore, "Household and Gender Relations."

80 This conclusion is also suggested by Peter Baskerville's work on enterprising women in Victoria in the nineteenth century, where, after the passage of the Women's Property Act, relatively large numbers of women became entrepreneurs or landholders. Baskerville, "She Has Already Hinted at Board," and "Women and Investment."

81 Walters, *Early Days Among the Gulf Islands*.

82 J.P. Booth to A.R. Robertson, 19 Sept. 1872, Provincial Secretary's Correspondence Inward, file 602/72, GR 526, BCA.

83 Inquest into the death of George Purser, file 18-1885, British Columbia Attorney General, Inquisitions, 1872–1937, roll B 2372, GR 1327, BCA. For a close look at the life of Mrs Purser, see Barman, "The Worth of an Everyday Woman," unpublished paper.

84 This is Harriet Harrison, who went on to become Harriet Staff, and was probably the daughter of Abraham Copeland, one of the first settlers on the island. File no. 329, British Columbia, Supreme Court (Victoria), Probates 1859–1974, GR 1304, BCA.

85 Pre-emption Record 1499, east half of range 1 west, section 8 [Ganges Bay], Saltspring Island Land Register. The fifty acre parcel of land was transferred from William Harrison, improved (no date) and purchased from the crown by Harriet (now married to Alfred Staff) in 1892. Harriet and Alfred were living apart in the 1891 census. Harriet was living on Saltspring with one of her sons in 1901.

86 In 1901 she had apparently left her husband Joseph and was living with her son Edward and his wife. Census of Canada, 1901, District No. 3, Vancouver Electoral District, Polling Sub-division Saltspring Island, Nominal.

87 "Left her husband many years ago and lived with a White man. Now she claims to be married to a half breed by the name of Sheppard and when he is not out sealing lives with him at Saltspring. He is not a member of any band." Canada, Department of Indian Affairs, Ref/vol. RG 10 vol 11,050; file: 33/3 part 7.

88 Louis Stark, box 67, British Columbia Attorney General's Office, GR 419, BCA.

89 Will included in Probate file no. 1754, British Columbia, Supreme Court (Victoria), Probates 1859–1974, GR 1304, BCA.

90 File no. 5-1892, British Columbia Attorney General, Inquisitions, 1872–1937, GR 1327, BCA. Darlington and Mrs Brown were convicted of murder.

91 Bouchard, "Family Reproduction in New Rural Areas."

92 For a discussion of how E.P. Thompson's work has undermined the concept of class, see Reddy, *Money and Liberty*, 1–33.

93 Thompson, *The Making of the English Working Class*, 1–33.

94 Reed, "Gnawing it Out"; Chase, *The People's Farm*. For an excellent Marxist analysis of rural life that explores the difficulties of that frame-

work, see Carter, *Farm Life in Northeast Scotland*. Daniel Samson maintains that while class relations are different in the country from in urban industrial areas, the concept of class simply needs complex revisions to accommodate rural society. Samson, *Contested Countryside*.

95 Thinking of the inadequacies of Marx's two-class model, Asa Brigg's three-class model, and R.S. Neale's five-class model, William Reddy argues "whenever it becomes a question of linking political comportment with social or economic status, endless subtleties and the constant discovery of new exceptions and subgroups have taken the place of the simple schemas of class conflict." Reddy, *Money and Liberty*, 28. Although E.P. Thompson recommends holding on to the concept "not from its perfection as a concept but from the fact that no alternative category is available, in the endless and seemingly inevitable visions and revisions of class," Reddy maintains that its resemblance to the "old commonsense original is so faint that one can legitimately object to retaining the old word." Reddy, *Money and Liberty*, 105; Thompson, "Eighteenth Century English Society," 149.

96 For the difficulties of elaborating the inequalities within the household in terms of liberal economic and political theory, see Sandwell, "Rural Reconstruction"; Hart "Imagined Utilities," esp. 113–14; Folbre, "Hearts and Spades," esp. 247; Moore, "Household and Gender Relations," esp. 132; Muszynski, "Structural Determinants," 103–20; Valenze, *The First Industrial*; and Sandwell, "The Limits of Liberalism."

97 8 June 1869 and 4 April 1879, Saltspring Islanders petition for better roads, "Petitions," F1355, Colonial Correspondence, GR 1372, BCA.

98 Thomas Lineker to James Douglas, 9 July 1860, F1000, 1 Colonial Correspondence, GR 1372, BCA; M. Franklyn, Magistrate, to Colonial Secretary, 28 December, 1866, F602/27, Colonial Correspondence, GR 1372, BCA; Douglas to Newcastle, 8 January 1861, MS quoted in Flucke, "Early Days on Saltspring Island," 183. See also 21 December 1868, petition regarding the murder of William Robinson, "Petitions," Colonial Correspondence, F1355, GR 1372, BCA.

99 See Frederick Lester to His Excellency Arthur Kennedy, May 1864, F988-1, Colonial Correspondence, GR 1372, BCA; from John Booth, Thomas Griffiths and Abraham Copeland, to Colonial Secretary, 26 October 1869, GR 1372; from Fred Foord et al. to His Excellency Lieutenant Governor Trutch, 20 July 1872, F565-72, GR 526, BCA.

100 "Research Report" on Saltspring Island Post Offices, by William E. Topping, Fellow, Royal Philatelic Society, London, typescript, SSIA. For a discussion on the importance of the money-order business, see, for example, Fletcher to National Post Office, June 1887, file 723, and August 1887, file 768. Divisional Inspectors' Reports, National Post Office of Canada,

source RG3, reel C-7227, NAC. Mr Fletcher to Post Master General, 20 May 1887, Post Office Inspectors' Reports, British Columbia, 1886–87, RG3, series 6 vol. 8, reel C7227, file no. 696, NAC.

101 *British Colonist*, 13 September 1885; *Henderson's British Columbia Gazetteer and Directory*, 1889, 275, 276, 348.

102 See, for example, Davidson, "The McLennan Family," Presentation to the Salt Spring Island Historical Society, 1989, Interviews, SSIA; and Akerman, "The Akerman Family," Presentation to the Salt Spring Island Historical Society, 1987, Interviews, SSIA.

103 See Fred Foord to John Morley, 26 July 1873, Add Mss 984.7.5, BCA.

104 See, for example, Hamilton, *Salt Spring Island*; and Kahn, *The History of Saltspring Island*.

105 George Mitchell, J. Akerman, J.C. Crane, J.C. Jones, Fred Foord, and T.C. Parry were elected. Mitchell, Akerman, Foord, and Parry owned extensive lands; Foord and Akerman went on to be among the wealthiest on the land by 1891, the earliest date at which assessment rolls are available. 16 January 1873, box 1, file 2, British Columbia, Provincial Secretary, Saltspring Island Correspondence and By-laws, GR 1707, BCA. For a full description of the elite of Saltspring Island, see Sandwell, chapter 5, "Reading the Land."

106 J.I. Little suggests that the formation of an elite within a population seems necessary to mobilize successful operation of municipal governments Little, *Society and State in Transition*; 13–14.

107 Barron, *Those Who Stayed Behind*, 31.

108 Burchell, Gordon, and Miller, eds, *The Foucault Effect*.

109 Curtis, "Preconditions of the Canadian State."

110 Samson, "Industry and Improvement," unpublished PhD thesis.

111 Loo, *Making Law, Order and Authority*.

112 Loo, *Making Law, Order and Authority*, 9.

113 "British Columbians actively sought the application of law and the construction and intervention of the courts. They did not see recourse to the courts as unnatural or as a sign of social breakdown, but as a natural outgrowth of human nature and the conflict that accompanied the pursuit of self-interest." Loo, *Making Law, Order and Authority*, 9.

114 Little, *Society and State in Transition*, 13–14.

115 Douglas to Newcastle, 8 January 1861, MS, BCA cited in Flucke, "Early Days on Saltspring Island," 183.

116 For a close look at the "modernizing" role of post offices, and resistance to it in rural America, see B. Kielbowicz, "Rural Ambivalence Towards Mass Society." Inspector Fletcher to the Postmaster General, 23 June 1887, Canada, Divisional Inspectors' Reports, Corrrespondence, National Post Office (Canada), British Columbia, 1887, RG3–D3, Series 6, reel C-7227, no. 723, NAC.

See also 14 January 1895, where the competency of Mr McFadden is questioned. Fletcher to Postmaster General, Canada, Divisional Inspectors' Reports, Correspondence, National Post Office (Canada), British Columbia, 1895, RG3, Series 6, vol. 9, file no. 198, NAC.

117 Seventh Annual Report on the Public Schools of the Province of British Columbia, 1877–78 (BCSP, 1878): 711–13.

118 Postal Inspector Wallace to the Postmaster General, 28 December 1882, Canada, Divisional Inspectors' Reports, Correspondence, National Post Office (Canada), British Columbia 1882–1884, RG3, Series 6, vol. 4, reel 7226, file no. 789, NAC.

119 A.R. Robertson to John P. Booth, Saltspring Island, 19 September 1872, British Columbia. Colonial Secretary, Correspondence Outward, January 1871 to December 1872, C/AB/30.1J/11, BCA. See also n8.

120 Arthur Walter to the Hon. Mr Smithe, Premier, 28 April 1885, British Columbia Premier's Office, Correspondence Inwards, box 1, file 3, GR 441, BCA.

121 For Sampson's arrest of his daughter, see Regina v Whyms [sic] and Anderson, December 21, 1881, box 22, file 1881–18, British Columbia Attorney General, GR 419. For his arrest of his wife, see Regina vs Mary Anne McFadden and Mary Ann Sampson, file 24/66, British Columbia Attorney General, Documents, 1857–1966, GR 419, BCA; also Franklyn to Colonial Secretary, 16 November 1866, file F602.24 reel B1329, British Columbia, Colonial Correspondence, BCA.

122 See, for example, Wilson and Stortz, "May the Lord Have Mercy on You"; and Wilson, "Lottie Bowron and Rural Women Teachers."

123 Frederick Lester to the Governor of Vancouver Island, May 1864, F988-1, Colonial Correspondence, GR 1372, BCA; see also "Saltspring Island" Second Annual Report of Public Schools for the Year Ending 31 July 1873 (BCSP, 1874), 11; "Saltspring Island School," Third Annual Report of Public Schools for the Year Ending 31 July 1874 (BCSP, 1875).

124 Sixth Annual Report on the Public Schools of the Province of British Columbia, 1876–77 (BCSP, 1877), 18.

125 J.P. Booth, Secretary, to SAG Lewis, 10 February 1882, in British Columbia Superintendent of Education, Correspondence Inward, GR 1445, BCA.

126 "Central Settlement, Saltspring Island," Public Schools Report, 1881–82 (BCSP, 1883).

127 In 1876 high rates of absenteeism at the Burgoyne Bay School were related to "local differences" while at the North End School, "local animosities have subsided; the teacher has overcome the prejudices that existed against him." Fifth Annual Report on the Public Schools of the Province of British Columbia, 1875–76 (BCSP, 1877), 104. Island schools were closed for a number of months in 1875, Public School Report, 1875–76

(BCSP, 1877), 104; in 1876, Public Schools Report, 1876–77 (BCSP, 1878); and in 1882, Public Schools Report, 1881–82 (BCSP, 1883).

128 G. Stainburn, teacher at Burgoyne Bay to C.C. McKenzie, Superintendent of Education, Burgoyne Bay, 4 October 1881, in British Columbia Superintendent of Education, Correspondence Inward, GR 1445, BCA.

129 Louis Stark to Mr Trutch, land agent, November 1869 and 22 November 1870, British Columbia Surveyor General, Correspondence Inward from Louis Stark, 1869, 1870, C/B/30.71K/S+s, BCA.

130 Although the Women's Institute, the Sunshine Guild, the Imperial Order of the Daughters of the Empire, and the Islands' Agricultural and Fruit Growers Association emerged on the island late in the nineteenth century or early in the twentieth, the only social or economic organizations on Saltspring Island in the years under study were the Farmer's Institute, and the Saltspring Island Lodge of the Independent Order of Good Templars. Only the minutes for the latter are available before 1891.

131 In the second meeting, after passing a motion to draft a code of laws, "considerable argument then ensued which however took no definite effect," and members had to wait until the next meeting till cooler heads could prevail. Minutes for 10 February 1886, Minute Book of Independent Order of Good Templars, Hope of Saltspring Lodge, Lodge No. 87, Vesuvius Bay, SSIA.

132 11 August 1886; January 1887; 26 July 1887; 31 Jan 1888; 9 March 1887; 24 May 1887; 31 May 1887; Minutes, Hope of Saltspring Lodge, SSIA.

133 1 September 1888, Hope of Saltspring Lodge. For a delightful blow-by-blow account of the Lodge, see Crofton, "The Rise and Sad Demise of Saltspring's Lodge of Hope."

134 For an overview of these, see Sandwell and Lutz, "Who Killed William Robinson?". See, for example, Dubinsky, *Improper Advances*; Peterson del Mar, "What Trouble I Have Seen"; and Lewthwaite, "Violence, Law and Community."

135 For an early history of the political furore on Saltspring Island, see Flucke, "Early Days on Saltspring Island," 161–99.

136 Petition submitted to Jonathan Begg, Returning Officer for Saltspring Island, by voters on Saltspring Island, 13 January 1860, file 142, microfilm reel B1309, GR 1372, BCA.

137 *British Colonist*, 2 and 9 April 1863.

138 *British Colonist*, 17 January 1874.

139 E. Pimbury to J.W. Trutch, 15 January 1874, file B1-F2, Saltspring Island Correspondence and By-Laws, 1871–1882, British Columbia, Provincial Secretary, Correspondence, GR 1707, BCA.

140 Flucke, "Early Days on Saltspring Island," 197.

141 Vict. 46, chap. 22, Statutes of the Province of British Columbia, 1883, Victoria, 1883, 89, quoted in Flucke, "Early Days on Saltspring Island," 199.

142 Fred Foord to Honorable Executive Council, In Answer to the Petition of Settlers of Burgoyne Bay, 1882, Box 1, file 2, Saltspring Island Correspondence and By-Laws, 1871–1882, British Columbia, Provincial Secretary, Correspondence, GR 1707, BCA.

CONCLUSION

1 Malin, *History and Ecology*, xxii. Malin's key arguments are summed up in Robert P. Swierenga's valuable editorial comments and introduction to this collection.

2 Lyle Dick's study of human settlement in what may be the most extreme environment, Ellesmere Island, confirms Malin's supposition that human culture allows people to adapt to most conditions, given the time, knowledge, and technology. Dick, *Muskox Land*.

3 See Sandwell, "Introduction: Finding Rural British Columbia," in Sandwell, ed., *Beyond the City Limits*.

4 As Simard puts it, "*Indians* and *Whites* do not exist ... Indian and White represent fabled creatures, born as one in the minds of seventeenth and eighteenth century European thinkers trying to make sense of the modern experience, particularly the European 'discovery' of new continents and their populations." Simard, "White Ghosts, Red Shadows," 333–69.

5 See, for example, Cole Harris, "The Simplification of Europe Overseas"; and Sacouman, "Semi-Proletarianization and Rural Underdevelopment in the Maritimes."

6 Bouchard, "Family Reproduction in New Rural Areas."

7 Samson, ed., *Contested Countryside*, 26.

8 Jean Barman has suggested this with her study of inter-racial marriages in rural areas of the province. Barman, "Invisible Women and Mixed-Race Daughters."

9 Cole Harris explores the humanitarian nature of colonial policy through a detailed discussion of the Douglas System in *Making Native Space*. Other writers have tended to ignore the advantages that colonialism brought to such groups as African-Americans and Hawaiians and to construct the ethnic diversity and relative equality evident in the mid-nineteenth century as a transitional or incidental characteristic of colonialism in British Columbia.

10 Saltspring Island has retained its antipathy to municipal government. In spite of repeated referenda on the subject, the island refuses to become a municipality.

This is not to deny the great appeal of islands as the focus of academic research (witness the Institute for Island Studies in Prince Edward Island)

or as a tourist destination. It is, however, to suggest that the discursive
power of island to constitute "other" has been overstated. For a particularly clear articulation of this contrast see Wilson, *A New Lease on Life*.

11 For a review of the centrality of the family in Canadian rural history, see
Sandwell, "Rural Reconstruction."

12 For a discussion of "liberalism" in Canadian history and historiography,
see McKay, "The Liberal Order Framework."

13 For a discussion of some of these, see Sandwell, "The Limits of Liberalism."

14 For a detailed explication of the need to re-evaluate the relevance of liberal economic and political theory to nineteenth-century Canadian history,
see Sandwell, "Rural Reconstruction."

Bibliography

A. PRIMARY SOURCES

Manuscripts

Archives of the Ecclesiastic Province of British Columbia, University of British Columbia, Vancouver
• Hills, George, Bishop of Columbia, Diaries, 1860–1887.

Archives of the Sisters of St Ann, Victoria
• St Ann's, Cowichan, Register of First Arrival at the school, Registers of First Communion, RG II, S36, box 1.

British Columbia Archives
Aldous, F.G., "Regarding the S.E. Quarter of Section 52, Saltspring Island," Field Notes, Map Division, Office of the Surveyor General, Victoria, 1943.
Blair, George, Diary, 1862, Add Mss. 186.
British Columbia, Attorney General, Correspondence, GR 419.
– – Inquisitions, 1872–1937, GR 1327.
– Colonial Correspondence Inward, GR 1372.
– Colonial Correspondence, "Petitions, 1868–1870," GR 1372.
– Colonial Secretary, Colonial Correspondence, Reel B1329.
– – Correspondence Out, January 1871 to December 1872, C/AB/30.1J/11.
– Department of Finance, Surveyor of Taxes, 1892–1894, Assessment Roll B 443, Gulf Islands Assessment District.
British Columbia, Department of Land and Works, Pre-Emption Records, Vancouver and Gulf Islands, GR 766.
– – Certificates of Improvement, Vancouver Island and the Gulf Islands, GR 765.
– – "Mr. Morley's Old Book, Land Records and List of Squatters," GR 514.
– – Correspondence Outward, 1859, CAA30.7J1.

– Department of Lands, Miners' Certificates and Leaves of Absence, Misc. Mining Receipts and Leaves Of Absence, Box 4, GR 1057.

– District of Salt Spring Island and Chemainus Sheriff's Office, List of Voters, 29 January 1866, GR 1666.

– District of Salt Spring Island and Chemeynes, List of Voters, 30 January 1862, GR 1666.

– Premier's Office, Correspondence Inwards, GR 441.

– Provincial Secretary, Correspondence Inward, GR 526.

– – Correspondence, Salt Spring Island Municipal By-Laws, Saltspring Island Correspondence and By-Laws, 1871–1882, GR 1707.

– Royal Commission on Agriculture, 1912 , testimony given at Ganges Harbour, April 10, 1912; box 1/4, GR 324.

– Salt Spring Island and Chemainus District, Poll Book, 27 July 1863, GR 1666.

– Superintendent of Education, Correspondence Inward, 1879–1891, GR 1445.

– Supreme Court (Victoria), Probates 1859–1974, GR 1304.

– Surveyor General, Correspondence Inward from Louis Stark, 1869, 1870, C/G/30.71k/s+2.

– Vancouver Island Colonial Surveyor, Correspondence and Papers re. Settlers on Salt Spring Is, 1859, '61, '62, '66, CAA/30.71/sa3.1.

– – Office of the Land Recorder for Salt Spring Island, Copy of the Pre-Emption Register to 17 October 1862; CAA/30.71/SA3.1.

– Vancouver Island, Supreme Court of Civil Justice, Bench Books of Criminal Cases Heard Before Judge Joseph Needham, 1867–1869, Trial of Tom for the Murder of William Robinson, 1869, GR 2030.

Brown, Robert, "Miscellaneous notes on Vancouver Island: Scrapbooks, 1863–64," vol. 1, Add Mss 794.

Canada. Census of Canada, 1881, District no. 191, Vancouver, Cowichan and Saltspring Island, Schedule no. 1 – Nominal.

– – 1891, District no. 3, Vancouver, M2 – S.D. 14, Saltspring Island, Schedule no. 1 – Nominal.

Fred Foord to John Morley, 26 July 1873, Add Mss 984.7.5.

Fry, Henry, "Field Notes, Survey of Saltspring Island, Saltspring Island Field Book," Map Division Office of the Surveyor General, Victoria, September 1907.

Green, Ashdown Henry, Diary of a Survey of Saltspring Island, 8 June – 22 November 1874, Add Mss 437.

Laing, F.W., Secretary to the Minister of Agriculture, "Early Agriculture in British Columbia," typescript, 1925, GR 509.

Mallandaine, Edward, "Reminiscences," Add Mss 470.

Robson, Ebenezer, Diaries, 16 September 1861 to 27 March 1862, H/D/R57, R57.3.

Wallace, Marie Albertina (née Stark), "1867–1966, Salt Spring Island, B.C."
    Xerox of typescript, Add. Mss. 91.

National Archives of Canada
Canada, Indian Reserve Commission, Census of British Columbia Indians,
    1876–77, RG 88 v 494.
– National Post Office (Canada), British Columbia, 1877–1880, Divisional In-
    spectors' Reports, Correspondence, RG3, Series 6, vol. 2, reel 7225.
– National Post Office (Canada), British Columbia, 1882–1884, Divisional In-
    spectors' Reports, Correspondence, RG3, Series 6, vol. 4, reel 7226.
– National Post Office (Canada), British Columbia, 1895, Divisional Inspec-
    tors' Reports, Correspondence, RG3, Series 6, vol. 9, reel 7320.
– National Post Office (Canada), British Columbia, 1897, Divisional Inspec-
    tors' Reports, Correspondence, RG3–D3, Series 6, vol. 9, reel 7232.

Special Collections, University of British Columbia Archives
Anglo British Company (ABC) Packers, Managers' Draft Books, 1901–1905.
Laing, F.W.,"Colonial Farm Settlers on the Mainland of British Columbia,
    1859–1871," MS.

Saltspring Island Archives
Aitken, Alexander, Diary, 1891–92.
Akerman Family, Family File.
Beddis, John, Diary, 1 January 1890 to 30 June 1890.
Begg, Jonathan, Correspondence to William and Margaret Chisholm, 1858–62.
Bullock, Henry, Bullock File.
Gyves Family, Family File.
Mahon Family, Family File.
Maxwell Family, Family File.
Minute Book of Independent Order of Good Templars, 1886–87, Hope of
    Saltspring Lodge, Lodge No. 87, Vesuvius Bay.
Register of Baptisms, Marriages and Burials, Union Church, Methodist
    Church, United Church of Canada, Burials on the Burgoyne Circuit, Victoria
    District, British Columbia.
Register of Births, Marriages, and Burials, 1891–1915, [Anglican] Diocese of
    Columbia.
Saltspring Island Archives (SSIA) on-line, http://saltspringarchives.com/
    index.html
Tolson, Leonard, "Memoirs," 1941.
Topping, William E., "Research Report on Saltspring Island Post Offices,"
    typescript, London, nd.
Trage Family, Family File.
Wilson, E.F.,"Our Life on Salt Spring Island, B.C., 4 February 1894 to
    24 November 1905," MS.

Primary Sources: Published

British Columbia as a Field for Emigration and Investment, Victoria: Wolfenden Press, 1891.

British Columbia Directory for the Years 1882–83, Victoria: R.T. Williams, 1882.

British Columbia Directory for 1884–85, Victoria: R.T. Williams, 1885.

British Columbia Directory, Victoria: E. Mallandaine, R.T. Williams, 1887.

Directory of Vancouver Island and Adjacent Islands for 1909, Victoria: Provincial Publishing Co., 1909.

Handbook of British Columbia and Emigrant's Guide to the Gold Fields with Map and Two Illustrations from Photographs by M. Claudet, London: W. Oliver, 1862.

Henderson's British Columbia Gazetteer and Directory for 1897, Victoria: 1897.

Henderson's British Columbia Gazetteer and Directory, Victoria: 1902.

Henderson's British Columbia Gazetteer and Directory, Victoria: 1905.

Henderson's British Columbia Gazetteer and Directory, vol. 13, Victoria: 1910.

Henderson's British Columbia Gazetteer and Directory, 1889, Victoria: 1889.

Henderson's Greater Victoria City Directory and Vancouver Island Gazetteer and Directory, 1914, Victoria: 1914.

Henderson's Victoria City and Vancouver Island Gazetteer and Directory, 1910–11, Victoria: 1911.

The Mercantile Agency Reference Book (and Key) for the Dominion of Canada, Toronto: Dun, Wiman and Co., July 1887.

The Mercantile Agency Reference Book (and Key) for the Dominion of Canada, Toronto: R.G. Dun and Co., 1900.

Williams British Columbia Directory, Victoria: 1889.

British Columbia. *British Columbia Public Accounts, 1885–1914*, Victoria: R. Wolfenden.

– Department of Agriculture, *Agriculture of British Columbia, Canada, Bulletin No. 8*. Published by the Authority of the Legislative Assembly, Victoria: 1919.

– – *Province of British Columbia, Canada: Its Climate and Resources, with Information for Emigrants*, Victoria: Wolfenden Press, 1883.

– – Reports 1891–95, *British Columbia Sessional Papers* (BCSP), 1892–96.

– "Petition Submitted to the Provincial Government by the People of Salt Spring Island, 1890," BCSP, 1891.

– Public Schools Reports, 1873–1900, BCSP, 1874–1901.

– Voters' Lists, Elections, 1875, 1876, 1877, 1878, 1879, 1881, 1882, 1885, 1890, 1893, 1894, 1898, 1900, 1903, 1906, 1908, 1911, 1913, BCSP.

Canada. Agriculture Canada, Research Branch, *Soils of the Gulf Islands of British Columbia, volume 1, Soils of Saltspring Island,* Report no. 43, Victoria: British Columbia Soil Survey, 1987.

– Dominion Bureau of Statistics, *Seventh Census of Canada, 1931.*

– – – Census of Agriculture in British Columbia, volume 8, 1931.

– – *Third Census of Canada, 1891.*

– – *Fourth Census of Canada, 1901,* Bulletin XII, Census of Agriculture, British Columbia, 1901.

Canada, *Manual Containing Instructions to Officers Employed in the Taking of the Third Census of Canada,* Ottawa: Government Printing, 1891.

Cartwright, E.A., *A Late Summer: the Memoirs of E.R. Cartwright,* London: Caravel Press, 1964.

Claydon, P.S.N. and V.A. Melanson, eds and comps, *Vancouver Voters, 1886: A Bibliographic Dictionary,* Vancouver: British Columbia Genealogical Society, 1994.

Environment Canada, *Saltspring Island: A Landscape Analysis,* Report BC-X-99, Victoria: Pacific Forest Research Center, 1974.

Hayman, John, ed., *Robert Brown and the Vancouver Island Exploring Expedition,* Vancouver: University of British Columbia Press, 1989.

Hendrickson, James, *Journals of the Colonial Legislatures of the Colonies of Vancouver Is. and British Columbia 1851–1871,* 5 vols, Victoria: Provincial Archives, 1980.

Mallandaine, Edward, *First Victoria Directory, Comprising a General Directory of Citizens,* Victoria: Hibben, Carswell, and Herre, 1860.

– *First Victoria Directory, fourth issue, and a British Columbia Guide,* Victoria: 1871.

– *Guide to the Province of British Columbia for 1877–78, compiled from the latest and most authentic sources of information,* Victoria: T. Hibben and Co., 1877.

– *British Columbia Directory,* Victoria: R.T. Williams, 1887.

Phillips, E. *Salt Spring Island, 1902, British Columbia,* pamphlet (n.p.), SSIA.

Wilson, The Rev. E. *Salt Spring Island, 1895: an Illustrated Pamphlet with Map,* Salt Spring Island: Vesuvius P.O., 1895.

Newspapers

British Colonist, 1859–91.

Chronicle, 1866.

Daily Press (Victoria), 1861.

Daily Province (Vancouver), 1927.

New Westminster Times, 1859–61.

Salt Spring Island Parish and Home, 1892–96.

Victoria Gazette, 14 July 1859–61.
Weekly British Colonist, 1860.

Interviews

Bennett, John, Interview, 1990, SSIA.

Brown, Ted, Interview, 1990, SSIA.

Davidson, Mary, "The McLennan Family," Presentation to the Salt Spring Island Historical Society 1989; Interviews, SSIA.

Dodds, Robert, Dorothy and Lassie, Interview, 1990, SSIA.

Hele, Robert and Diane, Interview, 1990, SSIA.

Horel, Charles, Interview, 1990, SSIA.

Reynolds, Valentine, Interview, 1990, SSIA.

B. SECONDARY SOURCES

Books

Accampo, Eleanor, *Industrialization, Family Life and Class Relations: Saint Chamond, 1815–1914,* Berkeley: University of California Press, 1989.

Anderson, Benedict, *Imagined Communities: Reflections on the Origin and Spread of Nationalism,* London: Verso, 1983, 1991.

Anderson, Kay J., *Vancouver's Chinatown: Racial Discourse in Canada, 1875–1980,* Montreal and Kingston: McGill-Queen's University Press, 1991.

Arnett, Chris, *The Terror of the Coast: Land Alienation and Colonial War on Vancouver Island and the Gulf Islands, 1849–1863,* Burnaby: Talonbooks, 1999.

Asch, Michael, ed., *Aboriginal and Treaty Rights in Canada: Essays on Law, Equality and Respect for Difference,* Vancouver: UBC Press, 1997.

Barman, Jean, *Growing up British in British Columbia: Boys in Private School,* Vancouver: UBC Press, 1984.

– *The West Beyond the West: A History of British Columbia,* Toronto: University of Toronto Press, 1991.

– Neil Sutherland, and J. Donald Wilson, eds, *Children, Teachers and Schools in the History of British Columbia,* Calgary: Detsilig Publishing, 1995.

Barron, Hal, *Those Who Stayed Behind: Rural Society in Nineteenth-Century New England,* Cambridge: Cambridge University Press, 1984.

Baskerville Peter, and Eric W. Sager, *Unwilling Idlers: The Urban Unemployed and their Families in Late Victorian Canada,* Toronto: University of Toronto Press, 1998.

Belshaw, John Douglas, *Colonization and Community: The Vancouver Island Coalfield and the Making of the British Columbian Working Class,* Montreal and Kingston: McGill-Queen's University Press, 2002.

Bordieu, Pierre, *Outline of a Theory of Practice*, Cambridge: Cambridge University Press, 1977.

Boydston, Jean, *Home and Work: Housework, Wages and the Ideology of Labor in the Early Republic*, Oxford: Oxford University Press, 1990.

Bradbury, Bettina, *Working Families: Age, Gender and Daily Survival in Industrializing Montreal*, Toronto: McClelland and Stewart, 1993..

Brown, Jennifer S.H., *Strangers in the Blood: Fur Trade Company Families in Indian Country*, Vancouver: UBC Press, 1980.

Burchell, Graham, Colin Gordon, and Peter Miller, eds, *The Foucault Effect: Studies in Governmentality, with Two Lectures by and an Interview with Michel Foucault*, Chicago: University of Chicago Press, 1991.

Cail, Robert E., *Land, Man and the Law: The Disposal of Crown Lands in British Columbia, 1871–1913*, Vancouver: UBC Press, 1974.

Canada, Environment Canada, *Saltspring Island: A Landscape Analysis*, Report BC-X-99, Victoria: Environment Canada, Pacific Forest Research Centre, 1974.

Carlson, Keith Thor, Albert McHalsie, and Jan Perrier, *A Sto:lo Coast Salish Historical Atlas*, Vancouver, Seattle, and Chilliwack: Douglas and McIntyre, University of Washington Press, and Sto:lo Heritage Trust, 2001.

Carter, Ian, *Farm Life in Northeast Scotland: 1840–1914: The Poor Man's Country*, Edinburgh: John Donald Publishing, 1979.

Carter, Sarah, *Capturing Women: The Manipulation of Cultural Imagery in Canada's Prairie West*, Montreal and Kingston: McGill-Queen's University Press, 1997.

Certeau, Michel de, *The Practice of Everyday Life*, Berkeley: University of California Press, 1984.

Chase, Malcolm, *The People's Farm: English Radical Agrarianism 1775–1840*, Oxford: Oxford University Press, 1988.

Clayton, Daniel W., *Islands of Truth: The Imperial Fashioning of Vancouver Island*, Vancouver: UBC Press, 2000.

Cohen, Marjorie Griffin, *Women's Work, Markets and Economic Development in Nineteenth Century Ontario*, Toronto: University of Toronto Press, 1988.

Comacchio, Cynthia R., *The Infinite Bonds of Family: Domesticity in Canada, 1850–1940*, Toronto: University of Toronto Press, 1999.

Cruikshank, Julie, *Life Lived Like a Story: Life Stories of Three Yukon Native Elders*, Vancouver: UBC Press, 1990.

Darroch, Gordon, and Lee Soltow, *Property and Inequality in Victorian Ontario: Structural Patterns and Cultural Communities in the 1871 Census*, Toronto: University of Toronto Press, 1994.

Dick, Lyle, *Farmers Making Good: The Development of the Abernethy District, Saskatchewan, 1880–1920*, Ottawa: Environment Canada, 1989.

– *Muskox Land: Ellesmere Island in the Age of Contact*, Calgary: University of Calgary Press, 2001.

Dirks, Nicholas, Geoff Eley, and Sherry B. Ortner, eds, *Culture, Power, History: A Reader in Contemporary Social Theory*, Princeton: Princeton University Press, 1994.

Drushka, Ken, *Working in the Woods: A History of Logging on the West Coast*, Vancouver: Harbour Publishing, 1992.

Dubinsky, Karen, *Improper Advances: Rape and Heterosexual Conflict in Ontario, 1880–1929*, Chicago: University of Chicago Press, 1993.

Duff, Wilson, *The Indian History of British Columbia, volume 1, The Impact of the White Man*, Victoria: Provincial Museum of British Columbia, 1964.

Elliot, Marie, *Mayne Island and the Gulf Islands: A History*, Mayne Island: 1984.

Elliott, Bruce, *Irish Migrants in the Canadas: A New Approach*, Kingston and Montreal: McGill-Queen's University Press, 1988.

Fink, Deborah, *Agrarian Women: Wives and Mothers in Rural Nebraska, 1880–1940*, Chapel Hill: University of North Carolina Press, 1992.

Fisher, Robin, *Contact and Conflict: Indian-European Relations in British Columbia, 1774–1890*, Vancouver: UBC Press, (1977) 1992.

Foucault, Michel, *Discipline and Punish: The Birth of the Prison*, New York: Vintage, 1979.

– *The Archaeology of Knowledge*, New York: Pantheon, 1972.

Furniss, Elizabeth, *The Burden of History: Colonialism and the Frontier Myth in a Rural Canadian Community*, Vancouver: UBC Press, 1999.

Gaffield, Chad, *Language, Schooling and Cultural Conflict: The Origins of French Language Controversy in Ontario*, Montreal and Kingston: McGill-Queen's University Press, 1987.

Gagan, David, *Hopeful Travelers: Families, Land and Social Change in Mid-Victorian Peel County*, Toronto: University of Toronto Press, 1981.

Gailey, Christine Ward, *Kinship to Kingship: Gender Hierarchy and State Formation in the Tongan Islands*, Austin: University of Texas Press, 1987.

Garner, Joe, *Never Fly Over an Eagle's Nest: A True Story of Courage and Survival During British Columbia's Early Years*, Nanaimo: Cinnabar Press, 1980.

Gough, Barry, *Gunboat Frontier: British Maritime Authority and Northwest Coast Indians 1846–90*, Vancouver: UBC Press, 1984.

Greer, Allan, *Peasant, Lord and Merchant: Rural Society in Three Quebec Parishes, 1740–1840*, Toronto: University of Toronto Press, 1985.

Guha, Ranajit, ed., *Subaltern Studies II*, New Delhi: Oxford University Press, 1983.

Hamilton, Bea, *Salt Spring Island*, Vancouver: Mitchell Press, 1968.

Harris, R. Cole, *Making Native Space: Colonialism, Resistance and Reserves in British Columbia*, Vancouver: UBC Press, 2002.

– *The Resettlement of British Columbia: Essays on Colonialism and Geographical Change*, Vancouver: UBC Press, 1997.

– and Elizabeth Phillips, eds, *Letters from Windermere, 1912–1914*, Vancouver: UBC Press, 1984.

Hayman, John, ed., *Robert Brown and the Vancouver Island Exploring Expedition*, Vancouver: UBC Press, 1989.

Howkins, Alun, *Reshaping Rural England, 1850–1925*, London: Harper Collins, 1991.

Inwood, Kris, ed., *Farm, Factory and Fortune: New Studies in the Economic History of the Maritime Provinces*, Fredericton: Acadiensis Press, 1993.

Jensen, Joan, *Loosening the Bonds: Mid Atlantic Farm Women 1750–1850*, New Haven: Yale University Press, 1986.

Johnston, Hugh J.M., ed., *The Pacific Province: A History of British Columbia*, Vancouver: Douglas and McIntyre, 1996.

Jolly, Margaret, and Martha MacIntyre, eds, *Family and Gender in the Pacific: Domestic Contradictions and the Colonial Impact*, Cambridge: Cambridge University Press, 1989.

Kahn, Charles, *The History of Salt Spring Island*, Madeira Park: Harbour Publishing, 1998.

Kilian, Crawford, *Go Do Some Great Thing: The Black Pioneers of British Columbia*, Vancouver: Douglas and McIntyre, 1978.

Klein, Kerwin, *Frontiers of Historical Imagination: Narrativing the European Conquest of Native America, 1890–1990*, Berkeley: University of California Press, 1997.

Knight, Rolf, *Indians at Work: An Informal History of Native Indian Labour in British Columbia, 1858–1930*, Vancouver: New Star, 1978.

Koppel, Tom, *Kanaka: The Untold Story of Hawaiian Pioneers in British Columbia and the Pacific Northwest*, Vancouver: Whitecap Books, 1995.

Lehning, James, *Peasant and French: Cultural Contact in Rural France During the Nineteenth Century*, Cambridge: Cambridge University Press, 1995.

Levy, Anita, *Other Women: The Writings of Class, Race and Gender, 1832–1898*, Princeton: Princeton University Press, 1991.

Lewis, Jane, ed., *Labour and Love: Women's Experience of Home and Family*, Cambridge: Blackwells, 1986.

Lillard, Charles, *Seven Shillings a Year: The History of Vancouver Island*, Saltspring Island: Horsdal and Schubart, 1986.

Little, J.I., *Crofters and Habitants: Settler Society, Economy and Culture in a Quebec Township, 1848–1881*, Montreal and Kingston: McGill-Queen's University Press, 1991.

– *Nationalism, Capitalism and Colonization in Nineteenth Century Quebec*, Montreal and Kingston: McGill-Queen's University Press, 1989.

– *Society and State in Transition: The Politics of Institutional Reform in the Eastern Townships, 1838–1852*, Montreal and Kingston: McGill-Queen's University Press, 1997.

Loewen, Roy, *Family, Church and Market: A Mennonite Community in the Old and the New Worlds, 1850–1930*, Toronto: University of Toronto Press, 1993.

Loo, Tina, *Making Law, Order and Authority in British Columbia, 1821–1871*, Toronto: University of Toronto Press, 1994.

Mackie, Richard Somerset, *The Wilderness Profound: A Victorian Life on the Gulf of Georgia*, Victoria: Sono Nis Press, 1995.

– *Trading Beyond the Mountains: The Hudson's Bay Company in the Pacific Northwest*, Vancouver: UBC Press, 1997.

Malin, James C., *History and Ecology: Studies of the Grassland*, Lincoln: University of Nebraska Press, 1984.

Martin, Ged, *Edward Gibbon Wakefield: Abductor and Mystagogue*, Edinburgh: Ann Barry, 1997.

May, Dean L, *Three Frontiers: Family, Land and Society in the American West, 1850–1900*, Cambridge: Cambridge University Press, 1994.

McCracken, Grant, *Culture and Consumption*, Bloomington: Indiana University Press, 1990.

McDonald, Robert A.J., *Making Vancouver: Class, Status, and Social Boundaries, 1863–1913*, Vancouver: UBC Press, 1996.

McKay, Ian, *The Quest of the Folk: Antimodernism and Cultural Selection in Twentieth Century Nova Scotia*, Kingston and Montreal: McGill-Queen's University Press, 1994.

Meek, Robert, *Social Science and the Ignoble Savage*, Cambridge: Cambridge University Press, 1976.

Mill, John Stuart, *On Bentham and Coleridge*, New York: Harper Torch, 1950.

Morton, James, *The Enterprising Mr. Moody, the Bumptious Captain Stamp*, Vancouver: J.J. Douglas, 1977.

Norcross, Elizabeth Blanche, *The Warm Land*, Nanaimo: Evergreen Press, 1959.

Ormsby, Margaret, ed., *A Pioneer Gentlewoman in British Columbia: The Recollections of Susan Allison*, Vancouver: UBC Press, (1976) 1991.

Osterud, Nancy, *Bonds of Community: The Lives of Farm Women in Nineteenth Century New York*, Ithaca: Cornell University Press, 1991.

Ovanin, Thomas K., *Island Heritage Buildings: A Selection of Heritage Buildings in the Islands Trust Area*, Victoria: Queen's Printer for British Columbia, 1987.

Pahl, R.E., *Divisions of Labour*, Oxford: Blackwell Publishers, 1984.

Palmer, Bryan D., *Descent into Discourse: the Reification of Language and the Writing of Social History*, Philadelphia: Temple University Press, 1990.

Parr, Joy, *Labouring Children: British Immigrant Apprentices to Canada, 1869–1924*, Montreal: McGill-Queen's University Press, 1980.

Pateman, Carole, *The Disorder of Women: Democracy, Feminism and Political Theory*, Stanford: Stanford University Press, 1989.

Pedlow, Ken, *Ruckle Provincial Park: A Documentary History*, Victoria: Province of British Columbia, Ministry of the Provincial Secretary and Government Services, Heritage Conservation Branch, 1984.

Perry, Adele, *On the Edge of Empire: Gender, Race and the Making of British Columbia, 1849–1871*, Toronto: University of Toronto Press, 2001.

Peterson del Mar, David, *"What Trouble I Have Seen": A History of Violence Against Wives*, Cambridge: Harvard University Press, 1996.

Poovey, Mary, *Uneven Developments: The Ideology of Gender in Mid-Victorian England*, Chicago: University of Chicago Press, 1988.

Pratt, Mary Louise, *Imperial Eyes: Travel Writing and Transculturation*, New York: Routledge, 1992.

Reddy, William, *Money and Liberty in Modern Europe: A Critique of Historical Understanding*, Cambridge: Cambridge University Press, 1987.

– *The Rise of Market Culture: The Textile Trade in French Society 1750–1900*, Cambridge: Cambridge University Press, 1984.

Reed, Mick, and Roger Wells, eds, *Class Conflict and Protest in the English Countryside*, London: Savage, 1990.

Richardson, David, *Pig War Islands: the San Juans of North West Washington*, Eastsound, Washington: Orcas Publishing, 1990.

Riley, Glenda, *The Female Frontier: A Comparative View of Women on the Prairie and the Plains*, Lawrence: University Press of Kansas, 1988.

Roy, Patricia E., *A White Man's Province: British Columbia Politicians and Chinese and Japanese Immigrants, 1858–1914*, Vancouver: UBC Press, 1989.

– *The Oriental Question: Consolidating a White Man's Province, 1914–41*, Vancouver: UBC Press, 2003.

Sabean, David Warren, *Property, Production and Family in Necklarhausen, 1700–1850*, Cambridge: Cambridge University Press, 1990.

Said, Edward, *Orientalism*, New York: Vintage Books, (1978) 1979.

– *Culture and Imperialism*, New York: Alfred A. Knopf, 1993.

Samson, Daniel, ed., *Contested Countryside: Rural Workers and Modern Society in Atlantic Canada, 1800–1950*, Fredericton: Acadiensis Press, 1994.

Sandwell, R.W., ed., *Beyond the City Limits: Rural History in British Columbia*, Vancouver: UBC Press, 1999.

Schwantes, Carlos A., *The Pacific Northwest: An Interpretive History*, Lincoln and London: University of Nebraska Press, 1989.

Scott, Joan, *Gender and the Politics of History*, New York: Columbia University Press, 1988.

Shanin, Teodor, ed., *Defining Peasants: Essays Concerning Rural Societies; Exploring Economies and Learning from Them in the Contemporary World*, London: Blackwells, 1990.

– *The Awkward Class*, Oxford: Oxford University Press, 1972.

Smith, Adam, *The Wealth of Nations, Books I–III*, originally published 1776; New York: Penguin Books, 1970.

Snell, Keith, *Annals of the Labouring Poor: Social Change and Agrarian England, 1660–1900*, Cambridge: Cambridge University Press, 1985.

Stevens, Homer, and Rolf Knight, *Homer Stevens: A Life in Fishing*, Madeira Park: Harbour Publishing, 1992.

Stewart, Mary Lynn, *Women, Work and the French State: Labour Protection and Social Patriarchy*, Kingston and Montreal: McGill-Queen's University Press, 1989.

Stoler, Anne Laura, *Race and the Education of Desire: Foucault's History of Sexuality and the Colonial Order of Things*, Durham: Duke University Press, 1995.

Strobel, Margaret, *Gender, Sex, and Empire*, Washington: American Historical Association, 1993.

Strong-Boag, Veronica, and Gillian Creese, eds, *British Columbia Reconsidered: Essays on Women*, Vancouver: Press Gang Publishers, 1992.

Struthers, James, *No Fault of their Own: Unemployment in the Canadian Welfare State*, Toronto: University of Toronto Press, 1983.

Sutherland, Neil, *Childhood in Canadian Society: Framing the Twentieth Century Consensus*, Toronto: University of Toronto Press, 1976.

– *Growing Up: Childhood in English Canada From the Great War to the Age of Television*, Toronto: University of Toronto Press, 1997.

Suttles, Wayne, *Coast Salish Essays*, Vancouver: Talonbooks, 1987.

Tennant, Paul, *Aboriginal Peoples and Politics: The Indian Land Question in British Columbia, 1849–1989*, Vancouver: UBC Press, 1990.

Thompson, E.P., *The Making of the English Working Class*, New York: Pantheon, 1963.

Toynbee, Richard Mouat, *Snapshots of Early Salt Spring and other Favoured Islands*, Saltspring Island: Mouat's Trading Co. Ltd., 1978.

University of Toronto, *Dictionary of Canadian Biography*, vol. XIII, 1901–1910, Toronto: University of Toronto Press, 1994.

Valenze, Deborah, *The First Industrial Woman*, Oxford: Oxford University Press, 1995.

Van Kirk, Sylvia, *"Many Tender Ties": Women in the Fur Trade Society, 1670–1870*, Winnipeg: Watson and Dyer, 1980.

Vincent, David, *Literacy and Popular Culture in England, 1750–1914*, Cambridge: Cambridge University Press, 1989.

Voisey, Paul, *Vulcan: the Making of a Prairie Community*, Toronto: University of Toronto Press, 1988.

Walbran, Captain John T., *British Columbia Place Names, Their Origin and History*, Vancouver: Douglas and McIntyre, (1909) 1977.

Walters, Margaret Shaw, *Early Days Among the Gulf Islands of British Columbia*, Victoria: Hebden Printing, n.d.

West, Elliott, *Growing Up With the Country: Childhood on the Western Frontier*, Albuquerque: University of New Mexico Press, 1989.

White, Richard, *It's Your Misfortune and None of My Own: A New History of the American West*, Norman: University of Oklahoma Press, 1991.

– *Land Use, Environment and Social Change: The Shaping of Island County*, Seattle, Washington: University of Washington Press (1980) 1992.

Whitney, Gordon G., *From Coastal Wilderness to Fruited Plain: A History of Environmental Change in Temperate North America from 1500 to the Present*, Cambridge: Cambridge University Press, 1994.

Wilk, Richard, E., *Household Ecology: Economic Change and Domestic Life among the Kekchi Maya in Belize*, Tucson: University of Arizona Press, 1991.

– *The Household Economy: Reconsidering the Domestic Mode of Production*, Boulder: Westview Press, 1989.

Williams, Raymond, *The Country and the City*, London: Chatto & Windus Ltd, 1973.

Wilson, Catharine Anne, *A New Lease on Life: Landlords, Tenants and Immigrants in Ireland and Canada*, Kingston and Montreal: McGill-Queen's University Press, 1994.

Woolf, Stuart, ed., *Domestic Strategies: Work and Family in France and Italy, 1600–1800*, Cambridge: Cambridge University Press, 1991.

Young, Robert, *Colonial Desire: Hybridity in Theory, Culture and Race*, London: Routledge, 1995.

Zelizer, Viviana, *Pricing the Priceless Child: The Changing Social Value of Children*, Princeton: Princeton University Press, 1985.

Zeller, Suzanne, *Inventing Canada: Early Victorian Science and the Idea of a Transcontinental Nation*, Toronto: University of Toronto Press, 1987.

Articles

Aminzade, Ronald, "Reinterpreting Industrialization: A Study of Nineteenth Century France," in S. Kaplan and C. Koepp, eds, *Work in France: Representations, Meanings, Organization and Practice*, Ithaca: Cornell University Press, 1986, 394–420.

Barman, Jean, "Invisible Women and Mixed-Race Daughters in Rural British Columbia," in R.W. Sandwell, ed., *Beyond the City Limits: Rural History in British Columbia*, Vancouver: UBC Press, 1999, 159–79.

Baskerville, Peter A., "'She Has Already Hinted at Board': Enterprising Urban Women in British Columbia, 1863–1896," *Histoire Sociale / Social History*, 26, no. 52 (Nov. 1993), 205–27.

– "Women and Investment in Late-Nineteenth Century Urban Canada, Victoria and Hamilton," *Canadian Historical Review*, 80, no. 2 (June 1999), 191–218.

Belshaw, John Douglas, "Cradle to Grave: An Examination of Demographic Behaviour on Two British Columbian Frontiers," *Journal of the Canadian Historical Association* (1994).

– "Rurality Check: Demographic Boundaries on the British Columbia Frontier," in R.W. Sandwell, ed., *Beyond the City Limits: Rural History in British Columbia*, Vancouver: UBC Press, 1999, 195–211.

Bittermann, Rusty, "The Hierarchy of the Soil: Land and Labour in a 19th Century Cape Breton Community," *Acadiensis*, 28, 1 (Autumn 1988), 33–55.

– "Farm Households and Wage Labour in the Northeastern Maritimes in the Early 19th Century," *Labour/ Le Travail,* 31 (Spring 1993), 13–45.

Bouchard, Gérard, "Co-Integration et Reproduction de la Société Rurale: Pour un Modèle Saguenayen de la Marginalité," *Recherches Sociographiques,* 29, no. 2–8 (December 1988), 283–309.

– "Family Reproduction in New Rural Areas: Outline of a North American Model," *Canadian Historical Review,* 75, no. 4 (1994), 475–510.

– "Family Structures and Geographic Mobility at Laterriere, 1851–1935," *Journal of Family History,* 2 (1977), 350–69.

– "Introduction à l'étude de la société saguenayenne au XIX et XXᵉ siècles," *Revue Historique Américaine Française,* 31 (1977), 15.

– "Mobile Populations, Stable Communities: Social and Demographic Process in Rural Parishes in the Saguenay, 1840–1911," *Continuity and Change,* 6 (1991), 59–86.

– "Sur un démarrage raté: industrie laitière et co-intégration au Saguenay, 1880–1940," *Recherches Sociographiques,* vol. 45, no. 1 (1991), 73–100.

Boyd, Robert, "Smallpox in the Pacific Northwest: The First Epidemics," BC *Studies,* 101 (Spring 1994), 5–40.

Boydston, Jeanne, "To Earn Her Daily Bread: Housework in Antebellum Working-Class Subsistence," *Radical History Review,* 35 (1986).

Bradbury, Bettina, "Women and Wage Labour in a Period of Transition: Montreal, 1861–1881," in David J. Bercuson, ed., *Canadian Labour History: Selected Readings,* Toronto: Copp Clark Pitman, 1987.

– "Pigs, Cows and Boarders: Non-Wage Forms of Survival Among Montreal Families 1861–91," in *Labour / Le Travail,* 14 (fall 1984), 9–46.

– "Gender at Work at Home: Family Decisions, the Labour Market and Girls' Contributions to the Family Economy," in Bettina Bradbury, ed., *Canadian Family History: Selected Readings,* Mississauga: Copp Clark Pitman, 1992, 177–98.

Carter, Sarah, "First Nations Women of Prairie Canada in the Early Reserve Years, the 1870s to the 1920s: A Preliminary Enquiry," in Christine Miller and Patricia Chuchryk, eds, *Women of the First Nations: Power, Wisdom, Strength,* Winnipeg: University of Manitoba Press, 1996, 51–76.

– "Categories and Terrains of Exclusion: Constructing the Indian Woman in the Early Settlement Era in Western Canada," in Joy Parr and Mark Rosenfeld, eds, *Gender and History in Canada,* Toronto: Copp Clark, 1996, 30–49.

Clarkson, Christopher, "Property Law and Family Regulation in Pacific British North America, 1862–1873," *Histoire Sociale/Social History,* vol. 30, no. 60 (November 1997), 386–416.

Clayton, Daniel,"Captain Cook and the Spaces of Contact at Nootka Sound," in Elizabeth Vibert and Jennifer S. Brown, eds, *Reading Beyond Words: Contexts for Native History,* Peterborough: Broadview Press, 1996, 95–123.

Cornell, Sean, "Early American History in a Postmodern Age," *The William and Mary Quarterly*, 3d. Ser., vol. L, no. 2 (April 1993), 329–41.

Craig, Beatrice, "Agriculture in a Pioneer Region: The Upper St. John Valley in the First Half of the Nineteenth Century," in Kris Inwood, ed., *Farm, Factory and Fortune: New Studies in the Economic History of the Maritime Provinces*, Fredericton: Acadiensis Press, 1993, 17–36.

Crofton, John, "The Rise and Sad Demise of Salt Spring's Lodge of Hope," *British Columbia Historical News*, 26, no. 3 (1993), 30–2.

Crosby, Marcia, "Lines, Lineage and Lies, or Borders, Boundaries and Bullshit," in Marcia Crosby, ed., *Nations in Urban Landscapes*, Vancouver: Contemporary Art Gallery, 1997, 23–30.

Cruikshank, Julie, "Invention of Anthropology in British Columbia's Supreme Court: Oral Tradition as Evidence in Delgamuukw v. B.C.," *BC Studies*, no. 95 (Autumn 1992), 25–42.

Curtis, Bruce, "Preconditions of the Canadian State: Educational Reform and the Construction of a Public in Upper Canada, 1837–1846," *Studies in Political Economy*, 10 (1983), 99–121.

Darroch, Gordon, "Scanty Fortunes and Rural Middle Class Formation in Nineteenth Century Central Ontario," *Canadian Historical Review*, 79, 4 (December 1998), 621–2.

– "Family Co-Residence in Canada in 1871: Family Life Cycles, Occupations and Networks of Mutual Aid," Canadian Historical Association *Historical Papers* (1983), 30–55.

– and Michael Ornstein, "Family and Household in Nineteenth Century Canada: Regional Patterns and Regional Economies," *Journal of Family History*, vol. 9, no. 2 (Summer 1984), 158–77.

Demeritt, David, "Visions of Agriculture in British Columbia," *BC Studies*, no. 108 (Winter 1995–96), 29–59.

Fink, Deborah, "Farming in Open Country, Iowa: Women and the Changing Farm Economy," in M. Chibnik, ed., *Farmwork and Fieldwork: American Agriculture in Anthropological Perspective*, Ithaca: Cornell University Press, 1987, 121–44.

Flucke, A.F., "Early Days on Saltspring Island," *British Columbia Historical Quarterly*, 15, nos. 2 and 4 (July-Oct. 1851), 161–202.

Folbre, Nancy, "Hearts and Spades: Paradigms of Household Economics," *World Development*, 14, no. 2 (1986), 245–55.

Fraser, Nancy, "Talking About Needs: Interpretive Contests as Political Conflicts in Welfare-State Societies," *Ethics*, 99 (January 1989), 291–313.

Freidmann, Harriet, "Patriarchy and Property," *Sociologia Ruralis*, 27, 2 (1986), 187–93.

– "World Market, State and Family Farm: Social Bases of Household Production in the Era of Waged Labour," *Comparative Studies in Society and History*, 20 (1978), 545–86.

Gaffield, Chad, "Children, Schooling and Family Reproduction in Nineteenth Century Ontario," *Canadian Historical Review*, 72, 2 (1991), 157–91.

– Canadian Historical Association Presidential Address "Historical Thinking, C.P. Snow's Two Cultures, and a Hope for the Twenty-First Century," *Journal of the Canadian Historical Association*, New Series, vol. 12 (2001), 3–25.

Galois, Robert, and R. Cole Harris, "Recalibrating Society: The Population Geography of British Columbia in 1881," *Canadian Geographer*, 38, no. 1 (1994), 37–53.

Goodman, David, and Michael Redclift, "Capitalism, Petty Commodity Production and the Farm Enterprise," *Sociologia Ruralis*, nos. 3–4 (1985), 231–47.

Gossage, Peter, "La marâtre: Marie-Anne Houde and the Myth of the Wicked Stepmother in Quebec," *Canadian Historical Review*, 76 (4 December 1995), 563–97.

Greer, Alan, "Wage Labour and the Transition to Capitalism: A Critique of Pentland," *Labour/Le Travail*, 21 (Spring 1985), 7–22.

Harris, R. Cole, "Industry and the Good Life Around Idaho Peak," *Canadian Historical Review*, 66, no. 3 (Sept. 1985), 315–43.

– "Voices of Disaster: Smallpox around the Strait of Georgia in 1782," *Ethnohistory*, 41: 4 (Fall 1994), 592–626.

– "The Simplification of Europe Overseas," *Annals of the Association of American Geographers*, 67: 4 (December 1977).

Hart, Gillian, "Imagined Unities: Constructions of 'The Household' in Economic Theory," in Sutti Ortiz and Susan Lees, eds, *Understanding Economic Process: Monographs in Economic Anthropology*, Lanham: University Press of America, 1992, 111–29.

Hendrickson, James E., "The Constitutional Development of Colonial Vancouver Island and British Columbia," in Peter W. Ward and Robert A.J. McDonald, *British Columbia: Historical Readings*, Vancouver: Douglas and McIntyre, 1981.

Hurst, James Willard, "The Institutional Environment of the Logging Era in Wisconsin," in Susan L. Flader, ed., *The Great Lakes Forest: An Environmental and Social History*, Minneapolis: University of Minnesota Press, 1983.

Inwood, Kris, and James Irwin, "Canadian Regional Commodity Income Differences at Confederation," in Kris Inwood, ed., *Farm, Factory and Fortune: New Studies in the Economic History of the Maritime Provinces*, Fredericton: Acadiensis Press, 1993, 93–120.

– and E. Roelens, "Labouring at the Loom: A Case Study of Rural Manufacturing in Leeds County, Ontario, 1870," D. Akenson, ed., *Canadian Papers in Rural History*, 7, Gananoque: Langdale Press, 1989, 222–41.

Irby, Charles, B., "The Black Settlers on Salt Spring Island in the Nineteenth Century," *Phylon*, (1974), 368–74.

Johnston, Hugh, "Native People, Settlers and Sojourners: 1871–1916," in Hugh Johnston, ed., *The Pacific Province: A History of British Columbia*, Vancouver: Douglas and McIntyre, 1996, 165–204.

Jones, David C., "The Zeitgeist of Western Settlement: Education and the Myth of the Land," in J. Donald Wilson and David C. Jones, eds, *Schooling and Society in Twentieth Century British Columbia*, Calgary: Detsilig Publishing, 1980.

Kielbowicz, Richard B., "Rural Ambivalence Towards Mass Society: Evidence from the u.s. Parcel Post Debates, 1900–1913," *Rural History*, 5: 1 (1994), 81–102.

Koroscil, Paul, "Resettlement in Canada's British Garden of Eden," in Catherine Kerrigan, ed., *The Immigrant Experience*, Guelph: University of Guelph Press, 1989, 129–64.

– Soldiers, Settlement and Development in British Columbia, 1859–1871," *BC Studies*, 54 (Summer 1982), 63–87.

Lamb, W. Kaye, "Early Lumbering on Vancouver Island," *British Columbia Historical Quarterly*, 2, no. 2 (1938), 95–121.

Leier, Mark, "W[h]ither Labour History?: Regionalism, Class and the Writing of b.c. History," *BC Studies*, no. 111 (Autumn 1996), 61–75.

Levi, Giovanni, "On Microhistory," in Peter Burke, ed., *New Perspectives on Historical Writing*, University Park: Penn State University Press, 1991, 93–114.

Lewthwaite, Susan, "Violence, Law and Community in Rural Upper Canada," in Jim Phillips, Tina Loo, and Susan Lewthwaite, eds, *Essays in the History of Canadian Law*, Toronto: Osgoode Society for Canadian Legal History, 1994, 353–86.

Little, J.I., "The Foundations of Government," in Hugh J.M. Johnston, ed., *The Pacific Province: A History of British Columbia*, Vancouver: Douglas and McIntyre, 1996, 68–96.

Loo, Tina, "Dan Cranmer's Potlatch: Law as Coercion, Symbol and Rhetoric in British Columbia, 1884–1951," *Canadian Historical Review*, 73, 2 (1992), 125–65.

Mackie, Richard S., "The Colonization of Vancouver Island, 1849–1858," *BC Studies*, no. 96 (Winter 1992–93), 3–40.

Marshall, Daniel P., "An Early Rural Revolt: The Introduction of the Canadian System of Tariffs to British Columbia, 1871–4," in R.W. Sandwell, ed., *Beyond the City Limits: Rural History in British Columbia*, Vancouver: UBC Press, 1999, 47–61.

McDonald, Robert A.J., "Lumber Society on the Industrial Frontier: Burrard Inlet, 1863–1886," *Labour/Le Travail*, 33 (Spring 1994), 69–96.

– "The West is a Messy Place," *BC Studies*, no. 111 (Autumn 1996), 88–92.

McKay, Ian, "The Liberal Order Framework: A Prospectus for a Reconnaissance of Canadian History," Canadian Historical Review, 81, 4 (December 2000), 630.

McPherson, Kathryn, "Feminist Reflections on the Writing of Canadian Working Class History in the 1980's," *Labour/Le Travail*, 27 (Spring 1991).

Medick, Hans, "The Proto-Industrial Family Economy: The Structural Function of Household and Family in the Transition From Peasant Society to Industrial Capitalism," in P. Thane and A. Sutcliffe, eds, *Essays in Social History, vol. 2*, (1986) 30; first published in *Social History*, 3 (1976), 291–316.

Moore, H.L., "Household and Gender Relations: The Modeling of the Economy," in Sutti Ortiz and Susan Lees, eds, *Understanding Economic Process: Monographs in Economic Anthropology*, Lanham: University Press of America, 1992, 131–47.

Muszynski, Alicia, "Structural Determinants in the Formation of the British Columbia Salmon Cannery Labour Force," in Greg Kealey, ed., *Class, Gender and Region: Essays in Canadian Historical Sociology*, St John's: Committee on Canadian Labour History, 1988, 103–20.

Myers, Tamara, "The Voluntary Delinquent: Parents, Daughters and the Montreal Juvenile Delinquents' Court in 1918," *Canadian Historical Review*, vol. 80, no. 2 (June 1999), 242–68.

Palmer, Bryan B.,"Class and the Writing of History: Beyond BC," *BC Studies*, no. 111 (Autumn 1996), 76–84.

– "Response to Joan Scott," *International Labour and Working-Class History*, no. 31 (Spring 1987), 14–23.

Parr, Joy, "Gender History and Historical Practice," *Canadian Historical Review*, 76, no. 3 (September 1995), 354–76.

– "Hired Men: Ontario Agricultural Wage Labour in Historical Perspective," *Labour/Le Travail*, 15: 41: 104 (1985).

Perry, Adele, "I'm Just Sick of the Faces of Men: Gender Imbalance, Race, Sexuality and Sociability in Nineteenth-Century British Columbia," *BC Studies*, nos. 105–6 (Spring/Summer 1995), 27–44.

– "Bachelors in the Backwoods: White Men and Homosocial Culture in Upcountry British Columbia, 1858–1871," in R.W. Sandwell, ed., *Beyond the City Limits: Rural History in British Columbia*, Vancouver: UBC Press, 1999, 180–94.

Pisani, Donald, "Squatter Law in California, 1850–1858," *Western Historical Quarterly* (Autumn 1994), 277–310.

Reed, Mick, "'Gnawing it Out': A New Look at Economic Relations in Nineteenth Century Rural England," in *Rural History* 1, 1 (1990), 83–94.

Russell, Peter, "Forest into Farmland: Upper Canadian Clearing Rates, 1822–1839," in J.K. Johnson, Bruce Wilson, eds, *Historical Essays on Upper Canada: New Perspectives*, Ottawa: Carleton University Press, 1989, 131–49.

– "Emily Township: Pioneer Persistence to Equality?" *Histoire Sociale/Social History*, 24, no. 44 (Nov. 1989), 317–31.

Sandwell, R.W., "Rural Reconstruction: Towards a New Synthesis in Canadian History," *Histoire Sociale/Social History*, vol. 27, no. 53 (May 1994), 1–32.

- "Peasants on the Coast? A Problematique of Rural British Columbia," in Donald Akenson, ed., *Canadian Papers in Rural History*, 10, Gananoque: Langdale Press, 1996, 275–303.
- "The Limits of Liberalism: The Liberal Reconnaissance and the History of the Family in Canada," *Canadian Historical Review*, vol. 84, no. 3, September 2003, 423–50.

Scott, Joan Wallach, "The Statistical Representation of Work: La Statistique de l'industrie à Paris, 1847–1848," in *Gender and the Politics of History*, New York: Columbia University Press, 1988, 113–38.

Simard, Jean-Jacques, "White Ghosts, Red Shadows: The Reduction of North American Natives," in James A. Clifton, ed., *The Invented Indian: Cultural Fictions and Government Policies*, New Brunswick, New Jersey: Transaction Publishers, 1990, 333–69.

Smith, Paul Chaat, "Home of the Brave," *"c" Magazine*, 42 (1994), 30–42.

Stephenson, Penelope, "Mrs. Gibson Looked as if She was Ready for the End of Term: The Professional Trials and Tribulations of Rural Teachers in British Columbia's Okanagan Valley in the 1920s," in Jean Barman, Neil Sutherland, and J. Donald Wilson, eds, *Children, Teachers and Schools in the History of British Columbia*, Calgary: Detsilig Enterprises, 1995, 235–57.

Strong-Boag, Veronica, "Moving Beyond Tired Truths: Or, Let's Not Fight the Old Battles," *BC Studies*, no. 111 (Autumn 1996), 84–7.

Sutherland, Neil, "I Can't Recall When I Didn't Help: The Working Lives of Pioneering Children in the Twentieth Century British Columbia," *Histoire Sociale / Social History*, 23, no. 48 (Nov. 1991), 263–88.

- "We Always Had Things to Do: The Paid and Unpaid Work of Anglophone Children Between the 1920's and the 1960's," *Labour/Le Travail*, 25 (Spring 1990), 105–41.

Taylor, Alan, "'A Kind of War:' The Contest for Land on the Northeastern Frontier, 1750–1820," *William and Mary Quarterly*, 46 (1989), 3–26.

Thomson, Duane, "The Response of Okanagan Indians to European Settlement," *BC Studies*, 101 (Spring 1994), 96–117.

Thompson, E.P., "Eighteenth Century English Society: Class Struggle Without Class," *Social History*, 3, no. 2 (May 1978), 133–65.

Van Kirk, Sylvia, "Women in Between: Indian Women in the Fur Trade Society in Western Canada," Canadian Historical Association, *Historical Papers*, (1977), 30–46.

- "'What if Mama is an Indian?' The Cultural Ambivalence of the Alexander Ross Family," in Jacqueline Peterson and Jennifer Brown, eds, *The New Peoples: Being and Becoming Metis in North America*, Winnipeg: University of Manitoba Press, 1985, 207–17.

Vibert, Elizabeth, "The Natives were Strong to Live: Reinterpreting Early Nineteenth-Century Prophetic Movements in the Columbia Plateau," *Ethnohistory*, 42:2 (Spring 1995), 198–229.

Wickwire, Wendy, "To See Ourselves as the Other's Other: Nlaka'pamux Contact Narratives," *Canadian Historical Review*, 75, 1 (1994), 1–20.

Wilson, J. Donald, "Lottie Bowron and Rural Women Teachers in British Columbia, 1928–1934," in Veronica Strong-Boag and Gillian Creese, eds, *British Columbia Reconsidered: Essays on Women*, Vancouver: Press Gang Publishers, 1992, 340–63.

– and Paul L. Stortz, "May the Lord Have Mercy on You: the Rural School Problem in British Columbia in the 1920s," *BC Studies*, no. 79 (Autumn 1988), 24–58.

Unpublished manuscripts, articles, and theses

Barman, Jean, "The Worth of an Everyday Woman: Maria Mahoi and Her Two Families," paper, Department of Educational Studies, University of British Columbia, 1996.

– "Taming Aboriginal Sexuality: Gender, Power and Race in British Columbia, 1850–1900," paper presented to the BC Studies Conference, 3 May 1997.

Bennett, Jason Patrick, "'The True Elixir of Life:' Imagining Eden and Empire in the Settlement of Kelowna, British Columbia, 1904–1920," MA thesis, Simon Fraser University, 1996.

Carlisle, Mary Margaret, "Early Agricultural Education in British Columbia: the Pioneering Role of the Farmers' Institutes," MA thesis, University of British Columbia, 1986.

Clarkson, Christopher, "Liberalism, Nation Building and Family Regulation: The State and the Use of Family Property Law on Vancouver Island and in the United Colony/Province of British Columbia, 1862–1873," MA thesis, University of Victoria, 1996.

Davidson, Mary, "The Little Church in the Valley: Burgoyne United Church, Fulford-Ganges Road, Salt Spring Island, B.C.," typescript, SSIA.

Dendy, David, "The Worm in the Apple," paper presented to the New Directions in B.C. History Conference, Prince George, B.C., May 1995.

Evans, Clint, "Unimportant or Overlooked? The Historical Role of Agriculture in British Columbia," paper presented at the 1991 Qualicum Conference, British Columbia.

Falcon, Paulette Yvonne Lynette, "'if the evil ever occurs' – the 1873 Married Women's Property Act: Law, Property and Gender Relations in 19th Century British Columbia," MA thesis, University of British Columbia, 1991.

Laing, F.W., "Colonial Farm Settlers on the Mainland of British Columbia, 1859–1871, UBC Special Collections 9, nd.

Lutz, John, "Losing Steam: Structural Change in the Manufacturing Economy of British Columbia, 1860–1915," MA thesis, University of Victoria, 1988.

– "The Lost Years: Aboriginal People and Work in British Columbia, 1885–1960," paper presented to the B.C. Studies Conference, November 1992.

– "Superintending the Songhees: Naming, Knowledge and the Extension of Dominion Over Aboriginal People, 1843–1913," paper presented to the 1993 Canadian Historical Association Annual Meeting.

– "Work, Wages and Welfare in Aboriginal-Non-Aboriginal Relations, British Columbia, 1849–1970," PhD thesis, University of Ottawa, 1994.

MacPherson, Ian, "Creating Stability in a Marginal Industry: the Social Origins of the Struggle for Orderly Marketing in British Columbia, 1900–1940," paper presented at the 1986 BC Studies Conference, University of British Columbia Special Collections.

Marshall, Daniel P., "Mapping the Political World of British Columbia, 1871–1883," MA thesis, University of Victoria, 1991.

Pilton, James, "Salt Spring Island" in "Negro Settlement in British Columbia 1858–1871," MA thesis, University of British Columbia, 1951.

"Saint Mark's Centennial, 1892–1992, Parish of Salt Spring Island" typescript, SSIA.

Samson, Daniel Joseph, "Industry and Improvement: State and Class Formations in Nova Scotia's Coal-Mining Countryside, 1790–1864," PhD dissertation, Queen's University, 1997.

Sandwell, R.W., "Farmers, Peasants and Profit-Maximizers: The Farmers and their Markets: Conceptual Issues," panel presentation to the Canadian Historical Association Annual Conference, St. Catharines, Ontario, 2 June 1996.

– "Reading the Land: Rural Discourse and the Practice of Settlement, Saltspring Island, British Columbia, 1859–1891," PhD dissertation, Simon Fraser University, 1998.

– and Lutz, John, "Who Killed William Robinson? Race, Justice and Settling the Land," a website, http://web.uvic.ca/history-robinson/index.html.

Stadfeld, Bruce, "Manifestations of Power: Native Response to Settlement in Nineteenth Century British Columbia," MA thesis, Simon Fraser University, 1993.

Stratton, Morton, "Agriculture: Farms, Farmers and Farming," in "A History of an Island Called Salt Spring," manuscript, SSIA.

Thomson, Duncan Duane, "A History of the Okanagan: Indians and Whites in the Settlement Era, 1860–1920," PhD thesis, University of British Columbia, 1985.

Wells, Ruth, "Making Health Contagious: Medical Inspection of the Schools in British Columbia, 1910–1920," MA extended research paper, University of Victoria, 1981.

Wilson, Catharine Anne, "Landlord, Tenants, and Immigrants: The Irish and the Canadian Experience," PhD thesis, Queen's University, 1989.

Wright, Arthur James, "A Study of the Social and Economic Development of the District of North Cowichan, 1850–1912," graduating essay, University of British Columbia, April 1966, UBC Special Collections.

Index

Names of individuals who are only briefly mentioned in the book do not appear in the index. However all the information about each individual and family that was available when I did my research has been compiled into a database and donated to the Salt Spring Island Archives. With the permission of the archivist, researchers with an interest in particular individuals can search this database by name or address.

and Aboriginal peoples, 122–3; alternatives on Saltspring Island summarized, 117–20; and class, 214–15.

Land Ordinance, 1860, 24–5; 1861, 29; 1870, 29. *See also* Homestead Act

landownership: and age, 199–200; centrality to culture of Saltspring Island, 231; and class analysis, 213–14, 216; provisional forms on Saltspring Island, 64–7; statistics for Saltspring Island, 56–7, 66, 199–200; and wealth, 90. *See also* land ideology, land policy, pre-emption system

land policy: difficulty of studying, 4, esp. n3; and families, 32–5, 73, 82, 122–3, 206–7; first pre-emptions in colonial British Columbia, 21–4; and gender, 206–7, 209–10; public pressure re instituting, 21–3, 25. *See also* land ideology, pre-emption system

land quality on Saltspring Island, 92–3

land settlement: and British Columbia historiography, 4–6, chapter 1

land speculation: evaluating evidence of land speculation on Saltspring Island, 79–82; fear of, in land policy formation, 72; and the Wakefield system, 20

Lehning, James, 155–6

liberal ideology, 34, 124, 155–7, 194, 226–7; citizenship and modernity, 217–24; and growth of the state on Saltspring Island, 215–24; and land ownership on Saltspring Island, 213–14; and

men's lives, 209–13; and rural Canada, 230; and women's lives, 207, 209–13

life-course, 199–205

literacy: of island population, 6n8

Little, J.I., 218

livestock. *See* agriculture

logging, 53; and the island economy, 129; and the pre-emption system, 111

Loo, Tina, 218

Lutz, John, 5, 159n1, 179

Mackie, Richard, 136

Malin, James, 123, 225

Married Women's Property Act, 206–7

Marshall, Daniel, 31

Maxwell, David, and family, 49–51, 70–2; cattle raising, 51; logging, 111; photograph, 100; work for provincial government, 130

McFadden family: attempted murder trial of Mary-Anne, 193–4, 204; diet, 136, 137; work, 128, 137

McLennan, Alexander, and family, 130; photograph, 19

medical services on Saltspring, 208

men: assessing patriarchal privilege, 205–13; bonding, 206; as breadwinners, 209–10; enfranchisement, 209; leisure, 205–6; limited liberal identity on Saltspring Island, 209–10; and the pre-emption system, 207, 209–10. *See also* occupation, occupational plurality, work

microhistory, 7–10; limitations of, 229

mining: comparison of mining population of Van-

couver Island with Saltspring, 141–3; potential on Saltspring Island, 52–3

municipal government on Saltspring Island, 216–17, 221–3. *See also* elections

murder. *See* violence

Naukana, 51–2, 169–70

North Vesuvius School. *See* schools

Norton, John, and family: overview of his landholdings and household, 61–2; photograph, 63; testimony at murder inquiry, 174, 177

occupation: difficulties with the concept, 123–5; census listings, 126–7. *See also* occupational plurality, work

occupational plurality: advantages over concept of "occupation," 123–5; centrality in Canadian economy, 133–4, 150; centrality in island economy, 128–38; importance in rural economies worldwide, 155; and independence of islanders, 223–4; in pioneer stages of settlement, 52–4

Oregon Territory, 20

Pateman, Carole, 207, 209

peasant economy: description and evaluation of Saltspring as, 5, 139, 152–8, 228

Pemberton, Joseph: colonial surveyor, 24, 27

Perry, Adele, 32, 34, 210

policing: first permanent constable, 216; McFadden/Sampson attempted murder trial, 194; and racism, 185–7; request